Date Due

AUG 31 '89		
MAY 1 0 1997		
MAY 1 4 1997		

SOCIAL SECURITY IN AMERICA

SOCIAL SECURITY IN AMERICA

POLICY PAPERS IN HUMAN RESOURCES
AND INDUSTRIAL RELATIONS 19

Philip Booth
School of Social Work
The University of Michigan

FOREWORD BY FEDELE F. FAURI

ANN ARBOR, MICHIGAN
MAY 1973

INSTITUTE OF LABOR AND INDUSTRIAL RELATIONS
THE UNIVERSITY OF MICHIGAN — WAYNE STATE UNIVERSITY

International Standard Book Number: 0-87736-119-3 (cloth)
0-87736-120-7 (paper)

Library of Congress Catalog Card Number: 73-620091

Copyright © 1973 by the Institute of Labor and Industrial Relations,
The University of Michigan—Wayne State University

Published 1973. Second impression March, 1974

Printed in the United States of America

G.R. Local 250
Plant No. 2

To Eugene and Daniel Booth

CONTENTS

LIST OF TABLES

FOREWORD

FEDELE F. FAURI

Social welfare programs in the United States have developed
slowly but steadily since the enactment of the Social Security
Act of 1935, effectively helping to promote the well-being and
happiness of a large segment of the American people. Stemming
from this one act, we now have old-age and survivors, unemployment, and disability insurance; federal grants to the states
for the needy aged, blind and disabled, and needy families with
children; federal grants for maternal and child health, crippled
children, and child welfare services; and Medicare, Medicaid,
and federal grants for vocational rehabilitation. In addition, the
framework developed by the social welfare leaders of the 1930s
has been broadened over the years to form a comprehensive
system of social insurance and federal grants-in-aid to states for
public assistance and welfare services as a permanent part of the
basic fabric of our social institutions.

These step-by-step advances have followed principles advo-
cated by President Roosevelt in his social security message of
1934; first, that the social security system be self-sustaining and
not supported by general taxation; second, that it be a national
system with maximum state and federal cooperation; and third,
that the credit structure of the nation be assured by retaining
federal control over the investment and safeguarding of the
reserves. Roosevelt's emphasis on fiscal responsibility and an
evolutionary approach to social welfare problems guided the

various congresses over the years as amendments expanded and liberalized the social security programs. Progress, which has come about through the give-and-take of the democratic process, has resulted in broadened social security legislation becoming a permanent part of the laws of the nation in assuring applicants and beneficiaries specific statutory rights that cannot be arbitrarily denied or withdrawn by administrative agencies and in making improvements under the leadership of both major political parties.

Old-age and survivors' insurance dramatically demonstrates the process that has been followed in the United States in the enactment of social welfare legislation. Accepted almost unanimously today, the program elicited predictions from early critics that social security would mean the loss of individual liberty and individual responsibility, be a burden on the economy, and effect national bankruptcy; although passed by a substantial majority in 1935, many Congressmen voted for it with reluctance, hoping that the Court would rule it unconstitutional. Yet over the years various Congresses steadily improved the program, while emphasizing fiscal responsibility and actuarial soundness.

A major program founded by the original social security law was the unemployment insurance system; it cushioned the burden of joblessness and loss of income that had been borne by the worker and his family. Forty years ago unemployment required a worker to liquidate his savings and other assets and to accumulate debts; if driven to take unskilled work, the skilled worker (and society) lost his occupational skill and morale. Public and private welfare resources were overstrained by the persistence of widespread unemployment and community distress. Over the years, unemployment insurance funds have been available in the localities where and when they are needed as unemployment has risen. Workers and their families have been protected against distress and insecurity; community purchasing power and labor standards have been maintained; and workers have been given confidence that they will have some income to pay their bills when unemployment strikes.

As a policy paper, this volume reviews the development and growth of social security programs and policies in the United States during the past 35 years, and details how effectively protection against risks to income security has been extended to millions of Americans. The author indicates the interrelations of public programs of income maintenance for long-term and short-run contingencies: old-age retirement, invalidity, survivorship, unemployment, work-injury, and sickness. He clarifies how our complex and expensive private employee "fringe" benefit structure supplements public programs under a conscious public policy of financial support that uses tax exemptions and deductions. Yet uneven and fragmented protection under a complex of public and private measures weakens the entire structure of assurance to the people.

This comprehensive survey is capped with the author's evaluation of proposed reforms and improvements. The description, comparison, and analysis reflect a long career in legislative planning and research, beginning with the research staff of the Social Security Board in 1936, when guidelines for policy and administration were developed. When the country was catching up on social security at the close of World War II, his understanding of federal and state programs aided me to provide technical advice on social security to House and Senate committees. In the 1960s, when I was Dean of the School of Social Work, he helped develop the curriculum and taught social policy and income maintenance to our advanced students. The volume's treatment of social security in this country is informed by the author's participation in development of new approaches and new programs here, as well as in supplying policy and technical assistance to developing countries while a member of the social security staff of the ILO.

Analyzing the progress that our social security system has made in recent decades offers useful insights into the significance of these changes for the future and serves as a backdrop for examining policy alternatives for meeting future security needs of the American people. Review of past developments suggests that, in general, we have followed Roosevelt's 1935 counsel to avoid hasty and extravagant actions. Incremental changes of the past 30 years have cautiously extended protection to additional population groups, although the social security system has grown faster and further than its founders might have anticipated. The magnitude of these changes, however, has been due as much to population and labor force growth, and rising levels of earnings and living standards as to the changes in the social security program themselves.

Recent changes may foreshadow even greater advances in the

future. Extensions of Medicare to the disabled and to victims of "black lung" and chronic kidney disease are likely to draw attention to other diseases, crippling to body and to family finances, that may be brought under the Medicare umbrella. Continued improvement in the adequacy of benefits paid to survivor families, plus other benefit trends indicated by recent developments, raise issues about rising worker-employer tax rates, assuming continued reliance on payroll tax financing. Increased federal participation in program areas hitherto regarded as state functions may indicate growing awareness of federal responsibility in these areas, and could remedy major deficiencies in social security programs that are of key importance to American families. These developments raise crucial issues about the direction of income security protection in the next quarter century and the alternative choices available to meet these needs.

As originally conceived, the social security system provides a floor of protection through wage-related benefits on which the worker can build additional security through savings, private pensions, home ownership, and other assets. It was not designed to pay post-retirement benefits to lift out of poverty those workers whose former earnings kept them in poverty during their job careers. Most of the aged today, however, must rely entirely on social security benefits after their earnings stop and only one in seven has a private pension of any substance. What are our alternatives in remedying these long-term low benefits to increase the income of the aged? Should we seek solutions within a single program or continue to use a multiheaded approach?

Social security is designed for and capable of helping people cope with slippage, rather than failure, in the economy, which has an adverse effect on their personal lives. But social security cannot be expected to bail out a society where most workers are not able to retain or find work beyond advanced middle age, and where lack of jobs, private and public, fails to provide opportunity for work and a decent living. Broadening and upgrading social insurance, reducing public assistance to a truly residual role, creating a national public assistance system with uniform benefit and entitlement conditions should go far to correct the major deficiencies in our present system. Support for extending health insurance to the rest of the population will make the wage earner's income go further to protect his living standards. Decent housing, the opportunity to work at decent wages that permit accumulation of savings and the obtaining of schooling, training, and experience are interdependent and basic requisites of an effective social security system.

Federal and state governments have taken important initiatives in the past two decades to extend income security, health, housing, training, and educational services to millions unable to obtain them through commercial or voluntary channels. We now face shifts in priorities, however, and new policies that may result in a less active federal role in human and community resource programs. Will such shifts in federal support and emphasis lead to retreat from the hoped-for advances in housing, health, manpower, and educational services, and thus weaken the underpinnings of effective income security measures? If so, can we expect that future increases in social security benefits will truly enable the beneficiaries to improve their living standards?

FEDELE F. FAURI
Vice President
The University of Michigan

PREFACE

Social security in this country, as we have come to realize, comprises a complex set of governmental and private arrangements against what Franklin Roosevelt called the "misfortunes which cannot be wholly eliminated in this manmade world of ours." The chapters that follow review, analyze, and explain major currents in social security program development in the United States during the past 35–40 years. In covering federal, federal-state, and employer measures dealing with the contingencies of retirement, invalidity, survivorship, unemployment, and disability, as well as health insurance, I may have cast my net over a larger target than can be satisfactorily captured in so brief a volume. The reader must judge whether the result is a reasonably successful one.

This book deals with the major public social insurance programs, the experience under them, and major social policy problems and issues. It also suggests areas of desirable program improvement and aims to inform the general reader, as well as students of social security. It should also be useful to people working in agencies operating social security programs who find, more and more often, that they need a broader understanding of the place of their own activities in the complex context of public and private programs.

In the course of this task, I have fortunately been able to draw upon a background of experience in legislative and pro-

gram planning of federal and federal-state social insurance programs beginning in late 1936; provision of technical assistance
to other countries in the capacity of an international social
security advisor; and discussion of problems and issues in social
security with classes of university students during the past decade.

Many former and present colleagues have made contributions
to this volume, directly and indirectly. John Carroll, Alfred
Skolnik, Tom Staples, Daniel Price, Peter Barth, Robert Goodwin, and Joseph Hickey, among others, read and commented on
sections of the manuscript. Fred Black and Jerry Cates, former
students, made useful suggestions on an early version. Special
notes of acknowledgement are due Saul Blaustein and Nelson
Cruikshank who read and criticized the entire manuscript. Other
staff members of the Departments of Labor and H.E.W. also
supplied additional information.

These chapters were initially composed in briefer compass as
part of a forthcoming volume, *The Government and Social
Welfare,* coauthored by Wayne Vasey and myself; I am grateful
to him for encouragement, valuable suggestions, criticisms, and
insights into social welfare policy. F. E. Peacock, Publishers,
gave permission to use these materials in their present form.

Marcia Myers, Maralyn Jennings, and Carol Etring typed and
retyped many versions of the manuscript and Virginia Chupp
and Rosalie Stluka provided valuable research assistance. Edward Surovell, Betty Lu Brydges, and Joyce Kornbluh made
valued and valuable suggestions in the translation of the manuscript into published form. Susan Wineberg prepared the index.
A special acknowledgment is due Louis Ferman for the initial
suggestion to undertake this volume and for his encouragement
throughout the entire undertaking.

With all others who discuss or write about social security in
the United States, I am indebted to the staff of the Social
Security Administration and its Office of Research and Statistics
for responding to numerous requests for program information
and interpretation; the work of that organization is a model of
excellence in the public service. For any errors of fact and
interpretation, the author alone is responsible.

April, 1973   PHILIP BOOTH

SOCIAL SECURITY
IN AMERICA

ABBREVIATIONS

AFDC	Aid to Families with Dependent Children
AFL-CIO	American Federation of Labor and Congress of Industrial Organizations
CCC	Civilian Conservation Corps
CWA	Civil Works Administration
DHEW	Department of Health, Education, and Welfare
DI	Disability Insurance
DOL	Department of Labor
EOA	Economic Opportunity Act
FERA	Federal Emergency Relief Administration
HI	Hospital Insurance
ILO	International Labor Office
MDTA	Manpower Development and Training Act
NCHS	National Center for Health Statistics
NCSS	National Center for Social Statistics, DHEW
OASDHI	Old Age, Survivors', Disability Health Insurance
OASDI	Old Age, Survivors', and Disability Insurance
OASI	Old Age and Survivors' Insurance
PIA	Primary Insurance Amount
PWA	Public Works Administration
RRB	Railroad Retirement Board
SMIB	Supplementary Medical Insurance Benefits
SRA	Social and Rehabilitation Services
SSA	Social Security Administration
SSA-ORS	Social Security Administration, Office of Research and Statistics
TDI	Temporary Disability Insurance
TRA	Trade Adjustment Act
UI	Unemployment Insurance
VA	Veterans Administration
WC	Workmen's Compensation

I

Social Change
and Program Development:
An Overview

A complex and varied array of public and private measures protect Americans against two major hazards—loss or interruptions of income and deficiencies in income that undermine family health and security and, where widespread, endanger the health and security of our society. To cope with these hazards, governmental income security measures in the United States have taken two principal forms: first, social insurance protection of wage earners and their families against the loss of income due to the contingencies of old age, survivorship, work injury, unemployment, and disability and against the cost of health services; second, public assistance, designed to assure a minimum level of subsistence to those with insufficient or no social insurance protection—the needy aged, families without a wage earner or those whose breadwinner, handicapped by illness or other disadvantage, cannot provide even a subsistence level of living for his family. We date these programs from the Social Security Act of 1935, when the federal government assumed responsibility for protection against major risks to worker and family security. Although the act was only a start in many areas, it formed the foundation for growth of a comprehensive program.

An array of private arrangements supplements these public measures. In areas such as health benefits that government has entered only partially, private plans cover risks that government has left largely unprotected. In retirement, unemployment, and work injury, for example, private plans supplement protection under government programs.

We should note the distinction between social security in the sense of a social goal, and social insurance as a *method* of attaining that goal. "Social security for the American pioneer was . . . described as a musket hanging over the fireplace."[1] In twentieth century society, and for the urban industrial sector of all countries, major risks to family security arise from interruptions in income caused by old age, unemployment, disability, and death of the family breadwinner. By contrast, for the rural poor and economically insecure city workers, risks lie in underemployment, malnutrition, ill health, immobility, and lack of marketable skills. Social insurance is an appropriate device for dealing with the former risks but it has little to contribute to the latter, which can be dealt with more effectively by preventive health measures, income deficiency payments, special education training and related services; measures such as these are outside the scope of this volume.

The depression of the 1930s enabled the country to overcome long-standing inhibitions against federal intervention in the social and economic life of the American people in the interests of their economic security. Earlier government measures to alleviate distress due to unemployment, old age, and family dependency had been piecemeal, limited to emergency situations, and, except for natural disasters, they were considered to be local or state matters. In large part they had been designed to supplement the efforts of voluntary agencies.[2] In fact, as Edwin Witte pointed out, "until 1931, poor relief was regarded . . . as exclusively a local responsibility — not one dollar was ever contributed for unemployment or any other form of relief by either

1. Sanford Cohen, "The Relevance and the Validity of Social Insurance in Developing Economies," in *The Role of Social Security in Economic Development,* Social Security Administration, Research Report no. 27 (Washington, 1968), p. 219.

2. See Roy Lubove, *The Struggle for Social Security, 1900–1935* (Cambridge: Harvard University Press, 1968). Idealization of voluntarism went hand in hand with limitation of governmental intervention. Community, employer, and industry approaches were thought of as the "American Way of Life."

the federal or state governments."[3] The national government provided disaster relief to individuals, but typically it was directed to protection of productive resources, e.g. factories, rescue of livestock, and devastated farm areas. In the last year of the Hoover Administration, through the Emergency Relief and Construction Act of 1932, federal advances and loans to states were authorized for relief work, marking the first use of federal funds for direct relief of distressed individuals and their families. Channeling these funds through state agencies had political acceptability, particularly since it avoided federal responsibility for providing services directly.

Movements supporting direct financial aid to the needy, including old age pensions, had met dogged opposition. Such pensions, it was said, "would kill all initiative and turn people into lazy, good-for-nothings who would rely on the state for their maintenance. Only the shiftless who squandered money faced a penniless old age."[4]

The variety of emergency federal measures introduced between 1933 and 1935 by the New Deal provided direct federal financial assistance to millions of families through the Federal Emergency Relief Administration (1933), which expended $2.5 billion in fiscal years 1934 and 1935. This positive commitment of federal resources to the care of the jobless used direct grants to the states, which distributed them through the localities. The federal-state operation influenced the shaping of public assistance under the Social Security Act.[5] In addition, the Civil Works Administration and Civilian Conservation Corps (1933) initiated large-scale work relief programs for needy families and individuals. The Works Projects Administration in 1935 marked

3. E. E. Witte, *Social Security Perspectives,* ed. R. J. Lampman (Madison: University of Wisconsin Press, 1962), p. 5. Public perceptions of the new programs are illustrated in the title of the address from which this quotation is taken: "Social Security: A Wild Dream or a Practical Plan?"

4. Henriette Epstein to Wilbur J. Cohen, 30 July 1970; from recollections of Henriette Epstein on the early efforts of the American Association for Old Age Security, formed by Abraham Epstein in 1927.

5. See Harry L. Hopkins, *Spending to Save* (New York: W. W. Norton & Co., 1936); R. E. Sherwood, *Roosevelt and Hopkins* (New York: Harper, 1948); and Josephine Brown, *Public Relief 1929–1939* (New York: Henry Holt & Co., 1940).

a new federal relief policy, moving away from direct financial assistance to needy families with employable adults toward work relief.[6]

General recognition of the inadequacy of these emergency measures and the need for permanent, comprehensive programs of public assistance and social insurance had taken shape by 1934. State programs for aid to the needy aged, widows, and orphans were beginning to spread, although handicapped by inadequate funds available to hard-pressed state and local governments, since many had used up their borrowing and spending authority.

COMMITTEE ON ECONOMIC SECURITY

In June 1934 President Roosevelt created the Committee on Economic Security, charging it to make studies and recommendations for providing "safeguards against misfortunes, which cannot be wholly eliminated in this man-made world of ours."[7] The committee was chaired by Secretary of Labor Frances Perkins, who provided active and effective leadership. It included Henry Wallace and Henry Morgenthau, the Secretaries of Agriculture and the Treasury, Attorney-General Homer S. Cummings, and Harry Hopkins, the Federal Emergency Relief Administrator. Its mission was carried out by a technical board headed by Arthur Altmeyer, Assistant Secretary of Labor, later chairman of the Social Security Board and Commissioner of Social Security, 1946-1953. An Advisory Council of 23 labor, employer, and public representatives was backed up by a professional staff headed by Edwin E. Witte. Witte provided a happy combination of expertise on labor legislation and the legislative process, the latter gained as head of the Wisconsin State Legislative Reference Service. The committee's recommendations were embodied in legislation introduced in January 1935. After

6. See Hilary M. Leyendecker, *Problems and Policies in Public Assistance* (New York: Harper, 1955); Grace Abbott, *From Relief to Social Security* (Chicago: University of Chicago Press, 1941); and Frances Piven and Richard Cloward, *Regulating the Poor* (New York: Pantheon Books, 1971).

7. Quoted in *Report to the President of the Committee on Economic Security* (Washington: Government Printing Office, 1935), p. v.

much debate, modification, and compromise, they were enacted as the Social Security Act of 1935.[8]

The coincidence of economic and social pressures and political developments account for adoption of the Social Security Act at this juncture of American history. There is little doubt that the act would not have been adopted in 1935 except for acute public awareness of widespread deprivation, dependency, and hopelessness during the Great Depression that convinced the people and their representatives in Congress that government action was essential to relieve the human distress caused by unemployment, old-age dependency, insecurity, and widespread poverty.[9] They recognized, too, that people who had scrimped during their working years to provide for their old age by savings, insurance, and company pension plans found themselves equally as destitute as others whose improvidence or meager earnings provided no surplus over their subsistence needs for prolonged unemployment or future retirement.

Belief in the Puritan ethic was rudely shaken since hard work, savings, industriousness, and prudent investment had failed to assure security. In its place the role of government in providing a first line of defense against economic insecurity was accepted, however reluctantly, by an entire generation.

Public awareness of the need for new approaches underlay the conviction that nationwide distress and poverty must never happen again—that a floor of security must be provided by governmental provision of at least a minimum subsistence during unemployment and old age from funds set aside from earnings during employment. The writing, lecturing, and counseling of a group of early social security experts contributed greatly to acceptance by labor, church, educational, and legislative leaders. They included Abraham Epstein, Isaac M. Rubinow, Paul H. Douglas, Eveline M. Burns, Barbara N. Armstrong, J. Douglas

8. See E. E. Witte, *Development of the Social Security Act* (Madison: University of Wisconsin Press, 1962); A. J. Altmeyer, *The Formative Years of Social Security* (Madison: University of Wisconsin Press, 1966).

9. For the story of the Great Depression as recalled by an improvised battalion of survivors, see S. Terkel, *Hard Times* (New York: Avon Books, 1970); and Charles McKinley and Robert Frase, *Launching Social Security: A Capture and Record Account, 1935-1937* (Madison: University of Wisconsin Press, 1971).

Brown, Edwin E. Witte, Michael M. Davis, I. S. Falk, and Edgar Sydenstricker, among others. The American Association for Social Security and the work of Epstein and Rubinow, especially, influenced legislative and labor groups.

Yet, political considerations of a broader nature played an equally important role in accounting for the adoption of the social security program at this juncture. As Frederick Lewis Allen points out,

> The bill might not have seen the light of day until much later than 1935, if ever, had not President Roosevelt been worried about the offensive against his administration, not from those who thought it was doing too much, but from those who thought it was doing too little—from Huey Long with his "share the wealth" slogan, and Dr. Francis E. Townsend with his extraordinary proposal for putting old people on the federal payroll. Yet when the Social Security bill came before Congress it slipped toward passage on a broad tide of acceptance.[10]

While social insurance was regarded as "the first line of defense against destitution," as Altmeyer put it, public assistance formed "a second line to be relied upon to the extent that the first line proved to be inadequate."[11]

In order to help ensure a sound foundation for the new social security system, the Committee on Economic Security insisted that other equally basic measures must be taken. No social security system could provide economic security except built upon a foundation of employment and earnings that assured adequate living standard for the population; nor would wages or benefits assure adequacy of income in the absence of economic policies directed at preventing inflation and deflation and ensure that the promised pensions would provide stable purchasing power. Since social security payments replace only a portion of prior income from earnings, it was essential that workers accumulate savings and that these be protected by assurance that bank deposits, private pensions, and other assets would be safe-

10. Frederick Lewis Allen, "Economic Security: A Look Back and a Look Ahead," in *Economic Security for Americans* (New York: Columbia University Press, 1954), p. 18.
11. Altmeyer, *Formative Years of Social Security,* p. 16.

guarded. "Maximum employment" was identified as the "first objective of a program of economic security" through public works and related measures. In addition to expansion of public health services, insurance mechanisms should cover the costs of medical care. The committee counted on all of these as essential to the nation's economic security, and essential to the successful operation of the measures which it was recommending.[12]

Despite much favorable public sentiment and support, the broad scope of the measure raised many questions of policy and strategy, in and out of Congress. Some advised the President to limit the measure for the time being to old-age assistance (the least controversial title), while others urged inclusion of health insurance and a national unemployment insurance program. Roosevelt chose to retain the complete "package" of 11 titles, lest all controversial items be left to an uncertain future "more favorable climate." Although the bill was passed by a substantial majority, many members of Congress voted "yea" reluctantly, but expecting the courts to find the act unconstitutional.

THE SOCIAL SECURITY ACT

The Social Security Act (Economic Security Act, as introduced) was an omnibus measure containing the framework for cash payment programs (both insurance and assistance) as well as providing federal grants-in-aid to support a variety of health and welfare, public health, vocational rehabilitation, and related services. The grants-in-aid for state public assistance plans, which aided the aged, the blind, and dependent children, were not to replace existing state programs with a federal scheme but aimed rather to shore up plans whose aid to the helpless and poor was intermittent, restrictive, uncertain in amount, grudgingly given, and frequently demanded sacrifices of the recipient's dignity.

12. *Report of the Committee on Economic Security,* especially pp. 3-10, 46-50. Recommendations on health insurance were omitted from the report and from administration legislative recommendations until after World War II. See also Peter A. Corning, *The Evolution of Medicare,* SSA—ORS Research Report no. 29 (Washington, 1969); E. M. Burns, "Health Care Systems" in *Encyclopedia of Social Work* (1971), pp. 510-523; Altmeyer, Formative Years of Social Security, p. 16.

The founders of the social security program were primarily concerned with two staggering social problems: old-age dependency and widespread unemployment. Old age is a universal risk; all of us grow old and hope for a decent and comfortable retirement. Unemployment strikes unevenly; some experience layoffs every year or two, while for others regular year-round employment is to be expected. The basic approach to both risks was to use social insurance; yet because pensions would not be payable for several years, for those already past age 65 and not working would not build up benefit rights and because some industries were not covered, assistance to the needy aged was necessary to form a second line of defense. The jobless who did not qualify for unemployment insurance would have to rely upon the national work relief program (WPA continued until 1942) and on local and state direct relief (general assistance) where provided.

In short, the insurance mechanism with wage-related benefits as a matter of right was provided for those in the workforce. For those out of the workforce (the aged, the blind, and dependent children), public assistance was employed, with benefits designed to meet the deficiency between an individual's needs and his resources (or means).[13] The following pages sketch the structure of old-age and unemployment benefits under social insurance.

Old-Age Benefits

The old-age benefit system (now OASDHI, old-age, survivors', disability, and health insurance) was founded on three basic principles: (1) a national (not state-by-state) system, (2) compulsory for those in covered employments, (3) providing benefits as a matter of right (without regard to individual means or needs). As a wage-related scheme, the monthly benefit varied with the workers' former wages to build up an initial reserve. Payments would not begin until 1942, and contributions, starting in 1937, would be 1 percent of wages paid by both workers and employers on the first $3,000 of earnings per year.[14]

13. Eveline M. Burns, *Social Security and Public Policy* (New York: McGraw Hill, 1956), chapter 1.
14. *Social Security Bulletin, Annual Statistical Supplement, 1969,* Table 33, p. 49. About 92 percent of all wage and salary payments in covered employment

Initially, the system would cover all workers in all commercial industrial firms, including firms with only one worker. Since the courts had held a separate railroad system unconstitutional, railroad workers were also included, and legislation for that industry was subsequently adopted.[15] The self-employed, plus workers in agriculture, domestic service, non-profit organizations, and state and local government were left out pending experience with the initially covered population. Workers would acquire benefit rights through their employment; a calendar quarter (the basic unit) of coverage required earnings of at least $50 in covered employment. Eligibility for benefits, at age 65, called for a minimum number of quarters of coverage since initiation of the program. Only the worker himself could receive benefits, following the pattern of an insurance annuity system. The founders' cautiousness was demonstrated in the benefit schedule that would pay a monthly benefit of $51.25 to a worker retiring at age 65 after 40 years of employment at an average wage of $100 per month.[16] Yet despite initial restrictiveness, the system would include more people initially than within old-age insurance plans of any other country.[17] Upon this reasonable and workable foundation, the program could develop and expand with experience and, in time, provide more adequate protection to a larger part of the work force.

Unemployment Insurance

Widespread and long-term unemployment was as devastating a problem as old-age dependency, but unemployment, being less universal than old age, was approached differently. The program's founders desired to combine payments to the jobless with a device for stabilizing employment or reducing unemployment.[18] In parallel measures, the several million jobless were to be absorbed in productive employment in public works (PWA)

were thus subject to contributions; as wages rose, this percentage declined to 80 percent in 1950.

15. Section 17 of the Railroad Retirement Act, adopted in 1937, excluded railroad employment from coverage of the Social Security Act.

16. Witte, *Social Security Perspectives*, p. 122.

17. Ibid., p. 120. Some 33 million worked in covered employment in 1937. See *Statistical Supplement* (1969).

18. The scheme allowed for financial incentives (experience rating) to employers to stabilize employment and to minimize labor turnover.

and work-relief programs (WPA). But workers employed in commerce and industry would receive unemployment insurance payments in their future periods of joblessness from funds set aside for this purpose during good times. Since cash benefits for the unemployed were only a second-best and temporary substitute for work and wages, the essential basis of employment security, the plan also called for a tie between unemployment benefits and employment services to assure that jobless workers were given job information, vocational counseling, and referred to appropriate job vacancies. They would be paid benefits only if no suitable job was available. But underemployment, especially if prolonged, "creates needs that are not met merely by the assurance of an adequate alternative flow of income. It is important that workers' skills should not deteriorate through nonemployment and those whose skills have become obsolete should be retrained for other employment."[19] Although a sound and workable retirement insurance scheme needed to be organized nationally because it was as unfeasible for workers at retirement age to combine pension rights built up over their working lifetime in several states (with differing plans) as it was hazardous in terms of state financing, such considerations did not hold for unemployment insurance.[20] State legislatures had debated specific proposals since the late 1920s, but only Wisconsin had adopted a program by 1934. Some specialists favored a federal approach, and other states awaited federal action for fear of placing their employers at a competitive disadvantage by subjecting them to a tax not being levied on their competitors in neighboring states. So held the accepted wisdom of that day (and of the present). Thus state inaction made federal action necessary, to "encourage" all states to act, if workers throughout the country were to be protected. Because federal courts were hostile to innovative federal and state intervention into areas of economic security, any approach had to ensure that the

19. Burns, *Social Security and Public Policy,* p. 9. This philosophy, plus the need for public construction of hydroelectric power facilities, flood control, and highways, supported the extensive TVA, PWA, and WPA programs of the pre-World War II period.

20. See J. Douglas Brown, *An American Philosophy of Social Insurance* (Princeton: Princeton University Press, 1972), which sets out the rationale of a national compulsory contributory old-age benefit system, providing benefits as a right.

plan would withstand the court's scrutiny. Federal courts already had rejected pension insurance, regulation of hours, and child labor, among others, and there was the potential danger that they would rule the social security measures unconstitutional. The strategy chosen by Roosevelt's advisers was a dual one—a federal old-age benefit plan, and unemployment insurance to rest on a federal-state basis.

The mechanism that persuaded all states to enact unemployment insurance programs by mid-1937 was a federal payroll tax of 3 percent that was applied to employers in commerce and industry with 8 or more workers during 20 weeks in the year. Significantly, no federal benefit plan was provided; instead, the states were to establish their own plans under federal guidelines. Employers' contributions paid under an approved state unemployment benefit program would be credited against their federal tax liability up to a maximum of 90 percent. If the employer was awarded a reduced rate of contributions because of his favorable unemployment record, his credit against the federal tax would be no less than if he was contributing at the normal rate. The remaining 10 percent was to cover 100 percent of the costs of state and federal administration of the programs, rather than a smaller share, as under other federal-state programs. Covering all state administrative expenses was necessary to assure at least minimum adequacy of services and staff throughout the country, especially in nonindustrial and rural states having little interest in or experience with, and only skeleton personnel and expertise devoted to, labor and social legislation. As an incentive to state action, employers' federal tax receipts would not be used to pay benefits in any state without an approved program. The tax-offset device, it was hoped, would be accepted by the Supreme Court, based on earlier precedents.[21]

Federal requirements were limited to essentials, ensuring that the employers did not receive federal tax credit for their state contributions unless paid under a genuine unemployment insurance law, that benefits would be paid when due, only for involuntary unemployment, and would not be denied by the

21. *Florida v. Mellon*, 273 U.S. 12 (1926). The Supreme Court upheld the federal and state laws in May 1937 decisions: *Steward Machine Co. v. Davis*, 301 U.S. 548 (1937) and *Carmichael v. Southern Coal and Coke Co.*, 301 U.S. 495 (1937).

imposition of conditions that would weaken recently recognized labor standards.[22] Jobless workers filed benefit claims through public employment offices to assure that they would be referred to suitable work, if available. Finally, if dissatisfied with the decision on his or her claim, a worker was assured a fair hearing before an impartial tribunal.

THE FIRST YEARS

The two social insurance programs under the Social Security Act had modest beginnings by 1970 standards since they defined both the risk protected against and the covered population in rather narrow terms. In 1939, 55 percent of all workers in civilian employment were covered under the retirement program and only 50 percent under unemployment insurance (see Table 1). This cautious approach was not surprising, considering the novel schemes, inexperienced staffs, uncertain public and taxpayer reception, and unsettled constitutionality of the federal legislation until 1937.

However, when the test cases came to the Supreme Court for decision as to whether Congress could levy on taxpayers in all states to build a fund for payment of old-age pensions and encourage states to set up unemployment compensation programs, the Court found for the government, 6 to 3. Judge Cardozo's notable opinion emphasized that old-age dependency and unemployment were national problems which required national, rather than the accustomed state-by-state, solutions:

> Needs that were narrow or parochial a century ago may be interwoven in our day with the well-being of the nation. . . . Spreading from state to state, unemployment is an ill not particular but general, which may be checked, if Congress so determines, by the resources of the nation. But the ill is all one, or at least not greatly different, whether men are thrown out of work because there is no

22. The worker could not be denied benefits for refusal of an offer of work (a) where wages, hours, and working conditions were substandard; (b) if the vacancy was due to a labor dispute; or (c) if he would be required to join a company union or to resign from or refrain from joining a bonafide labor organization.

Table 1.

Labor Force, Employment and Estimated Workers Covered under Social Insurance Programs, 1939, 1954, and 1970

Employment and Coverage Status	1939	1954 (in millions)	1970*
Total Labor Force	55.6	67.8	86.2
Paid civilian employment	43.6	59.5	77.6
Wage and salary workers	33.2	49.8	70.8
Self-employed	10.4	9.7	6.9
Covered by:			
Public retirement programs	27.2	51.0	74.5
Old-age, survivors, disability and health insurance[1]	24.0	45.3	69.2
Railroad retirement system[2]	1.2	1.2	.6
Public employee retirement systems[3]	2.0	4.5	4.7
Unemployment insurance[4]	22.4	36.6	55.8
Workmen's compensation	22.0	39.7	58.8
Temporary disability insurance[5]	—	10.6	14.4
Armed forces[6]	.4	3.4	3.0

*Monthly averages for 1939 and 1954; December data for 1970. Except where noted, data before 1960 are for the 48 states and the District of Columbia; beginning 1960, include Alaska and Hawaii.

1. Beginning 1955, includes persons under both a state or local government retirement system and OASDHI. Excludes those eligible for elective or optional coverage not under OASDHI, mostly state and local government employees. Excludes armed forces and railroad employees shown below.

2. Covered jointly under OASDHI and railroad retirement beginning 1951.

3. Excludes state and local government employees covered both by OASDHI and own retirement programs (counted under OASDHI) and armed forces.

4. State, railroad, and, beginning 1955, federal civilian employee programs. Excludes armed forces.

5. Railroad and state programs. Excludes government employees covered by sick-leave provisions.

6. Covered under OASDHI, beginning January 1957, and under the Ex-Servicemen's Unemployment Compensation Act, beginning November 1958.

Source: Social Security Programs in the U.S., SSA, 1971.
Social Security Bulletin, Statistical Supplement, 1970, Table 5.

Table 2.

Benefit Payments under Public Income-Maintenance Programs and Individuals Receiving Cash Payments, 1940–1970

Program	1940	1950	1960	1970
	Amount in benefits (millions)[1]			
Total, cash and medical	$4,356	$9,508	$27,739	$79,906
Cash payments[2]	4,191	8,676	25,873	64,322
Social insurance	1,113	4,085	19,134	49,978
Old-age, survivors, disability, and health insurance[3]	35	961	11,245	31,570
Railroad retirement[4]	118	311	962	1,756
Public employee retirement[5]	264	813	2,674	9,187
Unemployment insurance[5]	535	1,468	3,025	4,305
Workmen's compensation: net of medical[6]	161	415	860	1,877
Temporary disability insurance: net of medical[7]	–	117	368	721
Veterans' pensions and compensation	428	2,236	3,476	5,480
Public aid	2,650	2,354	3,263	8,864
Special types of assistance[8]	628	2,062	2,943	8,229
General assistance	392	293	320	632
Work programs[9]	1,630	–	–	–
Medical services	165	832	1,846	15,584
Old age, survivors, disability, and health insurance	–	–	–	7,099
Workmen's compensation	95	200	435	1,050
Temporary disability insurance	–	7	41	66
Veterans' health and medical care	70	573	848	1,793
	–	52	522	5,576

	Individuals receiving cash payments (thousands)[1][10]			
Social insurance:				
Old-age, survivors, disability, and health insurance	113	3,012	14,298	29,812
Railroad retirement	144	387	792	972
Public employee retirement[4]	249	596	1,448	3,033
Unemployment insurance[5]	1,024	1,432	1,794	1,635
Veterans' pensions and compensation	933	3,359	4,271	5,462
Public aid:				
Special types of assistance[8]	3,183	5,120	5,811	12,757
General assistance	4,038	1,105	969	1,056
Work programs	2,817	—	—	—

1. Includes benefits to dependents where applicable.
2. Includes lump-sum payments.
3. Excludes net payments in lieu of benefits (transfers) under financial interchange with railroad retirement system.
4. Excludes refunds of employee contributions to those leaving the service; includes benefits to retired military personnel and their survivors.
5. Benefits under state unemployment insurance laws, unemployment compensation for railroad workers, for federal employees, for ex-servicemen, veterans under the Servicemen's Readjustment Act of 1944 and the Veterans' Readjustment Assistance Act of 1952, and payments under the temporary extended unemployment insurance program and the Automotive Products Trade Act of 1965. Includes cash allowances to unemployed workers in training under the Manpower Development and Training Act of 1962.
6. Benefits paid under federal workmen's compensation laws and under state laws by private insurance carriers, by state funds, and by self-insurers; 1940 and 1950 data exclude Alaska and Hawaii.
7. Includes payments under private plans where applicable in the five jurisdictions with programs.
8. Includes the major federally aided programs of Old-Age Assistance, Aid to Families with Dependent Children, Aid to the Blind, and Aid to the Permanently and Totally Disabled.
9. Includes work relief earnings and other emergency aid programs. Number of recipients partly estimated.
10. For OASDHI, average monthly number; for railroad retirement, public employee retirement, public aid, and veterans' programs, number on rolls, June 30; for unemployment insurance, average weekly number. Data for workmen's compensation and temporary disability insurance not available.

Source: Social Security Bulletin, Stat. Supp., 1970, Tables 3, 10, 20, 21, 132. *Social Security Programs in the U.S.,* Social Security Administration, 1971. See *Social Security Bulletin,* May 1972, Table M-1, 2.

longer any work to do, or because the disabilities of age make them incapable of doing it. Preventing want in old age is plainly national in area and in dimension.[23]

Perhaps the system's major virtue lay in the fact that the program's founders had created so reasonable an approach that it would not merely survive the early strains placed upon it, but create public and congressional confidence. The social security program has now become the major element in the American family's economic security. The old-age benefit system was transformed within four years into a family-oriented scheme covering dependents and survivors. In the next three decades it achieved universal coverage of the population, protection against invalidity and health care of the aged, with benefits tied to the price level to assure against loss of purchasing power. The high quality of the program's administration elicited congressional and public confidence, and it was entrusted with heavier responsibilities as time went on.[24]

In related areas, advances came more slowly, especially where progress waited on state action. Unemployment insurance moved haltingly to extend coverage to the "other half" of the work force which was initially not covered. As wages rose, some states did extend coverage and increase benefits during the 1940s and 1950s, but others held back. For many states, fear of interstate competitive disadvantages led to gradual changes in benefits; lagging behind wages and prices, their programs have continued to exhibit increasing differences, rather than moves toward similar approaches to program goals.

Fear of competitive interstate disadvantages also contributed to the lag in workmen's compensation. Although that program's origins went back to the 1920s, it stood apart from the currents which caused the Social Security Act to move ahead and made little progress toward meeting the needs of the work-injured for compensation, medical care, and rehabilitation. In the mid-1950s, discouragement over the program's failure to make long overdue improvements led exasperated critics to speak of extreme changes. Some believed the workmen's compensation program would be better off returning to the earlier employer

23. *Helvering v. Davis,* 301 U.S. 319 (1937).
24. Brown, *Social Insurance,* pp. 23-24.

liability approach, while others looked to federal approaches, perhaps similar to unemployment or retirement insurance. Witte, a leader in the field, opined that fundamental change would be demanded if the state systems were not improved, but hoped that lagging improvements would be hastened by presidential recommendations.[25] The need for drastic changes and the alternatives suggested were repeated in 1972, as discussed in Chapter III.

President Roosevelt thought it advisable to omit health insurance from the recommendations for action on a social security program in 1935, which left an unfilled gap until the advent of Medicare, 30 years later. Roosevelt's plan to use the 1940 election to push for health insurance was laid aside because of the war in Europe;[26] it now stands as the key social security issue of the 1970s.

In 1940 we had begun to create a system of income support and social services designed to meet the basic needs of people under all but the most stressful economic conditions. Although only three of every five workers were covered by social insurance and generous provision had been made for most contingencies of income loss or special needs, protection against wage loss in the event of nonwork-connected disability was still in the future, and health insurance was not actively debated. But those who were shaping or recommending changes in policy felt that such gaps could be filled and inadequacies dealt with by future incremental change. Measured against the backdrop of the times in which the programs were enacted, changes of the past 30 years could be called impressive. Yet by the end of the 1960s discontent was being voiced in strident tones, and a Republican president was putting "welfare reform" at the top of his agenda for domestic policy. It was obvious that many of the social programs of the 1930s and 1940s were inadequate for the 1970s.

What had happened? The experience of the period suggests a number of explanations, but fewer answers. Urban decay, racial discrimination and protest, rural and inner-city poverty, all

25. Witte, *Social Security Perspectives*, pp. 383-384.
26. Corning, *Evolution of Medicare*. See also E. N. Feingold, *Medicare, Policy, and Politics* (San Francisco: Chandler Publishing Co., 1966), pp. 91-95; Joseph P. Lash, *Eleanor and Franklin* (New York: W. W. Norton & Co., 1971), pp. 465-467.

presented demands unmet by traditional incremental methods. As a government economist put it in 1969: "It is quite clear that our economic system has failed in raising those at the bottom of the income pyramid to even minimum acceptable living standards while providing a rising standard of living for the rest of us. Poverty in the country is not only relative, it is also absolute. It is stark and, for many, completely hopeless."[27]

The problem has not been one of failure to increase our expenditures for social welfare, either in relative or absolute terms. While the gross national product increased more than tenfold between fiscal 1940 and 1971, from $95 billion to $1,008 billion, social welfare expenditures went up nearly twentyfold, from about $9 billion to more than $170 billion per year, and accounted for 16.9 percent of GNP in 1971, in contrast to 9.2 percent in 1940. Per capita social welfare expenditures rose from $66 to $813, a twelvefold increase.[28]

The increased attention to human need, which these figures indicate, reflected heightened public sensitivity to its existence. To many social critics our affluence made the existence of widespread poverty a reproach whose persistence was acknowledged as an acute national problem in the 1960s. Initially we addressed the problem as "pockets of poverty in the midst of plenty." By mid-decade we regarded it as a challenge to be overcome and expressed some confidence in our ability to remove it: "The United States is the first major nation in history which can look forward to victory over poverty. Our wealth, our income, our technical know-how and our productive capacity put this goal within our grasp. As a nation, we clearly have the capacity to achieve this victory; what we need now is a commitment on the part of the people, the communities, private organizations and all levels of government."[29]

While the Economic Opportunity Act of 1964 (EOA) was the

27. Helen O. Nicol, "The Economic Basis for Social Welfare Planning" (address delivered at the National Roundtable Conference of the American Public Welfare Association, Dallas, Dec. 9-12, 1969).

28. Ida C. Merriam and Alfred Skolnik, *Social Welfare Expenditures under Public Programs, 1929-1966* (Washington: SSA—ORS, 1968), Tables I–IV; Alfred Skolnik and Sophie Dales, "Social Welfare Expenditures, 1970-71," *Social Security Bulletin,* December 1971, Tables 2-4.

29. U.S., Congress, House, Committee on Education and Labor, *Economic Opportunity Act of 1964: Report,* 88th Cong., 2d sess., 1964, H. Rept. 1458.

product of a great many forces, we should note that one of them, the Employment Act of 1946, pledged governmental action to provide employment opportunity to all who are able and available for work. The Area Development Act of 1961 anteceded and the Manpower Development and Training Act of 1962 (MDTA) complemented the EOA. Civil rights and federal aid to education carried this strain of legislation further.[30] Each dealt with another facet of a complex of problems and attempted to shape a multiheaded structural approach to employment opportunity for those who were without jobs because they had the wrong skills, lived in the wrong places, or had the wrong skin color. Had the objectives of the 1946 legislation been realized by appropriate and effective public and private measures leading to reasonably full employment at decent pay, our social welfare programs would not have encountered the same pressures to accomplish conflicting objectives, e.g., to provide wage-related benefits, income deficiency payments, and antipoverty guarantees through the same programs.

The substantial expenditures on social welfare do not necessarily indicate comparable commitment to the poor. Social security, education, and health spending, for example, while benefiting the least advantaged, provide greater benefit to the more affluent. The Kennedy and Johnson Administrations expressed a determination to redress the balance of opportunity for the poor. In so doing, government recognized the structural nature of poverty, unemployment and underemployment, and the failure of macroeconomic measures to reach those at the bottom. The urban renewal, Model Cities, and manpower programs adopted a more targeted approach to reach the poor and disadvantaged. Although the expenditures of these programs did not match the eloquence of their promises, they at least acknowledged the nature and extent of unmet human needs.

Between 1960 and 1971, the public assistance program, which is most directly related to needs of the poor, increased spending from $4.0 billion to $17.6 billion, a more than fourfold increase.[31] The fact that it took place during a period of

30. Civil rights and federal aid to education carried this strain of legislation further. See J. L. Sundquist, *Politics and Policy* (Washington: Brookings Institution, 1968), chapter 1.

31. *Social Security Bulletin,* May 1972, Tables M–26 and M–28.

affluence, although impressive, has also been a source of chagrin and perplexity. As a percentage of gross national product, this indicates a favorable response to claims of increasing commitment; in 1960-71, for example, expenditures for public assistance increased by 50 percent from 0.8 percent to 1.2 percent of GNP.[32] But by comparison with the numbers whose income qualified them for assistance, the figures also reflect continuing exclusion of even greater numbers of the poor. Some 15 million people received public assistance in June 1972, about one half of the 25 million counted as poor.[33]

The magnitude and character of societal changes in the past three decades required more than the social insurance, public assistance, and social services envisaged in the 1935 Social Security Act. Inadequate housing, mental health problems, lack of jobs, need for vocational training, and juvenile delinquency also invited federal action under successive administrations. These piecemeal efforts reflected a problem-by-problem approach rather than a clear commitment to planned solutions of our social ills.[34]

Seeds of social legislation of the mid-1960s lay dormant in the 1950s awaiting a favorable climate for germination and growth. As Sundquist states:

> In one of the most remarkable outpourings of major legislation in the history of the country, the Congress in 1964 and 1965 had expressed the national purpose in bold and concrete terms — to outlaw racial discrimination in many of its forms, to improve educational opportunity at every level, to eradicate poverty, to assure health care for older people, to create jobs for the unemployed, to cleanse the rivers and the air and protect and beautify man's outdoor environment.[35]

Despite this legislation no one maintained that we were in com-

32. Ibid., Table M-29.

33. G. Y. Steiner, *The State of Welfare* (Washington: Brookings Institution, 1971); Piven and Cloward, *Regulating the Poor;* and, from another perspective, Leonard Goodwin, *Do the Poor Want to Work?* (Washington, Brookings Institution, 1972). See also SSA-ORA, *Monthly Benefit Statistics,* July 1972.

34. A. M. Rivlin, *Systematic Thinking for Social Action* (Washington: Brookings Institution, 1971), chapter 2.

35. Sundquist, *Politics and Policy,* p. 3.

mand of our problem. Indeed, we appeared overwhelmed by environmental pollution, social unrest, continuing racial discrimination, continuing urban decay, fiscal crises of state and local governments, and a soaring welfare load, which were all resistant to efforts at solution.

Failure to reduce either family dependency on public assistance or the high unemployment concentrated in urban ghettos could not be charged to inadequate welfare and income maintenance programs. These could not create jobs, open opportunities, or eliminate discrimination. Nor could they restructure the tax system to finance the enlarged public services that would provide jobs and earnings for the jobless and wageless.

INCOME SECURITY EXPANSION

The three and a half decades after 1935 saw the income maintenance and social services programs under the Social Security Act expanded and tested under such changing conditions as wartime prosperity and full employment, and recurrent periods of recession, recovery, and readjustment. Women entered the labor force in larger numbers, men retired earlier, and youth acquired more schooling before joining the work force. Population moved from agriculture to industry, trade, and service, and from farm to the city and then to the suburbs.

The growing number and proportion of women in covered employment under social security, a fourfold increase since 1937, has had some impact on social security programs and their operations. Part-week and part-time work have become normal occupational statuses. When federal and state security legislation was designed, women constituted 27 percent of covered workers; in 1970, 38 percent, up by 40 percent. Now they constitute more than half (52 percent) of all beneficiaries, but they received but 46 percent of all benefits in 1971. Women receive lower retirement and disability benefits than men due primarily to fewer years of employment, largely in low-paid occupations and industries, as well as pay discrimination for the same work. Special disqualifications in unemployment insurance cut off benefits for wives who leave work to accompany their husbands to a new work location (or to a new military post) and cancel benefits when they leave work to bear children.

Long-standing complaints of sex discrimination arose from a variety of sources: lower occupational status and earnings, non-recognition of household management and child care as productive services (in national economic terms) and discriminatory program benefits and requirements such that a working couple benefits may be lower than they would be if only one of them had produced the aggregate family earnings, and the invidious disqualifications under unemployment insurance applying to wives and mothers. Various proposals to satisfy these complaints are under study.

The second half-century saw more aggressive action by organized labor and minority groups, which asserted claims to equality of opportunity and a larger share of employment, education, and other aspects of the nation's affluence. The working classes were achieving a greater measure of economic security and a share of the country's prosperity and were concerned that their increased family security would be endangered by long-term unemployment, sickness, premature old age, and death of the family breadwinner. Sensitivity to interruption of income has been accentuated by family living and spending patterns, which call for firm financial commitments not easily reduced or postponed: monthly payments for shelter and other necessities such as the family car, school or college tuition, insurance, and household appliances, as well as income and property taxes. Even relatively high-paid workers quickly find themselves in a bind when their earnings are interrupted or sharply reduced. Thus a strong interest in improved income maintenance accompanied advances in levels of living.

INTERRELATIONSHIPS

Before discussing more than three decades of social security development, we should remind ourselves of the relationship between the piecemeal efforts referred to earlier and our perception of the essential nature of the system. In fact, the social security system is a combination of diverse government and voluntary measures. Some risks to income security are covered by several programs, others by none at all. Benefits under some programs may apply to everyone, others to only specific occupation or age groups. Some programs are financed and administrated by either federal or state governments, others by both. Nowhere is there "any provision for consistency of policy or any central responsibility over the system as a whole."[36] But in a society where governmental responsibility for income security has grown unsystematically, it is no surprise that measures to close coverage gaps, improve benefits, and coordinate financing have not proceeded under a unified comprehensive policy or plan.

This complex of approaches presents administrative and policy problems that affect the programs' interrelationships. For example, an older worker, laid off, may have rights to both social security retirement and unemployment benefits. The victim of a work injury left with a permanent total disability may "be entitled" to workmen's compensation, social security disability benefits, and, in Rhode Island for example, temporary disability benefits. Either of them may also have acquired rights under his employer's retirement, paid sick leave, supplementary unemployment benefits, or other benefit plans. If in need, he might receive public assistance. Program expansion to encompass new risks complicates their interrelationships. Entitlement to one benefit rests upon entitlement to another: hospital insurance under Medicare rests upon entitlement to (not necessarily receipt of) social security or railroad retirement cash benefits. But receipt of one benefit may cause ineligibility for another benefit or a reduction in its amount. This is true of unemployment compensation in some states when beneficiaries become eligible for, or receive, workmen's compensation or OASDI benefits.

Such instances may be routine for the agencies involved, but are dramatic and painful for individual recipients. For example, the 20 percent increase in social security benefits effective in October 1972 had a "nightmarish" effect (to use the language of the *New York Times,* October 3, 1972) upon more than 180,000

36. Clair Wilcox, *Toward Social Welfare* (New York: Richard D. Irwin, Inc., 1969), p. 91; Lenore E. Bixby, "Women and Social Security in the U.S.," *Social Security Bulletin,* September 1972, pp. 6-7. See also *Report of the Task Force on Social Insurance and Taxes to Citizens Advisory Council on the Status of Women* (1969) and *Report of 1971 Advisory Council on Social Security,* mimeographed (SSA–ORS, 1971).

recipients of old-age assistance since the increased retirement benefit raised their monthly income above the eligibility level.[37]

Side effects of such program improvements may well be unavoidable, but they can be avoided or ameliorated by utilizing appropriate antidotes. Unfortunately, information and communication filter unevenly into the legislative process and those who wish to prevent ill effects may not have access to a majority of the congressional committees or legislative bodies concerned.

During the past three and a half decades, earnings from employment provided economic security for more people than ever before in our history, but most families, as well as the young and the aged, were increasingly dependent upon money income. In earlier years in our country the aged shared the food and shelter of their children and made their own contribution to family support and comfort in the home, the family farm, or other enterprise. Today, they must turn to social security.

As the labor force expanded by 55 percent between 1939 and 1970, civilian employment rose by over 75 percent, (see Table 1). Extension of coverage under the law, however, was more influential than other factors in accounting for the greater increases in social insurance coverage than in either the labor force or employment, as shown below:

Program	Increase in Coverage 1939-70 (percent)
OASDHI	185
Unemployment insurance	130
Workmen's compensation	165
Public employee retirement	135*
Railroad retirement	(-50)†

*Excluding dual coverage
†Decline

37. See pp. 125–128 for discussion of overlapping public and private benefit measures. A recent study indicates that 119 million beneficiaries could have been aided in fiscal 1972 by income transfer programs but that actually the programs included no more than 60 million individuals. James R. Stonery, *Public Income Transfer Programs: The Incidence of Multiple Benefits and the Issues Raised by their Receipt,* Joint Economic Committee, Subcommittee on Fiscal Policy, Paper no. 1 (Washington: Government Printing Office, 1972), p. 1.

Social security payments, as well as the number of beneficiaries, have risen more sharply than the covered work force. Although few people acquired rights to benefits in the early years until they had several years of employment, the number of aged and disabled receiving benefits began to mount as disability and health benefits were added and as early retirement benefits (at age 62) became more common. Between 1950 and 1970, the number of beneficiaries in the major programs (except for the railroad system) increased at least fourfold, and benefits went up even more, as shown below:

Increases in Numbers of Beneficiaries and Amount of Payments, 1950-70

	No. of Beneficiaries	*Amount of Benefit Payments*
OASDHI	10 times	30 times
Railroad retirement	2 times	5 times
Public employment retirement	5 times	12 times
Temporary disability insurance	na	6 times
Unemployment compensation	na	3 times
Workmen's compensation	na	4times

The marked increase in the number of retired government workers reflected improved pension plans even more than increases in government employment. Benefit payments under all social security programs had quadrupled in the 1940s, and then increased eleven-fold in the next two decades. Some 26 million workers and their dependents were receiving OASDHI retirement, disability, and survivors benefits by 1970. Payments doubled as an element of personal income, rising from 4 percent in 1950 to 8.9 percent in 1970.[38]

In the private sector, following the same trend, retirement coverage expanded threefold.[39] Thus both public and private sources provided a floor of protection for a growing part of the

38. *Statistical Supplement,* 1970, Table 4, p. 26.
39. From 10 million to 28 million; W. W. Kolodrubetz, "Employee Benefit Plans in 1968," *Social Security Bulletin,* April 1970, Table 1, p. 38. See also Table 14 below.

country's work force against the risks of income loss due to retirement, long-term disability, premature death, unemployment and work injury. As workers acquired entitlement to benefits, their utilization of the program was reflected in rising benefit rolls. For example, as the infirmities of aging added to workers' difficulties in meeting job requirements, the retired population increased.

During almost four decades of change the social security system, while continuing to emphasize replacement of lost earnings and the need to safeguard workers against any undermining of their living standards, also exhibited concern for poverty prevention to insure those at the margin of insecurity against slipping into poverty when their earnings were interrupted. Yet as protection of the skilled and regularly employed was improved by public and private measures, disparities between the "haves" and the "have nots" became more evident. In the following chapters we shall focus on such major issues as:

1. the extent to which the population at risk was covered;
2. the eligibility conditions whereby the covered population qualify for benefits;
3. the amount and duration of benefit payments, their adequacy in replacing wage loss or serving as a defense against poverty;
4. the financing of the system; and
5. the basic elements in the administrative structure and operations whereby people exercise their benefit rights.

II

Social Insurance for the Aged, Disabled, and Survivors

THE EXPANSION OF SOCIAL SECURITY

The old-age benefits program within 35 years became the keystone of the nation's social security framework, extending to virtually the entire population and providing family benefits for a wide range of contingencies, including the wage earner's prolonged total disability, retirement, need for medical care, and death. It has been suggested that the system's life insurance protection "may be one of the most valuable possessions of almost every family with children."[1]

The 1939 Amendments

The 1939 amendments constituted a major shift in the financing and benefit structures of the program, a shift which would not have been accepted by the Congress except for the analysis and unanimous support of the esteemed membership of the Advisory Council on Social Security. The 1937-38 Advisory Council, authorized by the Senate Committee on Finance, was the first of a series of tripartite advisory groups appointed to

---

1. Ida C. Merriam, "Income Maintenance: Social Insurance and Public Assistance," in *Social Security in International Perspective,* ed. Shirley Jenkins (New York: Columbia University Press, 1969), p. 59.

study and recommend program improvements.[2] Each subsequent Advisory Council has had a core of employee, employer, and public members who had served in prior bodies, just as the 1937-38 council included members from the 1934 Committee on Economic Security. Major program changes have grown out of the recommendations they developed; Nelson Cruikshank, former director of the AFL-CIO Department of Social Security, views the use of these bodies as contributing substantially to the wide public acceptance of the program.[3] As Brown has put it, the councils provided a significant linkage between the legislative and executive branches of government that was of key importance in the growth and development of this very complex system.[4]

The 1939 amendments shifted the social security system from an individual to a family security program and constituted the first major change after 1935. The 1937-38 Advisory Council had called for protecting the worker's wife and children during his retirement, and his widow and orphans, should he die prematurely.[5] The new amendments made benefits payable in 1940, rather than in 1942, as provided originally. Because the intent was to limit benefits to workers who had "substantially" retired, earnings of $15 per month or more called for suspension of benefits. Nominal earnings (less than $15 per month) were not viewed as inconsistent with retirement status. Financing was modified; a partial reserve with a contingency fund replaced the more substantial reserve originally projected. The contribution rate of 2 percent for worker and employer combined was to be increased at three-year intervals to a total of 6 percent in 1949.

The new provisions remained unaltered during the 1940s while the nation's energies concentrated on World War II and postwar readjustment. But it was recognized that changes would surely be needed to take account of (1) the higher wages and

2. It was followed by the Second Advisory Council, which served in 1947-48; others served in 1957-58, 1963-63, and 1969-71. The Act provides that subsequent Councils be appointed in 1973 and every four years thereafter. Brown, *Social Insurance,* pp. 47-48.

3. Cruikshank to author, 16 Oct. 1972.

4. Brown, *Social Insurance,* pp. 44-54.

5. Since traditionally the husband was the family breadwinner and the wife was the homemaker, benefits were provided for wives and widows (and to parents) with dependency on the worker presumed without requiring proof of financial support.

prices of the 1940s, which had made the benefit and tax schedules obsolete, (2) the expansion of the work force, (3) rising public assistance payment levels, especially since old-age assistance payments, by 1945, were substantially higher than retirement benefits, and (4) private fringe benefit plans providing retirement and other benefits.[6] Yet Congress froze contributions at 2 percent during the 1940s despite recommendations by the Social Security Board and its successors that the scheduled increases take effect.[7]

Postwar planning during wartime was not neglected. Great Britain, whose people had felt war's hardships directly, planned comprehensive health, welfare, educational, and housing services for the entire population. The Beveridge program was no less than the British public hoped for, and no less than the War Cabinet had promised. A universal economic security system plus a national health service was enacted soon after World War II.[8] Yet more urgent demands in the U.S. gave an uncertain priority to national action that might carry out recommendations of studies conducted by the executive departments, congressional committees, private industry, and other voluntary efforts.[9]

The 1950 Amendments

After the war, a substantial revision and catching-up in social security protection was overdue. The Federal Security Agency and Department of Labor, responsible congressional committees, and private organizations had plans for improvement.[10]

6. Witte, *Social Security Perspectives,* pp. 23–29, 32–38.

7. R. J. Myers, *Social Insurance and Allied Government Programs* (New York: Richard D. Irwin, Inc., 1965), pp. 56–57.

8. Sir William Beveridge, *Social Insurance and Allied Services* (New York: Macmillan Co., 1942); also V. N. George, *Social Security: Beveridge and After* (London, Kegan Paul, 1968) on the changing role of social security in Great Britain.

9. Postwar planning was also represented: Wilbur J. Cohen, ed., *War and Post-War Social Security* (Washington: American Council on Public Affairs, 1942); National Resources Planning Board, *After the War—Full Employment* (Washington, 1943); and George B. Galloway and Assocs., *Planning for America* (New York, 1941). As for postwar full employment problems, see S. K. Bailey, *Congress Makes a Law: The Story behind the Employment Act of 1946* (New York; Columbia University Press, 1950), pp. 9–12.

10. U.S., Federal Security Agency, Social Security Administration, and Department of Labor, *Annual Reports,* especially 1945, 1947, 1948. See also *Issues in Social Security,* a staff report to the House Ways and Means Com-

A variety of their studies and reports addressed matters left aside in earlier legislation, such as health and disability protection. Not all of these were to be made effective at once; some, more controversial, were deferred for reconsideration in 1954, 1956, and thereafter. Nevertheless, the 1950 amendments were among the most significant in the program's history.

Even after ten years of OASI, public assistance remained the major source of protection against the hazards of old age and premature death, leading Congress to initiate a far-reaching revision of the social security system. As the House Ways and Means Committee put it in reporting out the 1949 amendments (enacted in 1950):

> The Congress is faced with a vital decision. . . .
> Inadequacies in the OASI program . . . threaten our economic well being. The assistance program . . . cares for a much larger number of people than the insurance program. . . . If not strengthened and expanded [it] may develop into a very costly and ill-advised system of non-contributory pensions, payable not only to the needy but to all individuals at or about retirement age who are no longer employed.[11]

The 1950 amendments set significant precedents for the future:

1. Coverage was extended to some farm and domestic service workers, some of the self-employed and federal government employees; nonprofit organizations and state and local governments could elect voluntary coverage. Some 10 million additional jobs were brought under the system.

2. To catch up with wages and prices, benefits were increased 78.5 percent, and higher minimum and maximum amounts established.

3. As a major precedent, the benefit increases were paid to

mittee (1946); *Report of the Advisory Council on Social Security to the Senate Committee on Finance,* Senate Document 149 (1948); and Cohen, *War and Post-War Social Security.*

11. U.S., Congress, House, *Social Security Amendments of 1949: Report on H.R. 6000,* 81st Cong., 1st sess., 1949, H. Rept. 81-1300. See also W. J. Cohen and R. J. Myers, "Social Security Amendments of 1950: Summary and Legislative History," *Social Security Bulletin,* October 1950, pp. 3-14.

former as well as future retirees to assure that their monthly benefits provide better protection against higher living costs.[12] For low-wage workers who had retired in 1940, for example, the new benefits might be as high as their preretirement earnings.

4. The retirement test now permitted beneficiaries to earn up to $50 per month without deduction from benefits.

5. Finally, the contribution rate, frozen since 1936 at 1 percent each (employer and employee), was increased to 1.5 percent upon a wage base raised from $3000 to $3600; a long-range contribution schedule called for a 6.5 percent (combined) tax rate in 1970.[13]

The minimum benefit was doubled, from $10 to $20 per month, and the maximum family benefit from $85 to $150 — nearly twice the former amount (Table 3). Coverage was

Table 3.

OASDI – Selected Benefit Provisions, 1935–1971

	Primary Insurance Amount		Maximum Family Benefits
	Min.	Max.	
1935	$10.00	$ 85.00	—
1939	10.00	(not specified)	$ 85.00
1950	20.00	80.00	150.00
1952	25.00	85.00	168.75
1954	30.00	105.00	200.00
1958	33.00	127.00	254.00
1961	40.00	127.00	254.00
1965	44.00	168.00	368.00
1967	55.00	218.00	434.40
1969	64.00	250.70	434.40
1971	70.40	295.40	517.00
1972	84.50	354.50	620.40

Source: Statistical Supplement, 1970, p. 23; *Higher Social Security Payments*, DHEW Publication (SSA), 73-10324, July 1972.

12. By contrast, private pensions promising a fixed dollar amount cannot generally adjust benefits to price changes. The 1950 amendment thus moved from the "private" toward the "social" insurance principle and gave pensioners greater protection against inflation.

13. Myers, *Social Insurance and Allied Government Programs*, p. 57. See also J. A. Pechman, H. R. Aaron, and M. K. Taussig, *Social Security: Per-*

also extended to 10 million formerly excluded jobs; eight of every ten jobs were now covered, compared to six in ten in 1936.[14] Inclusion of low-paid farm and domestic workers helped those who had little likelihood of acquiring security in old age from savings or employer pensions. For them, the social security benefit would be their sole or principal support. Covering the self-employed, and especially those in small family businesses, was a major contribution to their older years when savings and other resources were minimal.

Changes Since 1950

The 1950s saw coverage extended to most categories of workers still excluded, leaving only self-employed physicians and a few others to be included in 1965 and thereafter. Self-employed farmers[15] and professionals were included in 1954 and 1956, and hired farm and domestic worker coverage was expanded. Members of the armed forces were also brought into the system, apart from their military service pensions. Covered workers in nonprofit and state and local government employment (coverage to be elected by the *employers*) increased substantially during the 1960s.[16] On the other hand, although

---

spectives for Reform (Washington: Brookings Institution, 1968), pp. 262–272; and *Statistical Supplement,* 1970, pp. 13–22, for the history of benefit, coverage, and financing provisions.

14. The number of workers reporting covered earnings increased as follows:

1937	33 million	1960	73 million
1950	48 million	1965	81 million
1951	58 million	1970	94 million
1955	65 million		

Social Security Bulletin, Aug. 1971, p. 27; *Statistical Supplement,* 1970, Table 34.

15. J. Chester Ellickson, "Social Security for Farm Operators: Acceptance and Role in Farm Population Adjustment," *Journal of Farm Economics,* Dec. 1958, pp. 1662–1670. Farmers initially preferred to be excluded, looking upon social security as both unnecessary and in conflict with their judgment that individuals should provide for their own economic security through thrift and industry. Increased familiarity with the system decreased this aversion. When the advantages of extended coverage brought them under the program in 1955, there were practically no objections; many already had some protection through their off-farm employment. The new approach to a minimum floor of security now appeared compatible with the older judgment of individual responsibility.

16. Coverage of 6.5 million (1960) and 9.5 million (1970) state and local government employees rose from 57 percent to 69 percent; about 95 percent of

total coverage had risen to 93 million by 1970, approximately 8
million workers in governmental, domestic service, and nonprofit employment were still unprotected by social security although many were under other government or private plans.

The maximum retirement benefits at age 65 were increased by
two thirds by 1958, then doubled by the 1971 amendments and
increased by 20 percent in 1972. Eligibility was extended to
workers with a more irregular work history – employment in one
of every four quarters, compared with the initial one in every
two. As evidence of protection of the marginally covered,
184,000, or 14 percent of all 1970 benefit awards were at the
minimum; it was only 7 percent in 1960, when employment in
one in three quarters was required.[17] The retirement test after
1952 took account of annual earnings before reducing the worker's benefit – this being more appropriate for the self-employed
than monthly earnings. The average monthly benefit awarded to
men rose from $76 in 1956 to $137 in 1970, and from $55 to
$104 for women, increases of 79 and 89 percent respectively.[18]
Men with reduced benefits averaged $119 in monthly benefits in
1970, an increase of 60 percent over the benefits of $75 in 1963,
the first year when early retirement pensions were payable.[19]

As might be expected, black workers' benefits are lower than
those paid to whites. Reflecting their lower earnings in covered
employment, black retired and disabled beneficiaries receive
benefits about 20 percent lower than those of whites, somewhat
less than the differential between men and women – 22-23 percent for both white and black beneficiaries. The difference between benefits awarded blacks and whites had narrowed by
1970, reflecting smaller differences in wages. While all beneficiaries received higher benefits than in former years, blacks
made greater gains than whites; this was more pronounced for
retirement than for disability benefits.[20]

Members of the armed forces were also given more adequate
protection; in 1946, World War II veterans had been awarded

---

5 million plus nonprofit employees were covered at the end of the 1960s.
SSA – ORS, *State and Local Government Employment Statistics, 1964-1968,*
(Washington, 1970); and special tabulations.

  17. *Statistical Supplement,* 1970, Table 54, p. 67.
  18. Ibid.
  19. Ibid., Table 53.
  20. Ibid., Table 67.

wage credits of $160 per month of service between September 1940 and July 1947, but the same benefit rights were extended to all the armed forces in 1956, and in 1967 wage credits were increased to a maximum of $300 per quarter, effective in 1968.[21]

OTHER PROGRAM CHANGES

While the system was approaching universality in numbers covered and eligibility for benefits was liberalized, social security was also broadened to protect workers against other risks of long-term loss of earnings, especially disablement.

Disability

During the late 1940s several unsuccessful attempts had been made to cover the risk of long-term total disability, treating invalidity as akin to premature retirement. In 1949, following recommendations of the Federal Security Agency, (predecessor of the Department of Health, Education, and Welfare), President Truman, and the 1948 Advisory Council on Social Security, the House acted to extend benefits to the permanently and totally disabled aged 50 and over; it also added a fourth category of public assistance for the needy who were totally and permanently disabled. Responding to strong objections to the insurance approach by medical, private insurance, and employer organizations, the Senate accepted instead the public assistance approach.

Commercial insurance carriers, medical organizations, and employer groups asserted that disability insurance was open to abuse and malingering, not readily controllable; resulting mounting costs (on behalf of a few people) would endanger the solvency of the retirement funds which millions of aged depended upon. In some part the position of these groups rested upon earlier unfavorable claims experience with disability coverage under private insurance; conceivably, many "undesirable risks" had been sold life insurance policies containing disability clauses.

Successive congresses also preferred the pattern of using pub-

---

21. Ibid., p. 13. This protection is financed from general revenues.

lic assistance rather than social insurance to protect the needy against such risks as disablement and the costs of health care. Ten years later, the Kerr-Mills program of 1960 provided grants-in-aid to states to cover the costs of medical and hospital care to the needy aged. During legislative consideration, this measure was substituted for a broader program of hospital insurance under social insurance. Supporters of the Kerr-Mills bill held that only those aged who could not meet their medical expenses without requiring public assistance were in sufficient need to justify federal intervention.[22]

Loss of income due to disability was insured under social insurance in 1956,[23] limited to workers at least 50 years old who had substantial employment prior to their disablement.[24] The age 50 requirement was removed in 1960. This extension did not protect those who became disabled early in their working careers and who could not acquire the requisite quarters of covered employment because they were incapable of engaging in even substantial part-time employment. To qualify for benefits, the worker must be unable to engage in any substantial gainful activity and have been disabled for at least five months before being eligible for the first monthly benefit. He must also be expected to remain disabled for at least 12 months (originally, to last indefinitely or until death).

Benefits are also payable to persons aged 18 or over if they had been disabled before age 18; the childhood disability benefit protects persons who could not have been capable of acquiring benefit rights through employment, and continues for the duration of the disability. Unlike other benefit procedures, determination of disability is made by state, not federal, agencies, in-

22. See W. L. Mitchell, "Social Security Legislation in the 86th Congress," *Social Security Bulletin,* Nov. 1960, pp. 3–29, especially pp. 5–14.

23. As an intermediate step in 1954, the "disability freeze" "eliminated, under cautious restrictions, a certified period of total disability in computation of the average-wage base for other [retirement and survivors'] benefits," akin to "waiver of premium" in life insurance. This action recognized that many workers built up rights to very low retirement and survivor's benefits when disabilities produced years of low and no earnings. Brown, *Social Insurance,* pp. 156–157.

24. The development of disability insurance proposals from the 1938 Advisory Council recommendations until enactment in 1956 is discussed in W. J. Cohen, *Retirement Policies under Social Security* (Berkeley and Los Angeles: University of California Press, 1957), pp. 43–68. See also Brown, *Social Insurance,* chapter 11.

cluding the vocational rehabilitation agency. That agency determines whether the applicant would benefit from vocational rehabilitation, and disability benefits may be denied any applicant who refuses to accept such services.[25]

Eligibility for disability payments was set far more restrictively than for retirement, being limited to the fully insured — at least 20 quarters of coverage within the last 40, and at least one quarter of coverage per year since 1950, prior to the year of disablement. Under the 1972 amendments, the 6-month waiting period was reduced to 5 months, effective January 1973, allowing additional payments to about 1 million beneficiaries; this change, in due course, may become the initial step toward further reductions in the waiting period, as has been proposed. The 1972 Senate bill, it may be noted, called for a 2-month reduction.[26]

Causes of premature and involuntary retirement are not limited to severe disability and declining job opportunities after age 50 since older workers may have greater difficulty in meeting job demands. Recognizing that the age of retirement is not the same for all workers, a 1956 amendment lowered women's pensionable age to 62, with an actuarial reduction; later on, coincident with the 1960 recession, men obtained the same age 62 retirement option.

The monthly benefit is reduced by 5/9 of 1 percent for each month the applicant is below 65; for those filing at age 62, the benefit is reduced by 20 percent. This reduction compensates for the fact that persons retiring at 62 would receive benefits for 3 more years than those retiring at 65, for 2 more years at age 63, and so on. It should be noted that early retirement is commonly exercised by disabled applicants who are not "disabled enough" to qualify for disability benefits.[27]

Despite coverage extensions, many who were past 65 (or near 65) in 1936 when the program started had never worked long enough in covered employment to become eligible, and many

25. The determination is reviewed by the SSA for consistency with national policy. SSA — ORS, *Social Security Programs in the U.S.* (Washington, 1971), p. 33.
26. U.S., Congress, Senate, *Social Security Amendments of 1972,* 92nd Cong., 2d sess., 1972, Senate Rept. 92–1230.
27. See L. D. Haber, "Disability, Work, and Income Maintenance: Prevalence of Disability in 1966," *Social Security Bulletin,* May 1968, p. 21.

who lacked enough resources for more than subsistence were not even eligible for state old-age assistance. Under a 1966 amendment, these noninsured persons obtained partial relief when a uniform monthly payment of $35 (increased to $58 in 1972) was made available to nearly three quarters of a million persons beyond age 72. This flat benefit, financed from general revenues rather than from payroll taxes, was a departure from the principle that eligibility depends upon prior covered employment. To be eligible, these very aged persons could not be receiving old age assistance, and government pensions were to be deducted from the benefit.[28] By 1972 the number receiving such benefits had declined to 450,000.

Under the 1972 amendments, workers who delay retirement beyond age 65 receive higher benefits; beginning in 1973, their benefits were increased by 1 percent for each year after age 65 that they postpone their retirement. Generally speaking, it is workers with good health, higher earnings, and more favorable employment or self-employment circumstances who continue working beyond age 65, and the increment will aid those already favored in the job market for their contribution to the economy through continued productivity and service.

RETIREMENT TEST

Retirement benefits have been designed to replace the wages lost upon retirement, rather than being paid at a given age to all eligibles. The amount of earnings disregarded as consistent with retirement status has been increased over the years in recognition of beneficiaries' actual needs and desires to earn additional income, and that in practice retirement often means gradual, rather than abrupt, cessation of work. Understandably, those whose benefits are reduced or suspended due to earnings contend that the benefit should be payable at 65, regardless — that it is an "earned" benefit, paid for by their past contributions. Past congresses received more proposals to abolish or liberalize the retirement test than any other provision.[29] The test is called an

28. SSA – ORS, *Social Security Programs in the U.S.,* 1971, pp. 28–29.

29. See W. J. Cohen, *Retirement Policies under Social Security;* and Philip Booth, ed., *Proceedings, Sixth Social Security Conference* (Ann Arbor: University of Michigan, Institute of Labor and Industrial Relations, 1969), pp. 57–58.

inequitable one in that receipt of nonwage income—such as dividends, interest, and rent, for example—does not bar receipt of benefits. Some assert that it discourages older workers' employment which would add to our goods and services, improve living standards, and add to the life satisfactions of aged workers.

Retention of the test has been defended by the Social Security Administration and the responsible congressional committees:[30]

1. Abolition would benefit a minority of the aged; most are unable to find work even before 65; one of every five men and two of every five women beneficiaries had not been employed for at least one year before getting retirement benefits.[31]

2. The earnings of many who defer retirement do not decline at age 65.

3. It would cost at least 0.7 percent of wages to pay benefits at age 65 to all; the additional benefits would go only to about 10 percent of the aged, those whose benefits are suspended or reduced.

4. At the same cost, benefits could be raised for the great majority who have little or no earnings.

In 1972 Congress accepted the oft-made proposal that the $1 benefit reduction for each $2 in earnings (applied in 1972 to earnings from $1680 to $2880 per year) be applied to all earnings without limit. Thus workers' total income can go up steadily as their earnings increase. It was also provided that the new limit on disregarded earnings (raised from $1680 to $2100) will be adjusted, annually, to changes in average earnings. It was estimated, in 1972, that this change would enable 450,000 additional aged workers to be entitled to benefits (formerly excluded

30. Myers, *Social Insurance and Allied Government Programs*, pp. 79–81; William Haber and Wilbur J. Cohen, *Social Security: Programs, Problems and Policies* (Homewood, Ill.: Richard D. Irwin, Inc., 1966), pp. 171–172; U.S., Congress, Senate, Special Committee on Aging, *Hearings on the Economics of Aging: Toward a Full Share in Abundance*, 91st Cong., 1st sess., Part 9, 1969, p. 1385. U.S., Congress, House, Letter from Wilbur J. Cohen (Secretary of H.E.W.) transmitting a report pursuant to PL 90–248, *Social Security Amendments of 1967*, 91st Cong., 1st sess., H. Doc. 91-4a, 9 Jan. 1969.

31. Virginia Reno, "Why Men Stop Working at or before Age 65," SSA–ORS, *Survey of New Beneficiaries*, Report no. 3 (Washington, 1971), Table 2, p. 19.

by earnings above $2,880) and 1.2 million would receive higher benefits than before.[32]

BENEFITS

Benefit Formula

Although benefits varied with wages and the number of family dependents, as of October 1972 the formula provided a minimum retirement and disability benefit of $84.50 and a maximum of $354.50 for a single worker (Table 4). This benefit, the Primary Insurance Amount (PIA), is the base for calculating the benefit for dependents and survivors. An additional 50 percent is added for his wife or a dependent child 18 and under, or if in school 21 and under. As shown in Table 5, survivors' benefits are a higher fraction of the basic benefit than dependents' benefits, since it is presumed that the family breadwinner no longer is present.[33] While the retirement benefit for a worker who had average monthly earnings of $150 is nine tenths of his wages, this fraction drops to about one half for those whose monthly earnings are $550 or more. However, family benefits (a couple with one child, for example) may exceed 100 percent of wages for low earners, but decline to 83–94 percent in the higher monthly wage brackets ($550 or more).

About 1.2 million of the 13.4 million retired worker beneficiaries at the close of 1970 were under age 65; 576,000 were men and 649,000 were women. Among all 13.4 million, the men were about 72.6 years old, while women were 72.0, only slightly younger; 25 years earlier, in 1945, both groups were only one year younger, suggesting that although many people (0.6–0.7 million per year) had elected early retirement in the past decade, this was being offset by greater longevity.[34]

32. U.S., Congress, Senate Committee on Finance and House Committee on Ways and Means, *H.R. 1, Summary of Social Security Amendments of 1972 as Approved by the Conferees*, 92nd Cong., 2d sess., 17 Oct. 1972, Conference Committee Print, p. 1.
33. For example, while the benefit for a dependent wife, husband, or child is 50 percent of the basic benefit, under the 1972 changes made by PL 92–603 (30 Oct. 1972), that for an age 62 surviving widow or widower is the same as the benefit the deceased husband (or wife) would have received. An aged widow and one child family receives the same benefit as an aged couple.
34. *Statistical Supplement*, 1970, Tables 67 and 77.

Table 4.

Examples of Monthly Cash Benefit Awards to Selected Beneficiary Families under 1972 Social Security Amendments

	less than $74	$250	$350	$450	$550	$650	$750
Average monthly:							
Average yearly earnings after 1950:	less than $923	$3,000	$4,200	$5,400	$6,600	$7,800	$9,000
Retired worker 65 or older / Disabled worker under 65	$ 84.50	$174.80	$213.30	$250.60	$288.40	$331.00	$354.50
Wife 65 or older	42.30	87.40	106.70	125.30	144.20	165.50	177.30
Retired worker at 62	67.60	139.90	170.70	200.50	230.80	264.80	283.60
Wife at 62, no child	31.80	65.60	80.10	94.00	108.20	124.20	133.00
Widow at 60	73.30	125.10	152.60	179.30	206.30	236.70	253.50
Widow or widower at 62	84.50	144.30	176.00	206.80	238.00	273.10	292.50
Disabled widow at 50	51.30	87.50	106.80	125.50	144.30	165.60	177.30
Wife under 65 and one child	42.30	92.50	157.40	217.30	233.90	248.30	265.90
Widowed mother and one child	126.80	262.20	320.00	376.60	432.60	496.60	531.80
Widowed mother and two children	126.80	267.30	370.70	467.90	522.30	579.30	620.40
One child of retired or disabled worker	42.30	87.40	106.70	125.30	144.20	165.50	177.30
One surviving child	84.50	131.10	160.00	188.00	216.30	248.30	265.90
Maximum family payment	126.80	267.30	370.70	467.90	522.30	579.30	620.40

Note: Generally, average earnings covered by social security are figured from 1951 until the worker reaches retirement age, becomes disabled, or dies. Up to five years of low earnings or no earnings can be excluded. Maximum earnings creditable for social security are $3,600 for 1951–54, $4,200 for 1955–58, $4,800 for 1959–65, $6,600 for 1966–67, $7,800 for 1968–71, $9,000 for 1972 and $10,800 for 1973. The maximum benefit for a retired worker in 1972 was $259.40 a month, based on average yearly earnings of $5,652. The higher benefits shown in the chart, based on average earnings shown in the columns on the right, generally will not be payable until some years to come.

Illustrative Monthly Benefits under OASDHI (1972) for Various Family Categories, and 1971 and 1972 Awards as Percent of Average Monthly Earnings

Beneficiary Category	Average Monthly Earnings and Monthly Benefits													
	$150	%	$250	%	$350	%	$450	%	$550	%	$650	%	$750[2]	%
Retired or disabled, 65 or older	134	90 (75)*	175	70 (58)	213	60 (51)	251	56 (42)	288	52 (44)	331	51 (42)	355 ·	50 (40)
Worker, age 65 with aged spouse	201[3]	134 (112)	262	105 (88)	320	90 (76)	377	84 (63)	432	79 (65)	497	77 (64)	532	71 (59)
Retired worker age 62	108	72 (60)	140	56 (47)	170	48 (41)	182	40 (34)	230	40 (34)	265	41 (34)	284	38 (32)
Worker and spouse, age 62	158	105 (88)	210	84 (69)	250	71 (60)	313	69 (58)	338	61 (51)	389	61 (50)	415	55 (47)
Worker, age 65, spouse with one child	201[3]	134 (112)	267[3]	107 (89)	371[3]	106 (88)	468[3]	104 (80)	520[3]	94 (79)	579[3]	89 (74)	620[3]	83 (69)
Widow, under 65, with one child	201	134 (112)	262	105 (87)	320	91 (76)	377	84 (73)	433	78 (66)	495	76 (64)	532	71 (59)
With two children	201[3]	134 (112)	267[3]	107 (89)	371[3]	106 (88)	468[3]	108 (78)	522[3]	95 (79)	579[3]	90 (74)	620[3]	83 (69)

*Figures in parenthesis are amounts payable under 1971 provisions, as a percentage of earnings.
1. Adapted from Table 4, above.
2. Benefits in these amounts will not be payable before the late 1970s because monthly wages above $650 were not taken account of until 1972.
3. Maximum family payment.

Special Minimum Benefits

The benefit formula varies workers' benefits according to their prior earnings, as we have learned, without taking account explicitly of the number of years in covered employment. According to the benefit formula, ever since the beginning, a worker who entered covered employment late in his working career, or had been in-and-out of covered work, could receive a lower benefit on that account than another (with identical annual earnings) who had a more regular, continuous employment history. But the second worker did not receive an augmented benefit on that account; to do so would have been thought inconsistent with prevailing concepts of wage-related benefits.

Under the 1972 amendments, however, minimum benefits were adjusted to years of service, but only for those with more than 20 years of covered employment; these long-service workers now receive an increment of $8.50 per month for every year worked after the twentieth, until a maximum of $170.00 per month is reached for 30 years or more of work.[35]   Like the annual increment for those retiring after age 65, these changes benefit workers with substantial covered employment; the augmented benefits take more account of long service than of higher earnings, a significant innovation. For example, a worker with 28 years of covered employment whose average monthly wage was $75 or less will receive a monthly benefit of $153, but another with similarly long service whose average monthly wages were twice as great ($150) will receive $202, or 33 percent more. The former differential in benefits, $84.50 vs $134.50, reflecting differential earnings alone, was 60 percent.

The benefit formula has been revised every two to four years since 1950 to maintain the buying power of the pensions of retired and disabled workers, their dependents, and survivors. For most beneficiaries, the benefit is all or most of their income. Although the 1954 scale of benefits for workers with average monthly earnings of $200–$250 was less than 40 percent of such earnings, these benefits increased to 50–65 percent by

35. Other countries where the basic pension is a percentage of prior wages also provide increments for each year of insurance or each year beyond a specified minimum number. SSA—ORS, *Social Security Programs throughout the World, 1971*, Research Report no. 40 (Washington, 1972), p. xvi.

1971,[36] and then to 60–70 percent, under the 1972 amendments (Table 5). The 1972 changes also increased the benefit for an aged retired worker with average wages of $450 or more to 50–55 percent of his earnings. The benefit increases of 1965–72 have more than kept pace with rising prices.

The same benefit formula applies to disabled and retired workers, but because the former must possess a more recent and regular employment history than the retired worker, disabled workers receive pensions averaging 10–15 percent higher than retirees, as shown in the following tabulation:

Average Monthly Payments for Retirement and Disability
Selected Beneficiaries, 1970

Worker Only	Retirement	Disability
Male	$129	$136
Female	102	113
Retired worker, wife and one child	228	264

Source: Statistical Supplement, 1970, Table 24.

Since 1967 a worker's disabled widow (or widower) aged 50 or over can receive disability benefits. The actuarial reduction at age 50, however, is much greater than at 62; for example, it reduces the monthly payment to 50 percent of the PIA, a substantial cut indeed where no family wage earner is likely to be present and contributing to family income.

Benefit Experience, 1940–72

At the close of 1971 the OASDHI program was paying benefits to nearly 15 million aged and disabled workers, 3 million dependent husbands and wives, plus 4.1 million child survivors and dependents (Table 6). Surviving widows and widowers, mothers, and parents accounted for another 3.8 million, and 534,000 additional aged men and women received the special age 72-plus benefit. Monthly cash benefits exceeded $2.6 billion,

36. Brown, *Social Insurance,* p. 168.

Table 6.

OASDHI Monthly Benefits in Current Payment Status by Type of Beneficiary, 1971 (in thousands)

Type of Beneficiary	Amount		Number	
	Amount	% of Total	Number	% of Total
Total	$2,628	100.0	26,229	100.0
Retired	1,577	60.0	13,349	51.0
Disabled	196	7.5	1,493	5.8
Dependent wives and husbands	175	6.7	2,952	11.2
Surviving widows and widowers	328	12.5	3,227	12.3
Children	280	10.7	4,122	15.7
Widowed mothers	45	1.7	523	20.0
Parents	3	*	29	*
Noninsured aged 72 and over	24	0.9	534	2.0

*Less than .05 percent

Source: Statistical Supplement, 1970, Table 25.

$36.8 billion for the year; including $7.2 billion in health insurance, the total came to $44 billion.

Minimum earnings requirements exclude only the most marginal members of the work force, except for agricultural workers who must meet more rigorous requirements. A farm worker must have earned $150 in wages in a year from a single employer, if on piece rates, or worked 20 days in a year on an hourly or other time basis. No such minimum earnings with a single employer are required of other workers. Domestic service workers must meet the standard $50 per quarter with all employers to obtain a quarter of coverage. Gaps due to coverage exclusions are widened by underreporting of employment and wages in seasonal or part-time work, where employers fail to keep payroll records, file reports, and pay contributions for piece-rate workers. Farm workers are likely to lose protection if employed by a crew leader or labor contractor rather than the farm operator; it is harder to assure compliance in reporting by a mobile crew leader than by a farm operator with a fixed location.

The 1971 Advisory Council on Social Security estimated that at least 0.5 million workers do not receive credit for their farm earnings because the farm operator is not treated as employer of the workers employed on his farm.[37]

Disabled Workers' Benefits

The requirements for disability benefits are very stringent, as we have seen;[38] a worker must be too disabled to engage in any substantial gainful work and, in addition, have had substantial recent employment. These restrictions, barring all but the most severely disabled, lead to denial of two of every three claims, or 192,000 of a total of 523,000 in 1968.[39]

Some court decisions in the 1960s had reversed earlier denials of disability claims, holding it improper to deny benefits where there was some "reasonable likelihood" that the disabled worker could find work within a "circumscribed" labor market. Congressional committees now opined that the rising costs of the program (up seven-fold in nine years) were related to the manner in which "disability" was being interpreted; "the number of allowances was larger than . . . the number estimated." In consequence, the definition was changed in 1967 to make it evident that a worker was not "under a disability" if still capable of engaging in substantial gainful work, whether or not such work existed in his locality or whether he would be hired to do it.[40]

While some 1.5 million workers were receiving disability benefits at the close of 1970, studies of the 1966 disabled population showed that about one half as many more severely disabled workers, ineligible for disability benefits, were receiving instead early retirement, survivors', or dependents' benefits.[41] The num-

37. *Report of the 1971 Advisory Council on Social Security*, p. 59.

38. L. D. Haber, "Identifying the Disabled: Concepts and Methods in the Measurement of Disability," *Social Security Bulletin*, Dec. 1967, p. 15.

39. SSA—ORS, *Social Security Disability Applicant Statistics, 1968*, June 1972, Table 1, p. 15.

40. U.S., Congress, Senate, Committee on Finance, *Social Security Amendments of 1967: Committee Report on H. R. 12080*, 90th Cong., 1st sess., 1967, Senate Rept. 744, pp. 47-49.

41. Another 400,000 were receiving disability benefits under public employee retirement plans. Sophie R. Dales, "Benefits and Beneficiaries under Public Employee Retirement Systems, 1969," SSA—ORS, Research and Statistics Note no. 6 (Washington, 1970), Table 1.

ber of severely disabled who are excluded has been estimated at three times the number who get benefits. Inability to meet the restrictive disability requirements has led aging workers who are unable to work steadily or at all and who are without other means of support to opt for early retirement benefits at age 62. Despite the actuarial reduction in their benefits (20 percent at age 62), most who elect early retirement do so because of physical incapacity to carry on their usual work activity — shifting to new and less demanding employment is increasingly difficult for older workers. Of 1.6 million severely disabled OASDI beneficiaries, more than one of every five were receiving early retirement benefits, according to a 1966 survey, because they could not qualify for disability benefits. Such protection, of course, is not available to those disabled persons under age 62. Many who are ineligible for disability benefits and are not old enough to receive early retirement benefits must resort to public assistance. Some 15 percent of the severely disabled aged 60–61 were receiving public assistance, according to the 1966 survey, but this dropped to about one third, or 5.5 of those aged 62–64, when (early) retirement benefits became available. The 1971 Advisory Council Report recommended changes in the law to enable these older workers to qualify for disability benefits.[42]

Survivors and Dependents

Dependents and survivors protection has added a major support to family security since 1940. Survivor beneficiaries increased from 73,000 to 6.5 million in 30 years. (Table 7); three of every eight widows were receiving benefits in 1968. But children in particular were benefited; 83 percent as many orphans as widows and widowers combined, were receiving benefits in 1971. While our orphan population has actually declined — from 1 in 16 to 1 in 20 children in the population between 1940 and 1966 — 2 of every 3 orphans received survivors' benefits in 1969. By contrast, the AFDC program aids a

---

42. L. D. Haber, "Disability, Work, and Income Maintenance: Prevalence of Disability in 1966," *Social Security Bulletin,* May 1960, Table 4; Haber, *Social Security Survey of the Disabled: 1966,* Table 4; and *Report of the 1971 Advisory Council on Social Security,* pp. 43–47.

Table 7.

OASDHI Number of Survivor Beneficiaries, Selected Years, 1940–1970 (in thousands)

	Total	Child Survivors	Widows & Widowers	Widowed Mothers	Parents
1940	73	48	4	20	1
1945	534	377	94	121	6
1950	1,094	653	314	169	15
1960	3,446	1,530	1,544	401	36
1969	6,229	2,599	3,090	510	30
1970	6,469	2,689	3,228	523	29

Source: Statistical Supplement, 1968, op. cit., Tables 27, 92; *1970,* Tables 91, 96. *Monthly Benefit Statistics,* Calendar Year Benefit Data, 1969 (2/27/1970) and 1970 (3/19/1971).

small proportion of child orphans; only 6 percent of all aided children in 1969 were orphans, compared to 21 percent in 1950. The 4.1 million child beneficiaries in 1971, including dependents of retired and disabled beneficiaries, accounted for over 43 of every 1000 children under 18 — about triple the 1950 recipient rate.[43] Until the 1972 amendments were adopted, widows and widowers at age 62 received benefits of only 82.5 percent of the worker's PIA: widows now receive the same benefit amount as their deceased husbands would have received, if still alive; it was then estimated that 3.8 million widows' and widowers' benefits were increased.

Adequacy of Benefits

Social security benefits vary with workers' former wages, but are proportionately greater for lower than for higher earnings (see Table 5). In addition, the statutory minimum and maximum disregard prior earnings and aim at other objectives, the minimum to take account of subsistence needs and the maximum to place a ceiling on benefit costs.

43. D. B. Eppley, "Decline in the Number of AFDC Orphans," *Welfare in Review,* Sept.–Oct. 1968, pp. 1–7; *Statistical Abstract of the U.S., 1971,* p. 296; and *Trend Report 1969: Graphic Presentation of Public Assistance and Related Data,* NCSS Report A–4 (1969), pp. 45–47.

One may ask how adequate social security benefits should be. Enough to provide for total living requirements of the beneficiary, assuming that he has no other income? Unlike public assistance, which aims at a subsistence objective and takes all of the recipient's resources into account, social security disregards the beneficiary's resources, other than current earnings. To the extent that low and irregularly employed earners are insured, and many are, benefits based on their prior earnings can leave a substantial gap below their subsistence needs. Although more and more we supplement cash payments with benefits in kind in the form of health care, and through subsidized housing and food programs, we must ask how nearly adequate are the benefits provided, in practice.

Comparing retirement benefits actually being paid to single persons with payments to couples and families (Table 8), a family with one child received only $30 more than a couple; single men received only two thirds and single women only one half as much as a couple. Widows with two children were paid half again as much as a couple, but those with three or more children received no more. Apparently, the deceased father of larger families had lower earnings than the father of fewer children. Widows with three or more children have more total income than one-child families, but only half as much per capita. Large families were twice as likely as small families to fall below the poverty line, the lower per capita benefits being due to the statutory family maximum. Yet although survivors' families were surely far better off than other broken families, which were not receiving survivors' benefits, they were less well off than husband-wife families.[44]

Aged adults not only get more adequate benefits than children, but aged couples are better off than older men and women who are unmarried. While a single retired beneficiary gets less than two thirds as much as a couple, he or she would need at least three fourths as much if all three were to subsist at the low-income maintainance level.[45] When we note that benefits

44. E. Palmore, G. Stanley, and R. H. Cormier, *Widows with Children under Social Security*, SSA—ORS Research Report no. 16 (Washington, 1966), pp. 62–63.
45. He would need 77 percent as much as the couple to subsist at the poverty level, using SSA standards. Mollie Orshansky, "Re-Counting the Poor: A Five Year Review," *Social Security Bulletin*, April 1966, Table 1, p. 23; See also Pechman, Aaron, and Taussig, *Social Security*, pp. 79–87.

Table 8.

Benefits in Current Payment Status, and Average Monthly Payment, by Family Groups with Selected Characteristics, 1970

Family type	Number of families, in thousands	Number of beneficiaries, in thousands	Average monthly amount
Retired Worker Families	13,363	16,571	$133
Worker only	10,553	10,553	114
Men	4,904	4,904	130
Women	5,629	5,629	102
Worker & wife	2,454	4,912	199
Worker & children	159	354	190
Worker, wife & children	205	756	230
1 child	94	281	228
2 or more children	72	352	220
Survivor Families	4,627	6,465	130
Widow or widower only	3,131	3,132	102
Widow, widower and children	59	123	198
Widowed mother & children	523	1,725	263
1 child	187	370	213
2 children	155	464	291
3 children	94	376	297
4 or more children	88	514	282
Children only	851	1,421	147
1 child	515	515	99
2 children	197	393	198
3 children	60	246	256
4 or more children	58	267	246
Disabled Worker Families	1,496	2,665	163
Worker only	1,054	1,054	126
Worker & spouse	43	86	199
Worker, wife & children	398	1,525	270
1 child	77	230	264
2 or more children	164	865	273
Total	20,007	26,236	

1. Details exclude 521,000 special-age-72 beneficiaries and 53,000 parents and remarried widows.

Source: Social Security Bulletin, March 1972, Table Q 17, p. 75; *Social Security Bulletin, Stat. Supp.* 1970, Table 96.

paid to seven of every ten single persons fell below the poverty threshold (July-December 1969 awards) compared to only three in ten couples' benefits, we see further evidence of the more generous treatment of couples; the data also make it clear that couples had greater life-time earnings.[46] The single person's benefit would have to be increased by 10–15 percent to meet the low-income criterion if the couple's benefit remained constant. If this appears unlikely, given the political facts of life, a greater increase in benefits for single persons than for couples would be desirable.

As a related test of adequacy, to what extent do social security benefits fall below the level of subsistence at which public assistance supplementation becomes effective? Benefits paid to 7.4 in every 100 failed to meet their needs without supplementation from old-age assistance in 1970.[47] One in every four OASI and one in every five DI beneficiaries receive another cash benefit from a public program. Most are receiving public assistance or VA pensions; the others receive public employee, military, or RRB pensions.[48] One proposal is a higher minimum benefit, reducing the need for dual support; for every second old-age assistance recipient is an OASI beneficiary receiving supplementary assistance. But benefit improvement concentrating on the minimum may carry undesired side effects. A higher minimum would result in larger payments to nonpoor families, many with another pension, since many at the minimum are secondary earners with a brief and irregular earnings history; for others, covered employment was in a secondary job, the principal employment giving them other pension rights.[49]

The special minimum benefit for low earners with long employment histories referred to earlier, effective January 1973, was justified by some supporters in terms of antipoverty strate-

46. V. Reno and C. Zuckert, "Benefit Levels of Newly Retired Workers: Findings from the Survey of New Beneficiaries," *Social Security Bulletin,* July 1971, pp. 3–31 and Table 12, p. 22. Couples were more likely to receive private pensions and to continue working after pensionable age.

47. *Statistical Supplement,* 1970, Table 16; this percentage has held fairly constant since 1960, although it was twice as high in 1950.

48. Stonery, *Public Income Transfer Programs,* pp. 26–30.

49. Pechman, Aaron, and Taussig, *Social Security,* pp. 91–94; *Lenore A. Epstein, "Workers Entitled to Minimum Retirement Benefits under OASDHI," Social Security Bulletin,* March 1967, pp. 3–10.

gy. Insofar as the new higher minimum benefit aids workers with a record of long employment in covered work who have subsisted on very low earnings, it can be regarded as an antipoverty measure. But to the extent that average monthly earnings of $75–$150 per month over a 20–30 year period characterizes workers who have not been self-sufficient on the basis of their covered employment but have been members of multiearner households or have held jobs for many years which were outside the social security system (as in noncovered government employment),[50] the allocation of substantial social security funds to improve their benefits can be questioned on policy grounds. If the impact of the change is limited to some 150,000 aged, their dependents and survivors, however, and $20 million per year (in 1974) as estimated by the Conference Committees in late 1972,[51] the changes may be of greater significance in principle than in substantial effect on poor and nonpoor beneficiaries. If broadened substantially, as was proposed in the Senate bill ($10 per month for each year of coverage in excess of 10 years),[52] for example, it would pose questions of greater magnitude.

Another undesirable side effect would appear if higher minimum benefits, justified on antipoverty grounds, were to lessen effective support or reduce the resources for paying more nearly adequate benefits to workers in the middle-wage brackets ($550–$650 per month) whose benefits are barely half of former wages. Those forced to retire before age 65 get much lower benefits in relation to their earnings (Table 5). The disparity in the benefit/earnings ratio between workers earning $250–$350 and $550–$650 per month, for example, reflects a greater burden carried by high earners in favor of those with lower wages. The more generous weighting of benefits for low earners could be financed in part from general revenues, rather than through a lower benefit/earnings ratio for the higher wage group.

Benefit increases since 1950 have irregularly offset the impact

50. U.S., Senate Committee on Finance, *Social Security Amendments of 1972*, Report 92–1230, pp. 153–155.

51. U.S., Senate Committee on Finance and House Committee on Ways and Means, *H.R. 1, Summary of Social Security Amendments of 1972 as Approved by the Conferees*, p. 1.

52. U.S., Senate Committee on Finance, *Social Security Amendments of 1972*, Report 92–1230.

of price changes, which erode the real value of pensions. The nine benefit changes since 1950 (Table 3) have taken account of price increases, but in each case after the fact. Such changes at two- or three-year intervals do not help the beneficiary recoup his pension's loss of buying power during prior years. Waldman and Pechman point out that benefits awarded in 1954 were increased 14 percent by 1966, but matching wage and price changes would have called for increases of 56 percent and 23 percent, respectively.[53] However, the benefit increases of 13, 15, 10, and 20 percent in 1967, 1969, 1971, and 1972 respectively, more than offset price inflation for workers retiring in those years.

As a 1971 Ways and Means Committee's Report put it: "Congress has legislated eight benefit increases since . . . January, 1940, . . . and . . . the cumulative effect of these benefit increases greatly exceeds the rise in the cost of living over the same period."[54]

In comparing benefits paid to all beneficiaries in recent versus prior years, however, the effect of the more than fourfold increase between 1940 and 1970, for example (from $22.60 to $108.10), is a very different one. In constant dollar terms, the 30-year change was from $55 to $118.10, an increase of less than half the change in actual dollars. "For retired workers and aged widows, more than half the increase has been eaten away by inflation."[55] Similarly, while gross wages in manufacturing between 1940 and 1972 quadrupled, the ceiling on wages creditable for benefits was three times as high, $9,000 compared to $3,000 (see Table 9). Since under the 1972 amendments benefits can be increased more frequently through automatic adjustments to price changes, beneficiaries obtain more effective protection against loss of the purchasing power of their benefits; somewhat greater changes would be necessary to enable retirees to share

53. S. Waldman, "OASDI Benefits, Prices and Wages: 1966 Experience," *Social Security Bulletin*, June 1967, p. 10; Pechman, Aaron, and Taussig, *Social Security*, pp. 100–101.

54. U.S., Congress, House, Ways and Means Committee, *Social Security Amendments of 1971*, 92nd Cong., 1st sess., 1971, H. Rept. 92–231, p. 40.

55. D. N. Price, "OASDHI Benefits, Prices, and Wages: Effect of the 1967 Increase," *Social Security Bulletin*, Dec. 1968, pp. 32–34. Also *Statistical Supplement*, 1970, Table 13.

Table 9.

Schedule of Taxable Earnings, Contribution Rate and Premium for OASDHI, 1937–79[1]

Year in effect	Annual maximum earnings[2]	Combined employer-employee				Self-employed Total
		Total	OASI	DI	Hosp.	
1937–49	$3,000	2.00	2.00			
1950	$3,000	3.00	3.00			
1951–53	$3,600	3.00	3.00			2.250
1954	$3,600	4.00	4.00			3.000
1955–56	$4,200	4.00	4.00			3.000
1957–58	$4,200	4.50	4.00	0.50	0.5	3.375
1959	$4,800	5.00	4.50		0.5	3.750
1960–61	$4,800	6.00	5.50		0.5	4.500
1962	$4,800	6.25	5.75		0.5	4.700
1963–65	$4,800	7.35	6.75			5.400
1966	$6,600	8.40	7.00	0.70	0.7	6.150
1967	$6,600	8.80	7.10		1.0	6.400
1968	$7,800	8.80	6.70	0.95	1.2	
1969	$7,800	9.60	7.45	0.95	1.2	6.900
1970			7.30	1.10		
1971		10.40	8.10			7.500
1972	$9,000					
1973	$10,800	11.70	8.30	1.40	2.0	7.700
1974–1977	$12,000					

1. As of December 31, 1972.
2. Taxable and creditable.

Source: Adapted from *Statistical Supplement, 1970*, p. 21; see also Public Law 92-603, Oct. 30, 1972.

in the economic well-being of workers currently in the labor force. As Price points out, however, the latter adjustments require policy decisions on such questions as the proportion of wage increases to be reflected in benefits, applying such benefit increases equally to all or some beneficiaries, financing, and, of equal importance, the priority to be given these adjustments compared to meeting other program needs.[56]

56. D. N. Price, *ibid.*

Early Retirement

Older workers apply for reduced benefits more frequently as they find it difficult to retain their jobs or to find new ones when laid off. Aged men were 2.5 percent of all jobless in 1960–61 but bulked twice as heavily (5.6 percent) among those out of work for 6 months or more. For example, while one of every five awards in 1960 was made at reduced amounts, this had gone up to every second award in 1970.[57] To illustrate the impact, reduced benefits for a worker retiring in 1970 at 62 with average monthly earnings of $450 were 40 percent of his prior wages, compared to the 56 percent for workers filing at 65; all 1970 reduced awards for men averaged $114, a one-sixth reduction.[58] Moreover, the actuarial-reduction for workers 62–64 is applied, in reality, to substantially lower pension amounts (based upon lower earnings) than those awarded at age 65. Median annual social security income under July-December 1968 awards to men age 62 were $1,150, compared to $1,760 awarded at age 65, a difference of nearly 35 percent. This is nearly double the 20 percent difference that would exist if the two groups had identical earnings.[59]

We have noted above that many workers opt for early retirement when their age and infirmities handicap them in holding a present job and, even more, in finding another job after a layoff. For others, combined employment (or self-employment) on a part-time basis and a second pension can make early retirement more nearly voluntary, in fact. However, the latter option is more commonly available to higher than to low earners, for they are more likely to be entitled to a private pension replacing a substantial proportion of former wages. To make retirement voluntary for low earners would require substantial extensions of private pension coverage plus such reforms as vesting and portability.[60]

57. *Social Security Bulletin*, Dec. 1971, Table Q6, p. 67. More than one half the men and nearly two thirds of the women awarded retirement benefits in July–December of 1969 claimed entitlement at age 62; only 1 in 10 became entitled at age 65. Reno and Zuckert, "Benefit Levels," p. 6.

58. *Statistical Supplement*, 1970, Table 96.

59. P. Lauriat and W. Rabin, "Men Who Claim Benefits before Age 65: Findings from Survey of New Beneficiaries, 1968," *Social Security Bulletin*, Nov. 1970, pp. 16–18.

60. See also P. Henle, "Trends in Retirement Benefits Related to Earnings," *Monthly Labor Review*, June 1972, pp. 12–20; *Report of the 1971 Advisory Council on Social Security*.

In summary, comparing benefits for retirement, survivorship, and invalidity, which of these are the most adequate, and why? Benefit arrangements for the retired are the best. Survivors come off poorly per capita, because they appear in family-size packages, including children, but the system has been judged from the start on how well it has done for retired persons, who are rarely accompanied by children. The disabled also come off less well, because their needs, which extend beyond cash wage replacement, cannot be served adequately by a system that has ignored medical and rehabilitative services; the effectiveness of Medicare coverage of the disabled, effective July 1973, is still to be seen.

Furthermore, benefits under the long-term benefit programs have been most generous to married couples—less so to single workers—and provide clearly inadequate benefits to families, even when considered as a floor. More than half the beneficiaries in survivor and disabled worker families are members of families with children (Table 8), and every third beneficiary in the system is a member of a survivor or disabled worker's family. Every second beneficiary in the families of widowed mothers is a member of a family with three or more children. Members of disability and survivor families with three or more dependents, and receiving benefits in 1970 that were limited to $280–$300 per month by the statutory family maximum, are the major victims of a benefit structure that meets only bare subsistence needs of larger families. Some with the higher program benefits receive private pensions (or other public pensions) at more than nominal amounts. Because those who get the lowest benefits are less likely to have supplementary earnings or other income, they must look to the public programs for subsistence or amenities above that level; exceptions are found among workers getting the minimum benefit who also receive public employee pensions.

HOSPITAL AND MEDICAL INSURANCE: MEDICARE

Discussion of Medicare requires reference to the key role that organized labor has played in its enactment and in social security as a whole. Since 1935 organized labor has taken a major position in the development of all social security legislation, especially Medicare. Amendments broadening coverage, extending benefits, and taking on new risks (such as disability and health insurance) have had significant labor support. Similarly, the state organizations and international unions have pushed for improving state legislation on unemployment and temporary disability insurance and workmen's compensation. In support of the interests of its membership and frequently going beyond Administration proposals, labor has also supported program improvements for groups outside its ranks, including farm workers, for example. The key Medicare proposal was introduced by Congressman Aime Forand in 1957 and reintroduced in 1959. It was designed by the AFL-CIO, which was the major interest group supporting it, with other groups adding their support as the legislative battle proceeded. The American Medical Association, in association with other professional, business, and insurance organizations, comprised the major opposition, which supported proposals for private health insurance for the aged.

The 1965 amendments established health insurance for the aged—hospital and physicians' services (Medicare) for those eligible for OASDI (and RRB) monthly benefits. They marked a major success in a struggle dating back more than twenty years, preceding the 1948 Truman proposals for comprehensive health insurance. While earlier proposals were more inclusive, a legislative move beginning with the limited Forand proposal of 1957 permitted supporters to focus on a more modest and practicable objective. In fact, a bill proposing that health insurance should begin with social security beneficiaries was introduced in 1952 by Senators Murray and Humphrey and Representatives Celler and Dingell.[61] The proposal was defended on the grounds that the aged needed and utilized hospital care more frequently than younger people but were least able to afford commercial insurance. While some supporters regarded the compromise as inadequate, the opposition treated it as a victory for "socialized medicine." Medicare was a major issue in the election campaigns of 1960 and 1964, but the 1964 landslide produced a large enough congressional majority to pass the legislation.[62]

61. Corning, *Evolution of Medicare,* pp. 71–78.
62. For legislative history, see Richard Harris, *A Public Trust* (New York:

Hospital and related posthospital care is financed by worker and employer contributions; those insured under it are also covered by a second plan (formerly optional), which provides specified physicians' in-hospital and out-patient services but financed by subscriber and government contributions. Health service benefits under OASDHI follow private health insurance approaches by covering the costs of specified hospital and medical services. This is distinct from either a cash wage-loss payment to the beneficiary or the direct provision of hospital and physicians' services, as under the British National Health Service. Nor is it a prepayment plan such as HIP in New York and Kaiser-Permanente in California.

Its scope was broadened significantly in 1972 to go beyond the aged to disability beneficiaries, a group whose medical care costs, like the aged, are an especially heavy charge against their limited resources. This protection was made available (effective July 1, 1973) to workers receiving disability benefits for at least 24 consecutive months, as well as to disabled widows and dependent widowers over age 50, and to child disability beneficiaries (plus qualified railroad retirement beneficiaries). Since the disabled use about seven times as much hospital care and three times as much physicians' services as the nondisabled, the extension reaches a group generally unable to get private health insurance protection. This major advance protected more than 1.7 million beneficiaries most exposed to slipping into poverty because of health care costs.

In order to cover those aged persons who were not entitled to Medicare, mainly because they had not been under social security long enough to acquire retirement protection, any person age 65 or over was permitted to enroll voluntarily under Parts A and B of the Medicare program, effective July 1, 1973. State and local governments can purchase Medicare protection for their older employees and, more importantly, for retired persons. The premium, beginning at $33 per month, is subject to adjustment if cost experience justifies. This 1972 amendment took account of the people covered by local and state govern-

New American Library, 1966); H. M. Somers, *Medicare and the Hospitals* (Washington: Brookings Institution, 1967), chapter 1; Corning, *Evolution of Medicare:* and Sundquist, *Politics and Policy,* chapter 7. Harris provides the most complete legislative history.

ment pension plans, but not by social security, who had not obtained health insurance protection on a group or individual basis. Whether pensioners will be able to pay the $33 monthly premium (from their fixed incomes) without assistance from former employers (or public assistance) remains to be seen.

Hospital Insurance (HI)

Basic protection was provided against the costs of in-patient services, related post-hospital extended care (as in a nursing home), and home health services for persons eligible for social security or railroad retirement monthly benefits, whether or not they were receiving them, at age 65. The same benefits, financed from general revenues under special transitional provisions, cover those who became 65 before 1968 but were not eligible for retirement benefits. The following services were included:

1. In-patient hospital services for 90 days per benefit period; the patient was to pay a "deductible amount" of $40, plus "co-insurance" of $10 per day after 60 days.[63]
2. Post-hospital extended care in a skilled nursing home for up to 100 days in a benefit period. After the first 20 days the patient pays $5 per day for the remaining 80 days. This was raised, by stages, to $8.50 per day, as of January 1, 1972.
3. Post-hospital home health services for a maximum of 100 visits per year for homebound persons, including visiting nurse services and other types of therapy.

Supplementary Medical Insurance Benefits (SMIB)

Medical benefits (Part B) to supplement hospital insurance are available to those persons eligible for Part A hospital insurance; they must pay a monthly premium of $5.80, matched by the Treasury. Aged public assistance recipients can be insured if the state pays the premium; some states have done so, having expended $138 million for this purpose in fiscal year 1972. Under the 1972 amendments, enrollment in Part B (physi-

63. The deductible was successively raised—the latest as of January 1972, to $68 and $17 per day after 60 days, and $34 per day after 90 days, per spell of hospitalization. *Statistical Supplement,* 1970, p. 22.

cian's services) was made automatic (as of July 1973) for the aged and disabled as they become eligible for hospital insurance coverage. The annual deductible was increased, effective January 1973, from $50 to $60. The plan calls for coinsurance of 20 percent of the "reasonable charges" for the following services:

1. Physicians' and surgeons' services, whether on an in-hospital or outpatient basis, clinic, home, extended care facility, or elsewhere.
2. Home health services, for up to 100 visits per year.
3. Outpatient hospital services, including x-ray, laboratory, and other diagnostic tests.
4. Outpatient physical therapy.
5. Limited ambulance services.
6. Surgical dressings, splints, casts; rental or purchase of such durable equipment as oxygen tents, hospital beds, wheel chairs, and prosthetic devices (other than dental).
7. In-hospital radiology and pathology services.

Among expensive, excluded services are prescription drugs and blood transfusions, but coverage has been extended to in-hospital x-ray and pathology services.

The 1971 Advisory Council proposed that SMIB costs be met through contributions during the individual's working life, rather than by premiums paid from his reduced income after retirement.

Medicare Operations

What has been the impact of Medicare in extending health services to the aged? Have the benefits relieved the aged sick of rising costs? In examining these aspects, we should not overlook other advantages of the program which do not lend themselves readily to numerical measurement. For example, as one analyst has observed, Medicare "has enhanced the dignity of the nation's elderly by providing coverage for their needed hospital care, and allowing them to be cared for in hospitals without regard to their personal resources." With the greater availability of medical services, use of hospital services (days of care) increased by one fourth between 1965 and 1967; the increase was greatest for the disadvantaged: those above 75, blacks, and low-income single persons. As an indication of greater freedom of choice afforded the aged, hospital stays in facilities where no charges were incurred (payment by welfare or VA), dropped from 17 percent to only 3 percent. Out-of-pocket expense for hospital charges declined from 38 percent to 7 percent in spite of higher prices and greater utilization.[64] The aged visited doctors' offices more frequently, obtaining treatment in less impersonal settings than, for example, emergency room facilities. The proportion of blacks making clinic visits declined from 25 percent to 14 percent. Out-of-pocket expense for combined in-hospital and ambulatory care declined from 77 percent to 47 percent of the total between the two years (15 percent in dollar terms), despite the increase in average total charges for medical care from $298 to $415.[65]

These aggregate figures might suggest that Medicare did not relieve the aged, as a group, of most of the burden of their medical costs, for even though their out-of-pocket expense dropped from 53 percent to 26 percent of total expenditures between the 1966 and 1971 fiscal years, the dollar amounts of expense carried from their own resources remained about the same — declining only from $234 yearly to $225.[66] From another perspective, however, Medicare's contribution was far more important. Most peoples' medical costs derive from numerous short-term hospital and medical episodes, where deductibles and coinsurance account for a greater share of total expenditure than from larger medical bills. But older people do have prolonged spells of illness and hospitalization involving expensive treatment, with bills running from $2,000 to $20,000 or more. Because a greater share of the aged person's costs are covered by Medicare in such cases, the threat of very large medical bills is largely removed. The leveling off of out-of-pocket expense for

64. Regina Lowenstein, "Early Effects of Medicare on the Health Care of the Aged," *Social Security Bulletin,* April 1971, pp. 3–9 and Table 7, p. 11. See also, Howard West, "Five Years of Medicare — A Statistical Review," *Social Security Bulletin,* Dec. 1971, p. 22.

65. Lowenstein, "Early Effects of Medicare," pp. 4, 13; See also Table 10. Private insurance covered 19 percent in 1965, but declined to 8 percent in 1967.

66. Barbara S. Cooper and Nancy L. Worthington, "Medical Care Spending for Three Age Groups," *Social Security Bulletin,* May 1972, Table 9.

the aged, despite increased use of services and higher prices, was made possible in large part by increased public spending on the aged; public funds paid for 68 percent of health costs of the aged in 1971, compared to 30 percent in 1967. By contrast, for persons under 65, whose out-of-pocket expense went up by 31 percent, public spending accounted for one fourth of the health bill.[67]

Few analyses of the SMIB program are available, but it is apparent that the aged made much use of the program — four of every five eligibles or 15 million did so in 1967. Since SMIB insures only 80 percent of charges for specified services after the first $50 (now $60), unsurprisingly it reimbursed less than one half of the charges incurred in that year. But only 8.5 million persons incurred reimbursable charges of over $50.[68]

How did the aged sick meet the remaining deductible and coinsured expenses? Half of them relied upon their own resources entirely; others used private insurance and public assistance. Those who covered more than the average share of costs from their own resources had the most education, higher incomes, were working, and were in two-person households. One fifth of the enrollees who used SMIB services were welfare recipients and half of these reported that welfare agencies paid all or some of their expenses. Those with the lowest income more often relied on welfare agencies for payment of charges — 14 percent of those with incomes under $3,000, compared to 7 percent with incomes of $3,000–$5,000.[69] Such findings support our common understanding — many who use medical care the most have the least resources to pay for it.

Although intending no full appraisal of the impact of Medicare upon the accessibility and utilization of health care services, it is apparent that a disproportionate share of services and expenditures are devoted to the aged. Not only do older people require more care and more long-term treatment, they also use the more expensive types of care; thus it is not surprising that

67. Cooper and Worthington, "Medical Care Spending," Table 9, p. 3.

68. J. Green and J. Scharff, "Use of Medical Services under Medicare," *Social Security Bulletin,* March 1971, pp. 4–5, Tables 1–2, pp. 6, 9. Another 6 million had charges averaging $20, not enough to meet the deductible. See also Lowenstein, "Early Effects of Medicare," Table 10.

69. Ibid., Table 3, pp. 10–11, Table 2, and pp. 9, 14. SMIB recipients are largely outside the welfare rolls.

although the aged comprise one tenth of the population, one in every four dollars was spent on their behalf.[70]

The first post-Medicare years saw particularly sharp annual increases in medical care costs — 12–13 percent for 1968–70, and 80 percent for the six-year period. However, 1971 showed a lower rate of increase, 10.9 percent. The change may reflect more effective controls on use of nursing homes and for reimbursement of physicians services, even though doctors' fees continued to increase. The length of hospital stays for aged patients declined 3 percent per year in 1970 and 1971. Whether these are straws indicating the start of a downward trend in health care spending for the aged is yet to be seen. More even balancing of financial support for health care for the young, especially children, need not require reduced care for the aged.

THE FINANCING OF OASDHI AND ITS IMPACT

OASDHI benefits and administration are financed primarily from contributions paid by employees, employers, and the self-employed. The government's share of the cost of SMI benefits and of hospital benefits for the noninsured is financed from general revenues. The monies are paid into separate trust funds for retirement, disability, hospital, and supplementary medical benefits; additional income is derived from interest earnings. The combined employer-employee contribution rates (exclusive of Medicare), as shown in Table 9, increased from 2 percent in 1937 to 9.7 percent for 1973–77. The allocation for disability insurance, costs having increased far more than anticipated, has risen from 0.5 percent in 1957–58 to 1.1 percent in 1970–72, and again to 1.4 percent in 1973–77. The taxable wage base, though lagging behind wages, was raised from the $3,000 limit in 1937 to $9,000 in 1972 and to $10,800 in 1973 and $12,000 in 1974; thereafter it will be adjusted to changes in average wages. Liberalization of the benefit schedule, increased longevity and growth of the aged population, among other factors, account for

70. In 1971 and 1966–71. See Cooper and Worthington, "Medical Care Spending," p. 3, and adapted from Table 9, p. 14. By contrast, those age 18 and below, numbering 36 percent of the population, accounted for 16 percent of all health spending in fiscal 1971.

The Aged, Disabled, and Survivors 65

the increased benefit expenditures, which in turn required greater contributions. Hospital and related health insurance benefits
are financed by a separate contribution for this purpose — 1.2
percent in 1968–72 and 2.0 percent in 1973–77.

Payroll taxes as the major source of financing of the social
security system have been criticized and defended, with specific
issues receiving varying attention from time to time. But the
subject of financing has assumed major importance, if for no
other reason, as Brittain puts it, than that the payroll tax has
been the fastest growing major tax in the postwar United
States.[71]

Will future retirees get their money's worth for the contributions they have paid? On the one hand, no one drawing OASDI
benefits in 1971, for example, had paid more in contributions
than a minor fraction of the value of his benefit protection.[72]
Retirees from the beginning have received essentially full-rate
benefits; so have those who were brought into the system later
on. As benefits for current and future retirees are raised, the
value of the benefits paid to those who retired in the past — some
of them twenty or more years ago — as well as to new retirees,
will exceed their contributions. The arguments of many critics,
according to Wilcox, for example, "assume that the economy
will be static, that average earnings will be the same, and that
average benefits, therefore, will not increase."[73] Beyond this,
some critics seem to ignore the value of employers' contributions toward financing of retirement benefits and the value of
dependents' survivors' and disability benefits — few workers, indeed, could invest their own contributions well enough to match

71. Among recent discussions of the subject, see J. A. Brittain, "The In-
cidence of Social Security — Payroll Taxes," *American Economic Review,*
March 1971, pp. 110–111; and *The Payroll Tax for Social Security* (Washing-
ton: Brookings Institution, 1972), especially chapters 1 and 5. See also discussion in Pechman, Aaron, and Taussig, *Social Security;* articles by W. J.
Cohen, R. M. Ball, and G. R. Rohrlich, among others, in the *Encyclopedia of
Social Work,* 1971; and R. J. Lampman, *Ends and Means in Reducing Income
Poverty* (Chicago: Markham Publishing Co., 1971).
72. Ida C. Merriam suggests a 10 percent figure in "Income Maintenance:
Social Insurance and Public Assistance," pp. 74–76. See also Joseph A. Pech-
man, "The Rich and the Poor and the Taxes They Pay," *The Public Interest,*
Fall 1969, p. 30; and Edwin L. Dale, Jr., "The Security of Social Security,"
New York Times Magazine, 14 Jan. 1973, pp. 8–10, 40–45.
73. Wilcox, "Toward Social Welfare," pp. 128–129.

the "return" on the combined worker-employer contribution. Summarizing findings from detailed calculations, Pechman concludes that young workers of today will receive retirement benefits equal to, or greater than, the value of their taxes.[74]

Is the payroll tax regressive, in that contributions paid by low-income workers are a greater percentage of their earnings than of workers with higher earnings? While federal personal and corporate income taxes supply the major progressive elements in the total tax system, all other federal, state, and local taxes taken together have a regressive effect — this is especially true of sales, excise and property taxes.[75] Social security taxes, as such, add to this regressive effect, for the uniform rate cuts more deeply into the income of low earners than of people who earn over the taxable wage base. As the base has been raised, the impact has become less regressive. Yet many low-income families subject to social security taxes pay no personal income taxes; social security takes more than the income tax from three of every five who pay both. Increasing concern about the current and possible future level of social security taxes, in the light of further benefit improvements, has led to support for supplementation from general revenues or other tax sources.[76]

Fuller consideration of the impact of the payroll tax would necessitate viewing the tax and the benefit features, taken together, as an insurance premium. As already noted (Table 5), the weighting of the benefit schedule favors the lower earners, thus reducing its regressive character. Brittain has identified flaws in the concept that contributions are premiums. He points out that the government has both supported the insurance principle "in support of taxes, and rejected it [in court proceedings] in denial of benefits." Yet it is widely accepted that the insurance analogy has a powerful pragmatic rationale — that "Congress will approve substantial benefit increases only if they are

74. Pechman, Aaron, and Taussig, *Social Security*, Appendix A, p. 249.
75. Lampman, *Reducing Income Poverty*, p. 99; and J. A. Pechman, *Federal Tax Policy*, rev. ed. (Washington: Brookings Institution, 1971), pp. 179–183. Sales and excise taxes account for $34 of every $100 state and local tax dollars, and property taxes, $40 of every $100. *Statistical Abstract*, 1971, p. 402.
76. On these proposals, see *Report of the 1971 Advisory Council on Social Security;* W. J. Cohen in the *Encyclopedia of Social Work*, 1971; Pechman, Aaron, and Taussig, *Social Security*, pp. 212–213, and J. A. Brittain, *The Payroll Tax for Social Security*.

financed by the payroll tax and viewed as insurance benefits." It is unlikely, he points out, that benefits would have reached their present level except for acceptance of the tax as a premium.[77]

More recently, Pechman has repeated earlier suggestions that the payroll and income taxes be integrated. As he and others might agree, however, drastic revision is not likely without a broader overhaul of our tax structure. Recent increases have lifted the combined social security tax rate to nearly 12 percent of payrolls, applicable to a $10,800 tax base (in 1973); it has thereby become more difficult, fiscally and politically, to shift the burden of raising the necessary $45–$65 billion per year to the personal (and corporate) income tax. This is the case all the more since the corporate income tax has been scaled down, producing far less revenue in recent years than the payroll tax.

Do payroll taxes, taken together with social security benefits, redistribute income from high to low income groups? Social security taxes and benefits redistribute income in several directions: over time, from workers as contributors to themselves as beneficiaries (forced savings); from single persons to families; from younger and from working to older and nonworking people; and from higher- to lower-income groups.[78] Because it is difficult to trace social security taxes and benefits within the stream of other taxes and benefits, we deal with them here as part of a larger whole, but with particular reference to people who would be below the poverty line but for receipt of transfer payments. Covering virtually the entire population, the system pays more benefits to the nonpoor than to the poor; no means test excludes them. On the other hand, social security is "one of the most important vehicles . . . developed for preventing poverty," and makes a greater contribution to lifting the poor out of poverty than any other public transfer system.[79] In 1967, for example, the pretransfer poor received $49.2 billion — half of this in social insurance and public assistance — and in return paid $10.7 billion through public and private channels. Their net gain

77. Ibid., pp. 9–11.
78. George F. Rohrlich, "Social Policy and Income Distribution," *Encyclopedia of Social Work*, 1971, pp. 1391–92. Milton Friedman contends that "in overall effect" it redistributes income from lower to higher income persons" (Wilbur J. Cohen and Milton Friedman, *Social Security: Universal or Selective* [Washington: American Enterprise Institute, 1972], p. 22).
79. Cohen, "Social Insurance," p. 1283.

was thus $38.5 billion. The nonpoor, by contrast, received $82.8 billion but paid out $121.3 billion.[80]

From OEO data, it is estimated that three out of every four pretransfer poor families (12.3 out of 16.1 million) received public and private transfers averaging $1,840, and half of these were taken out of poverty by transfers.[81] The 6.1 million taken out of poverty were the more well off and, particularly, those favored by social security and public assistance, namely the aged and the family breadwinners with irregular employment. Among aged families (half of the pretransfer poor), for example, seven in ten were taken out of poverty.[82] Nearly all of the remainder, while not removed from poverty, had their poverty deficit largely reduced. To sum up, OASDI benefits in 1966 removed more than two in three otherwise poor beneficiaries out of poverty, and reduced the income gap for the remainder.

HOW SECURE IS SOCIAL SECURITY?

One of the most common questions concerns the security of the social security resources — assurance to the contributor-beneficiary that he or his survivors will receive the promised benefits. The commercial insurance carrier whose reserves should be sufficient to pay all insured risks is visualized as having the resources to meet all conceivable future contingencies. Contrasting this with $45 billion in social security reserves, only enough to meet a single year's liabilities, the worker becomes concerned. As to this point, the 1971 Advisory Council Report on Social Security Financing notes that concepts of actuarial soundness are not the same for commercial insurance and compulsory social insurance. The latter does not need the reserves necessary for an "institution that cannot count on current income to meet current obligations." As the Council put it, "The test of actuarial soundness of a social insurance system is whether expected future income from contributions and interest . . . will be sufficient to meet anticipated . . . benefits and administrative costs."[83] Earlier Councils had recommended that

80. Lampman, *Reducing Income Poverty,* pp. 117–118.
81. Ibid., p. 11.
82. Ibid., pp. 114–115.
83. *Report of the 1971 Advisory Council on Social Security,* p. 97.

the system be operated on a pay-as-you-go basis, with current income sufficient for current expenditures. This would take account of an unanticipated drop in income or other emergencies and would avoid calling on the congress for emergency taxes to meet deficits.[84]

In keeping with this objective, assets of the retirement and disability trust funds at the year-end have exceeded the coming year's expenditures by a comfortable margin, as shown below:

OASDHI Trust Funds:
Contributions, Benefits, and Reserves, Fiscal 1968–72
(in billions)

Fiscal year	Contributions	Benefits*	Assets at end of period
1967–1968	$ 25.4	$ 22.8	$28.1
1968–1969	29.5	26.1	31.9
1969–1970	34.1	28.1	37.7
1970–1971	36.5	34.5	40.7
1971–1972	40.6	38.6	43.8

*Excludes transfers to RRB, from general revenues, interest earnings and net administrative expenses; in absence of these adjustments, figures shown do not balance exactly.

Sources: Social Security Bulletin; December 1972, Table M-56, pp. 43–44; *1970 Annual Report, Board of Trustees of the Federal OASI and DI Trust Funds,* p. 25; *Social Security Bulletin,* December 1970, pp. 24–25.

As expenditures and contributions rose, the higher tax rates and higher wage base led to a greater fund balance at the end of fiscal year 1970 than seemed warranted by anticipated benefits. This, among other reasons, led Congress to make the March 1971 10 percent benefit increase effective retroactively to January 1, but delayed the effective date of the $9,000 taxable wage limit until January 1972. An increase in the tax rate was postponed until 1973.[85]

The program's contribution to our economic security has facilitated such expansion that in fiscal terms its expenditures

84. Adapted by Pechman, Aaron, and Taussig, *Social Security,* p. 208, from *Final Report of the 1938 Advisory Council on Social Security.*

85. U.S., Congress, Senate, Committee on Finance and House Committee on Ways and Means, *Social Security Amendments of 1971: Conference Report,* 92nd Cong., 1st sess., Rept. 92–42, p. 11.

constitute the next largest item, after defense, of government spending; its taxes, the second largest source of revenue. Every fifth federal dollar of income and expenditure is a social security dollar. Policy decisions affecting social security income and expenditures figure increasingly in overall federal budget planning. In weighing national priorities, the Federal Advisory Council's recommendations have dealt with the interests of the contributors-beneficiaries-voters as affected by social security *vs.* federal budget considerations.[86] "The Social Security trust funds should be maintained at [such] a level [as to] reduce the possibility that policy decisions relating to the social security program will be unduly influenced by overall Federal budget objectives."[87]

ADMINISTRATION

The OASDHI system is administered by the SSA and, except for one aspect of disability insurance, is federally administered. Collection of contributions is a U.S. Treasury Department responsibility. Since workers' retirement benefits are determined on the basis of their earnings history as well as age and marital status, collection, maintenance, and processing of earnings records of the covered population has made the Baltimore operation one of the world's most advanced computer centers. The social security account number, identifying the covered worker and beneficiary population, now is applied to the entire population. Benefit and claims operations are decentralized to some 900 district and branch offices, plus smaller localities, in order to be accessible to older and disabled people in sparsely populated areas.[88]

86. For an international perspective see also Paul Fisher, "Developments and Trends in Social Security throughout the World" (Address to the 17th General Assembly, International Social Security Association, Cologne, Sept., 1970), pp. 17–25.

87. *Report of the 1971 Advisory Council on Social Security,* p. 105.

88. Recent innovations designed to bring the huge organization closer to the public include use of staff of labor unions and employing firms to inform and take claims from fellow employees and members, and neighborhood offices staffed with employees "who have an understanding of the culture, life style and language of the people in the area." (J. S. Futterman, "Administrative Developments in the Social Security Program since 1965," *Social Security Bulletin,* April 1972, p. 7).

The SSA enjoys a reputation for efficiency above that of most governmental and private organizations. From the start, its staff selection and training have emphasized the priority of the needs of applicants and beneficiaries. As recent examples, letters, the radio, and television as well as home visits were used in a "Medicare Alert" campaign in 1966 to ensure that all aged persons understood the advantages of enrolling in the new health insurance program; in the fall of 1972 beneficiaries were similarly sought out and called upon at home (by Red Cross volunteers) to inform them that they might be eligible to use food stamps. The confidence which the SSA has built up within all branches of government and the general public has facilitated policy decisions to broaden and enlarge the program and, in consequence, the responsibilities and functions of the agency.

Its record and reputation for effectiveness are safeguarded through headquarters staff supervision of decentralized operations through regional and area subheadquarters. Comments from congressmen (on the receiving end of constituents' complaints) reflect this confidence; one member of Congress expressed himself thus during hearings on the SSA appropriation request for 1971-72:

> More American citizens probably form an opinion of the American government through your office than any other federal activity. . . . A person going to the post office does not have an emotional situation. . . . Here, there is the language difficulty and many who are physically handicapped. . . . There is no doubt that millions of our citizens will love our country and admire our institutions by the impression your Department leaves.[89]

OTHER RETIREMENT, SURVIVOR AND DISABILITY PROGRAMS

Railroad Retirement Benefits[90]

The retirement benefit system for railroad workers antedates the Social Security Act. Although the railroad plan enacted in

89. Quoted in *OASIS*, Aug. 1971, p. 2.
90. This discussion is drawn from *Annual Reports of the Railroad Board*, plus *Social Welfare Expenditures under Public Programs, 1929-1966*, SSA – ORS Research Report no. 25 (Washington, 1968), pp. 39-42.

1934 was invalidated by the courts, 1935 legislation did become operative and assumed the obligation for pensions to retired workers on the benefit rolls of the railroads' plans, for many of these were virtually insolvent. Within four years after benefits became payable, more than 100,000 railroad workers retired and $250 million in benefits were paid.

Entitlement to retirement, disability, and survivors' benefits requires ten years of railroad service, a more restrictive requirement than under OASDHI. As railroad employment declined (Table 1) during the past quarter-century, contribution rates, applied to a contrasting base, have risen to meet benefit obligations. They reached 19.9 percent of earnings in 1971, including 1.2 percent for hospital benefits, and are scheduled to reach 21.6 percent in 1987.[91] A key program development is a special relationship with OASDHI whereby workers ineligible for railroad plan benefits could receive social security benefits by combining their railroad and social security rights. Although the two plans are similar, railroad benefits are guaranteed, since 1959, to be at least 110 percent of what would be payable under the Social Security Act if all of the workers' railroad service since 1937 had been under OASDI. Retirement benefits are payable earlier than under social security, at age 60 (with 30 years of service) or at age 62 (with fewer years) but with an actuarial reduction. As an additional benefit to long-service workers supplemental annuities ($45–$70 per month) are payable to workers retiring after June 1966. Railroad workers are also covered by Medicare.[92]

Railroad workers' concern for their own staff benefit system has produced more favorable treatment than under social security. Their seniority and related job protection assures them higher earnings and more regular work than most other workers get and rationalizes more generous benefits. It is not surprising, therefore, that the railroad unions, intensely interested in their own system, have been effective in securing their legislative objectives. Surely the needs of railroad workers are served more satisfactorily by an organization concerned primarily with their interests. However, the costs to the industry and to the nation of such "special" protection have been increased by the decline in

91. SSA – ORS, *Social Security Programs in the U.S.,* p. 115.
92. RRB collects the taxes for railroad workers, but the SSA deals with the providers of health services for beneficiaries under both systems.

railroad employment to one third of its World War II number, and to the point where retired and disabled beneficiaries and their dependents and survivors exceed the number at work. Resulting higher costs have led to suggestions that the railroad and general schemes be merged.

Agencies and programs which center on the client group — the veterans' programs are another example — have resisted proposals for integration; as Eveline Burns points out, the success of this resistance "illustrates the influence that can be exerted by the combination of a powerful lobby of interested beneficiaries and a client-oriented agency."[93]

The President's Commission on Railroad Retirement recommended substantial corrective actions to prevent future financial insolvency.[94] A revised tax and benefit structure for workers and employers was called for, and the railroad workers' system restructured into a two-tier arrangement, with social security forming the basic level of protection, plus a separate railroad system of retirement benefits to augment social security benefits. It proposed that dual benefits enjoyed by a minority of railroad beneficiaries, but imposing heavy costs, should not accrue in the future. The railroad unions, however, favored employer (rather than the present joint) financing of benefits above the level which the social security system provides. Substantial differences in the positions of the interested parties require resolution if necessary congressional support for long-term benefit and tax increases for the railroad system is to be obtained.

Public Employee Retirement[95]

Staff benefits for public employees have increased in importance with the growth of public employment, which expanded

93. Burns, *Social Security and Public Policy*, p. 254, footnote. See also Steiner, *The State of Welfare*, chapter 7.

94. U.S., Congress, House, President's Commission on Railroad Retirement, *The Railroad Retirement System: Its Coming Crisis, Report to the President and the Congress*, 92nd Cong., 2d sess., 1972, H. Doc. 92-350, pp. 3–50.

95. This discussion draws on the following sources: Joseph Krislov, *State and Local Government Retirement Systems, 1965*, SSA–ORS Research Report no. 15 (Washington, 1966), pp. 1–3; SSA–ORS, *State and Local Government Employment Statistics, 1964–1968* (Washington: Government Printing Office, 1970), Table 1A, p. 6, and special tabulations; and Alfred M. Skolnik and Sophie R. Dales, "Benefits and Beneficiaries under Public Employee Retirement Systems, Calendar Year 1971," SSA–ORS, Research and Statistics Note no. 13 (Washington, 1972).

from 8.8 to 13 million between 1960 and 1970. State and local education, welfare, and health services account for most of this growth. Retirement and other staff benefits, together with security of tenure, formerly had been a major element in attracting people to public service, for they helped to compensate, in part, for lower earnings. Some of the oldest retirement systems in the country are in the public sector, with teachers among the first beneficiaries. While the gap between earnings in private and public employment has narrowed, this has not lessened the growth of fringe benefits in the public sector. In some cases, pension and other fringe benefits may be equal or superior to those available in private employment. The generous treatment of the federal civil servant as to retirement benefits is due in part to congressional interest in improving a system in which members of Congress themselves are covered.

Aside from retirement, advances have been spotty as to health care, unemployment, and disability protection. The federal civil service has led the public sector in protection against work injury (with the very first such legislation) and vacation pay, and in more recent years with survivors', unemployment, and health care benefits. Wage loss protection against short-term disability under paid sick leave plans is a major benefit in all public employment. Although California, New York, Michigan, and some other states and major cities may approach the federal level of benefits or even exceed it in some respects, state and local employees generally have less comprehensive and generous protection than federal workers. Future development as to state and local employee protection is rather uncertain, given the mounting financial pressures upon these government units.

Protection of state and local government workers against the contingencies of old age, disability, survivorship, and health care has been improved substantially by the addition of social security protection to their staff benefit plans, the trend having begun on a small scale during the early 1950s. Federal employees not under civil service retirement or other federal employee retirement plans are covered by social security. Although the social security system was expected initially to protect only those who were not under a state or local retirement system, by the late 1950s, election of social security coverage was permitted on an increasingly wider scale; it permitted election by employees who were under a pension plan, with or without the agreement, as required earlier, of the government unit itself. As of 1972 all but six state retirement systems permitted social security supplementation and 70 percent of all state and local government employees were under social security. Of 9.5 million state and local government workers included in 1969 data, 1.6 million had only social security protection, and another 4.9 million had both social security and state or local retirement plan protection. Only a few of these, less than 15 percent of the workers, were under plans which offset the normal retirement benefit, wholly or in part, by the amount of the social security benefit.

Despite the fact that federal employees are outnumbered three to one by employees of state and local governments, the federal systems currently pay more benefits to a greater number of beneficiaries. The more comprehensive coverage, greater maturity, and more generous benefits under the federal schemes accounted, in 1970, for twice as many benefit dollars ($6.1 *vs.* 3.3 billion) and 40 percent more beneficiaries (1.8 *vs.* 1.3 million) than under the state and local systems.

Current concerns as to the future development of public employee retirement plans give greater attention to growing duplication of coverage. For example, should benefits be adjusted to the price level and for productivity in state and local government employee plans (as is being done under social security) where workers enjoy dual protection? In addition, as in other pension planning, there is concern about solvency of reserves and long-range planning of investment of mounting reserves which totaled some $60 billion in 1970, compared to $20 billion in 1960. The increased interest in early retirement, aside from police and fire systems, requires personnel planners—as well as actuaries—to concern themselves with issues of pensionable age and minimum years of service as they affect retention of both experienced and junior staff members. The multiplicity and fragmentation of protection among hundreds of plans in individual states requires coordination or integration of these systems in order to achieve more adequate protection of all workers.

III

Social Insurance for the Sick, Injured, and Jobless: Other Programs

Financial problems of long-term interruptions in family income due to retirement, disability, and premature death are alleviated by benefits for those outside the active working force – the aged, the infirm, their children, and their widowed parents. By contrast, unemployment and disability contingencies and programs dealt with here concern benefit payments to people whose earnings are interrupted by a short-term layoff, illness, or injury, and who anticipate returning to work after a few weeks or months. Unlike OASDHI, which is a national uniform program, unemployment and disability benefits have the character of state programs, despite federal underpinning of unemployment insurance.

UNEMPLOYMENT INSURANCE

Before we examine the history, purposes, and objectives of unemployment benefits, we should examine how well it serves us, to better understand its shortcomings and proposals for reform. Unemployment insurance is only one of several devices for compensating wage loss due to involuntary unemployment, but despite deficiencies it is the most effective of all. It reaches about one third of the jobless at any one time, as seen when we compare two commonly used monthly figures: the estimated number of jobless (4.7 million)[1] in December 1971 with the number getting benefits (1.6 million).[2] Since World War II, the percentage of unemployed receiving unemployment insurance has varied from 35 percent to 55 percent. The gap has been narrowed by extensions of coverage and duration and liberalized eligibility. Some of the gap, hard to measure, results from the worker's failure to claim benefits because (1) a layoff may be very short, (2) prompt return to work is expected, (3) he expects to be found ineligible, or (4) his benefit rights are exhausted. Perhaps most jobless nonclaimants are new entrants to the labor force or reentrants who are unable to qualify for benefits.

Other measures, mostly in the private sector, either reach fewer jobless or carry them for a shorter time. Dismissal pay, for example, assures some 5 million workers a lump sum indemnity in event of separation. Another half million have the equivalent of a work guarantee — usually a minimum number of hours or weeks of work. But such benefits are available only to workers with long seniority and thus a lesser risk of unemployment. Public assistance gives short-term help when other resources are exhausted. Only half the states provide AFDC-U to family breadwinners, and others also provide temporary direct (local) relief, supplementing unemployment insurance. In April 1972, for example, 920,000 persons were getting direct relief at an average of $67 per month.[3]

1. The monthly estimate of unemployment is the most satisfactory series available on the size and composition of the group not at work and seeking work. The definitions have been criticized on the grounds that they include some individuals who should be omitted and exclude others who ought to be included. "There is approximately a 20 percent undercount of [unemployment among] non-white males between . . . 20 to 44 years . . . We may be understating their economic plight, such as their rate of unemployment." (U.S. Department of Labor, Bureau of Labor Statistics, *Pilot and Experimental Programs on Urban Employment Surveys,* Report no. 354, March 1969, p. 2). See also, President's Committee to Appraise Employment and Unemployment, *Measuring Employment and Unemployment* (Washington: Government Printing Office, 1962); S. L. Wolfbein, *Employment and Unemployment in the U.S.* (Chicago: Science Research Associates, 1964); and *Manpower Report of the President,* 1972, pp. 35–40 (and prior reports).

2. The number of beneficiaries in December 1971, 1.6 million, is the average weekly number of individuals receiving benefits in that month; another measure, the "insured unemployed," stood at 2.2 million for the same month. The latter overstates the number of beneficiaries because it includes persons whose claims are awaiting determination or are in waiting period status. See Gloria P. Green, "Measuring Total and Insured Unemployment," *Monthly Labor Review,* June 1971, pp. 37–48.

3. *Public Assistance Statistics,* NCSS Report A-2, April 1972.

It was noted earlier that the program was adopted when unemployment was at a record peak; it was expected to encourage employment stabilization and reduce unemployment.[4] Employers would be induced to reduce layoffs by having their taxes reduced when they had few separations and having them increased if they had many, the system referred to as experience-rating. In addition, the benefit flow into communities hard hit by layoffs could reduce spreading unemployment by maintaining consumer purchasing power. We have learned, however, that economic activity is more greatly influenced by fiscal, credit, spending, and monetary policies than by individual employers' unemployment insurance contribution rates; yet experience rating has had a pervasive impact on benefits, financing, and administration.[5]

Responsibility for the system is divided between federal and state authorities as to coverage, financing, and benefits. The system is essentially state in character; state authorities deal directly with jobless workers and their former and prospective employers. States determine who shall be entitled to benefits, of what amount, and for how long. These policies are at the heart of the system's effectiveness. State laws must meet federal requirements for two purposes: so that employers' contributions under state law can be offset against their tax liability under the payroll tax levied by the Federal Unemployment Tax Act, and so that the state can receive federal grants for the cost of administration. Review of state laws for conformity with federal law is vested in the Department of Labor's Unemployment Insurance Service. The federal agency must certify that state operations comply with such federal requirements as payment of benefits when due and workers' right to appeal when their claims are denied.

The Federal-State Employment Service "partner" helps the jobless obtain work and provides job information, counseling, referral, and placement services. If the claimant refuses offered

4. See Lubove, *The Struggle for Social Security*, chapter 7.

5. See, for example, R. A. Lester, *The Economics of Unemployment Compensation* (Princeton: Industrial Relations Section, 1962); William Haber and M. G. Murray, *Unemployment Insurance in the American Economy* (Homewood, Ill.: Irwin Publishing Co., 1966); R. Munts, "Objectives for Today's Economy," *Manpower*, Aug. 1969, pp. 18–21; and numerous additional references in SSA-ORS, *Basic Readings in Social Security* (Washington: Government Printing Office, 1970), p. 63.

work, his benefit claim can be questioned. The service helps employed workers move into better jobs and assists the unemployed to find new work. As manpower policies have evolved, priorities have shifted in stages, from temporarily jobless experienced workers to unemployment insurance claimants, and, in recent years, to applicants disadvantaged in competing for job openings. More recently, it has emphasized jobs and training for public welfare recipients. While federal manpower policy has aimed at a nationwide service, state and local interests tend to determine priorities on a narrower base.[6]

In providing benefits to help workers over temporary periods of unemployment, unemployment insurance assures them flexibility in choosing among available job opportunities to take account of their work experience, preferences, and present circumstances. Insulated from naked economic pressure to accept the first available job, the needs of the individual worker and of the labor market are well served by this flexibility. Similarly, the employer is assured freedom in making decisions whether to retain or dismiss workers in serving his own economic ends. Thus experienced workers on layoff for a model change can remain in the proximity of the plant, available for recall; assurance of benefits makes it unnecessary to scatter in search of other jobs. By contrast, a controlled labor market restricting both the worker's freedom to leave one job or seek another and the employer's freedom to hire and fire allows no such flexibility to either. Government itself may have less flexibility in adopting trade or fiscal policies which affect the labor market. It is true that this freedom of choice, used unwisely, can lead to unwise decisions, but it affords reasonable protection to those affected; the safety mechanism that unemployment insurance provides fits and supports our private-enterprise oriented society.

Administration

The law which the state agency administers is enacted by the state legislature, and the staff are state employees. Unlike most other federal-state programs, administration is financed by feder-

6. See Sar A. Levitan and Garth L. Mangum, *Federal Training and Work Programs in the Sixties* (Ann Arbor: Institute of Labor and Industrial Relations, 1969); Stanley H. Ruttenberg and J. Gutchess, *Manpower Challenge of the 1970s* (Baltimore, Johns Hopkins University Press, 1970).

al funds, not by state appropriations. However, orientation is focused on state interests, even though the program is federally financed; indeed, resistance to federal "interference in state affairs" may be sharpened by the closeness of the fiscal and administrative relationships.

Administration is beset with other competing interests. While unions work for higher benefits, employer-contributors wish to avoid higher costs. Caught between labor and industry, the agencies may more often mediate between them than shape and carry forward an independent policy line. They are likely to assume a neutral or passive official posture regarding workers exercising their rights to benefits, in contrast to an activist posture with regard to prevention of improper payment of benefits. The stance of the unemployment insurance agency will reflect the extent that labor, industry, or agriculture influence state programs regarding coverage extension, eligibility, benefits, and financing policy. Equally, such a stance permeates local office attitudes toward claimants, whether personnel aid claimants "to perfect their claims" (as the British put it), or make the often uninformed jobless client carry the burden of proving his entitlement.

Early Experience

The federal-state system was put to the test of compensating for substantial unemployment immediately following its creation, since millions were out of work between 1938 and World War II. Heavy unemployment during 1937–41, however, was reflected only partially in program operations. Most states had adopted legislation in 1935–36, the last in June 1937. Wisconsin issued the first unemployment insurance check in August 1936, but it was January 1939 before benefits were payable in as many as 49 of the 51 jurisdictions including Hawaii, Alaska, and the District of Columbia. In 1940, 5 million jobless workers (of the 23 million in covered employment) received benefits amounting to more than $500 million. Despite this contribution to their income, protection was far from adequate; every second claimant was still out of work when his benefit rights ran out. The high exhaustion rate was due in part to claimants' prolonged unemployment and the general lack of steady work, in addition to the limited duration of benefits payable: only 4 states allowed more than 16 weeks of benefits. But expectations as to the role of the system were modest. As Secretary of Labor Perkins put it: "We always admitted that . . . the system would not be adequate for all; . . . by far the largest number [of the unemployed] had had intermittent employment. Even if the allowance were small . . . it would sustain savings and credit, . . . serve to piece out the intermittent unemployment which members of a family might have . . . [and] would be worth in peace of mind . . . more than its cash value would indicate."[7]

Coverage

Due to legislative coverage extensions plus more rapid growth of the covered than noncovered sectors of the labor force (manufacturing expanded while agriculture declined), covered employment rose from 20 million (36 percent of the work force) in 1938 to 36 million (55 percent) in 1954, and then in 1970 up to 56 million (85 percent) under the 1970 amendments. Yet in 1971 more than 12 million wage and salary jobs remained outside the system, mostly in state and local government, agriculture, and domestic service. The raw statistic of 12 million uncovered jobs has wider significance; millions of workers who move back and forth from covered to noncovered employment as job opportunities dictate have no benefit rights from noncovered work to add to their rights from covered jobs in order to qualify for benefits (when earnings in covered employment fall short), or for higher weekly payments, or for more benefit weeks. The system is thus less effective in providing family security and in supporting purchasing power. To include farm and domestic workers would protect the lowest earners in the work force.

From the start, states have tended to limit "covered" employment and wages (for purposes of contributions and benefit rights) to the scope of the terms in the federal act. The original restricted coverage limited the program's effectiveness; after World War II attempts to broaden the federal act were unsuccessful until 1954 when the federal act covered firms with four or more workers. The earlier organized state and employer opposition to federal coverage of firms with fewer than eight

7. *Employment Security Review*, Aug. 1955, p. 7.

workers had subsided by 1954, because many states had already taken such action; compliance would now require conforming changes by only the remaining states—always a telling point for a congressional committee. Despite ad hoc extensions to special groups such as civil servants and ex-servicemen, 15 more years passed before the next major coverage extensions, for example, to employers with one or more workers.

Benefits

Qualifying requirements. To assure that the system compensates for wage loss of workers who are active in the labor force, unemployment insurance attempts to compensate for recent work interruptions, not those long past; persons who have never worked have no benefit rights. Therefore, minimum weeks of work or earnings during the reference period (usually the preceeding year) or both are needed to qualify. These requirements have been raised by stages since 1939, when wages were low and interruptions in employment common. Three states permit workers to qualify who have earned less than $300, and 25 states require less than $500 in a year; in 1972 only 11 states required earnings of $700 or more (Table 10). The states requir-

Table 10.

State Unemployment Insurance Eligibility Requirements, Base-Period Earnings and Weeks-of-Employment, 1972

No. of states*	Base-period earnings	No. of states	Weeks of employment		
			14-16	17-19	20
Total 52		Total 14	3	4	7
3	Under $300	2	1	1	
10	300-399	1	1		
12	400-499	3			3
9	500-599	1		1	
7	600-699	2			2
7	700-799	3		2	1
4	800 & over	2	1		1

*Includes Puerto Rico and District of Columbia.

Source: Adapted from *Comparison of State Unemployment Insurance Laws,* August 1972, Table 301.

ing some employment during 20 or more weeks (as 7 did), as well as requiring substantial earnings, are more likely than others to bar workers who have been jobless for a prolonged period.

More than 85 of every 100 claimants meet qualifying requirements, supporting the conventional view that only workers with the lowest earnings or irregular or part-time work are excluded. But this overlooks certain labor market realities – that new entrants or reentrants to the work force do not acquire benefit rights until as many as six to nine months or longer after they have entered covered employment; frequently, they will experience layoffs and unemployment (but without protection) as they try to break into the job market. And in the depression of 1970–72 hundreds of thousands of aircraft workers and others were jobless for six to nine months or longer; without further employment they were unable to requalify after exhausting their initial benefit entitlement.

Amount of benefits. The benefit for a week of unemployment varies with the worker's prior wages, between the minimum and maximum, under formulas weighted in favor of low earners in many states. The formulas in most cases aim to replace at least 50 percent of weekly wages, which most states compute as a fraction (approximating 1/26) of wages in the calendar quarter of highest wages, to reflect full-time work in a recent four-quarter reference base period; other states use a fraction of annual earnings or average weekly earnings (See Appendix).[8] The statutory maximum benefit, a ceiling on payments, lagged behind as wages rose; the $15 maximum payable under most of the original laws was as much as was then thought feasible. During the 1940s and thereafter, as wartime employment reduced the ranks of the unemployed, labor shortages developed, and prices rose. Wages tripled from a weekly average of $25 in 1939 to $74.50 in 1954 and then nearly doubled again to $141 in 1970. Although weekly benefits in the early years of 1938–40 averaged as much as 40–42 percent of average wages, they lagged behind as wages

8. Operational convenience, reflecting employer reporting and agency record keeping practices of the period influenced the initial choices among alternatives; later on, utilization of electronic record keeping equipment has not altered the states' preferred formulas. See also G. S. Roche, *Benefit Entitlement in Unemployment Insurance* (Kalamazoo: W. E. Upjohn Institute for Employment Research, forthcoming).

rose. By 1950 the average benefit-wage ratio had declined to 35 percent, where it has remained until the present with minor fluctuations (Table 11). In 1970, it was 36 percent.

The decline was due to the constraints of the statutory maximum, which lagged behind increasing earnings. Workers with higher wages get less than half (often a fourth to a third) of their former earnings. Although a few (11) states pay dependents' allowances to augment the benefits of family breadwinners, their impact has been a minor one because of payment ceilings and restrictive definitions of "eligible" dependents.

If weekly benefits are to restore at least half of prior weekly earnings for the great majority of claimants, the maximum ben-

Table 11.

Average Weekly Benefit as Percent of Average Weekly Wage in Covered Employmnt for Selected Years, and by State, 1970

United States	Average weekly wage (total wages)	Average weekly benefits Amount	Ratio to average weekly wage
Total: 1940	$ 27.00	$10.56	.39
1950	60.00	20.76	.34
1960	93.00	32.87	.35
1968	127.00	43.43	.34
1969	134.00	46.17	.34
1970	141.00	50.31	.36
Alabama	113.80	35.30	.31
Alaska	206.49	45.55	.22
Arizona	129.36	42.72	*.33
Arkansas	99.07	34.96	.35
California	147.43	51.87	.35
Colorado	126.22	51.05	.40
Connecticut	150.09	55.76	*.37
Delaware	142.20	45.79	.32
Dist. of Col.	138.82	50.02	*.36
Florida	122.57	33.76	.28
Georgia	116.54	33.76	.28
Hawaii	123.71	52.04	.42
Idaho	111.97	43.81	.39
Illinois	147.53	45.91	*.31
Indiana	138.12	37.67	*.27
Iowa	122.00	48.56	.40
Kansas	188.18	46.57	.39

Table 11. (continued)

Average Weekly Benefit as Percent of Average Weekly Wage in Covered Employment for Selected Years, and by State, 1970

United States	Average weekly wage (total wages)	Average weekly benefits	
		Amount	Ratio to average weekly wage
Kentucky	199.87	40.56	.34
Louisiana	126.34	42.49	.37
Maine	109.38	38.12	.35
Maryland	124.86	45.15	*.36
Massachusetts	128.24	47.81	*.37
Michigan	159.14	50.42	*.32
Minnesota	130.42	43.77	.34
Mississippi	102.44	32.51	.32
Missouri	131.23	32.51	.32
Montana	112.41	34.22	.30
Nebraska	114.95	39.38	.34
Nevada	137.99	44.24	*.32
New Hampshire	114.68	41.64	.36
New Jersey	153.34	54.88	.36
New Mexico	113.30	35.40	.31
New York	150.76	50.88	.34
North Carolina	106.49	30.00	.28
North Dakota	106.90	42.61	.40
Ohio	146.18	46.83	*.32
Oklahoma		32.20	.27
Oregon	128.90	41.42	32
Pennsylvania	131.03	46.20	.35
Rhode Island	118.24	46.52	*.31
South Carolina	105.86	36.24	.34
South Dakota	101.25	36.76	.36
Tennessee	113.02	35.56	.32
Texas	124.37	37.80	.30
Utah	112.93	40.71	.36
Vermont	120.25	45.19	.38
Virginia	113.96	34.64	.32
Washington	143.39	34.64	.24
West Virginia	130.73	31.65	.24
Wisconsin	134.90	51.04	.38
Wyoming	115.40	43.28	.39

*Includes dependents' allowances.

Source: Handbook of Unemployment Insurance Financial Data, 1938-1970.

efit must be nearer 65 percent than 50 percent and must keep pace with earnings; but this is not so in most states. At the end of 1971, for example, 27 states, accounting for one of every three workers, had maximums of 50 percent or more of the state average weekly wage (Table 12); for only three of these (Utah, Hawaii, and the District of Columbia) the maximum provided as much as 65 percent of the average wage, the goal set out in

Table 12.

Number and Percent of States and of Covered Employment by Maximum Weekly Benefit Amount (MWBA), December 1971, as a Percent of Average Weekly Wage (AWW)[1]

MWBA[2] as a percent of AAW in covered employment	States		Covered employment[3]	
	Number	Cumulative number	Percent	Cumulative percent
Under 35%	5	5	18.0	18.0
35–39	4	9	8.7	26.7
39–44	7	16	17.5	44.2
45–49	9	25	21.6	65.8
50–54	15	40	17.3	83.1
55–59	3	43	8.4	91.5
60 +	9	52	8.5	100.0

1. Based on average weekly wage in covered employment for 12 months ending June 30, 1971.
2. Excludes dependents' allowances.
3. Based on average monthly covered employment for 12 months ending June 30, 1971.

Source: U.S. Department of Labor, Manpower Administration, Unemployment Insurance Service.

President Nixon's unemployment insurance message to Congress in July 1969. By contrast, the maximum benefit in five states, accounting for nearly one fifth of all workers, was less than 35 percent of weekly wages (see also Appendix).

As one result of the restricted benefits produced by obsolete benefit maximums, more than one half of all 1971 claimants (and at least 6 of every 10 in 14 states) were paid a weekly benefit, which for them was not wage-related but a uniform amount – the maximum set by statute (see Table 13).[9] In effect, the states are paying the same benefit to those who earn at least the average weekly wage, and half the states pay the maximum benefit to workers earning less than average wages. Only lower-paid workers receive benefits varied in relation to their former earnings. If the margin between benefits and wages is to protect the work incentive, it is difficult to rationalize why a worker earning the 1970 average wage of $140 per week should have a greater margin between his benefit and his wages than if he earned $75 per week. Yet most states pay the latter worker approximately half of his wages, but the former nearer one third. Such an anomaly is inequitable. In addition the laws do not pay adequate benefits to the jobless worker and his family. A flexible maximum, adjusted annually or semiannually to the state's wage level, avoids the restrictive effects of a fixed benefit ceiling during periods of rising wages. Although 26 states by the end of 1971 had changed to such a formula with maximums of at least half the average wage, most of the others paid benefits of less than half wages to workers at the statewide average wage.[10]

Duration of benefits. The number of weeks of benefits payable to jobless workers has, over time, approached program objectives more closely, tiding the great majority of jobless workers over their spells of unemployment. In 1971, for example, when the average insured claimant was entitled to 24.5 weeks of benefits, he was without work and receiving benefits only three fifths as long; many others, however, were unemployed still longer. Maximum weeks payable had climbed from an average of 20 weeks in 1946 to 26 in 1971. Those claimants still jobless when their benefits rights ran out, however, accounted for 30 percent in years of high unemployment compared to 16–20 percent in good times.

Since World War II, even in good years, one in every five claimants was still out of work when his benefit rights ran out. The 1971–72 depression, however, found the system seriously

9. Arizona, Florida, Illinois, Indiana, Iowa, Louisiana, Michigan, Minnesota, Mississippi, Montana, Nebraska, North Dakota, Ohio, South Dakota, Wyoming, and Texas. In Ohio, Michigan, Indiana, and Illinois, 70 percent or more received the maximum basic benefit, excluding dependents allowances.

10. For a review of the 1971 amendments to state laws, see J. A. Hickey, "Report on State Unemployment Insurance Laws," *Monthly Labor Review,* Jan. 1972, pp. 22–30.

Table 13.

Percent of Newly Insured Claimants[1] Eligible for the Maximum Weekly Benefit Amount, 1971, by State

Total, 52 states	Percent eligible for MWBA, 1971[2]	Total, 52 states	Percent eligible for MWBA, 1971[2]
Alabama	49	Montana	69
Alaska	53	Nebraska	69
Arizona	65	Nevada	58
Arkansas	28	New Hampshire	19
California	47	New Jersey	55
Colorado	24	New Mexico	41
Connecticut	31	New York	41[3]
Delaware	57	North Carolina	15
Dist. of Columbia	44	North Dakota	62
Florida	50	Ohio	80
Georgia	54	Oklahoma	41
Guam	—	Oregon	54
Hawaii	36	Pennsylvania	57
Idaho	49	Puerto Rico	15
Illinois	72	Rhode Island	31
Indiana	80	South Carolina	32
Iowa	64	South Dakota	60
Kansas	56	Tennessee	39
Kentucky	53	Texas	67
Louisiana	62	Utah	41
Maine	37	Vermont	46
Maryland	48	Virginia	38
Massachusetts	40	Virgin Islands	—
Michigan	76	Washington	52
Minnesota	56	West Virginia	20
Mississippi	60	Wisconsin	43
Missouri	57	Wyoming	67

1. Claimants who established a benefit year.
2. In states where the MWBA changed during the year, percentages include claimants at both prior and current amounts.
3. Represents percent of beneficiaries receiving MWBA and is therefore not strictly comparable with other states.

Source: U.S. Department of Labor, Manpower Administration.

Table 14.

Claimants Who Exhausted Benefit Rights, as Percent of All Insured Claimants and Actual and Potential Duration for Beneficiaries, Selected States — (With Highest & Lowest Average Actual Duration of Benefits for Exhaustees), 1971

	Number	Exhaustions[1] as percent of first payments	Average potential duration	Average actual duration (weeks) All beneficiaries	Exhaustees[2]
Lowest actual duration (less than 20 weeks)					
Indiana	46,123	27.3	21.0	11.0	18.0
Idaho	5,675	26.3	20.1	11.0	16.7
Georgia	28,472	32.3	20.7	10.2	17.1
Iowa	18,348	34.0	21.7	12.8	17.9
Florida	41,541	38.5	19.8	12.4	17.3
Maine	16,050	33.9	20.8	12.7	17.8
Nebraska	7,490	30.2	22.6	13.3	19.2
Texas	56,496	36.6	22.4	13.8	19.7
Virginia	11,969	21.8	21.5	10.4	19.1
South Dakota	1,919	29.3	21.3	11.2	17.9
Highest actual duration (25 weeks or more)					
District of Columbia	5,763	31.5	30.6	17.9	28.5
Alaska	4,605	26.7	27.2	16.9	26.4
New Mexico	5,341	28.1	29.1	16.0	27.0
Pennsylvania	80,420	18.8	29.1	13.7	27.2
Hawaii	8,384	34.9	26.0	17.9	26.0
New York	206,403	27.2	26.0	15.8	26.0
Vermont	42,185	27.3	26.0	12.7	26.0
Maryland	24,372	24.7	26.0	12.7	26.0
Connecticut	70,807	30.8	25.8	16.3	25.7
Massachusetts	92,944	34.1	27.5	17.8	26.2
New Hampshire	2,795	10.0	26.0	11.1	25.8
Total U.S.	2,020,205	30.1	24.5	14.4	22.7

1. Claimants exhausting benefits in 1971 as percent of first payments, July 1, 1970–June 30, 1971.
2. A final week of compensable unemployment in claimant's benefit year results in exhaustion of benefit rights for that benefit year.
Source: Adapted from Special Tabulation, Manpower Administration, Unemployment Insurance Service.

inadequate for many more of the jobless. Even though average entitlement ranged from 20 to 31 weeks among the various states, the number who exhausted their benefit rights increased from one in every four in 1970 to one in every three in 1972. The highest exhaustion rates, as might be expected, were found in the states where workers had the least entitlement. Those exhausting their rights were out of work half again as long as the average, 22.7 versus 14.4 weeks.

During the 1960s a number of states did extend benefit duration beyond 26 weeks, especially for workers with steadier work histories. Additional benefit weeks were "triggered" whenever the rate of unemployment in the state rose above a specified level. The substantially increased unemployment in 1971–72 brought into force new state and federal programs for extending benefit protection in recession periods to long-term jobless who had exhausted their "normal" benefit rights. Although extended benefits under the 1970 federal legislation did not take effect nationwide until January 1972, such benefits were paid in late 1970 in the 5 states which had acted earlier, and in 22 states during 1971. Some $640 million had been paid to the long-term jobless under the state plans prior to 1972. Federal reimbursement required that the rate of unemployment in the state be as high as 4 percent for at least three months and at least 20 percent above its own average unemployment rate for the same period during the two preceeding years. Since many of the 22 states paid extended benefits under less restrictive conditions, they could not obtain federal reimbursement. As the recession continued into 1971, the strain on the state programs made the inadequacy of protection even more evident; while exhaustions rose to 2 million in 1971, payments had more than doubled since 1969 (from $2.1 to $5.0 billion).

Disqualification and Contested Claims

Since in principle the programs compensate involuntary unemployment, they withhold benefits where unemployment was not involuntary. Claims are contested, for example, when an employer asserts that the claimant refused work, or quit, or when the agency initiates a question as to entitlement. If the claimant had left work voluntarily or refused offered work without good cause, or was dismissed for misconduct, he is subject to disqualification, i.e., his payments are postponed or even reduced. Nor are benefits payable for unemployment due to a labor dispute.[11] Benefits are withheld when the claimant is receiving vacation pay or wages in lieu of notice because it is felt he has lost no earnings for that period. In fraud cases entitlement may be reduced or even canceled. Yet a quit could be nondisqualifying, for example, where the worker left to take a better job which he then lost. During the past 30 years disqualification periods have become longer, although they vary with the circumstances of each case. Periods of benefit suspension have been lengthened by requiring that the claimant have a minimum period of employment following the quit, for example, before benefits are reinstated. The practice works greater hardship, of course, when unemployment is severe, but the intent is to discourage quits when jobs are easier to get. Reducing the worker's benefit rights by the number of weeks of disqualification introduces a punitive element.

The Social Security Act requires state laws to provide for a hearing before an impartial tribunal for workers whose claims are denied. It also bars complete cancellation of benefit rights, except in cases such as fraud; however, cancellation of rights to all but one week of benefits, for example, is permitted.[12] Most states provide two stages of appeal, plus administrative reconsideration, when claimants protest the original decision.

How do contests affect the program's effectiveness in compensating for involuntary unemployment? It is difficult to assess their impact in meaningful quantitative teams, since a contest may be initiated by the agency staff or by a former employer, upon initial filing, in any week for which a continued claim is filed, and after the claim has been terminated as well. If a contest arises on the initial claim, benefits may be withheld pending determination, redetermination, or appeal; if arising later, benefits may or may not be suspended, depending upon

11. Two state laws pay benefits to workers for unemployment due to labor disputes, but only after the eighth week in New York and the seventh week in Rhode Island.

12. See Haber and Murray, *Unemployment Insurance,* especially chapters 8, 15. See also Roche, *Benefit Entitlement.*

circumstances. Delayed benefit payments, while contests are pending, weaken the program's effectiveness in providing funds to the jobless while unemployed. Although fewer claims are involved in formal "appeals" than in "contests," the former process is lengthier, and the case for continued payment can be more compelling.[13] When the claimant is back at work before the final decision has been issued, if no benefits had been paid while he was unemployed, the program's purpose has surely been vitiated.[14]

Supplemental Unemployment Benefits

Just as unions had demanded additional retirement protection from their employers beyond that provided by OASDI, heavy unemployment, low benefits, and inadequate duration in the mid-1950s led to dissatisfaction in security-conscious labor organizations. Neither federal exhortation of the states nor union lobbying had extracted improved benefits from the states. Turning from government to the employers in major industries, the workers obtained contractual protection in the steel, automobile, rubber, and a few other industries to supplement state benefits and to bring total wage-loss compensation up to two thirds of wages and to 52 weeks. By the close of the 1960s the plans protected about 2.5 million workers. Those so protected, with two or more years of service, typically, could receive between 60–80 percent of their earnings from public plus private benefits; for many, compensation rose to or more than 90 percent of take-home pay. These plans provide about 5 of every 100 industrial workers with more adequate unemployment protection, but the majority depend entirely upon the state programs.[15]

13. In 1970, only 47 percent of appeals to a referee were decided within 45 days; in 1969, nearly 250,000 claimants were involved in appealed benefit decisions (Department of Labor, *Unemployment Insurance Statistics*, Sept.–Oct. 1969, Table 16).

14. In *California Department of Human Resources Development v. Java*, USLW 4491 (26 April 1971), the U.S. Supreme Court upheld the right of a claimant, whose claim had been allowed originally, to continue to receive benefits while an employer's appeal to a referee is pending.

15. See Becker, *In Aid of the Unemployed*, especially chapter 6; also Joseph M. Becker, *Guaranteed Income for the Unemployed: The Story of SUB* (Baltimore: Johns Hopkins University Press, 1968).

Financing

Unlike the OASDHI program's employer-worker contributory systems, unemployment insurance is financed by federal-state taxes assessed upon employers; only three states collect
worker contributions, and these at lower rates than from employers. The first 35 years of the program have demonstrated
that under the original tax structure the program could finance
higher benefits for more weeks than originally estimated. But
benefit costs remained so low during World War II and thereafter that contribution rates were reduced, under experience
rating, to less than 1.5 percent of total payrolls between 1945
and 1960 (compared to 2.0 to 2.7 percent in 1939–1942). Benefits rose as high as 1.5 percent of total payrolls during only 5
years between 1940 and 1960, but fell below 1 percent during
12 of these years. Benefit reserves (the excess of contributions
over benefits, plus interest) climbed to 6 percent of payrolls by
1941 and even higher by 1954; thereafter, reserves declined
because of lower contributions, leveling off at or below 3.5
percent during the 1960s.

The program has been less costly, however, than commonly
understood, for the contribution rates apply to taxable payroll,
which in most states has meant the first $3,000 of workers'
wages per year; the taxable wage base, under federal law, remained at $3,000 from 1936 until the 1970 amendments raised it
to $4,200, effective January 1, 1972. Those states which in-
creased the taxable wage base on their own account were able to
raise the revenues desired with lower tax rates. As program
costs rise, the choices between a higher tax rate affecting all
employers and a higher taxable wage base especially affecting
high wage employers become more and more important.

The higher tax base has been regarded as more equitable in
unemployment insurance financing, as well as in OASDHI.
Since 1940 an increasing proportion of rising payrolls has been
untaxed, giving high average-wage firms an advantage in this
respect, over those whose workers earned $3,000 (now $4,200)
on the average. The percentage of all wages taxable has declined
steadily, from 93 percent in 1940 to 46 percent in 1970,[16] and

16. The percentage of wages that were taxable, in selected years, was as
follows:

the difference between taxable and "total" wages has increased; however, most public discussion refers to "taxable" wages, and thus influences public understanding of program costs. In 1971, for example, while the average contribution rate was 1.7 percent of employers' taxable wages, it was only half as much (0.8 percent) of total wages. Similarly, benefits were 2.2 percent of taxable but only 1.3 percent of total wages.[17] Despite recent increases, the record demonstrates the relatively low year-by-year cost of the programs compared to other employee benefits. These rates of taxes and benefits may blur the fact that a number of states' reserves had declined because of earlier tax reductions, just as benefits were going up. Total reserves declined from 3.5 percent to 2.5 percent of total payrolls between December 1968 and December 1971. In some states this placed benefit financing in an uneasy position.

State and federal costs for administering unemployment insurance are financed from the proceeds of the Federal Unemployment Tax Act.[18] Unlike administrative financing, the benefit reserve of each state is maintained separately in the U.S. Treasury. Consequently, the benefit reserves of a state, which are ample for its current or future benefit expenditures, are not accessible to assist a neighboring state whose reserves are depleted by a continuing benefit drain. A small pooled fund (Reed Fund) is available for loans (at interest) to states in danger of insolvency, and it has been used, although by few states, in years of severe unemployment such as 1958, 1961, and 1971–72.

1945	88 percent	1960	60 percent
1950	79 percent	1965	53 percent
1955	68 percent	1969	46 percent (estimate)

U.S., Congress, House, Ways and Means Committee, *Unemployment Insurance: Hearings*, 91st Cong., 1st sess., 1969, p. 163.

17. Department of Labor, *Unemployment Insurance Statistics*, March 1971, and March 1972, Table 6.

18. State agencies administering unemployment insurance programs are in a somewhat different position from other departments of state government as to their capacity to expand operations (and staff) when their work loads increase suddenly. The impact of an unanticipated rise in unemployment upon claim and benefit loads (resulting in greater administrative costs) in only a few states can be met, usually, by U.S. Department of Labor allocations drawn from a national fund. Other state departments may have to request a supplemental appropriation through the governor. When several agencies found themselves in a similar position, as in 1970–72, supplemental funds were requested from Congress.

Declining reserves have hampered states in meeting the needs of their jobless. Proposals to improve benefits and expand coverage are resisted, not only in states facing depleted reserves, but in adjacent states equally reluctant to raise taxes despite a better financial situation.

Experience Rating

The impact of experience rating on the program has affected areas other than adjustment of employers' contribution rates. Tax rates have been modified, in theory, on the basis of employers' success in leveling out peaks and valleys in employment and in reducing turnover; in fact, the key factor is the amount of benefits (as related to past contributions and payrolls) paid to former employees. Thus employers have as direct an incentive to oppose more generous benefit provisions and to contest benefit awards as to try to control labor turnover. The latter alternative appears to have been regarded as too onerous, while the former is more in keeping with a basic aversion to "paying" people for "not working." Moreover, experience rating has tended to negate an original program objective, removal of the threat of interstate competitive disadvantages in levying unemployment insurance taxes. However, interstate tax competition remains.[19] Improved benefits and tax increases in the states are opposed as placing employers at a competitive disadvantage.[20] While such concerns may lead employers to resist benefit improvements, however, the threat of higher taxes may not produce an incentive effective enough to reduce layoffs or achieve employment stabilization. Could Boeing have avoided tens of thousands of layoffs following suspension of the SST contract in

19. For discussion of interstate competition, see C. Spivey, *Experience Rating in Unemployment Compensation,* Bureau of Economic and Business Research, Bulletin 84 (Urbana: University of Illinois, 1958); R. A. Lester, *Economics of Unemployment Compensation* (Princeton: Industrial Relations Section, 1962), especially chapter 6, "Interstate Competition in Unemployment Compensation"; Haber and Murray, *Unemployment Insurance,* chapter 17; and J. A. Becker, *Experience Rating in Unemployment Insurance* (Baltimore: John Hopkins University Press, 1972).

20. The validity of this argument was questioned in respect to workmen's compensation by John F. Burton, Jr., *Interstate Variations in Employers' Costs of Workmen's Compensation* (Kalamazoo: W. E. Upjohn Institute for Employment Research, 1966).

1971, or U.S. Steel the layoffs following the 1971 General Motors strike, under the incentive of experience rating? Differentials in unemployment insurance tax rates seem to have less influence on employer behavior than the rhetoric of legislative debates would suggest. The impact of employer decisions as to turnover are less influential in both micro and macro terms than governmental measures to provide economic supports and to increase employment and spending, and monetary and credit policy.[21] In this broader perceptive one asks whether unemployment insurance program policy, including financing, should not be guided more directly by national rather than individual state concerns. Such a position was taken in a recent Canadian policy statement: "Provincial . . . governments cannot by themselves bring under control the forces that cause unemployment; to do so requires the full panoply of economic powers . . . fiscal, monetary, debt management, trade, and balance of payments policies. . . . The viability of unemployment insurance . . . depends upon the successful use by the federal government of these instruments of economic policy: if they fall under federal jurisdiction, so should unemployment insurance.[22]

Other Federal Unemployment Insurance Legislation, 1940–72

Federal legislation on unemployment insurance historically has been concerned with extending coverage from the narrow original base to assure federal benefit protection to groups with a special claim on the nation, such as war veterans and federal employees, to making loans or advances available to states whose benefit reserves were near exhaustion, and in recession periods, to providing more protection to workers whose benefit rights did not tide them over their unemployment. Numerous proposals for substantial changes as to the division of federal and state responsibilities, such as federal benefit or fund solvency standards, have failed to overcome state resistance to change, as for example in the taxable wage base.

21. See Herbert Stein, "Unemployment, Inflation and Economic Stability," in *Agenda for the Nation,* ed. Kermit Gordon (Washington: Brookings Institution, 1968), especially pp. 288–292; R. Munts, "Today's Economy," pp. 18–19.

22. Government of Canada, *Income Security and Social Services* (Ottawa: Queen's Printer for Canada, 1969), p. 80.

War veterans. World War II veterans, in 1944, were granted Servicemen's Readjustment Allowances under the comprehensive GI Bill of Rights. Many of the 15 million veterans had no state benefit rights, having entered military service directly from school. Some 9 million claimed benefits ($20 per week for up to 52 weeks) for an average of 19 weeks, but only slightly more than 10 percent did so for the 52-week maximum. Following the Korean conflict, a similar program paid $26 per week, but for a shorter period — 26 weeks. Veterans were absorbed more rapidly into the work force — only 900,000 of the 4 million veterans filed claims and 650,000 received benefits for an average of 13.6 weeks.[23] It took until 1958 to set up a permanent program whereby all servicemen with at least 90 days service could obtain benefit protection: their service was treated as though covered under the state programs, and benefits were paid through the states but reimbursed by the federal government. Vietnam veterans are protected on the same basis; in 1972 veterans' organizations discussed a new national scale of benefits to give better protection to Vietnam veterans suffering severe unemployment.

Federal civilian employees. Although the civil service is often thought of as assuring absolute security of tenure, successive expansions and contractions of the federal establishment displaces workers as functions change and budgetary reductions occur. Evidence that many workers displaced in 1953–54 remained jobless for months persuaded the 1954 Congress to bring civil servants under the unemployment insurance umbrella. This group now claims benefits under the law of the state where last employed, with federal financing of benefits based upon federal service.[24]

Extended benefits. The 1958 and 1961 recessions called forth temporary federal programs to protect claimants who were still jobless when their state UI benefits ran out. As many as 2.6 million claimants in 1958 (one third of all beneficiaries) exhausted their benefit rights but were still out of work. After some

23. Similar temporary arrangements were made (1946) for the nearly 170,000 merchant seamen in federally operated (or charter) wartime service during World War II and during the Korean conflict.

24. Title XV of the Social Security Act protects federal civilian employees and, since 1958, exservicemen as well.

recovery in 1958–60, the number exhausting benefits again rose to 2.5 million in 1961, accounting for three of every ten beneficiaries. Between 1957 and 1961, exhaustees were entitled to an average of five months of benefits; the system would indeed have to provide more substantial protection to tide experienced workers over long-term unemployment during recessions, especially for those displaced by automation, occupational obsolescence, or employers' age limits.

Congress, after much discussion, provided two ad hoc benefit extensions for the long-term jobless. First, the 1958 Temporary Unemployment Compensation Act made federal advances to the states (June 1958–July 1959) which agreed to extend benefit duration by 50 percent, but only one in three states did so, leaving unprotected nearly one third of the exhaustees.[25] In 1961 federal action under a new TEUC Act went further, requiring extended benefits in every state. Despite these two ad hoc extensions, federal responsibility for extended benefits on a standby basis came slowly.

In 1969 President Nixon submitted proposed unemployment insurance amendments, enacted in 1970, including extended duration of benefits for persons exhausting their state benefits. The first of the plan's two parts provided federal funds to match state-extended benefits in all states whenever the national rate of insured unemployment rose above 4.5 percent for three consecutive months. States were required to adopt conforming laws by January 1972. Under the second part, matching (50–50) federal funds were made available to states voluntarily extending benefits; rising unemployment in any state would trigger payment of extended benefits provided the unemployment rate went above 4 percent and was at least 20 percent higher than the average unemployment rate in the state during the preceeding two years. The 20 percent requirement was removed in October 1972, when much continuing high unemployment was not being compensated; the same amendment extended the program until June 30, 1973. Since the new program permits workers to receive extended benefits for half as many weeks as their regular state entitlement (up to a total of 39 weeks), those

25. Five other states on their own account extended duration of benefits. Philip Booth, "The Temporary Extended Unemployment Compensation Act of 1961: A Legislative History," *Labor Law Journal,* Oct. 1961, pp. 910–911.

entitled to 20 weeks of regular state benefits, for example, could get 30 weeks in all.

Continued heavy unemployment in 1971–72 led to several extensions of the program.[26] The Emergency Unemployment Compensation Act of 1971 allowed up to 13 additional benefit weeks (from January 30 to September 30, 1972) to claimants who exhausted both their regular and extended benefits. The extension applied only where a state's unemployment rate reached 6.5 percent or more for 3 months. In the face of an impending cutoff while high unemployment prevailed, the emergency extension was renewed in June 1972 permitting continued operations until March 31, 1973.

The weakness of the extended benefit program was due to several causes. First, federal reimbursement was limited to 13 weeks per worker no matter how long he or she remained out of work. Second, the federal "trigger" mechanism did not help states where despite great numbers of jobless beneficiaries, the unemployment rate did not remain 20 percent above the two prior years. Third, the unemployment rate used as the federal measuring tool was the "insured" (compensated) unemployment figure, which dips substantially below "total" unemployment as workers' benefit rights expire.

Other Benefits to the Unemployed

Closely related to unemployment insurance are other public programs for maintaining the flow of income to displaced workers. They are not readily classified under a simple heading since they differ in content, level, and duration. The three mentioned here are financed from federal funds, and allowances are paid through the state employment security agencies.

Allowances authorized by the Trade Expansion Act of 1962 and the Automotive Products Trade Act of 1965* help workers displaced as a result of increased imports due to trade concessions.[27] They equal 65 percent of the displaced worker's

26. For a description of these legislative changes, see SSA-ORS, Research and Statistics Notes nos. 3 (25 Feb. 1972), 7 (31 March 1972), 12 (24 Aug. 1972), and 24 (12 Dec. 1972). Also "Extension of Emergency Unemployment Compensation Act," *Social Security Bulletin,* Sept. 1972, p. 20.

27. M. G. Murray, *Income for the Unemployed* (Kalamazoo: W. E. Upjohn Institute for Employment Research, 1971), pp. 19–20.

*Now expired.

average wages (up to a maximum of 65 percent of average
wages in manufacturing) and are payable for up to 52 weeks
with 13 additional weeks for workers age 60 or older, plus up to
26 additional weeks for those whose retraining courses last
longer than one year. The maximum benefit in 1971 was $87 per
week. Until 1969 the U.S. Tariff Commission had found no
cases where the petitioning workers' unemployment was due to
trade concessions; by 1970–71 it had certified barely a dozen or
so.[28]

The Disaster Relief Act of 1969 provided unemployment
assistance payments to individuals unemployed because of major disasters; workers covered by unemployment insurance can
file for benefits under this program after exhausting their entitlement. Self-employed individuals, although not under unemployment insurance, are also protected.

Weekly training allowances have been payable since 1962 to
persons in training courses approved under the Manpower Development and Training Act of 1962. The allowances are linked
to unemployment insurance in several ways: unemployment
benefits cannot be denied to claimants enrolled in approved
training courses, but duplication of benefits and allowances is
not permitted.[29] The worker may claim the allowances, even if
eligible for unemployment insurance; if being paid the latter, the
paying state is reimbursed by MDTA. This removes the burden
of income support from state unemployment insurance to the
federal program.

Of the three programs, only payments under the Trade Adjustment Act are substantially higher than unemployment insurance benefits payable in most states. MDTA allowances, like
TRA payments, constitute federally financed unemployment
payments which otherwise would be compensated for the most
part (but not necessarily in the same amounts nor for the same
number of weeks) under a state program. A question of policy is

28. Industrial Union Department, AFL-CIO, *The Developing Crisis in International Trade* (Washington: AFL-CIO, 1970), pp. 118–130. See also *Comparison of State Unemployment Insurance Laws*, section 800–820.05.

29. The amount of the allowance is the state's average unemployment insurance benefit or the worker's own benefit amount, if higher. Subsistence and
transportation allowances are also payable. Murray, *Income for the Unemployed*, pp. 32–36.

raised by the more generous TRA payments, although payable to a small number of workers, in that the "program does set a possible precedent that might be broadly applied . . . [to] income support outside unemployment insurance for all unemployment that results from overt govermental action. . . . Whether it is wise to single out such workers for special treatment is debatable."[30] Murray refers to possible effects upon unemployment insurance including raising state benefits to comparable higher levels or, by contrast, lessening union support for overall state improvements where union members receive special treatment.

Unemployment Insurance for Railroad Workers

A separate national unemployment insurance program for railroad workers, administered by the Railroad Retirement Board, was adopted shortly after the railroad retirement system became operative. It has provided a nationally uniform scale of benefits more generous than the state UI programs. While large reserves accumulated under the original contribution rate of 3 percent and low wartime unemployment, a higher 1958 benefit schedule and reduced contribution rates soon worsened the financial picture. As railroad employment declined in the mid-1950s benefit claims increased, reserves fell, and despite increased tax rates (to 3.75 and 4.0 percent in 1959 and 1963 respectively) the reserves were exhausted. Continued heavy benefit expenditures led to borrowing from the retirement fund until employment stabilized at lower levels in the mid 1960s.

Summing Up

Although it is an accepted element of the American social security system recognized for its contribution to worker security, unemployment insurance operates in a milieu of sharp public controversy, far more so than OASDI, although less so than public assistance. Perceived by many as constructive in safeguarding the public interest in workers' occupational and earnings status, and in replacing wages lost due to involuntary unemployment, it is questioned by others since it does "pay benefits

---

30. Ibid., p. 20. Murray suggests that it would be preferable to obtain more adequate protection for all workers through unemployment insurance.

to people for not working." In doing so it conflicts with the popular aversion to public payments to able-bodied men and women who are not indigent. Those who hold such views resist broadening the system: "After 35 years, the principle of unemployment insurance is universally accepted while its application is widely disparaged.... The worker who has a job ... feels that if he's working and everyone around him is, then surely the ... beneficiary is capable of finding a job if he really wants one."[31]

However, in paying $6 billion to more than 5.8 billion claimants in fiscal year 1972, the program gained recognition among a broad sector of the work force receiving benefits for the first time, notably the technical, professional, and managerial staffs of the electronic, aircraft, and space industries. Their work history had been spent in expanding industries; they had known little unemployment, but many now were without jobs for longer than their benefit rights lasted. Conceivably, this development might produce a new source of support for strengthening the program against long-term unemployment.

In comparison with OASDHI benefits, more than half of which go to the poor, the poor receive about one of every four dollars in unemployment and workmen's compensation benefits; "they raised out of poverty about half of the poor people who received such benefits."[32] The major contribution of unemployment insurance, especially vital in such depression years as 1971–72, is helping to protect those jobless for three to six months or longer from slipping into poverty and dependency.

As a sidelight on the program's changing reputation, public attention was drawn to the "problem of abuse" of unemployment insurance in the 1950s and early 1960s by people "preferring benefits to jobs;" this attention has been more or less displaced by sharper criticism of public assistance and especially recipients of AFDC. The earlier attacks were directed at "students, pregnant women ... seasonal workers and/or vacation-

---

31. Quoted from a letter from a state unemployment insurance administrator to L. P. Adams in *Public Attitudes toward Unemployment Research* (Kalamazoo: W. E. Upjohn Institute for Employment Research, 1971), pp. 53–54; see also M. S. Gordon and R. W. Amerson, *Unemployment Insurance* (Berkeley: University of California Institute of Industrial Relations, 1957), p. 74.
32. Rohrlich, "Social Policy and Income Distribution," pp. 1391–92.

ers who had abused the system."[33] Criticism of public assistance recipients and of the system itself, especially after 1966, laid the groundwork for reform proposals, including President Nixon's Family Assistance Plan.

Another basic question concerns the tax-credit device that underlies federal-state financing. When the law permits employers' contributions under state law to be credited against their federal tax liability, responsibility for assuring protection against unemployment devolves upon the state, for its law and program are certified as meeting federal requirements. We have seen how state laws and practices exclude millions of workers from protection, that benefits replace less than half of jobless workers' wages and do not last long enough to tide a great many over their unemployment. Is tax credit properly extended to programs which fall so short of the objectives for which the federal tax was levied? Shall we now reexamine the basis for 35 years of approval of state programs that do not provide adequate protection? Or, as proposed by President Johnson in 1965, should a nationwide floor assure at least minimum adequacy of coverage, benefits, and financing in all states?[34]

OTHER DISABILITY INSURANCE

Workmen's compensation and temporary disability (cash sickness) insurance are two of several social insurance measures for compensating workers for wage loss due to disability. In this country, disability and the disabled, either as social problems or as the focus of remedial programs, are viewed and dealt with under a complex and fragmented set of measures. Workmen's compensation is concerned only with work-connected injury or

33. See D. Macarov, *Incentives to Work* (San Francisco: Jossey-Bass, Inc., 1970); also Haber and Murray, *Unemployment Insurance,* pp. 137–139; J. M. Becker, *The Problem of Abuse in Unemployment Benefits* (New York: Columbia University Press, 1953); K. O. Gilmore, "The Scandal of Unemployment Compensation," *Reader's Digest,* April 1960, pp. 37–43; and a rejoinder in Haber and Cohen, *Social Security,* pp. 309–322. See also L. P. Adams, *Unemployment Insurance,* chapter 6.

34. M. G. Murray, *Proposed Federal Unemployment Insurance Amendments* (Kalamazoo: W. E. Upjohn Institute for Employment Research, 1966); U.S., Congress, *Unemployment Compensation: Hearings on H.R. 8282,* Parts 1–5.

disease; the state laws authorize commercial insurance carriers to underwrite the risk of work injury and permit employers to self-insure the risk, and to pay any benefits due. In seven states, however, employers must insure with the state's "exclusive" fund. The laws provide for money payments plus medical and rehabilitation services, the latter regarded as no less essential than the cash benefits. When a work injury occurs, the carriers, employers, and responsible governmental agencies need be concerned to assure that the injury *is,* in fact, work-connected and that *it* caused the worker's disablement (or death).

By contrast, temporary disability insurance is designed to compensate only nonwork-connected disability. In practice, however, it does provide workers with wage-loss compensation whether or not the disability is work-connected, while any issue of possible work connection is pending. For long-duration and total disabilities (again, overlapping with workmen's compensation), disability insurance under social security provides compensation but, like temporary disability insurance, no medical or rehabilitation services. Other public disability programs include those of the Veterans Administration, the Railroad Retirement system, the Longshoremen's and Harbor Workers Compensation Act, the Federal Employees Compensation Act, and public assistance (for needy adults with total-permanent disability).[35] Beyond all this, of course, are the private group insurance and self-insurance compensation plans and millions of individual health insurance poliies.

Social change of many kinds has added to the risk of disability away from places of work. Increased use of power machinery in and around the home, as well as chemicals and fuels, combines with the massive rise in traffic injuries and fatalities on the street and highway to increase the need for nonwork-connected wage loss protection and health care services. Increasingly, too, we find it difficult to assign or deny a definite work-connected causation to disabilities that are progressive and slow in manifesting themselves, for example vascular and muscular conditions and diseases of the sense organs. But no nationwide social insurance measures other than Medicare meet the contingency

35. In addition, railroad workers and seamen utilize the Federal Employees' Compensation Act. See A. M. Skolnik and D. N. Price, "Another Look at Workmen's Compensation," *Social Security Bulletin,* Oct. 1970, pp. 5–25.

of short-term disabling injury or illness when not work-connected (except for some 14 million workers in seven jurisdictions covered by temporary disability insurance), or for loss of
work due to childbirth or for disablement of homemakers. In
short, the nonprotected area is greater than the covered area.

The fact is that we do not know how many persons are or
have become disabled, from what causes, for how long, nor what
number receive compensation or other services under any gov-
ernmental/private auspices and with what outcome. In workmen's compensation, for example, some states cannot say how
many workers have received benefits, nor do they publish current data on payments in cash and in kind. These deficiencies
were underscored in the 1972 report of the National Commission on State Workmen's Compensation Laws:

> For many of the most important questions in workmen's
> compensation, data comparable among the states are not
> available. For instance, state agencies have no consistent
> data on the number of employees covered; . . . most states
> do not have data on the promptness of payment to injured
> workers. Almost no state has information on the number of
> workers receiving the maximum benefit. . . . The particular
> lack of comparable data hinders objective analysis of
> state . . . programs.[36]

As a result it is difficult to determine the extent to which the
programs, in fact, reach the disabilities from which workers
suffer. We must gather and analyze information from many
sources in order to present reasonably comparable and meaningful data as a basis for policy and program decisions.[37] Workmen's compensation and temporary disability insurance are
difficult to compare; their concern with wage-loss compensation
for workers' disability constitutes almost their only point of
similarity. Yet when we do compare cash sickness plans, both
private and public, with workmen's compensation as to the

36. *Report of the National Commission on State Workmen's Compensation
Laws* (Washington: Government Printing Office, 1972), p. 112. The Commission
was authorized by the Occupational Health and Safety Act of 1969 (PL 91-596).
37. See M. Berkowitz and W. C. Johnson, "Towards an Economics of
Disability: The Magnitude and Structure of Transfer and Medical Costs," *Journal of Human Resources,* V, no. 3: 271–279.

portion of the premium dollar spent on benefits, versus overhead and litigation, workmen's compensation comes off second best. This is especially so for litigation, a source of great expense, waste, and delayed payment, which adds a bitter taste to the adversary relationship. The considerations, among others, argue for combining the two approaches in a single system for compensating short-term disability.[38]

WORKMEN'S COMPENSATION

In the face of 60 years of workmen's compensation experience in the United States, one ought to be justified in the expectation that the various state and federal programs, in operation and effectiveness, would permit ready generalization and evaluation. Unfortunately, perusal of standard publications in the field finds classification of goals, objectives, defined risks, and benefit schedules approached with caution, and generalizations qualified by reservations.[39]

The fragmentation of protection is such that an identical injury to a railroad worker, merchant seaman, government clerk, and longshoreman would be compensated under four different legal systems involving different concepts and legal issues of liability, as well as varying amounts of benefit. Farmhands and factory workers suffering the same injury must turn to different remedies in most states.[40]

Compensation for work injury, our earliest form of social insurance, provides cash, medical, and rehabilitative benefits to workers injured on the job and income to the survivors of the family breadwinner if injured fatally. Occupational diseases, increasingly recognized as work injury, have been brought within its scope, but benefit protection is less complete because of the

38. Merton C. Bernstein, "Rehabilitating Workmen's Compensation," in *Social Security: Policy for the Seventies, Proceedings of the Seventh Social Security Conference*, ed. Philip Booth (Ann Arbor: Institute of Labor and Industrial Relations, 1973).

39. For example, H. R. Somers and A. R. Somers, *Workmen's Compensation* (New York: John Wiley & Sons, 1954); E. F. Cheit and M. S. Gordon, eds., *Occupational Disability and Public Policy* (New York: John Wiley & Sons, 1963); E. F. Cheit, *Injury and Recovery in the Course of Employment* (New York: John Wiley & Sons, 1961); Burton, *Costs of Workmen's Compensation*.

40. Cheit, *Injury and Recovery*, pp. 2–3.

difficulty of establishing in given cases that a worker's ailment is a work-connected disability.

While our first workmen's compensation law (1908) was a federal law protecting federal workers, state laws appeared in the next decade. By 1930 nearly all states and territories had programs, but the last state did not act until 1948. In replacing court action against the injured worker's employer as a remedy for injury, lost wages, and reduced earning power, workmen's compensation promised more expeditious action. It replaced an adversary court proceeding with a state agency responsible for assuring that the worker received adequate medical care and rehabilitation services, as well as compensation for lost wages.

These expectations were realized only in part. By midcentury deficiencies in state programs were recognized. According to one critical analysis, "every recent evaluation . . . has emphasized the gaps and weaknesses in the protective and restorative standards of the laws and has viewed with increasing impatience the rate at which they moved toward their objectives."[41] One father of the workmen's compensation movement pointed out in 1957 that its benefits were replacing only one third of wages, that it "works least well for the workers who suffer the most serious injuries," and that "unless we improve workmen's compensation, we still have . . . a very strong demand for fundamental changes," including federalization.[42]

Of the $3.47 billion paid in benefits in 1971, one of every three dollars ($2.3 billion) compensated for wage losses, the remaining $1.15 billion covering medical, hospital, rehabilitation, and related services. Benefit costs, however, account for as little as two of every three dollars of employers' premium payments, the remaining one third paying for administrative, sales, and other overhead expenses.[43] This is about eight times the proportion of total expenditures utilized for administration of disability insurance under social security. But the proportion of the premium dollar accounted for by benefits varied according to

41. Ibid., p. 319.
42. Witte, *Social Security Perspectives,* pp. 383–384.
43. A. M. Skolnik, "Workmen's Compensation Payments and Costs, 1971," SSA-ORS Research and Statistics Note no. 25 (Dec. 1972). Administrative costs of disability insurance under social security were less than 4 percent of contributions in F. Y. 1970. *Social Security Bulletin,* Sept. 1971, Table M-6, p. 31.

type of plan; 61 percent of all 1971 premium income went into cash and medical benefits, the corresponding figures for private carriers and state funds were 54 and 71 percent, respectively.[44] It should be noted that 1971 benefits increased by 20 percent over 1970, double the rate of increase between 1969 and 1970; the sharper increase was due to the substantially greater amount of payments under the federal "black lung" program, discussed below. Commercial carriers accounted for nearly three of every five dollars (58 percent) of 1971 benefit expenditures compared to nearly three in every ten dollars (29 percent) for state funds. Self-insurance accounted for 13 percent.

In litigated cases a "substantial proportion" of the award is paid to the injured worker's legal counsel, according to a report of the National Commission on State Workmen's Compensation Laws, and more than 25 percent in 5 of the 25 states which could provide information on this topic.[45] In no other social insurance program does so small a proportion of the premium costs reach the beneficiary.

Coverage

Initially, most states left employers free to elect to insure their workers against the risk of work injury, and, despite the trend toward compulsory coverage, 23 of the state laws still permitted elective coverage as late as 1970. Half the states cover all firms regardless of size. The 23 laws that cover only the larger establishments exclude a great many workers, because 14 of them exclude firms with 4 to 15 workers.[46] Domestic service, state and local government, and nonprofit organizations are commonly excluded, and only one in three states protect agricultural workers on the same basis as others.[47] By 1970 the system covered some 59 million (about 85 percent) of all wage and salary workers and $433 billion in wages and salaries. The

44. A. M. Skolnik, "Workmen's Compensation Payments and Cost, 1971," *Social Security Bulletin,* Jan. 1973, pp. 32–33.
45. *Report of the National Commission on State Workmen's Compensation Laws,* p. 107.
46. U.S. Department of Labor, Wage and Labor Standards Administration, *State Workmen's Compensation Laws,* 1969 rev., pp. 14–15.
47. Ibid. *Report of the National Commission on State Workmen's Compensation Laws,* Table 2.5, p. 46.

degree of extensiveness of coverage varied greatly: one third of the states (with one fifth of all potential coverage) covered fewer than 7 of every 10 potentially covered workers; at the other extreme, 11 states (with 55 percent of the potential coverage) protected 85 percent of their work force. Recent increases in coverage are due to labor force growth, the shift from elective to compulsory laws, and extension to some governmental, farm, and service workers.

Illustrating other obstacles to comprehensive protection, some 11 states have retained language limiting application to specified "hazardous" employments.[48] By midcentury all but one state had made some provision for occupational diseases, compared to 26 in 1940. On the other hand, it took until 1969 for all coal miners to obtain protection against one of the industry's most crippling diseases—"black lung" (pneumoconiosis)—but this was secured through the federal Mine Health and Safety Act of 1969, intended to cover miners in states whose laws excluded this disease. Since the program provides higher benefits than are paid under state laws to miners and widows, it is operative in all states where coal miners, their dependents, or survivors may be residing.[49] One may ask why it took so long for pneumoconiosis to be covered, although long recognized as a serious hazard in other countries. Coal mining is a major industry in a dozen states, each autonomous as to compensation legislation; coverage of this risk would have increased operators' costs. In addition, substantial medico-legal differences of opinion do exist as to causation of disability from this and related diseases manifesting themselves gradually over a period of years. Thus it may not be surprising that only three states specifically covered pneumoconiosis by mid-1966, and only four more by 1969, when the federal legislation was adopted. Although the temporary federal assumption of state

48. In excluding agriculture, however, as eight of these do, they exclude one of the most hazardous of all industries; in 1963, for example, California farm workers had the third highest rate of work injuries (next to mining and construction)—89 per 1,000 workers—and twice the average for all industries. G. P. Kleinman, *Occupational Health of Agricultural Workers in California* (Berkeley: Department of Public Health, 1965), p. 3.
49. SSA-ORS, "Black Lung Benefits Program: 2 Years of Experience," Research and Statistics Note no. 21 (7 Dec. 1972). See *Statistical Supplement, 1970,* Table 135: also Research and Statistics Notes no. 19 (6 Nov. 1970) and no. 8 (20 April 1972).

responsibility (as it was regarded) for "black lung" disablement was hedged about by constraints, many were removed and the program expanded broadly by the Black Lung Benefit Act of 1972; it also increased benefit levels, and established certain presumptions in the claimant's favor. Applicants whose claims had been previously denied were "promptly advised" that their cases would be reviewed under the new rules. Benefits, now related to federal salary levels, have been raised to an average of $189 in December 1971.[50] The scanty coverage of black lung beneficiaries by state programs is demonstrated in the fact that only 2.3 percent of miners' and widows' benefits in December 1971 were reduced because of receipt of other benefits.

A similar history relates to the hazard of radiation disease for workers in uranium mining and processing of enriched radioactive materials. Inadequate safety standards and safeguards devised by industrial medical experts coexist with hazards understated by the Atomic Energy Commission, as well as by its contractors. Industry and technology, in creating hazards, had moved beyond medicine and labor law administration in prevention, treatment, and compensation. While all states now cover radiation disability, this in itself does not ensure that workers are protected. As a recent U.S. Department of Labor compilation puts it, coverage is adequate in only about a half dozen states.[51]

Benefits

As in unemployment insurance, benefits under workmen's compensation vary from state to state, and the statutory weekly maximum plays a key role in limiting the percentage of a worker's prior earnings replaced by his benefits. In 1940 the maximum benefit was at least two thirds of the statewide average wage in all states; by 1967, however, the maximums had fallen so far behind as to be less than half of weekly wages under more than half of the laws. Taking account of 1971 amend-

50. SSA-ORS, "Black Lung Benefits Program," p. 4; see also *Wall Street Journal*, 24 Sept. 1971, p. 1 and 21 June 1972.
51. See Leo Goodman, "Radiation Hazard in Modern Industry" (John Fogarty Memorial Lecture under the auspices of APHA-Medical Care Section and D.C. Public Health Association, Washington, D.C., April 26, 1967): U.S. Department of Labor, Bureau of Labor Standards, *Summary of State Workmen's Compensation Laws*, Labor Law Series no. 10 (Jan. 1970), p. 3.

ments, only ten laws provide a maximum, including dependents' benefits, equal to two thirds or more of the statewide average wage.[52] Setting a new approach in 1969, Connecticut's maximum benefit is adjusted annually to wages; 13 other states have followed suit.[53] Benefit improvement reflected dependents' allowances, unlimited benefits in death and permanent disability cases, waiting periods, and removal of dollar limits on medical care.

We find a similar interstate disparity in the period for which benefits are payable; much complexity and differentation has developed in the ceilings on dollar amounts or weeks of duration. Disabilities can be temporary or permanent, partial or total, or fatal. And the complex benefit patterns bear little consistent relationship to wage loss, impaired working capacity or ability to participate in and contribute to community or family. A basic weakness in compensating total-permanent disability is noted in the observation that while the *injury and resulting disability may be permanent, the benefits are temporary* in half the states, despite utilization and results of medical and rehabilitative care. The federal-state system of vocational rehabilitation, though not aimed primarily at work related disability, is a major source of services for the work-injured.

Adequacy of benefits. A variety of criteria might be used to evaluate adequacy of benefits. While the statutory maximums establish a ceiling for individual workers' payments, the formula, in principle, provides for a weekly amount of two thirds of the worker's weekly wage; this fraction has been recommended by the so-called Model Act published by the Council of State Governments. The laws of the states approximated this standard in 1972, when 32 contained the two thirds fraction, 6 others used 65 percent, and none fell below 60 percent. However, the Commission found that computing the benefit as a percentage of "spendable earnings" took better account of dependents' allowances, the impact of income taxes, and the increasing importance of wage supplements. It recommended that a new formula approach be adopted, 80 percent of "spendable earnings" (a well-understood Department of Labor concept). If accepted by

52. Department of Social Security, AFL-CIO, *Security in Time of Need,* Publication 145 (Washington, 1969), p. 15; *Report of the National Commission on State Workmen's Compensation Laws,* Table 3.6.

53. F.C. Johnson, "Changes in Workmen's Compensation in 1971," *Monthly Labor Review,* Jan. 1972, p. 51.

the states, it would produce a slightly higher benefit than the two-thirds formula for workers with dependents.[54]

If the state benefits are so low compared to wages, how do they compare to the poverty line, a more modest criterion but surely one which every state could be expected to meet, especially since the law is aimed at employed workers in industry and commerce, not the poor. It may appear surprising, therefore, that for 38 jurisdictions in 1968, the maximum payment to the head of a four-person family for permanent-total disability fell below the 1968 ($68.37) poverty line (Table 15, col. 2). As the Berkowitz and Burton data indicate, even in 11 of the 20 highest wage states, the maximum benefit was no more than the income which a four-person family required to avoid poverty (col. 4)[55] — so low a benefit was especially inadequate because the disabled family breadwinner's return to work was uncertain.

Administration. Administration of these vitally important programs has been lodged in different agencies. In 20 states a single agency administers all labor legislation, while in 26 others the workmen's compensation function is handled by a separate agency, and in 5 is "administered" by the courts. These arrangements suggest key differences in the stance of various states as to their responsibility for injured workers. For example, some may give priority to the worker's interests by initiating remedial action, pending determination of the liability of employers and carriers. Others, by contrast, assume a more "judicial" stance, take less initiative, and appear to mediate the interests of the several parties: injured worker, employer, and insurance carrier.[56]

54. *Report of the National Commission on State Workmen's Compensation Laws*, pp. 56–60.

55. M. Berkowitz and J. F. Burton, Jr., "The Income Maintenance Objective in Workmen's Compensation," *Industrial and Labor Relations Review*. Oct. 1970.

56. The incidence of work accidents and injuries remains uncertain because of varying reporting practices, left largely to voluntary action by employers, which results in underreporting (varying among industries and states). The reporting requirements of state safety and health authorities also vary. In all likelihood, the image of the American workplace as "much safer than the home or street" may well contain as much fiction as fact: see Ralph Nader and Jerome Gordon, "Safety on the Job," *New Republic*, June 15, 1968, pp. 23–25; U.S. Congress, Senate, Committee on Labor and Public Welfare, *Occupational Safety and Health Act, 1970: Hearings on S2193 and S2788*, 91st Cong., 2d sess., Parts I and II. Also, P. Nonet, *Administrative Justice* (New York: Russell Sage Foundation, 1969), a case study of interrelationships of law, administration, and politics in the history of the California Industrial Accident Commission.

Table 15.

Workmen's Compensation Benefits for Permanent Total Disability, by State, and the Poverty Line, 1968

	Maximum weekly benefit[1] (4-person family)	Maximum weekly benefit[2] divided by poverty (4-person family)	Poverty rank (4-person family)	Average weekly wage rank
Alabama	$ 44	64%	45	39
Alaska	73	107	7	1
Arizona	150	219	1	18
Arkansas	49	72	35	51
California	53	78	25	3
Colorado	54	79	23	23
Connecticut	76	111	6	10
Delaware	50	73	30	8
District of Columbia	70	102	9	13
Florida	49	72	35	30
Georgia	50	73	30	34
Hawaii	113	165	2	24
Idaho[2]	53	78	25	42
Illinois	68	100	12	5
Indiana	51	75	28	12
Iowa	48	50	39	27
Kansas	49	72	35	29
Kentucky	49	72	35	30
Louisiana	45	66	42	22
Maine	65	95	14	45
Maryland	70	102	9	24
Massachusetts	83	121	5	21
Michigan	87	127	3	2
Minnesota	60	88	17	18
Mississippi	40	59	49	50
Missouri	52	76	27	14
Montana	50	73	30	39
Nebraska	45	66	42	37
Nevada	68	100	12	11
New Hampshire	58	85	20	34
New Jersey	86	126	4	6
New Mexico	45	66	42	34

Table 15 (continued).

Workmen's Compensation Benefits for Permanent Total Disability, by State, and the Poverty Line, 1968

	Maximum weekly benefit[1] (4-person family)	Maximum weekly benefit[2] divided by poverty (4-person family)	Poverty rank (4-person family)	Average weekly wage rank
New York	70	102	0	3
North Carolina	42	61	47	47
North Dakota[2]	60	88	17	46
Ohio	56	82	21	6
Oklahoma	40	59	49	28
Oregon[3]	54	79	23	18
Pennsylvania	60	88	17	16
Rhode Island	50	73	30	33
South Carolina	50	73	30	48
South Dakota	44	64	45	49
Tennessee	42	61	47	42
Texas[3]	35	51	51	26
Utah	55	80	22	39
Vermont[3]	61	89	16	30
Virginia	51	75	28	37
Washington[3]	65	95	14	8
West Virginia	47	69	41	16
Wisconsin	73	107	7	14
Wyoming	48	70	39	42

1. Maximum weekly payment for permanent total disability for a disabled workman with a dependent wife and two dependent children below age 18, as of January 1, 1969 (rounded to nearest dollar). The laws are those in effect on January 1, 1969. Chamber of Commerce of the United States, *Workmen's Compensation Laws,* 1969 ed. (Washington, 1969), pp. 22–23.

2. Ratio of maximum weekly benefit (col. 1) to the "poverty line" for a non-farm family of two adults and two children whose head is male. The poverty line for 1968 was estimated as $68 per week for-a-4-person family, U.S. Bureau of the Census, *Current Population Reports,* "Revision in Poverty Statistics, 1959 to 1968, "Series P-23, No. 28.

3. Including dependents' allowance.

Source: Reprinted with permission from the *Industrial and Labor Relations Review,* Vol. 24, No. 1, October 1970. Copyright c. 1970 by Cornell University. All rights reserved.

In a climate of new interest in adequacy of workmen's compensation, more studious attention is being given the protection of the severely disabled under OASDHI. The national concern is expressed in the report of the National Commission on State Workmen's Compensation Laws and congressional expansion of the black lung program. The Commission reports that coverage, benefits, and administration of the state programs are inadequate, and that insufficient improvement has occurred during recent years. Too much of the burden of wage loss and of medical care costs falls upon the worker and his family. The majority of the Commission supported the principles of state responsibility for work injury compensation and of employer liability, rather than broad social responsibility for these costs. Yet recognizing the slowness of change in state programs, it recommended that Congress establish a national commission to assist the states in achieving improvements in line with its recommended criteria of adequacy. Finally, if they do not achieve stated "essential elements of a modern workmen's compensation program" by July 1, 1975, Congress should then require compliance by federal legislation. Notwithstanding its rejection of federal assumption of administration, it held unanimously that "congressional intervention may be necessary" to bring about the reforms essential to survival of a state workmen's compensation system. Despite federal financial aid to state and federal-state income-maintenance programs, federal reluctance to accept formal program responsibility remains the dominant stance.

TEMPORARY DISABILITY INSURANCE

Wage and salary workers are estimated to have lost an average of seven days of working time in 1970—days when they were unable to work or to look for work because of a short-term disability, not work-connected, which lasted less than six months. Wages and salaries of some $13.9 billion were lost in 1970 because of such disabilities and, if another $1.5 billion income losses of the self-employed were added, the total would come to $15.5 billion.[57] Put in other terms, disabilities for an

57. See D. N. Price. "Cash Benefits for Short-Term Illness, 1948–70," *Social Security Bulletin,* Jan. 1972, pp. 19–29.

average worker, other than work injuries, account for seven working days per year, far more than the impact of work-connected disability.[58] Although workers are protected against the latter by an array of state and federal workmen's compensation laws, public concern for the greater risk of temporary nonwork-connected disability has not taken legislative form except in seven jurisdictions. Social security provides protection against long-term disability, but most protection against short-term disability is afforded by group insurance under employee-benefit plans.

One of every three workers, about 24 million, when their work and earnings are interrupted by nonwork-connected illness or injury, must absorb the entire wage loss and medical expense from their own resources. Lack of protection has more serious consequences when disability occurs during layoff. Protection against short-term disability thus constitutes the major gap in public protection against income loss to which workers are exposed. This risk was among the first covered by European social security programs, which generally have also provided maternity benefits for women workers.[59]

About 47 million, or two of every three, wage and salary workers in the country do have some type of protection, although government plans required by law covered only 14.4 million workers in 1970 compared to 10.6 million in 1954. The great majority are protected through group insurance purchased by employers from commercial carriers and paying specified weekly benefits. Employers may provide benefits directly, as in paid sick-leave plans; in addition, self-employed and white-collar

58. Precise comparisons are difficult to make, but rough approximations are of value. Job-connected disabilities account for nearly one fifth of all accidental injuries according to J. G. Trumbull, C. A. Williams, Jr., and Earl F. Cheit, *Economic and Social Security,* 2nd ed. (New York: Ronald Press, 1962), p. 249. Data from the Health Interview Survey for 1969, though on a different base, show rough correspondence; while there were some 66 days of bed disability per 100 persons in that year due to injury, 13 days (or 1 in 5) arose from injuries "while at work." (*Current Estimates, 1970,* NCHS Series 10, no. 72 [May 1972], Table 12.) From another survey of 21 million persons sustaining injuries that required medical attention or covering restrictions of activity for one or more days, about one half (or 10.3 million) incurred these injuries on the job. (C. H. Brooks, *Work Injuries among Blue Collar Workers and Disability Days, July 1966–June 1967,* NCHS, Series 10, no. 68 [Feb. 1972], p. 1.)

59. See SSA-ORS, *Social Security Programs throughout the World—1971,* Research Report no. 40 (1972), pp. xviii–xxiii.

workers purchase sickness insurance policies. Paid sick leave, utilized typically by white-collar and office employees, and especially by government workers, covers about nine tenths of the latter (federal, state, and local). All these approaches supplement one another, as Price points out—e.g., sick leave may supplement group insurance coverage.

The few legislated programs (national, federal, or state) operative in only seven jurisdictions, protect a minority of all workers, as we have noted. The governmental programs, except for Puerto Rico and Hawaii, date back to 1942–49; the latter two were enacted 20 years later. The laws adopted in the 1940s reflect the greater attention given at that time to employee fringe benefits plus shifting of worker contributions (in Rhode Island, New Jersey, and California) from unemployment to disability insurance. Despite legislative proposals and study commission reports in other states, new legislative enactments were stalemated; in the 1950s, the stalemate was due to conflicting approaches by interested groups: commercial underwriting, as in workmen's compensation, *vs.* the state as the carrier, as in unemployment insurance. The former remains the preferred employer/insurance carrier/medical organization approach. In addition, some groups continue to push for a federal-state approach, as in unemployment insurance, while others favor disability insurance under social security but with the waiting period gradually reduced from five months to a few weeks.

The major role which commercial carriers play in the state programs, other than in Rhode Island and in the railroad system, has been opposed by the organized labor movement, which has chosen to "take the route of collective bargaining."[60] It is fair to say that in programs such as these, which include worker contributions, labor has preferred the Rhode Island approach or the more limited role of private carriers in the California program, to the dominant role of private insurance, as under the workmen's compensation pattern. To be sure, collectively bargained cash sickness insurance plans which cover the great majority of workers are underwritten by commercial carriers. These insurance arrangements are effected by employers, however, and do not call for worker contributions.

60. Cruikshank (formerly Director, AFL-CIO Department of Social Security) to author, 16 Oct. 1972. See also James O'Brien, "Protecting the Worker On and Off the Job," *American Federationist,* Sept. 1972, p. 23.

Characteristics of the state programs display considerable similarity.[61] However, three provide different protection for workers disabled during unemployment, or while in noncovered employment, and some, like California's coverage of farm workers, protect workers who are not covered by unemployment insurance.[62] Except for New York and Hawaii, they are operated by the unemployment insurance agency. Only the railroad and Rhode Island "exclusive funds" bar employers from "contracting out" of state plan coverage to obtain insurance from an approved commercial carrier, or to self-insure, as permitted in the other jurisdictions.

Weekly benefits were similar to those under unemployment compensation in mid-1971, although some had been higher in earlier years. Except in two states, benefits compensate for only loss of earnings; California provides a hospitalization benefit of $12 per day for 20 days per disability period, while New York permits a mix of cash benefits and services as the "actuarial equivalent" of the statutory benefit.

The programs are financed by a variety of worker and worker-employer contributions. The cost of the statutory benefits is covered by worker contributions of 1 percent in Rhode Island and California. The New Jersey worker contribution of 0.25 percent is supplemented by variable employer contributions. Workers pay a maximum of 0.5 percent in the remaining jurisdictions, the employers contributing either the same or whatever is required to finance the benefit schedule. Where employers have "contracted out" their state plan liability to an approved self-insured or commercially insured plan, workers' contributions cannot be any more than they would be under the state plan.[63]

Although the railroad system covers virtually all railroad workers, and the other six programs cover more than four of every five workers in their jurisdictions, private plans have nev-

61. For program details, see U.S. Department of Labor, *Comparison of State Unemployment Insurance Laws*, Sections 600–630. See also SSA-ORS, *Social Security Programs in the U.S.*, pp. 86–97.

62. Philip Booth, "Sickness Insurance and California Farm Workers," *Social Security Bulletin*, May 1968, pp. 3–13. Nathan Sinai, *For the Disabled Sick: Disability Compensation* (Ann Arbor: University of Michigan School of Public Health, 1949).

63. U.S. Department of Labor, *Comparison of State Unemployment Insurance Laws*, Section 600.

er protected more than half the workers in the remaining states. Paid sick leave plans, protecting some 15 million workers, play a disproportionately large role in public employment, but cover only a minority of workers in private employment. Yet they accounted for nearly two of every five benefit dollars paid; they replaced two thirds of wages lost by workers covered by such plans in 1948, but this had risen to 77 percent in 1970. Private plans, although covering more workers, provide less protection for short-term illnesses because of noncompensated waiting periods and part-pay benefit schedules. These benefits replaced one fifth of all lost wages in 1970, double that of 1948; the compulsory programs, however, replaced nearly 20 percent of former wages, one third more than in 1948.[64]

Taking public and private plans together, plus paid sick leave, the total of $5.5 billion of benefits accounted for 36 percent of lost income in 1970, twice the 17 percent 1948 rate of replacement. The rate of increase has gone up by 1 percent per year since 1965. In five states with publicly operated programs, the state fund has overtaken the competitive private plans; prior to 1955–58, 40–45 percent of all payments in the five states combined were made from state funds, but this increased to 55 percent by 1964, and to 57 percent in 1971.[65] The declining role of private plans reflects their difficulty in matching state law benefit increases, for they are unable to charge higher premiums than charged in the state-plan contribution rate; each employer's risk must be able to stand on its own, whereas the social insurance approach combines all risks, good and bad, and· can protect all workers in the state through a uniform (and lower) rate.

EMPLOYEE BENEFIT PLANS

One might ask why a book on social security should discuss private employee-benefit plans, except perhaps to call attention

64. Price, "Cash Benefits," p. 27. In 1968 unemployment insurance, though covering 80 percent of all wage and salary workers, also compensated 20 percent of wages lost, due to unemployment. Program differences bring the two figures closer together when we note that spells of unemployment were longer than spells of illness; the latter, when covered by sick leave plans, replaced full wages. Every fifth unemployment beneficiary exhausted his unemployment benefit while still jobless.

65. Ibid., p. 24. See also Price, "Income Loss Protection Against Illness, 1971," Research and Statistics Note no. 23, 1972.

to their role in supplementing public protection against loss of earnings and health costs and to explain how government encourages their existence and growth. Labor, fraternal, and cooperative organizations have long regarded funeral, disability, and retirement benefits as an inducement to recruitment of members. Today formal employee benefits play a major role in worker security. Many plans dating back a half-century or more speak to employers' interest "to prevent suffering and distress among their faithful workers"; pensions facilitate retirement of older workers, permitting replacement by the younger, more vigorous (and temporarily lower paid) workers.[66] Employee-benefit plans appeared early, but provided spotty protection before governmental measures entered the field. Most existing plans were created under collective bargaining arrangements. During World War II government encouraged employers to introduce and extend employee benefit protection, for wage controls inhibited wage increases. More recently, employer contributions to pension and group insurance plans were held to be outside the area of wage increases under regulation by the controls administered by the Pay Board of the Cost of Living Council, under the Economic Stabilization Act of 1970.

In combination with social insurance and public assistance, employee benefit plans fill out income security protection beyond that of public programs. Government encourages such protection against contingencies it has been slow to cover, such as insurance against medical care costs, and to supplement public benefits, such as retirement. While governmental programs have been financed by payroll taxes and from general revenues, the tax system promotes private measures to advance social welfare objectives; Titmuss perceptively calls this "fiscal welfare."[67] The system has employed a broad array of tax exemptions, exclusions, and deductions which reduce tax collections (revenue foregone). As Assistant Secretary of the Treasury Weidenbaum put it, these represent "an alternative to an equivalent increase in federal expenditures that would otherwise be required for the same purpose."[68]

66. Philip Taft, *Economics and Problems of Labor* (Harrisburg: Stackpole, 1942), pp. 222–244.

67. R. M. Titmuss, "The Social Division of Welfare," in *Essays on the Welfare State* (London: Allen and Unwin, 1959), pp. 24–59.

68. Statement of June 2, 1970, before U.S. Congress Joint Economic Com-

Although employee benefit plans extend to a variety of contingencies, and individuals receive tax benefits for others, the greatest number of workers are protected against the costs of hospital and surgical care (Table 16). Somewhat fewer have group life insurance and only half as many have retirement protection. Unsurprisingly, health care plans have experienced most growth. By 1970 hospital and surgical benefit protection covered 60 million workers and over 90 million dependents; retirement plans covered 30 million workers. Both of these triple the 1950 figure. Contributions to private plans were nearly $35 billion; benefits (26B) were about half of major (comparable) public income program payments ($50 billion), exclusive of veterans' benefits and public assistance.[69]

If, as noted, employer contributions to their own plans receive favorable tax treatment, what magnitude of tax savings are concerned? The 1968 Treasury estimates for selected areas show savings of $5.3 billion as to pension plans, $0.4 billion for group life insurance, and $1.1 billion for hospital, surgical, and other medical care. If these tax savings are alternatives to direct expenditures for related purposes, as Weidenbaum suggests, we should take note of Eveline Burns' comment that "private agencies are invested with a public interest when they receive a public subsidy."[70] In these terms, how effective are private

mittee, Subcommittee on Economy in Government, in *Annual Report of the Secretary of the Treasury, 1970,* Exhibit no. 14, p. 306; see also Henry Aaron, "Tax Exemptions, the Artful Dodge," *Transaction,* March 1969, pp. 4–6; and Aaron, *Tax Incentives,* Reprint no. 20 (Washington: Brookings Institution, 1971). In 1949 the Presidential Board of Inquiry in dealing with a dispute in the steel industry held that "industry, *in the absence of adequate government programs,* owes an obligation to the workers to provide for . . . medical and similar benefits. . . . This obligation is . . . of the fixed costs of doing business." (Emphasis supplied.) (Quoted in M. C. Klein and M. F. McKiever, *Management and Union Health and Medical Programs,* PHS Publication no. 329 [Washington, 1953], pp. 7–8).

69. Includes OASDHI, RRB, public employee retirement, unemployment, workmen's and temporary disability benefits. *Statistical Supplement, 1970,* Table 10, p. 29; W. W. Kolodrubetz, "Trends in Employee Benefit Plans in the Sixties," *Social Security Bulletin,* April 1971, Tables 5–6, pp. 25–27. Those who received the $5.9 billion in private plan retirement and survivor benefits, for example, are also likely to be eligible for OASDHI benefits. By contrast, few of the beneficiaries of the $11 billion in private plan health benefits are age 65 or more and thus not entitled to Medicare benefits.

70. Vera Schlackman, "Eveline Burns – Social Economist," in *Social Security in International Perspective,* ed. Shirley Jenkins (New York: Columbia University Press, 1969), p. 16.

Table 16.

Estimated Number of Wage and Salary Workers and Dependents under Employee-Benefit Plans, 1950–70

	Millions of Workers and Dependents					
	1950		1960		1970	
	Workers	Dependents	Workers	Dependents	Workers	Dependents
Hospitalization	24	30	41	63	60	93
Surgical Expense	18	20	39	60	59	92
Life Insurance	19	*	34	3	52	9
Temporary Disability	20	n.a.	25	n.a.	31	—
Retirement	10	n.a.	21	n.a.	30	—

*Less than 0.5 million.

Source: Adapted from W. W. Kolodrubetz, "Two Decades of Employee Benefit Plans. 1950–1970," *Social Security Bulletin,* April 1972. Tables 1, 4; "Employee Benefit Plans in 1968," *ibid.,* April 1970, Table 1, p. 38; "Trends in Employee-Benefit Plans in the Sixties," *op. cit.,* pp. 23–24.

plans in meeting workers' needs for the protection they presume to provide? We use retirement plans as an illustration.

The 1960s saw improvements in retirement benefits, but eligibility depended on a combination of substantial periods of service and attainment of age 55 or 60. Formerly, fewer participants could expect to continue in employment long enough to receive a pension, but the number qualifying increased as vesting has become somewhat more common: early vesting and portability, offering more protection, are still quite rare. Yet one analysis points out that only 57 of any 100 men starting work at age 25 would have acquired nonforfeitable pension benefits after 20 years of service (at age 45); if they were 5 years older (age 50), 75 would have such benefits.[71]

Many students of private pensions have found that the degree of protection which the plans provide to workers is often illusory. A smaller proportion of wage and salary workers continues in the employment of a single firm for the 40 years from ages 25

71. H. E. Davis and A. Strasser, "Private Pension Plans, 1960–1969: An Overview," *Monthly Labor Review,* July 1970, pp. 45–47.

to 65 than even the best of employers presume, as a leading authority has pointed out.[72] Vesting only after 20 years of employment, for example, has undermined the protection which workers are often thought to possess. Beyond this, as indicated above, in 1970 more than half the work force was employed in establishments without private retirement protection (Table 16).

As noted above, higher private and public pensions appear to go together; by contrast, low earners are far more dependent upon social security. These differences accentuate other disparities — the greater security of higher wage, single-employer, regularly employed workers, in contrast to others whose working life is punctuated by unemployment, job changes, and low earnings. The former especially, if among the 3 million with supplemental unemployment benefits, have attained the security of a virtually guaranteed annual wage during employment. In later years their retirement income (private plus public pensions) approaches their preretirement income, taking into account tax savings available to the aged.[73]

Aside from disparities in treatment, students of employee-benefit plans have drawn attention to weaknesses and abuse. In the 1950s the first controls required registration and reporting to the U.S.Department of Labor. However, rapidly increasing numbers and assets of benefit plans and their complex organization and activities proved to be beyond the effective control of that department. For example, assets of private pension plans had reached $152 billion by the end of 1971 and together with state and local government plans, another $64 billion, totaled $216 billion.

Criticisms included mismanagement of reserves, imprudent investments, unsecured loans to "insiders" and the many older workers who failed to qualify for pensions. As the 1970s began, the demand for more effective controls and standards increased,

72. Brown, *Social Insurance,* p. 75. Factors that contribute to turnover on the employer's side include business conditions, product and technological change, mergers, shifts in location, and administrative policy; on the worker's side, shifting factors of health, interests, pay rates, growth in capacity, living and transportation arrangements, and personal incompatibility.

73. Social security benefits are tax-exempt, for example. E. R. Livernash, "Wages and Benefits," in *A Review of Industrial Relations Research,* vol. 1, ed. Woodrow Ginsberg et al. (Madison: Industrial Relations Research Assoc., 1970), p. 119, 127.

stimulated, in part, by mergers and bankruptcies in 1969–71 which left insufficient funds available to pay pensions even to workers with 30–40 years of service and within a year or two of pensionable age.[74] Yet a comprehensive program for regulating private pension plans failed to pass in the closing days of the 92nd Congress.

Insurance carriers have credited governmental programs with stimulating interest in private plans which supplemented the floor of income protection and health services. Medicare has increased interest in private supplements to hospital protection. Some observers are concerned that private plans may retard worker mobility, accentuate fragmented protection, and retard the growth of public programs; others anticipate continued expansion of public schemes.

Summing Up

Private plans today account for an increasingly large proportion of the wage package; they have grown from 5 to 19.6 percent of total compensation in private employment and in 1929 and 1967 have increased twice as fast as straight-time pay (9.6 percent annually compared to 3.9 percent). It is estimated that they may reach 50 percent of payrolls by 1985.[75] A more recent government survey puts spending on wage supplements in private industry in 1970 at 22.2 percent of basic wages and salaries. In contrast to such public programs as unemployment insurance with 0.9 percent, workmen's compensation with 1.1 percent, and social security 4.2 percent of payrolls (5.8 percent in 1970), private pension, and retirement plans accounted for 3.7 percent; life, accident, and health insurance, 3.2 percent; and vacation and holiday leave, 6.6 percent in 1970. Such enrichment of nonwage benefit protection increases the distinction between regularly employed, higher earners, typically in larger

74. Harry Gersh, ed.; *Employee Benefits Fact Book, 1972* (New York: Martin E. Segal Co., 1972); pp. 12, 453; see also U.S., Congress, Senate, Committee on Labor and Public Welfare, Subcommittee on Labor, *Retirement Income Security for Employees: Hearings on S-3598,* 92nd Cong., 2d sess., Parts 1–3, 1972; and Merton C. Bernstein, *The Future of Private Pensions* (New York: Free Press, 1964).

75. R. Oswald and J. D. Smythe, "Fringe Benefits: On the Move," *American Federationist,* June 1970. Livernash, "Wages and Benefits," pp. 120–121.

firms, and those who have no coverage or protection by strong unions, irregular employment, and low earnings. As the latter become "far more conspicious and deprived, [pressure] for public benefits can be expected to mount steadily to alleviate this differential condition."[76]

But the multiplicity of programs requires more than regulation of the private sector. Increasing numbers of workers can now acquire dual (or triple) benefit rights when their employment history includes coverage under federal, state or local plans, private group and/or individual programs, plus the general social security system. Other workers less well situated have little or no protection against sickness, unemployment or retirement in old age. As a recent overview of the international scene pointed out:

> The coexistence of separate plans for manual or white-collar workers, of those in private and public employment, of . . . urban and rural workers, of . . . [wage and salaried] and self-employed workers had led to a proliferation of extremely diverse schemes which, in turn, produced a serious and unwieldy fragmentation of income and health protection. [Benefit disparities of privileged groups caused them to] . . . turn against unification for fear of losing the differential advantage through the expected leveling of benefits. . . . The high cost of duplicating administrative machinery and the unsatisfactory distribution of risks . . . the pressure of sharply increasing subsidies to funds covering the workers in declining industries with shrinking contributions and a growing number of beneficiaries [has led to increased interest in more rational integration, or, at least, coordination of fragmented programs.][77]

Complicating factors include the political and economic influence of special interest groups, trade union and veterans' organizations, for example, which participate in the adminis-

76. Livernash, "Wages and Benefits," p. 121. Another study (1959–1966) indicated that fringe benefits enjoyed by two fifths of all union members were liberalized or introduced each year, but only for between one fifth and one fourth of nonunion members.

77. Paul Fisher, "Developments and Trends in Social Security throughout the World," (Address to the 19th General Assembly of the International Social Security Association, Cologne, Sept. 1970, pp. 13–14.

trative or policy structures of many plans. Yet the constraints upon social security programs, which must limit benefits provided for higher-paid workers, calls attention to the role of private pension plans in assuring appropriate higher benefits (beyond the capacity of social security) to employees with longer service and higher earnings, of $20,000–$30,000 or more per year, for example. If private plans are to supplement social security benefits for such workers, they will have to remedy their deficiencies, especially vesting and portability.[78]

Recent growth of public pension plans for state and local government workers, particularly those performing services essential to big-city living (policemen, firemen, sanitation workers), have produced more generous pensions payable at earlier ages than those in private plans or for most government civilian workers. These plans, over time, will not only claim substantial portions of state and local tax resources, but induce emulation. Their generous provision for favored groups poses practical obstacles to better coordination among public/private programs; conceivably, sharpened concern as to the financial effects of such developments may increase interest in coordination, if only as a brake on higher benefits. Continued piece-by-piece integration of local and state pension plans within social security is more likely, plus coordinating work injury, nonwork-connected and short- and long-term disability benefit plans, and tying medical and rehabilitation benefits under work injury schemes together with health insurance programs built on a broader base. Such a course is more in keeping with public policy and is more feasible in the light of congressional reluctance to embark on comprehensive revamping of public and private organizational structures.

It is not appropriate, at one extreme, to advocate integration of all public plans within a single institution, although to some specialists, shifting the entire responsibility to the social security system's "greater pool of risks and resources" might offer many advantages. Integration of groups of risks, such as hospital or health care, for example, could reshape the organization and delivery of health services to the American people. Yet it is widely accepted that social security should provide a floor of

78. See Brown, *Social Insurance*, chapter V.

basic protection upon which groups and individuals build additional protection for themselves. Public tax policy has long fostered such supplementation. Substantial integration of income maintenance and health service programs in the foreseeable future appears unlikely, even leaving aside the concerns of such interest groups as insurance carriers, unions, and veterans' organizations.

IV

Agenda for Change

Since the 1930s many governmental measures have been designed and have functioned to protect and improve the economic
security of Americans during and after their working careers.
Measures for underpinning security and preventing hardship
have helped workers deal with short- and long-term interruptions of earnings due to illness, unemployment, disability,
or premature death. In addition, we have supplemented income
maintenance for two of our lowest income groups, the aged and
disabled, by insurance against their health care costs. These
groups need and make the most use of such health services. The
heart of these public income security measures consists of the
rights to benefits and other services which people accrue
through their active participation in the work force. They are
supplemented by an array of private employee benefit plans
which add to workers' security, but especially aid those workers
with higher earnings and a more regular employment history,
who may also possess above-average protection under public
programs.

In discussing our basic social security system—the first line of
defense against economic insecurity, we should avoid the pre-
sumption that its protection is comprehensive and universal. It
does approach universality most closely in terms of numbers,
but we have already seen that the restricted range of risks
afforded protection constitutes the system's major limitations. In

fact, millions counted as poor in our society have become or remained poor because their work has been uneven, seasonal, casual, and poorly paid, or because they have not acquired social security rights founded on their own employment, or on their status as dependents or survivors of insured workers.

In this sense we perceive that maintenance of income has been the primary objective of the system thus contributing to prevention of poverty; alleviation of poverty among those already poor has been a secondary objective. Yet social security has done more to alleviate poverty among the aged, widows, and orphans than any other public program.

Almost four decades of experience with the benefits which workers and their families gain from our social security programs highlight the advantages which accrued from extension of coverage to additional contingencies and additional people. Widely shared perceptions of our programs' inadequacies have made us more sensitive to the gaps in protection against interruptions in income, lack of access to basic health and welfare services, and the stresses and waste of poverty and deprivation.

The following pages review briefly the substantial and significant protection afforded by the existing system, the system's shortcomings, and the importance of remedying them. In addressing the policy issues involved in achieving fuller protection, we recognize that the gains of the past were not achieved all at once and that new approaches and comprehensive reform proposals, however vital, are likely to be accepted and effected piece-by-piece as we reach agreement on means for attaining widely accepted goals. As Robert Ball points out, our own development compared to that of European countries is that of a "democratic society waiting for consensus, in contrast to a society where the state has greater control of decisions."[1]

Earlier pages have depicted the substantial protection afforded to millions of American workers and their families. More than 90 of every 100 workers and their families are protected under public programs against loss of earnings due to retirement, severe and prolonged disability, and premature death; 85 of every 100 jobs carry protection against work injury

1. William G. Bowen et al., *American System of Social Insurance* (New York: McGraw Hill, 1968), p. 239.

and unemployment. Most workers regularly employed in larger firms have acquired supplementary protection under employee benefit plans against sickness and health costs; smaller numbers are protected against financial losses in retirement. Millions in the "other America" have not gained access either to jobs which assure regular work or to sufficient earnings to attain a decent average existence. For them, work insecurity and low earnings provide little in benefits under either public or private programs.

When the economy and the society fail to enable millions of people to be financially self-sufficient during their working lives, it is not to be expected that income maintenance plans which rest upon such work history can do better for them when their work is interrupted or their working careers are over. Social insurance was not developed to compensate for or remedy chronically inadequate wages or chronic unemployment. This can be prevented or corrected by improved work opportunities created in the private and public sectors. Remedying the human distress of poverty is a task assigned to social assistance programs. What then has been provided by social insurance?

As the primary source of income protection, the OASDHI system paid cash benefits of $36.8 billion in 1971 to 27.3 million people: 20.6 million retired and disabled workers and their dependents and 6.7 million dependent survivors. Medicare provided $7.7 billion in health care services to aged people. In addition, some 7 million jobless received $6.0 billion (a new high point) in unemployment benefits. Additional millions were receiving workmen's compensation and short-term sickness benefits under public-private and private plans. Despite the broad scope of income support and income maintenance, many people are left unprotected against major risks to income security. The presumed needs defined by public programs and the measures devised to meet them necessarily reflect the distribution of income support requirements of the population. When we note that more than four of every five dollars in social insurance payments in 1971 were for the aged and disabled, their dependents and survivors, we may be taken aback by the apparent imbalance between their numbers and the far larger working age population. That an imbalance does exist is evident, but this imbalance reflects certain facts of our existence — that most people, from their twenties on to their mid-sixties, ordinarily rely on earnings for their support, while orphaned children, the aged, and invalids cannot do so. Distribution of the $76 billion in cash benefit payments in 1971 reflects the greater needs of the aged and long-term disabled population for continuing income. They received $56 of the $65 billion in social insurance payments because most of them will receive payments continuously for many years, some for the rest of their lives. With contrasting emphasis, $7.5 billion in public assistance went to AFDC recipients to support families with young children, but less than half as much, $3.2 billion, was paid in old-age assistance and aid to the needy disabled.[2] The unemployed and most of the work-injured population will receive insurance payments for relatively short periods, even if continued for six months or a year, when they are temporarily without work and earnings.

The system does, in fact, offer far less protection to those with short-term disabilities, especially if not work-connected. Working women who lose work and wages because of pregnancy and maternity in some 70 other countries are protected by sickness and maternity benefits; no similar protection exists in the United States.[3] As to other risks, work injury protection varies greatly from state to state; only one third of those jobless at any given time receive unemployment benefits. Under most of these, to generalize broadly, cash benefits replace between one third and one half of former earnings and the buying power of benefits does not keep pace with prices or rising productivity. Aside from deficiencies in cash benefits, more serious danger of undermining the living standards of those with interrupted earnings lies in the absence of public provision for medical and other rehabilitative services; only the work-injured, the aged, and severely disabled (as from July 1973) have such protection. Private plans provide more health care for those in the work force, especially for the regularly employed, higher seniority, better paid workers.

To remedy deficiencies and close gaps, we need to understand the cause and nature of such uneven protection as it applies to population groups and to risks of earnings loss. Our experience suggests that a major difficulty lies in the absence of consensus

2. *Social Security Bulletin,* May 1972, Table M-25.
3. *Social Security Programs around the World, 1971,* p. xviii.

within the body politic as to where responsibility lies for assuring social protection. Nowhere can we find agreement that the ultimate responsibility for health care, for example, rests in either the public or the private sector. If the former, does the responsibility rest at the local, state, or federal level, or should it be shared among them? To generalize, we can obtain substantial agreement as to goals of social policy, but effective action to achieve a given goal is often frustrated by disagreement on the means to be employed. Goals formulated in broad general propositions – e.g., to conquer poverty, to open up health opportunities for the aged, to tide the jobless over between jobs – can win wide acceptance. But to bring them about requires agreement on specifics, making choices among concrete alternatives on which reasonable men disagree – e.g., whether to provide hospital insurance to all aged eligible for social security benefits, to the needy and affluent alike, whether under a national plan, or to utilize state plans directed only to the need? Again, shall we provide six months unemployment benefit protection to all who are eligible, extended to as long as nine to twelve months during recessions under a nationwide program, or instead have each state provide benefits for so long a period as it may determine is necessary?

ALLOCATION OF WELFARE FUNCTIONS

When we examine the factors which have influenced decisions as to location of these responsibilities, without pretending to be exhaustive, we note that our society turns first of all to the private voluntary sector, or to the primary (local or state) unit of government,[4] or to the public assistance approach. Where we find substantial consensus that a given function is beyond the private sector's capacity (e.g., insurance carriers in the late 1920s disclaimed interest in writing unemployment insurance

4. This is expressed succinctly in the following statement: "Only when private enterprise cannot or will not do what needs to be done should government step in. When government action is required, it should be undertaken, if possible, by that unit of government closest to the people. For example, the progression should be from local to state to federal government, in that order." From Richard M. Nixon's 1963 application for admission to the New York Bar, quoted in *Washington Monthly,* Feb. 1969, p. 60.

and union unemployment benefit plans were unable to cope with depression unemployment), we turned to the public sector. A similar turn to the public sector occurred when, in the 1960s, private insurance carriers were unable to provide hospital insurance for the aged at a price the latter could afford to pay.[5]

Where local and state government fails (as in medical assistance to the aged under the 1960 Kerr-Mills approach) to develop a viable program covering all states, we turned to federal auspices. And when we obtained consensus that the assistance approach failed to provide adequate benefit protection or nationwide coverage (as in categorical aid to the needy total-permanent disabled) we turned to social insurance (invalidity insurance) in the mid-1950s.

While this rationalization of a complex decision-making process is oversimplified, it does provide insight as to factors which influence decisions and conditions which facilitate the process. Several criteria have influenced state and federal legislators in determining whether given programs should remain state and local responsibilities. These criteria have included:

State differentials:

state-by-state differentials in taxes (or premiums) and benefits preferred to nationwide uniformity (workmen's compensation);
federal reluctance to intervene (public education; health services).

States' rights:

state responsibility long accepted and defended by private and governmental interest groups (workmen's compensation).

Federally aided state programs:

federal grants-in-aid, encouraging state assumption of responsibility (public assistance).

Similarly, the *private, voluntary sector* continues to carry responsibility where governmental intervention is opposed or

5. See discussion between Eveline Burns and Henry Chase on the increasing role of government in income maintenance, versus that of the private sector in G. F. Rohrlich, ed., *Social Economics for the 1970s* (Cambridge, Mass.: Dunellen, 1970), pp. 66–87.

not fully accepted, as in employee health and welfare plans and maternity wage-loss benefits, and where disagreement persists as to the proper level of governmental responsibility, despite acceptance of the desirability of some form of governmental intervention, such as in liability for traffic injuries.

Federal governmental responsibility has been accepted when it has been widely conceded that:

insurance or assistance benefits paid to individuals and families should not vary from state to state;

a mounting burden of costs ought to be shifted from the states to the national government;

the potentially protected population moves among states during its working life;

a federal tax on employers in all states is necessary in order to overcome fears of interstate competitive disadvantage;[6]

state-by-state protection is unsuitable, inefficient, or ineffective as to coverage, eligibility or benefits;

state action has failed to provide nationwide protection against a hazard which has acquired nationwide notoriety, as with pneumoconiosis.

When we turn from the private/governmental area of responsibility to the form of protection, different factors enter: the *social insurance* approach has been accepted when it becomes generally agreed that:

benefits should be available as a right, rather than based upon need or means;

benefits should be available nationwide to the poor and nonpoor, to urban and rural people alike;

coverage should be compulory; and

benefits should be financed by an earmarked source of revenue.

Concerning the shifting of responsibility for income maintenance and income support from state to federal authority during recent years, it is interesting to note that the same has occurred

6. Arthur Larson has described the tax credit divide whereby the states were induced to levy taxes on employers for financing of unemployment benefits as one example of "beneficient bullying." See *Economic Security for Americans,* The American Assembly, Arden House Conference (New York: Columbia University Press, 1954), p. 39.

in education, transportation, health, and law enforcement, for example. To some observers the shift represents a "catching up" process after long years of neglect of urban problems by rural-dominated state legislatures. Thus while a majority of the population of 39 states was urban in 1960, their legislatures had a majority of rural representatives. By 1970 the nation was 74 percent urban.[7]

As the population became more and more urbanized, and cities and suburbs gained more congressional representation, the country turned to the federal government for resolution of problems long neglected. Among various influences, federal responsibility has been preferred to that of the states by some critics on the ground of superior efficiency and honesty. Thus, in a comment on a revenue-sharing proposal, the *New York Times* observed: "Since most state governments are inefficient and some corrupt, the people would be better served if the same money were spent by the generally more honest and more competent federal bureaucrats."[8] These and other factors, pressures, interests, and conditions, alone or in combination, interact and result in varying outcomes. Responsibility for a given program may be allocated wholly to a single level of government (as to the federal government, in OASDHI), to a federal-state arrangement (as in unemployment insurance or public assistance), or to combined governmental/private groups (as in the contracting-out of workmen's compensation underwriting to commercial insurance carriers). The influence of different combinations of factors has led to different decisions at various times as to (1) allocation of responsibility to private or governmental authority, (2) to what level of government, and (3) the form of protection, whether or not a program is to be on a universal basis, or only for people in needy circumstances. Since these decisions are made by federal and state legislatures and require appropriations, allocations, and administrative machinery to be made effective, the multiplicity and combination of forces and conditions which make for legislative policy decisions (or inaction) has not been systematized within the compass of this analytical framework.

7. Philip Hauser, "Meeting Human Needs," *Public Welfare*, Winter 1972, p. 12.
   8. Editorial, *New York Times*, 26 March 1972, p. E-12.

While we recognize the existence of uneven protection and remedial proposals, what are our choices in considering recommendations for program improvement? Where should priority be given, admitting that not every pressing problem is likely to be resolved or that, as economic, social, and political conditions and influences change, a given solution may serve for a limited time only and then itself become a "problem" requiring solution.

EXTENSION OF COVERAGE

Although coverage of the basic OASDHI program is virtually universal, millions of workers remain excluded from unemployment and workmen's compensation protection. This is particularly true of workers in agriculture, domestic service, state and local government, and, in workmen's compensation, those employed in smaller firms. Federal legislation to fill the gaps left by the 1970 unemployment insurance coverage extension is necessary to bring the remaining 12 million excluded jobs within the system. It cannot protect the affected workers and their families from slipping into poverty when unemployment strikes, without making coverage more nearly universal. Only then can their entire earnings and employment experience be taken into account for eligibility and benefit purposes.

Workmen's compensation, as presently organized, would require individual state action to offer protection against new occupational risks, as well as older ones, since industrial technology has outpaced the efforts of safety, health, compensation legislation and industrial medicine to match new hazards. This is especially true where compensation legislation has clung to classification of compensable disabilities in specific "scheduled" terms. The continued unprotected risks to the working population strongly suggest the need for federal action to fill gaps in state legislation. More fundamentally, allocation of responsibility among federal and state governments and industry groups for assuring safety in the workplace remaining undetermined in early 1973.

More effective progress toward comprehensive coverage against wage loss could be assured through measures covering all disabilities, whether or not work-connected, approaching a truly comprehensive disability insurance program. Such protection would include disability due to pregnancy and child birth, an incredible gap in a society where one of every four women with children under the age three is in the labor force; in 1970 the labor force included two of every five women with children under 18.[9] Yet while health and safety regulations and employers' rules require women to remain away from work during the later stages of pregnancy, only the U.S. among western nations fails to insure her loss of earnings, making it feasible for her to absent herself and to avoid danger to herself and the new-born child.

ELIGIBILITY FOR BENEFITS

Although the OASDHI program has broadened its eligibility requirements to include millions of low-wage workers with a casual, part-time, and irregular employment history, this approach has not been applied to all occupational and industry groups. Farm workers, in particular, face special obstacles to acquiring eligibility for benefits. Hundreds of thousands, especially if paid at piece rates, cannot demonstrate the required minimum employment with a single "employer" who may be a labor contractor or crew leader, a requirement not applied to nonfarm employment. Removal of these obstacles would enable a half-million farm workers to qualify for benefits; this change, recommended by the 1971 Advisory Council on Social Security, is long overdue.

Removal of other barriers to eligibility would enable hundreds of thousands of severely disabled workers to receive social security disability protection. To require, as the law now does, that the worker be so severely disabled as to make any gainful employment impossible is almost punitive, for it bars benefits even though work which he could perform does not exist in his locality, or would not be open to him if it did so exist. Such barriers to protection can scarcely be rationalized as reducing malingering; they should be removed. In addition, eligibility conditions should take account of older workers' difficulty in finding new work or reemployment due to progressive disability; such earnings loss might better be dealt with by dis-

9. *Manpower Report of the President,* 1971, p. 44.

ability benefits than by unemployment measures. Although disability beneficiaries continue to receive payments when they return to work on a trial basis, such flexibility does not help those who cannot satisfy the initial qualifying requirements. By removing the restrictions on eligibility which were unwisely tightened in 1967, and by reducing the five-month waiting period to three months or less, hundreds of thousands of severely disabled workers with reduced or no earnings could get more adequate income protection; it would be unnecessary for them to opt for reduced retirement benefits at age 62 to obtain some continuing income.

Frustrating problems of entitlement arise in workmen's compensation and disability insurance as to whether a worker's disabling condition was or was not work-connected, even when it is accepted that his earnings loss is due to the disabling condition. The increasing frequency of off-the-job injuries for which no adequate protection exists and the absence of disability protection under social security for the first five months of disability make a more universal approach all the more desirable. An all-embracing disability approach could employ a stage-by-stage reduced waiting period under social security, or combine state unemployment and workmen's compensation schemes, or both. These would make wage-loss protection available more widely to disabled workers, whether disabled for shorter or longer periods or for a work-connected cause. Policies as to eligibility in OASDHI and unemployment insurance, for example, that bar from benefits many who have had a close attachment to the work force and give protection to others without such attachment are closely intertwined with other policy issues as to the level and, in unemployment insurance, the duration of benefit protection for workers who have barely qualified, as distinct from those with a work history of steady employment and earnings. Such questions do not arise as to entitlement to benefits-in-kind—for example, the right of those who barely qualify for OASDHI benefits to enjoy the same Medicare protection as the $15,000-per-year earner. The interrelations of qualifying employment and earnings with benefit levels bear upon such basic questions as use of benefits as antipoverty devices, benefit/wage ratios, whether weeks of benefit entitlement (in unemployment insurance) should exceed weeks of past employment, and whether benefits should be paid during the off-season to seasonal workers; as in unemployment insurance, what limits on duration of benefits in recession periods should apply to persons with a steady work history compared to those who have barely qualified, and what benefit entitlement, if any, should be available to new entrants (and reentrants) to the work force possessing no record of recent employment. This recital makes it clear that quite different concepts as to social insurance goals and means underlie such differences on eligibility program issues. Further, the worker security problems involved there extend beyond the realm of social insurance to include wage and employment policy, occupational health and safety, private employee benefits plans, and expansion of social insurance to encompass sickness and health risks.

IMPROVING THE LEVEL OF BENEFITS

In examining alternative proposals for improving social security benefit structures, we must address issues about choices which are not necessarily mutually exclusive, for they can combine different but nonconflicting approaches. For example:

Should we pursue wage-related benefits, providing differential payments to low and high earners, or benefits providing, at the minimum, amounts sufficient to lift beneficiaries out of poverty?

Should benefits be adjusted to the presumed needs of larger families? If so, should dependents' allowances or family allowances be employed to deal with the presumed needs of larger families?

Should benefits be adjusted automatically to changes in the price level?

Should benefits under state or federal-state programs be made subject to national minimum levels?

The question whether benefits would be strictly wage-related or provide above-poverty-line subsistence is not an "either-or" choice; statutory minimum and maximum benefits take account of individual or family subsistence needs as well as wage relatedness. The issue has been aired most frequently in discussion of the OASDHI program, with figures such as Pechman and

Schorr[10] supporting above-poverty-line minimum benefits; and Cohen, Brown, Tobin, and Burns,[11] among others, holding more strongly to the wage-related principle (though at substantially higher than current levels), with public assistance or other measures providing supplementation where the insurance benefit falls below subsistence. The new minimum OASDHI benefit for workers with substantial (20-year) covered employment is not likely to reach most workers with below-poverty-line benefits, and many of them are likely to continue to need supplementation from old-age assistance. Social security neither does nor can carry the entire burden of ameliorating and preventing poverty. We must increase its effectiveness in preventing workers and their families from slipping into poverty by increasing pensions, unemployment, and disability benefits to the point where the role left to public assistance is essentially residual. Federalization of the adult (aged, blind, and disabled) assistance programs, effective in 1974, should provide a more adequate level of supplementary assistance than heretofore; since it is limited to only every third public assistance recipient, similar improvement of family dependency remains our major gap in family security.

Benefits under both federal and state insurance programs have not taken account of wage-earners' family requirements, in that most do not include dependents' allowances (only 11 state unemployment insurance laws and 5 workmen's compensation laws do so), and, where they do, in OASDHI for example, benefit ceilings limit allowances to a maximum of two children. No higher benefit is paid to larger families, even though more than 40 percent of the children in survivor benefit families are in families with three or more children. Benefit ceilings which reduce larger families to below-poverty benefit levels should be lifted if recourse to public assistance is to be minimized.

Because dependents' allowances in social insurance represent a departure from wage-related benefits, and because amounts are limited because of this constraint, they fall short of providing

10. A. Schorr, "Income Maintenance and Social Security," in *Social Welfare Forum* (New York: Columbia University Press, 1970), p. 37; and Pechman, Aaron, and Taussig, *Social Security.*

11. James Tobin in *Agenda for the Nation*, ed. K. Gordon (Washington: Brookings Institution, 1968), pp. 94–96; Cohen, *Encyclopedia of Social Work*, 1971, pp. 1284–94; Brown, *Social Insurance.*

adequately for larger families. Thus an alternative approach in the form of children's allowances has been recommended by Eveline Burns and others. If the presumed needs of children were met by children's allowances and financed from general revenues, the standard benefit could provide a higher proportion of prior earnings. Children's allowances go to more of the non-poor than the poor, but the resulting higher costs of using this device to aid large families among the poor can be shifted to the well-to-do through the progressive income tax, as suggested by Brazer,[12] among others.

In OASDHI, as well as unemployment insurance and workmen's compensation, where benefits lag behind prices, the newly adopted escalator clauses provide more effective protection for the purchasing power of benefits, especially when they are the sole or major income of beneficiaries and their families. Benefits were the major source of income of at least one fourth of beneficiary couples and two fifths of single persons newly entitled to OASDHI benefits in July–December 1969.[13]

Although adjustment to price level changes may serve the needs of those receiving short-term benefits (such as unemployment and workmen's compensation), the adequacy of long-term benefit programs requires consideration of other issues. The failure to adjust benefits to secular wage changes (productivity gains) hurts families relying on long-term pensions, especially those receiving retirement, invalidity, and survivors' benefits. When monthly benefits are payable for as long as 20 years or more, the wage base on which the benefit was determined will have become obsolete as wage levels reflect gains in the economy's productivity; periodic updating of the wage base for recipients of long-term pensions, as has been done in other countries, would avoid penalizing pensioners for their longevity by forcing them to subsist on pensions calculated on an obsolete wage history.

The failure of state action to bring unemployment insurance

12. H. Brazer, "The Federal Income Tax and the Poor: Where Do We Go from Here?" *California Law Review,* April 1969, pp. 422–449; see also, Dorothy S. Projector, "Children's Allowances and Income Tested Supplements: Costs and Redistributive Effects," *Social Security Bulletin,* Feb. 1970, pp. 3–14.

13. Lenore Bixby, "Income of the Aged: Overview from the 1968 Survey," *Social Security Bulletin,* April 1970.

benefits up to widely accepted standards, despite prodding by five Presidents, makes federal minimum benefit standards necessary.

LENGTHENING THE DURATION OF BENEFITS

Although social security payments may be adequate in replacing prior earnings or meeting subsistence needs where unemployment or disability is of average length, workers without earnings for longer periods still face major financial problems. For example, while unemployed workers at any given time in 1971 were out of work an average of 11–12 weeks, more than one-half million were jobless for more than six months, and during that year 2 million were still without work when their unemployment benefits were exhausted.[14] When such inadequate protection belies the promise of social insurance to safeguard workers and their families against slipping into poverty and dependency, it thereby fails to prevent the undermining of living standards, the basic purpose of social security and its contribution to society's health and welfare.

Unemployment insurance is particularly subject to the strain of downturns in economic activity, which adds to unemployment; this must be compensated for by adequate duration of benefits. The 1970 standby extended benefit program for periods of recession – unemployment might have been able to cope with a less severe recession, but it failed to tide hundreds of thousands of jobless over their unemployment during 1971–72. Even when supplemented by two emergency extensions of up to 13 more weeks each, the additional protection was inadequate for many jobless, for the new extensions were operative in fewer and fewer states. The AFL-CIO contended that while 2 million workers exhausted their benefits in 1971, only 400,000 received extended benefits.[15]

The program's failure to tide many workers over their prolonged unemployment calls attention to other weaknesses in unemployment insurance and other measures to deal with unem-

---

14. *Manpower Report of the President*, 1972, Table A-20; *Social Security Bulletin*, Sept., 1972, Table M-23.
15. *AFL-CIO News*, 1 April 1972.

ployment. We have already noted that as few as one third of the jobless at any given time receive unemployment compensation. Alongside the restricted coverage, eligibility, and other benefit provisions, the system carried more than $10 billion in reserves over from 1971 to 1972.

But correction of deficiencies in benefit and financing provisions by federal minimum standards, although necessary and overdue, will not address other persistent problems of fitting manpower and income maintenance policy together more effectively. Unemployment insurance is not suited to carry responsibility for remedying deficiencies in education and training of the hundreds of thousands who find themselves disadvantaged in getting decently paid jobs promising training and advancement; nor can it meet the retraining needs of those whose skills have been made obsolete by changing technology, or of the women who reenter the work force as their children begin to require less home care. Where appropriations fall short of meeting needs for expanded counseling, reeducation, and training, and for adequate allowances for those in training and education courses, utilization of unemployment insurance reserves for this purpose would prove more constructive than continuing to hold them in frozen benefit reserves.

Finally, our past measures for job creation have been far too modest and cautious to absorb disadvantaged jobless workers and to meet the underfinanced requirements of the public sector. We must go beyond the effort of the Emergency Employment Act of 1971, which provided jobs for only 3 percent of the jobless.[16]

OTHER BENEFIT ISSUES

Our attitude toward the appropriate pensionable and retirement ages for older workers reflects an incongruent mixture of

16. Sar A. Levitan, "Manpower Policy for a Healthy Economy," mimeographed (Paper presented at the International Conference on Trends in Industrial and Labor Relations, Tel Aviv, Jan. 9, 1972, pp. 13–14). Increased spending on education and training as a public investment is supported by Herbert Stringer, *Continuing Education as a National Capital Investment* (Washington: W. E. Upjohn Institute for Employment Research, 1972). See also L. Levine, *The Role of Unemployment Insurance in National Manpower Policies* (Kalamazoo: W. E. Upjohn Institute for Employment Research, 1972).

goals of public policy. Employment discrimination against the aged is a violation of their civil rights, as a matter of law, and we are increasing public spending to promote and expand their employment opportunities. Yet when we provide for an "early" pensionable age (at a reduced benefit amount) are we, with the other hand, encouraging early retirement? Rather than pursuing conflicting policy goals, are we not enabling older workers to choose between continuing at work and obtaining access to continuing income at an earlier age should they retire earlier, voluntarily, or under pressure from a combination of declining work capacity and shrinking work opportunities? But many who "choose" early retirement have suffered very real disadvantages. Compared to those retiring at age 65 or later, they have lower earnings, more irregular employment records, and are more likely to suffer physical disability. For them, early retirement is involuntary, and their lower lifetime earnings produce a lower than average pension; these already lower pensions also are subject to actuarial reduction, often to a subpoverty level. More nearly adequate protection can be provided by selective benefit increases to single persons and larger families and higher minimum benefits, or some combination of these.

A more important issue, however, relates to increasing the flexibility of both the retirement and pensionable age: gradually reduced work schedules and work effort requirement would enable older workers to continue to work and to earn, according to their working capacity as they age. More effective elimination of age discrimination plus expanded occupational health services would make it possible for older workers to continue working as long as they are capable of doing so. Disability which is "compensable" should take account of its often gradual onset and its impact on earnings and employment opportunities.

WOMEN WORKERS AND SOCIAL SECURITY

As the number of women in jobs under social security has increased, the adequacy of their social security protection is being reexamined.[17] Movement into the work force has been especially marked for married as compared to single women. In

17. See Bixby, "Women and Social Security," pp. 3–11.

1940, 27 percent of the women participated in the labor force; the figure was up to 43 percent by 1971, and to 50 percent for those between 20 and 65.[18] Married women (with husband present) entered the work force even more rapidly, the proportion increasing from 15 to 41 percent in 1940–1971, thus increasing the number of multiworker households. More specifically, 51 percent of all wives had some work experience in 1970, the majority being full-time workers working at least 27 weeks in that year.[19]

A few examples will illustrate incongruities in treatment of women under social security, although the issues deserve fuller treatment than attempted here. The OASDHI system looks upon a couple, both working, as a family unit and pays a wife's benefit at 50 percent of the husband's PIA to the spouse, as it would if she had never worked. However, if she is entitled to a higher benefit on her own account, her benefit is computed as though she were single. Dependent's benefits, if the couple has minor children, are computed in terms of the husband's benefit. Pechman, noting that the couple's joint income tax liability is based upon their aggregate earnings, suggests that benefits, too, should be based upon total family earnings to produce higher retirement income. We also hear it suggested that women should acquire benefit rights on the basis of services in child care, household management, etc., just as other persons receive when performing such services for pay. Such questions as these surely will receive more attention in the future.

The unemployment insurance system contains several characteristics carried over from original presumptions. The system, when established, seemingly provided benefits to replace a portion of the income of the displaced *sole* family wage earner. Although the wage-related benefit was the same, in principle, whether or not he was a member of a multiearner household, no family member was treated as his "compensable" dependent (where dependent's benefits are paid) if she had more than nominal earnings, or was eligible to receive unemployment benefits. Increased participation of married women in the insured

18. *Manpower Report of the President*, 1972, pp. 192–196.
19. Ibid., pp. 192–193; and U.S. Department of Labor, Bureau of Labor Statistics, *Work Experience of the Population in 1970*, Special Labor Force Report no. 141 (1972), Table A-6.

labor force should lead to reexamination of presumptions such as these, especially when we note that wives participate in the labor force in greater numbers when their husbands are out of work; among unemployed husbands, 50 percent had wives working or seeking work in 1970, but among employed husbands the figure was only 44 percent.[20]

Other provisions raise sharper questions of unequal treatment; 23 states disqualify women who leave work (or are laid off) during pregnancy.[21] The penalties, in terms of lost or deferred benefit, go beyond standard provisions withholding benefits from claimants who are physically or mentally unable to work or who are unavailable for work. In the same category are provisions disqualifying claimants (usually women) who leave work to marry (11 states) or to move to another area with a spouse (7 states). While the courts are increasingly finding that such provisions deny "equal protection of the laws" to women workers, general reexamination of the rationale behind such provisions is yet to take place.

FINANCING

Social security programs, financed primarily by payroll taxes, account for nearly one fifth of all federal revenues and federal spending. They rank second to the personal income tax in tax collections and second to national defense in spending. Social security and social welfare do not occupy an equally important position in state and local revenues; state and local governmental transfer payments accounted for about one tenth of their expenditures in 1970,[22] and drew upon general revenues more than upon payroll taxes.

The payroll tax is widely accepted as an appropriate source of social security financing, both here and abroad, although other western countries tend to use tripartite financing, and supple-

20. U.S. Department of Labor, Bureau of Labor Statistics, *Marital and Family Characteristics of the Labor Force,* Special Labor Force Report no. 144 (1972), Table P.

21. U.S. Department of Labor, *Comparison of State Unemployment Insurance Laws,* Table 407. In eleven other states they are deemed to be unavailable for work.

22. *1971 Economic Report of the President,* p. 280.

ment payroll taxes with earmarked sales and income tax revenues. The tax has come under increasing criticism in this country, as bearing heavily on low earners, because it does not take account of ability to pay. As the taxable wage limit has risen from the original $3,000 base — to $4,200 (in 1972) in unemployment insurance, and to $10,800 (in 1973) for OASDI — its incidence became less regressive and will become even less so with further increases in 1974 and thereafter.

Other changes and reforms in social security financing referred to above concern more adequate financing of benefits as well as more equitable distribution of benefit costs. Higher taxes of whatever form are rarely applauded by taxpayers who feel overburdened with taxes. Yet as a nation with among the lowest tax burdens of all highly industrial states, objections to more adequate social services, requiring more revenues, must yield to compelling social needs of the poor, the cities, the ill-housed, and of those receiving substandard health and medical care.

The following suggested changes in social security financing make no claim to originality; they draw upon proposals which advisory councils and specialists have frequently put forward to strengthen the financial base and distribute costs more equitably.

In the OASDI program, for example:

1. The taxable wage base, increasing to $12,000 in 1974, is to be adjusted thereafter in accordance with average wages. An increase to $15,000 by 1975, however, would go further toward taxing the full earnings of higher-paid workers, as is done for the lower paid. While the moderate increase in revenues obtained thereby would not make it possible to reduce contribution rates appreciably, the change appears justified in terms of equity.

2. Low-income workers who pay contributions at a greater proportion of their earnings than do higher earners and whose payroll taxes, a first claim on wages, already account for 6 percent of their gross income, should be given some relief from the incidence of a tax levied without relation to ability to pay and, for a great many, at a higher level than the personal income tax. Although complete relief from social security contributions would be inconsistent with the contributory nature of the program, partial tax relief should be allowed.

3. General revenues now cover as much as one fifth of the costs of Medicare (according to the 1971 Advisory Council

Report) but a far smaller portion of the cost of cash benefits. A persuasive case has been made for increasing general revenue financing of Medicare to one third to provide relief from the substantial costs of protecting those already aged in 1965, a cost which bears heavily on the currently employed. Wage earners and their employers have carried the cost of cash benefits since 1936 for those who retired early in the program's history, because they were already along in years when benefits first became payable and for those brought into the system when coverage was broadened substantially during the 1950s. General revenues should help to cover the costs of cash benefits, relieving current earners and their employers of some part of the entire burden. General revenue financing of one fifth of cash benefit costs has been recommended, thus making desirable benefit improvements possible at lower cost to current and future contributors.

4. Finally, in addition to bringing the disabled under Medicare, the cost of physicians' services under Part B of that program bears far too heavily upon the aged who pay the monthly premiums out of reduced incomes—for most, from their retirement benefits. It seems thoroughly preferable to finance such protection from current contributions paid during workers' working life as is done for other parts of the OASDHI program.

In unemployment insurance, as well, several desirable changes in financing under discussion for some years have not been acted upon, even under the 1970 amendments; inaction has impaired the program's capacity to protect jobless workers suffering wage loss. Employers in industries experiencing low unemployment, often because of the very nature of the industry, qualified for exemption from contributions entirely, or for tax rates under .5 percent. In order to distribute the system's costs more equitably, no employer should be permitted to pay less than a minimum rate of contributions—perhaps no less than 1 percent of payrolls. The federal law permits employer contribution rates to be reduced only upon the basis of the benefits paid to their former workers. The undesirable effects of this federal standard have been mentioned earlier, for it has helped create an adversary relationship between employers and workers concerning rights to benefits, and contributed to the reintroduction of interstate competition in taxes and benefits. Increasingly, students of the program agree that the federal law should permit employer tax rates to be modified upon the basis of other criteria which would measure employment turnover, for example, without regard to payment of benefits. It would be equally desirable for individual employer's rates to vary above and below the industry's average rate. But the justification for employer experience rating in unemployment insurance still is questionable and should be reexamined, perhaps by a congressional or presidential body (for the first time since 1934).[23]

SUMMING UP

In identifying the challenges and opportunities of the social security programs in the 1970s, pressures for alleviation and prevention of poverty pressed heavily against programs delivering wage-related benefits. As Alvin Schorr put it, "wage-related benefits do most for those who have earned the most . . . [and] conversely, the more that the program does for people who are poor, the less it seems to be related to prior earnings."[24]

Yet we need not assume the position that wage-related benefits should be put aside in favor of benefits calculated to meet individual and family needs in order for social security to do more for poverty prevention and alleviation. One fifth of the aged, disabled, and survivors, directly exposed to the risk of poverty and dependency by loss of earnings, would be poor except for their social security payments; specifically, three of every four aged who receive social security would be poor were it not for their benefits.[25] This is not to say that social security payments have done enough, or as much as they could, to prevent people from slipping into poverty when the family breadwinner's earnings disappear. It is certain that social security could do more. The 1972 benefit increase of 20 percent went beyond adjusting for price changes since the preceeding benefit

23. See Becker, *Experience Rating.*
24. National Conference on Social Welfare, *Social Welfare Forum* (New York: Columbia University Press, 1970), p. 37.
25. Ibid., p. 39.

increase. Others have favored more substantial benefit increases.[26]

Recent history of moves to improve the benefit levels of wage-related and means-tested programs demonstrates more favorable treatment of the former. Taking the most recent experiences, for example, while average monthly benefits in the adult public assistance programs increased about 5 percent between 1969 and 1971, and AFDC rose about 15 percent, average OASDI benefits had increased by 30 percent.[27] Even the nationwide uniform maximum monthly assistance payment of $130 for adults and $195 for a couple, adopted in October 1972, although higher than the minimum OASDI benefit, does not assure the recipient a higher income than the social security beneficiary would have. The public assistance payment is a maximum, including other income less earnings or other disregarded resources. The social security payment, by contrast, is a minimum, to which workers may add earnings (subject to the retirement test), plus other retirement pensions and unearned income. The social security approach posseses a more important quality; it avoids the stigma and restrictions of assistance plans, which increasingly have put pressures on recipients to accept substandard jobs, even if paying less than minimum wages. Increased social security benefits should make it possible for fewer people, rather than more of them, to be forced to resort to public assistance for supplementary help and, as Schorr has put it, avoid "catching up in the net of public assistance or income testing a larger proportion of the population than is absolutely necessary."[28]

Health care and income maintenance for the disabled remain the most frustrating and gnawing gap in social security protection of American workers and their families. Fortunately, recent renewal of interest in comprehensive health insurance ap-

26. W. J. Cohen urged a 25 percent increase in 1972 and again for 1974. "A Look Ahead: Social Welfare in the Decade of the 70s," *Public Welfare*, Winter 1972, p. 59.
27. See *Social Security Bulletin*, April 1972, Table M-24, p. 50; SSA-ORS, *Monthly Benefit Statistics: Calendar Year Benefit Data*, 1971 (Washington, 1972).
28. National Conference on Social Welfare, *Social Welfare Forum*, 1970, p. 42.

proaches offers the potentiality of lowered financial barriers to medical care and reforms in the organization and delivery of services. Equally, it may pry open the door to an all-embracing approach to work-connected and nonwork-connected, short- and long-term disability, putting aside distinctions (once designed to assure protection to those who fell into defined categories), which have been encrusted with procedures which obstruct coverage and benefit protection. A breakthrough for progress in this direction may be facilitated by recent federal initiatives, including social security protection of the victims of coal miners' "black lung" and possible action on the report of the 1972 National Commission on State Workmen's Compensation Laws.

Reform of unemployment insurance and equally belated reformulation of the relationship of compensation, retraining, and education of the unemployed calls for similar federal initiative and a congressionally directed study of these programs.

President Nixon's message of April 1973 on unemployment insurance reforms, including a national minimum standard for weekly benefits and coverage of certain farm workers (both long overdue), may lead to even broader improvements. One might hope that the Congress would see fit to add improved duration of benefits for the long term jobless, recognizing the weaknesses of the 1970 extended benefit program that was demonstrated in the 1971–1973 depression. In breaking with longstanding reluctance to require the states to meet federal weekly benefit standards, it may not be surprising that the President also called for federal prohibition of benefit payments to strikers, a controversial provision found in only two states.[29]

Thus the promise of more adequate social security protection for American workers and their families can come closer to realization through increasing the capabilities of these programs to provide more adequate safeguards "against misfortunes which cannot be wholly eliminated in this manmade world of ours."[30]

29. See *Congressional Record,* 12 April 1973, pp. H.2652–2654; and *The New York Times,* Editorial, 17 April 1973.

30. From Executive Order creating Committee on Economic Security, quoted in *Report to the President of the Committee on Economic Security,* 15 Jan. 1935, p. v.

APPENDIX A

Selected Benefit Provisions of
State Unemployment Insurance Laws, 1972

State	Method of Computing[1]	Minimum Weekly[2] Benefit	Maximum Weekly[2] Benefit
		High-quarter formula	
Alabama	1/26[1]	$15.00	$60.00
Arizona	1/25	10.00	60.00
Arkansas	1/26	15.00	67.00
California	1/24-1/27	25.00	75.00
Colorado	1/22[4]	14.00	86.00
Connecticut	1/26 + d.a.	15.00-20.00	86.00-129.00
Delaware	1/25	10.00	65.00
D.C.	1/23 + d.a.	14.00-15.00	105.00[2]
Georgia	1/25	12.00	55.00
Hawaii	1/25	5.00	90.00
Idaho	1/26	17.00	68.00
Illinois	1/20-1/25[1]	10.00[2]	51.00-97.00[2]
Indiana	1/25 + d.a.[1]	20.00[2]	45.00-65.00[2]
Iowa	1/20	9.00	68.00
Kansas	1/25	16.00[5]	64.00
Kentucky	1/23	12.00	68.00
Louisiana	1/20-1/25	10.00	70.00
Maine	1/22	12.00	63.00
Maryland	1/24 + d.a.	10.00-13.00	78.00[2]
Mississippi	1/26	10.00	49.00
Missouri	1/25	12.00	63.00
Montana	1/26	12.00	52.00
Nebraska	1/19-1/23	12.00	60.00
Nevada	1/25	16.00	77.00
New Mexico	1/26	13.00[5]	61.00
North Dakota	1/26	15.00	62.00
Oklahoma	1/26	16.00	60.00
Pennsylvania	1/21-1/25[6]	12.00-17.00	85.00-93.00
South Carolina	1/26[4]	10.00	59.00
South Dakota	1/22-1/24	12.00	55.00
Tennessee	1/26	14.00	57.00
Texas	1/25	15.00	63.00
Utah	1/26	10.00	81.00
Virginia	1/25	20.00	70.00
Washington	1/25	17.00	78.00
Wyoming	1/25	10.00	63.00
		Annual-wage formula	
Alaska	2.3-1.1 + d.a.	$18.00-23.00	$60.00-85.00
New Hampshire	1.7-1.2	14.00	75.00
North Carolina	2.0-1.1	12.00	60.00
Oregon	1.25	20.00	62.00
West Virginia	1.6-0.8	12.00	75.00

Social Security in America

Average-weekly-wage formula

Florida	50	$10.00	$64.00
Massachusetts[3]	50 + d.a.	12.00-18.00	74.00-111.00
Michigan	63-55 + d.a.[1]	16.00-18.00[2]	56.00-92.00
Minnesota	50	15.00	64.00
New Jersey	66⅔	10.00	76.00
New York	67-50	20.00	75.00
Ohio	50 + d.a.[1]	10.00-16.00	57.00-87.00
Rhode Island	55 + d.a.	12.00-17.00	79.00-99.00
Vermont	50	15.00	77.00
Wisconsin	50	22.00[5]	88.00

1. When state uses a weighted high-quarter formula, annual-wage formula or average-weekly-wage formula, approximate fractions or percentages are taken at midpoint of lowest and highest normal wage brackets. When additional payments are provided for claimants with dependents, the fractions and percentages shown apply to the basic benefit amounts.

2. When 2 amounts are given, higher figure includes dependents' allowances. (Augmented amount for minimum weekly benefit includes allowance for 1 dependent child; in Michigan, for 1 dependent child or 2 dependents other than a child. In Illinois and Indiana to claimants with HQW in excess of those required for maximum basic wba. Augmented amount for maximum weekly benefit includes allowances for maximum number of dependents; in D.C. and Maryland, same maximum with or without dependents.)

3. For individuals with an aww of $66.00 or less, benefit formula in Massachusetts is based on a weighted schedule of approximately 1/21-1/26 of HQW. An aww formula is used for all other claimants.

4. Wba expressed in law as percent of aww in HQ; in Colorado 60 percent of 1/13 of HQW; 50 percent in South Carolina (aww defined as 1/13 of HQW). Colorado provides an alternative method of computation for claimants who would otherwise qualify for a wba equal to 50 percent or more of the statewide aww if this yields a greater amount—50 percent of 1/52 of BPW with a maximum of 60 percent of statewide aww in selected industries.

5. Minimum computed annually in New Mexico at 10 percent of aww. In Kansas and Wisconsin, minimum computed at 25 percent of maximum wba—Kansas computed annually and Wisconsin semiannually.

6. Or 50 percent of full-time weekly wage, if greater.

Source: U.S. Department of Labor, *Comparison of State Unemployment Insurance Laws*, Revised August 1972, adapted from Table 304.

APPENDIX B

Significant Events in Social Security Legislation

1934

June 8 President Roosevelt's message to Congress on Social Security; Committee on Economic Security appointed.

1935

Jan 17 Report of Committee on Economic Security sent to Congress with legislative recommendations.

Aug 14 Social Security Act signed. (PL 74-271 [date of enactment])

Aug 23 Members of Social Security Board appointed.

Aug 29 Railroad Retirement Act signed. (PL 74-399)

1936

Jan 1 Federal unemployment tax of 1 percent levied on employers of 8 or more (raised to 2 percent in 1937, and 3 percent in 1938).

Aug 17 Wisconsin issues first unemployment insurance check.

1937

Jan 1 Old age benefit tax of 1 percent levied on employers and workers.

May 24 Supreme Court holds federal and state taxes for old age benefits and unemployment insurance constitutional (301 U.S. 495, 548, 619).

1938

June 25 Railroad Unemployment Insurance Act becomes law.

1939

July 1 Social Security Board absorbed by Federal Security Agency.

Aug 10 Benefits payable to dependents and survivors of retired workers; date of payment advanced to 1940; contribution rates held to 1 percent through 1942 (successively postponed through 1949). (PL 76-400)

1940

Jan 1 OASI benefits first payable

1942†

April 29 Rhode Island enacts first state temporary disability insurance (TDI) law for workers covered by unemployment insurance.

1944

June 22   GI Bill of Rights provides servicemen's readjustment (unemployment) allowances for unemployed and self-employed veterans of World War II. (PL 78-346)

1946

July 16   Social Security Administration replaces Social Security Board.

July 31   RR Act and RRUI Act establish survivors, sickness, and maternity benefits. (PL 79-572)

Aug 10   OASI benefits for survivors of World War II veterans; temporary unemployment insurance benefits to seamen with wartime employment; states permitted to use worker's unemployment insurance contributions for TDI. (PL 79-719)

1949

Aug 20   Bureau of Employment Security transferred to Labor Department.

1950*†

Aug 28   10 million more workers covered, including regular farm and domestic workers and most nonfarm self-employed and federal workers; on a voluntary basis, to state and local government workers not under retirement system; retirement test and eligibility liberalized; wage credits (noncontributory) of $160 per month for military service, Sept. 1940-July 1947. (PL 81-734)

1951

Oct 30   RRB and SSA programs coordinated with financial interchange; SSA covers RR workers with less than 10 years service. (PL 82-234)

1952*

July 16   Unemployment benefits for Korean vets. (PL 82-550)

July 18   OASI retirement test liberalized; military wage credits extended through 1953 (and later to April 1956). (PL 82-590)

1953

April 11   Department of HEW replaced Federal Security Agency.

Aug 5   Federally employed seamen covered by unemployment insurance. (PL 83-196)

1954*†

Aug 5   Loan (Reed) fund established for states with depleted unemployment insurance reserves. (PL 83-567)

Sept 1   Social Security coverage of self-employed farmers and additional farm and domestic workers; voluntarily, of members of state and local retirement systems; retirement test liberalized; benefit rights of disabled protected through "disability"; (PL 83-761).

Unemployment insurance coverage of employers of four or more and of federal civilian workers (PL 83-767); vets added in 1958. (PL 85-848)

1956

Aug 1   Monthly benefits to permanent-totally disabled age 50-64 (age 50 limit dropped in 1960); child's benefit to disabled children of retired or disabled workers if disability began pre-age 18; early retirement at age 62 for women workers and wives, at reduced benefit; coverage of self-employed professionals (MDs in 1965) and armed forces (on contributory basis). (PL 84-880)

1958*†

June 4   Extended unemployment insurance to workers exhausting state benefits through March 1959 (later to June 30, 1959). (PL 85-441)

Aug 28   Dependents' benefits for disabled workers; retirement test liberalized. (PL 85-840)

1959

May 19   RRB and RRUI benefits, contribution rates, and wage base modified; permanent plan of extended RRUI benefits. (Pl 86-28)

1960†

Sept 13   Retirement test and qualifying requirement liberalized; disability coverage extended. (PL 86-778)

1961*

March 24   Extended unemployment insurance benefits (to March 31, 1962) to workers exhausting state benefits. (PL 87-6)

June 30   Early retirement for men, age 62, with reduced benefits; eligibility and retirement test liberalized. (PL 87-64)

1965*†

July 30   Hospital and supplementary physicians' services (Medicare) for those eligible for retirement or RRB benefits; liberalized retirement test and disability definition; widow's benefit at age 60 at reduced rate. (PL 89-97)

1966

March 15   Flat rate noncontributory benefit for noninsured age 72 and over. (PL 89-368)

1968

Jan 2   Retirement test liberalized; disability definition tightened; armed forces wage credits increased; medicare benefits modified. (PL 90-248)

1969*†

Dec 30   Benefits increased for persons age 72+ and for other beneficiaries. (PL 91-172)
Federal Coal Mine Safety and Health Act provided cash and medical benefits for victims of pneumoconiosis (black lung). (PL 91-173)

1970

Aug 10   Unemployment insurance coverage of firms with one or more, and to state and nonprofit employment; tax base and tax rate increased; permanent extended benefit program set up. (PL 91-373)

Aug 12   RRB benefits increased; study of railroad retirement system authorized. (PL 91-377)

Dec 29   Occupational Safety and Health Act requires study of state workmen's compensation. (PL 91-596)

1971*†

March 17	Benefits, taxes, and wage base increased. (PL 92-5)
July 2	Increased RRB benefits. (PL 92-46)
Dec 29	Additional unemployment insurance benefits to those exhausting state rights. (PL 92-224)

1972*†

June 30	Emergency unemployment benefits extended 6 months. (PL 92-329)
July 1	OASI benefits tied to price index; taxable wage base tied to average wages. (PL 92-336)
Oct 20	Revenue Sharing Act places ceiling on federal funds for matching state social service expenditures, effective July 1, 1972. (PL 92-512)
Oct 27	Longshoremen's Compensation Act increased coverage and benefits for dock workers and privately employed workers in D.C.; benefits tied to average weekly wages; flexible maximum benefit set at $167 until 9/30/73. (PL 92-576)
Oct 30	Medicare extended to disabled and persons with severe kidney disease; higher benefits for long service workers and delayed retirement; widows benefit increased; programs for old age assistance, aid to the blind and disabled replaced as of Jan 1, 1974 by national Supplementary Security Income program, with minimum benefits federally financed and administered by SSA. (PL 92-603)

---

* Benefits for OASDI increased, see Table 3.
† OASDI tax rates and taxable wage base modified; see Table IX.

SELECTED REFERENCES

Books

Adams, Leonard P. *Public Attitudes towards Unemployment Insurance*. Kalamazoo: W. E. Upjohn Institute for Employment Research, 1971.

Altmeyer, Arthur J. *The Formative Years of Social Security*. Madison: University of Wisconsin Press, 1966.

Bailey, Stephen K. *Congress Makes a Law: The Story behind the Employment Act of 1946*. New York: Columbia University Press, 1950.

Becker, Joseph M. *Guaranteed Income for the Unemployed: The Story of SUB*. Baltimore: Johns Hopkins University Press, 1968.

Becker, Joseph M., ed. *In Aid of the Unemployed*. Baltimore: Johns Hopkins University Press, 1965.

Becker, Joseph M. *Experience Rating in Unemployment Insurance: Virtue or Vice*. Kalamazoo: W. E. Upjohn Institute for Employment Research, 1972.

Beveridge, Sir William. *Social Insurance and Allied Services*. New York: MacMillan Co., 1942.

Bowen, W. G., et al., eds. *The American System of Social Insurance*. New York: McGraw-Hill, 1968.

Brittain, John A. *The Payroll Tax for Social Security*. Washington: Brookings Institution, 1972.

Brown, J. Douglas. *An American Philosophy of Social In-*

surance: Evaluation and Issues. Princeton: Princeton University Press, 1972.

Burns, Eveline M. *Social Security and Public Policy.* New York: McGraw-Hill, 1956.

Carroll, John J. *Alternative Methods of Financing Old Age, Survivors, and Disability Benefits.* Ann Arbor: Institute of Public Administration, 1960.

Cheit, Earl F. *Injury and Recovery in the Course of Employment.* New York: John Wiley & Sons, 1954.

Cohen, Wilbur J. *Retirement Policies under Social Security.* Berkeley and Los Angeles: University of California Press, 1957.

Cohen, W. J. and Milton Friedman. *Social Security: Universal or Selective?* Washington: American Enterprise Institute, 1972.

George, V. N. *Social Security: Beveridge and After.* London: Kegan Paul, 1968.

Gersh, Harry, ed. *Employee Benefits Fact Book, 1972.* New York: Martin E. Segal Co., 1972.

Goodman, L. H., ed. *Economic Progress and Social Welfare.* New York: Columbia University Press, 1966.

Gordon, Kermit, ed. *Agenda for the Nation.* Washington: Brookings Institution, 1968.

Haber, William and Wilbur J. Cohen. *Social Security: Programs, Problems, and Policies.* Homewood, Ill.: Irwin, 1960.

Haber, William and M. G. Murray. *Unemployment Insurance in the American Economy.* Homewood, Ill.: Irwin, 1966.

Harris, Richard. *A Sacred Trust.* New York: New American Library, 1966.

Lampman, R. J. *Ends and Means in Reducing Income Poverty.* Chicago: Markham, 1971.

Lester, R. A. *The Economics of Unemployment Compensation.* Princeton: Industrial Relations Section, 1962.

Levitan, Sar A. *Programs in Aid of the Poor for the 1970s.* Baltimore: Johns Hopkins University Press, 1969.

Lubove, Roy. *The Struggle for Social Security, 1900-1935.* Cambridge: Harvard University Press, 1961.

Macarov, D. *Incentives to Work.* San Francisco: Jossey-Bass, 1970.

Murray, M. G. *Income for the Unemployed: The Variety and*

Fragmentation of Programs. Kalamazoo: W. E. Upjohn Institute for Employment Research, 1971.

Murray, M. G. *Proposed Federal Unemployment Insurance Amendments.* Kalamazoo: W. E. Upjohn Institute for Employment Research, 1966.

Myers, R. J. *Social Insurance and Allied Government Programs.* New York: Irwin, 1965.

National Conference on Social Welfare. *Social Welfare Forum, 1970.* New York: Columbia University Press, 1970. (Especially papers by Eveline Burns and Alvin Schorr)

Pechman, J. A., H. R. Aaron, and M. K. Taussig. *Social Security: Perspectives for Reform.* Washington: Brookings Institution, 1968.

Rivlin, A. M. *Systematic Thinking for Social Action.* Washington: Brookings Institution, 1971.

Rohrlich, G. F., ed. *Social Economics for the 1970s.* Cambridge, Mass.: Dunellen, 1970.

Schorr, Alvin L. *Explorations in Social Policy.* New York: Basic Books, 1968.

Shottland, Charles. *The Social Security Program in the U.S.* New York: Appleton Century Crofts, 1970.

Somers, H. M. *Medicare and the Doctors.* Washington: Brookings Institution, 1966.

Somers, Herman and Ann Somers, *Workmen's Compensation.* New York: John Wiley & Sons, 1954.

Steiner, G. Y. *The State of Welfare.* Washington: Brookings Institution, 1971.

Sundquist, James L. *Politics and Policy.* Washington: Brookings Institution, 1968.

Titmuss, R. M. *Essays on the Welfare State.* London: Allen and Unwin, 1959.

Titmuss, R. M. *Income Distribution and Social Change.* Toronto: University of Toronto Press, 1962.

Vasey, Wayne. *Government and Social Welfare.* New York: Holt, Rinehart, and Winston, 1958.

Wilcox, Clair. *Toward Social Welfare.* New York: Irwin, 1969.

Witte, Edwin E. *Development of the Social Security Act.* Madison: University of Wisconsin Press, 1962.

Witte, Edwin E. *Social Security Perspectives.* Madison: University of Wisconsin Press, 1962.

Journal Articles

Aaron, Henry. "Tax Exemptions, the Artful Dodge." *Transaction,* March 1969, pp. 4–6.

Berkowitz, Monroe and J. F. Burton Jr. "The Income Maintenance Objective in Workmen's Compensation." *Industrial and Labor Relations Review,* Oct. 1970 pp. 22–23.

Berkowitz, Monroe and W. C. Johnson. "Towards an Economics of Disability: The Magnitude and Structure of Transfer and Medical Costs." *Journal of Human Resources* 5: 271–279.

Booth, Philip. "Sickness Insurance and California Farm Workers." *Social Security Bulletin,* May 1968, pp. 3–13.

Booth, Philip. "The Temporary Extended Unemployment Compensation Act of 1961: A Legislative History." *Labor Law Journal,* Oct. 1961, pp. 909–921.

Brittain, John A. "The Incidence of Social Security Payroll Taxes." *American Economic Review,* March 1971, pp. 110–111.

Burns, Eveline M. "Health Services for All: Is Health Insurance the Answer?" *American Journal of Public Health* 59:9–18.

Cohen, Wilbur J. "Social Insurance." *Encyclopedia of Social Work, 1971,* p. 1283.

Cohen, Wilbur J. and R. J. Myers. "Social Security Amendments of 1950: Summary and Legislative History." *Social Security Bulletin,* Oct. 1950, pp. 3–14.

Davis, H. E. and A. Strasser. "Private Pension Plans, 1960–1969: An Overview." *Monthly Labor Review,* July 1970, pp. 45–57.

Fisher, Paul. "Developments and Trends in Social Security throughout the World." Address to the 17th General Assembly, International Social Security Asso., Cologne, Sept. 1970, pp. 17–25.

Haber, Lawrence D. "Disability, Work, and Income Maintenance: Prevalence of Disability in 1966." *Social Security Bulletin,* May 1968.

Haber, Lawrence D. "Identifying the Disabled: Concepts and Methods in the Measurement of Disability." *Social Security Bulletin,* Dec. 1967, p. 15.

Hickey, Joseph A. "A Report on State Unemployment Insurance Laws." *Monthly Labor Review,* Jan. 1972, pp. 22–30.

Johnson, Florence C. "Changes in Workmen's Compensation in 1971." *Monthly Labor Review,* Jan. 1972, p. 51.

Kolodrubetz, W. W. "Trends in Employee-Benefit Plans in the Sixties." *Social Security Bulletin,* April 1971, pp. 25–27.

Lowenstein, Regina. "Early Effects of Medicare on the Health Care of the Aged." *Social Security Bulletin,* April 1971, p. 3.

Mitchell, W. L. "Social Security Legislation in the 86th Congress." *Social Security Bulletin,* Nov. 1960, pp. 3–29.

Munts, Raymond. "Unemployment Insurance: Objectives for Today's Economy." *Manpower,* Aug. 1969, pp. 18–21.

Nash, D. C. "The Contribution of Life Insurance to Social Security in the United States." *International Labor Review,* July 1955, pp. 24–25.

Okner, B. A. "Transfer Payments: Their Distribution and Role in Reducing Poverty." Address, Association for the Study of Grants Economy, American Association for the Advancement of Science, Dec. 1969.

Orshansky, Mollie. "Re-Counting the Poor: A Five Year Review." *Social Security Bulletin,* April 1966, p. 23.

Oswald, Rudolph and J. D. Smythe. "Fringe Benefits—On the Move." *American Federationist,* June 1970.

Pechman, Joseph A. "The Rich and the Poor and the Taxes They Pay." *The Public Interest,* Fall 1969, p. 30.

Price, Daniel N. "Cash Benefits for Short Term Illness, 1948–1970." *Social Security Bulletin,* Jan. 1972, pp. 19–29.

Reno, Virginia and C. Zuckert. "Benefit Levels of Newly Retired Workers: Findings from the Survey of New Beneficiaries." *Social Security Bulletin,* July 1971, pp. 3–31.

Rice, Dorothy P. "Financing Social Welfare: Health Care." *Encyclopedia of Social Work, 1971.*

Skolnik, Alfred. M. "Twenty-Five Years of Workmen's Compensation Statistics." *Social Security Bulletin,* Oct. 1966, p. 6.

Skolnik, Alfred M. and Sophie R. Dales. "Social Welfare Expenditures 1970–1971." *Social Security Bulletin,* Dec. 1971.

Skolnik, A. M. and D. N. Price. "Another Look at Workmen's Compensation." *Social Security Bulletin,* Oct. 1970.

List of Figures

List of Tables

Foreword

In the spring of 1970, the high cost of medical care was the subject of heated public debate. A number of legislative proposals testified to mounting demand for a response from government to escalating medical costs. But much of the research on the problem then focused on the roles of the medical profession and of hospitals in the delivery of health care and on the access of the poor to medical facilities. So the Trustees and staff of the Twentieth Century Fund were much interested in John Krizay's proposal to study the effects of health insurance on the cost structure of health care and on the allocation of resources in the United States. His objective was to determine whether private insurance carriers, which are heavily involved in financing medical costs, have the motivation or the means to control the quality and cost of health care, and whether they could contribute to the efficiency and quality of a universal health care system if the United States were to adopt one.

Mr. Krizay, director of the Office of Monetary Affairs in the Department of State, is an economist who developed a special interest in health care financing as the result of an expensive illness in his own family. At the suggestion of the Fund, he conducted his research in collaboration with Andrew Wilson, a senior economist and consultant at the Agency for International Development (AID) with considerable expertise in the economics of health care. Their differing vantage points have proved invaluable, permitting them to deal with health insurance from the perspectives of the insured, the insurers, and the providers of medical care.

In this report, Krizay and Wilson make some fundamental points that are often glossed over in the debate on health care financing. First, there is no such thing as "free" medical care; the public must pay for any expansion of government-subsidized health care. Second, the potential demand for "free" health care is unlimited. Taking these facts into account, the authors have boldly confronted the problem of arriving at a system of health care financing designed to make high quality medical facilities available on an equitable basis at costs that are both low yet apparent to the public as they are incurred.

President Nixon's 1974 State of the Union message calling for a universal system of health care financing, was a reflection of growing public demand. In their exposure of the issues to which any such system must respond, Messrs. Krizay and Wilson have made a significant contribution to public debate.

As in all Fund projects, the authors enjoyed complete independence. Their views are their own, not the Fund's. We are grateful, however, for their careful analysis of this important area of public concern and for the clarity with which they have presented their views.

M.J. Rossant, Director
The Twentieth Century Fund
February 1974

Preface

As research on this study proceeded, it became clear that there was no need for yet another study leading simply to another proposal for a national health insurance plan. It also became evident that there was an oversupply of literature exposing the nature of the "national health crisis," analyzing its origins, and hurling accusations at those who caused it or now benefit from its perpetuation.

National figures of every political persuasion have put forward their analyses and offered their solutions. As is often the case when debate over public issues becomes heated, there has been a tendency to seek out culprits, to designate someone or some group as the cause of the problem. It is difficult to admit that issues arise out of developments society was slow to note or reluctant to face, or that solutions may be complicated and need to be carefully considered.

From the reporting on the health insurance debate, one can take his choice of the causes of rising medical costs: excessive profits of insurance companies; collusion between Blue Cross and hospitals or Blue Shield and doctors; "cheating" of Medicare, Medicaid and private insurers by physicians and hospitals; excessive incomes of physicians. One reads of loopholes in health insurance plans that enable carriers to avoid paying claims, of the "failure" of the private sector to produce a more effective health insurance program, and of the inefficiency of the private sector compared with the public sector. It is said that physicians' fees should be controlled, that hospitals should be forced to accept "community planning," that peer review among doctors should be mandatory, and that "preventive medicine" should be the foundation of any national health insurance program.

This study attempts to unravel these various arguments and put them into an orderly context. The intended audience is the interested general public and those whose work affects the health care system—physicians and other providers; those employed in supporting the providers; health insurance executives and sales-people; and officials of firms, labor unions, and other employer and employee organizations who determine the quantity and quality of health insurance that millions of people enrolled in group plans will have. This audience is usually better informed about its constituency than about the interests of other components of the health care system.

A most important element of this study is its perspective. We assume, to begin with, that the nation will shortly adopt some kind of national health insurance plan. We therefore examine medical services and health care inflation less from the standpoint of personal cost than from that of cost to the entire community.

One of the most important unstated assumptions of the health insurance debate is that the public's need for health care resources is finite, ending when everyone is "well." But health, unlike beauty, is not entirely in the eye of the beholder. It has a large subjective component. As a result, the demand for medical services seems to increase as their availability increases. People are reluctant to consider the formulation of a policy that involves the rationing of medical services. And yet, freed of all economic restraints, consumer demand for medical services might well prove impossible to satisfy. Society may wish to apply a growing share of its resources toward making more medical services available. But in so doing, it should be fully aware that the same resources could be used to enhance the comfort of people in other ways. Medical service is but one way to better health and health care is but one way to a better life. Hence the basic question that prompts this study is *what share of total resources the nation should decide to commit to health care and how it should reach that decision* in its efforts to provide universal protection against the costs of health care.

The basic research for this study was done in late 1970 and early 1971, when the latest full-year statistics available were for 1969. It is therefore assumed throughout the analysis that 1969 data represent the current situation although later data are used in illustrative statements. The authors have determined, in examining more recent data, that a change in the figures would not appreciably affect the analysis. Up-to-date figures on the subjects covered in the analytical portions are readily available from the sources cited.

Many people contributed to this study and they deserve more prominent mention than is possible here. Those members of the staff who put the study together, checked the figures and sources, reorganized the manuscript, and typed it merit particular praise. Zula Peperis not only ran the office and typed the manuscript during the first year of the study but also did some of the basic research for documents, clippings, and other sources. In the second year the experienced editorial talents of Frances Klafter brought order and organization to the study, and Ellen Wernick assisted in preparation of the final manuscript for publication. Members of the part-time staff Dorothea D. Benedict, Jerry Brightman, Tom Fleming, Dorothy Lawrence, and Jim Harvitt all gave valuable assistance. John Victor Bower, who took time out from his graduate studies at George Washington University to do the research for Chapter 4, was particularly helpful. Finally, Judi Jacobson and Beverly Goldberg of the Twentieth Century Fund editorial staff deserve credit for having reduced a mammoth manuscript to manageable book length. Outside the staff, the officials of Blue Cross-Blue Shield, the Health Insurance Institute, various private carriers—especially Connecticut General, Travelers, and Prudential—as well as various officials of AT&T, Liggett and Myers, General Mills, and many other firms were most cooperative in discussing with us the problems of buying, selling, and paying for health insurance. Group Health Association of America and the Group Health Association, Inc. of Washington, D.C., gave us time and wisdom that was invaluable in interpreting the prepaid group movement, and private conversations with physicians and hospital officials too numerous to mention individually provided other insights that helped in interpreting the data we had assembled. Officials of the U.S. Civil Service Commission, the Office of Management and Budget, and especially the U.S. Department of Health, Education, and Welfare, provided not only valuable information but pertinent comments on parts of the draft.

1 Why Health Insurance Reform

In the half century or more that America has flirted with the idea of national health insurance, the nature of health care and its financing requirements have changed drastically. Especially since World War II, advances in medical science have made possible the diagnosis and treatment of many serious illnesses and chronic ailments that previously had gone undetected or untreated. The medical advances of the recent past and those now on the horizon indicate that new developments will not be predominantly cost saving; they are more likely to require additional resources for medical care. For this and other reasons, the national health bill is likely to continue to rise. National health insurance has thus become necessary to protect not only the poor—the traditional beneficiaries of national health insurance programs—but everyone else, except the very wealthy.

While protecting individuals against the cost of medical care, health insurance also amplifies those forces that are already causing a greater share of total national resources to be used for medical services. When services are free or substantially free, the user tends to use them more frequently. At the same time, it becomes easier for suppliers to develop and offer new services with little or no concern for their cost. This is, in fact, one of the objectives of national health insurance—to make available more medical services of better quality to more people. But, given the subjective nature of illness and the differences in approach and intensity of treatment and diagnoses, the establishment of a universal national health insurance program presents the problem of determining what share of the nation's total resources are to be used for health care. Once this service is made "free" to consumers, how will they collectively signal suppliers that they prefer the resources be used for this purpose rather than for air conditioning for low-income housing, better transportation, or better education, to suggest a few activities that also enhance comfort? If arbitrary limits are placed on expenditures for medical services, such as under government operated programs, the quantity and quality of services made available might be less than consumers would want, and that presents problems of distributing what is made available. On the other hand, if the traditional economic restraint—price—is left to operate even partially, the very objective of national health insurance may be frustrated. The challenge facing the health insurance movement in this era of advancing technology, therefore, is not so much one of finding a way to protect our citizenry against the cost of medical services but more one of finding a way to apply the optimal limits to the use of these services once protection against its cost is provided.

1

The National Health Insurance Movement

Long before advances in medical technology began raising the cost of medical care, establishment of a compulsory, universal system of payment for medical services had become a public issue in the United States. The 1912 campaign platform of the Progressive party included compulsory health insurance, which issue survived the party on the national scene. Over the years countless bills providing for some form of compulsory health insurance have been introduced in state legislatures, and numerous national health insurance bills have been proposed to the United States Congress.[1]

The failure of the movement, until the mid-1960s, to generate active, widespread public support and effective legislation is often attributed, somewhat unfairly, to the American Medical Association. In fact, when universal health insurance first became a national issue, the AMA did not oppose it, and important elements within the association even argued in favor of it. Not until 1920 did the AMA resolve to oppose all compulsory health insurance plans on principle. And although, for the next fifty years, it adhered to this position strongly and vociferously, it was not alone. During this period other powerful organizations inside and outside the medical profession (the American Bar Association among them) also opposed the establishment of a compulsory health insurance system.[2] But even if they had not opposed it, the public would still probably not have supported it. In the days before specialization, medical treatment was simpler and less costly, if less effective. Even when relatively heavy costs were incurred, the personal nature of doctor-patient relationships militated against arguments for the establishment of a bureaucratized national health care system.

These circumstances have changed; today many people support the principle of a universal health insurance system, and no important groups—not even the AMA—overtly oppose it. A number of factors have contributed to this change in attitude.

First, labor unions have been in the forefront of the health insurance reform movement because when they have succeeded in obtaining health insurance through collective bargaining, its rapidly rising cost has hindered their efforts to increase take-home pay and other fringe benefits. The unions are therefore seeking both broader health insurance coverage and a reform that would eliminate basic health insurance as an issue for collective bargaining. The AFL-CIO supported a national health bill sponsored by Representative Martha W. Griffiths, while the United Automobile Workers (UAW), under the leadership of the late Walter Reuther, drafted its own proposal, which was introduced in the Senate by Senator Edward M. Kennedy and others. A compromise version of these bills, introduced in the House in the 92nd Congress as H.R. 22 (the Griffiths-Corman bill), and in the Senate as S. 3 (the Kennedy bill), now has the support of both unions.

Second, employers, many of whom pay for all or a substantial part of their employees' health insurance, have also reacted to the rising cost of the premiums. A number of businessmen now favor health insurance reform.[3]

Third, state governments, under whose jurisdiction insurance regulation falls, are sensitive to public criticism of the rising cost of health insurance. They have also found that the growing financial burden of Medicaid, the costs of which they share with the federal government, conflicts with other spending objectives. These considerations led the National Governors' Conference, meeting in Colorado Springs, Colorado, in September 1969, to come out in favor of national health insurance.[4]

Fourth, in the past twenty years, as shown in Figure 1-1, most of the population has become enrolled in "voluntary" health insurance plans. This term is used somewhat loosely here since Workmen's Compensation, for example, which covers the medical costs of work-connected injuries, is usually compulsory. Hospital insurance for the aged (Medicare Part A) is also compulsory for all who are covered by Social Security. Most employment-related group health insurance plans cover employees automatically, and are thus, in fact, com-

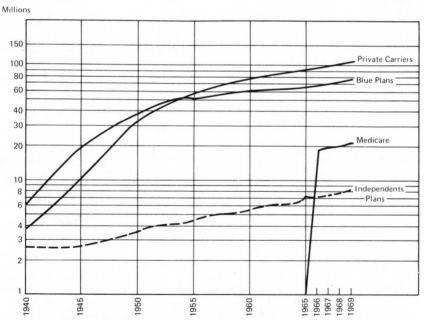

Figure 1-1. Gross Enrollment in All Health Insurance Plans that Include Hospital Coverage, by Type of Carrier, 1940-1969. Sources: *Source Book of Health Insurance Data* (New York: Health Insurance Institute, 1970); and *Health Insurance Statistics*, HI-11, January 31, 1969, HI-17, April 15, 1970, HI-24, February 19, 1971 (Washington: Social Security Administration, U.S. Department of Health, Education, and Welfare).

pulsory. Nevertheless, extensive experience with health insurance programs has made the idea of a national program less frightening to both patients and providers of health care. At the same time, the rise in medical costs has filled those who have little or no health insurance coverage with a sense of urgent need.

Fifth, between 1950 and 1969, when the overall rise in consumer prices was 52 percent, medical costs rose by about 111 percent (and by another 6 percent the following year).[5] Some medical costs increased far more sharply than others. Hospital daily service charges, for example, increased 450 percent from 1950 to 1969, and an additional 12.5 percent from 1969 to 1970.[6] Since costs have risen so rapidly, the substantial growth in health insurance coverage, both private and public, has failed to reduce the share of income that the average American family must spend for medical care. From 1950 to 1969, as shown in Table 1-1, the proportion of the population covered by some kind of health insurance rose from about 50 percent to nearly 90 percent, but out-of-pocket health care expenditures remained at roughly 3.5 percent of disposable personal income.

Table 1-1

Share of Expenditures for Civilian Personal Health Care, Paid by Insurance and Directly by Consumers, Selected Years, 1950-1969

	Total Expenditures[a]	Percent of Total Paid by Insurance				Direct Consumer Expenditures	
Year	(Billions)	All Insurance	Private Insurance[b]	Medicare	Consumers	Per Capita[c]	As Percent of Disposable Personal Income
1950	$10.8	11.1	11.1		66.7	$48	3.52
1955	15.1	18.5	18.5		61.6	57	3.42
1960	22.9	23.6	23.6		57.2	74	3.82
1965	34.9	26.6	26.6		52.1	95	3.91
1966	37.5	29.3	26.1	3.2	51.7	100	3.85
1967	42.5	35.3	24.2	11.1	44.9	97	3.53
1968	47.5	38.1	25.5	12.6	41.3	99	3.38
1969	53.5	39.4	26.5	12.9	40.1	108	3.49

[a]Includes, in addition to the expenditures itemized, public sector expenditures for civilian personal health care and expenditures of private philanthropy for civilian personal health care. For a detailed breakdown of personal health care expenditures in 1969 and the relationship of these expenditures to total national health expenditures, see Appendix B.

[b]Includes benefits under conventional health insurance and prepaid practice plans plus the portion of Workmen's Compensation benefits paid for medical services, which in the years shown ranged from $0.2 to $0.9 billion.

[c]Civilian resident population.

Sources: Barbara S. Cooper and Mary F. McGee, "National Health Expenditures, Fiscal Years 1929-70 and Calendar Years 1929-69," *Research and Statistics Note*, No. 25—1970 (Washington: Social Security Administration, U.S. Department of Health, Education, and Welfare, December 14, 1970), Tables 4, 8 and 9.

Sixth, under the present system, most health insurance coverage is tied to employment. Changing jobs can drastically alter the degree and quality of protection for an employee and his entire family.

Seventh, roughly one-fourth of all health insurance enrollees are not covered by group policies, through employment or otherwise. Their individual health insurance policies are much more expensive and generally provide less complete coverage than group policies. Those who are not wealthy enough to pay these high premiums or cannot obtain individual coverage because they are "adverse risks" must depend on essentially welfare arrangements such as Medicaid.

Eighth, the coverage most commonly included in both group and individual plans has led to distortions in the use of medical services by encouraging hospitalization and routine and predictable surgical procedures while excluding outpatient care and less common but often more costly procedures. Administrative costs are made unnecessarily high by confusion about coverage, lack of uniformity, the number of individual policies, and claims-handling procedures that can involve the insurance carrier, the patient and the physician in time-consuming paper work.

Clearly, then, the pressure to reform the present voluntary health insurance system or to replace it with a compulsory national system of a kind yet to be determined is justifiable. While the present system affects providers, users, and insurers in different and often conflicting ways, it does have benefits that none will readily yield. Therefore, the procedures the system has created for the provision of and payment for health care services and the vast organizations that conduct these procedures must be understood if reform is to be constructive.

The Insurers

Although the rhetoric of public debate has built up the image of health insurance as an industry run for profit, private companies account for only about half the gross enrollments in health insurance plans; government and nonprofit organizations account for the rest, as shown in Figure 1-1. More than 1000 private carriers—mostly life insurance companies—sell health insurance, although the top 20 companies account for 73 percent of the premium volume of the private carriers.[7] Health insurance constitutes a large and growing share of the premium income of these carriers, even though its contribution to their total assets is surprisingly small.

Blue Cross and Blue Shield are not private companies but nonprofit organizations whose tax-exempt status gives them some advantage in competing with the private carriers. Actually, Blue Cross-Blue Shield consists of 75 Blue Cross plans and 72 Blue Shield plans, each of which is autonomous, local, and only loosely affiliated nationally.

The third largest component of the health insurance system is the federal government, which entered the health insurance business in 1966 with the

Medicare program for people who are 65 years of age and over. The program was established largely because the Blue plans and the private companies tended to exclude poor insurance risks, and thus most people in this age group, from health insurance coverage at rates they could afford. Medicare Part A today automatically covers approximately 21 million Social Security beneficiaries, age 65 and over, plus certain categories under 65, for extensive hospital expenses and some nursing home care, while Medicare Part B covers approximately 95 percent of this number on a voluntary basis for a broad range of medical services provided by physicians and others. The program is underwritten by the federal government but administered by the Blue plans and some private carriers, who act as fiscal intermediaries. Unlike the private companies and the Blue plans, which offer a wide variety of group and individual coverage, Medicare offers uniform coverage for hospital and medical expenses.

The fourth component of the health insurance system is the so-called "independent plans," which include prepaid group plans, numerous small employer-employee and union group plans, individual practice plans, and various health clinics and dental plans.

The best known independents are the prepaid group plans that are often referred to as "community group practice plans" and cover an estimated 1.5 to 2.0 percent of all health insurance enrollees.[8] These plans include, for example, the Kaiser-Permanente Medical Care Program, the Health Insurance Plan of Greater New York (HIP) and the Group Health Cooperative of Puget Sound, Seattle. In most health insurance plans the subscriber (or his employer) pays the subscription fee or premium to an insurance company or Blue plan, which then reimburses him or the provider for the medical expenses covered by the policy. But in prepaid group plans the insurer is the medical service provider. The subscriber pays the subscription fee directly to the institution that provides the care. Hence the provider has an incentive to economize, and many of these organizations have apparently achieved substantial economies.

The employer-employee and union groups cover nearly 6 million people (nearly 3 percent of the insured population) in more than 400 plans.[9] A few large plans such as the United Mine Workers Welfare and Retirement Fund, the National Association of Letter Carriers Health Benefits Plan, the National Postal Union Health Benefit Plan, and others account for most of the enrollment.

The individual practice plans are, by and large, sponsored by medical societies. They are somewhat similar to Blue Shield plans except that the participating physicians agree to provide services through individual practices to a group of subscribers for a fixed fee, usually less than the prevailing rate. Group Health Insurance, Inc., of New York City and the Foundation for Medical Care of San Joaquin County in California are the most notable of the few such plans with sizable membership. Individual practice plan enrollees comprised only about 1 percent of the insured population in 1969.[10]

Health insurance is also provided through a number of other channels.

Workmen's Compensation insurance, the most significant of these, accounted for approximately 4.8 percent of total benefits paid by all health insurance, public and private, in 1969.[11] Automobile insurance, homeowners' insurance, and the accident policies sometimes required for school children, swimming pool members, and participants in summer camps also provide some medical expense coverage.

Disability or income loss insurance sold by private carriers in effect complements the income loss coverage provided under Workmen's Compensation plans. Although it does not provide payments for medical services, it influences the use of medical services, is frequently referred to as health insurance, and is listed as such in the statistics reported by private carriers.

Insurance is not the only alternative to out-of-pocket financing for medical services. Certain so-called "institutional" programs provide medical services for some 20 to 25 million persons, usually without direct charge to the patient. The largest of these programs in number of beneficiaries is Medicaid, a program created, along with Medicare, by the government in 1966, which pays the medical bills of welfare recipients and other medically indigent who meet federal and state eligibility requirements. Exactly how many people are covered by Medicaid plans is not known, but some 15 million people (3 million of whom are Medicare enrollees whose Medicare Part B premiums were paid by Medicaid) were served by the program in the fiscal year 1970. Medicaid is not an insurance program, because it involves no contribution or premium payment by or on behalf of the beneficiary, and unlike most other institutional health programs, it has no medical facilities of its own.

In addition, the Veterans' Administration and the U.S. Public Health Service have their own systems of hospitals. The military services provide medical care to members and retirees of the armed services and their dependents, both on base and off base, through a financing arrangement called "Civilian Health and Medical Program for the Uniformed Services" (CHAMPUS). State, county and local hospitals care for tuberculosis patients, mental patients and others. Medical care is also provided by universities and colleges to students, by the federal government to Indians and migratory workers, and by various levels of government to inmates of correctional institutions and other specialized groups.

The Insured

The spectacular growth in health insurance coverage since 1950 is reflected in Tables 1-2 through 1-4, which show estimated enrollment in various types of health insurance plans from 1950 through 1969. Particularly impressive has been the increase in comprehensive coverage, which was virtually nonexistent in 1950. Few countries with compulsory health insurance have achieved more complete enrollment.[12] It is likely that the voluntary system will improve total enroll-

8

Table 1-2
Estimated Net Enrollees in All Public and Private Health Insurance Plans that Include Hospital Coverage, Selected Years, 1950-1969

| Year | Net Total Enrollees[a] | | | | Estimated Net Enrollees Under Age 65 in Private Plans (Millions)[a] | | Medicare Enrollees (Millions) |
| | High (Based on HIAA Estimates) | | Low (Based on HEW Estimates) | | | | |
	Number (Millions)	Percent of Resident Civilian Population	Number (Millions)	Percent of Resident Civilian Population	High (HIAA)	Low (HEW)	
1950	76.6	50.3					
1955	105.5	63.6					
1960	130.0	71.9					
1965	153.1	78.7					
1966	167.5	85.2			148.6		18.9
1967	173.2	86.9	156.9	78.8	153.8	137.6	19.4
1968	179.1	89.0	162.4	80.7	159.3	142.8	19.8
1969	184.4	90.7	167.3	82.3	164.4	147.4	20.0

[a]Estimated duplicate coverage among private plans and between private plans and Medicare has been netted out.

Note: Discrepancies in addition are due to rounding.

Sources: Estimates of Health Insurance Association of America (HIAA)—Source Book of Health Insurance Data (New York: Health Insurance Institute, 1970), p. 17; estimates of U.S. Department of Health, Education, and Welfare (HEW)—Marjorie Smith Mueller, "Private Health Insurance in 1969: A Review," Social Security Bulletin, February 1971, Table 6, p. 7, and Table 8, p. 9; and—Health Insurance Statistics, HI-11, January 31, 1969; HI-17, April 15, 1970; and HI-24, February 19, 1971 (Washington: Social Security Administration, U.S. Department of Health, Education, and Welfare. For discussion of methodology used in estimating net enrollments see Appendix C.

Table 1-3
Estimated Net Enrollees in Public and Private Surgical Insurance Plans, Selected Years, 1950-1969

Year	Net Total Enrollees[a]		Net Enrollees Under Age 65 in Private Plans (Millions)[a]	Medicare Part B Enrollees (Millions)
	Number (Millions)	Percent of Resident Civilian Population		
1950	54.2	35.9		
1955	88.9	53.4		
1960	117.3	64.9		
1965	140.5	72.2		
1966	154.9	78.7	137.4	17.6
1967	160.6	80.6	142.8	17.8
1968	165.9	82.5	147.3	18.7
1969	172.4	84.8	153.3	19.1

[a]Enrollment figures are based on HIAA estimates. HEW estimates are somewhat lower. Estimated duplicate coverage among private plans and between private plans and Medicare Part B has been netted out.

Note: Discrepancies in addition are due to rounding.

Sources: *Source Book of Health Insurance Data* (New York: Health Insurance Institute, 1970), p. 18; Marjorie Smith Mueller, "Private Health Insurance in 1969: A Review." *Social Security Bulletin*, February 1971, Table 7, p. 8, and Table 9, p. 10; and *Health Insurance Statistics*, HI-11, January 31, 1969; HI-17, April 15, 1970; and HI-24, February 19, 1971 (Washington: Social Security Administration, U.S. Department of Health, Education, and Welfare).

ment even more. But it is well to remember that enrollment itself is not a good measure of adequacy or efficiency of health insurance programs.

Some people receive medical care under both health insurance and institutional programs, and some families are covered by two or more insurance plans, with either complementary or duplicate coverage. Health insurance plans and institutional care combined probably provide 95 percent of the population with some protection against medical expenses.[13] Nonetheless, some 10 to 15 percent of the population still had no health insurance coverage of any kind in 1969. While some of these people are protected by one or more of the institutional programs described above, at least 5 percent of the population is totally unprotected against medical expenses. The largest unprotected group probably consists of the "medically indigent" who are just above the welfare line. While many people in this group are eligible for Medicaid under national Medicaid rules, they do not meet state eligibility requirements, since only 22 states provide Medicaid coverage for people not on welfare. Other groups without protection of any kind against medical expenses include some itinerant workers (mainly farm help), some self-employed, some people employed by

Table 1-4

Estimated Net Enrollees in Public and Private Comprehensive Health Insurance Plans, Selected Years, 1950-1969

Year	Total Enrollees[a]		Enrollees in Private Plans (Millions)		Enrollees in Medicare, Part B (Millions)
	Number (Millions)	Percent of Resident Civilian Population	Insurance Companies	Blue Cross-Blue Shield	
1950	b	b	b		
1955	5.2	3.1	5.2		
1960	31.2	17.3	27.4	3.7	
1965	66.5	34.2	51.9	14.6	
1966	79.9	40.6	56.7	14.4	17.6
1967	96.3	48.4	62.2	16.3	17.8
1968	103.3	51.3	66.9	17.8	18.7
1969	111.7	55.0	72.3	20.3	19.1

[a]These figures include some duplication of coverage in the age group 65 and over, 1.9 million of whom are reported to be enrolled in private major medical plans. However, it is likely that some persons in this age group with private major medical policies are not enrolled in Medicare Part B. Of total Part A enrollment (automatic for Social Security recipients), some 800,000 were not enrolled in Part B (which is voluntary) in 1969. Some persons 65 and over are enrolled in neither Part A nor Part B.

[b]Negligible.

Note: Discrepancies in addition are due to rounding.

Sources: *Source Book of Health Insurance Data* (New York: Health Insurance Institute, 1970), p. 21; Marjorie Smith Mueller, "Private Health Insurance in 1969: A Review," *Social Security Bulletin*, February 1971, Table 11, p. 12; and *Health Insurance Statistics*, HI-11, January 31, 1969; HI-17, April 15, 1970; and HI-24, February 19, 1971 (Washington: Social Security Administration, U.S. Department of Health, Education, and Welfare).

individuals or small organizations, some students (especially those too old to qualify as dependents under their parents' health insurance plans), perhaps some wealthy people who feel no need for protection against medical expenses, dependent adults who are not family members, and early retirees.

The Providers of Medical Care

The health care labor force provides the medical services and ultimately receives the benefits paid out by health insurance plans, the payments made under the various institutional programs described earlier, and direct payments from consumers. Expenditures for their services accounted for 7.6 percent of the gross national product in 1971.

About 10 percent of the 4 million persons who comprise the health care labor force are doctors and dentists. About 50 percent are nurses' aides and others engaged in nursing activities. The remaining 40 percent are employed in doctors' offices, hospitals, laboratories, nursing homes, clinics, and other medical facilities in some 350 occupations, including technicians and therapists in various specialties; paramedical personnel trained to relieve physicians of much of their routine workload; medical writers, librarians and research workers; dieticians; ambulance attendants; maintenance and other service workers.[14]

Advances in medical technology have created large numbers of jobs requiring special skills. Between 1950 and 1969, for example, the number of persons engaged in clinical laboratory services increased from 30,000 to 114,000, the number of occupational therapists from 2,000 to 7,000, and the number of speech and audio pathologists from 1,800 to 12,700. Although health insurance policies cover many of these specialized services, most benefits are actually paid to two broad categories of providers—hospitals and doctors.[15] And although payments to hospitals account for more than a third of all health care expenditures and more than half of all health insurance benefit payments, doctors have far more influence than hospitals on health care costs. This is true in any system because it is the doctor who recommends the kind of treatment the patient shall receive, prescribes drugs, and determines whether hospitalization is indicated. The doctor and the patient, therefore, make the major cost-affecting decisions—decisions heavily influenced by the kind of health insurance covering the patient.

Health Care Financing Systems in Other Countries

The two basic plans that have been used in various countries for financing medical costs on a universal, share-the-risk basis are "national health insurance" and "national health service." Each has many variations, and the distinctions between the two are not always clear.

The national health insurance plans now in effect in other countries generally include such conventional elements of the insurance concept as risk-sharing by participants through premium payments and some responsibility on the part of the insured to maintain eligibility. The criteria for eligibility vary from country to country, but a premium payment is usually required of each participant, whether he pays it or it is paid on his behalf. The government usually tries to set premium levels high enough to meet claims, so that the system may be actuarily sound and self-sustaining. The administrators also try to control costs and utilization and seek efficiencies so that the system will operate within its means, although the income of national health insurance plans is often supplemented out of general revenues.[16] The adoption of a national health insurance plan seldom requires restructuring of the health care system or changing the method of remunerating the provider, except that the government may establish official fee schedules for physicians and set hospital rates. Nonetheless, controlling costs and utilization is a chronic problem.

National health insurance plans, generally speaking, are based on the welfare approach, with the objective of protecting the financially weak. In this respect they often differ very little from national health service plans such as Great Britain's. National health service plans are financed by the national treasury out of general revenues, earmarked revenues, or both, rather than by premiums. The government pays physicians on a capitation or salary basis and provides for hospital expenditures in the budget. The amount budgeted annually for health services is, thus, theoretically, the maximum that can be spent for medical services and constitutes a form of cost control. But budgets are not immutable, and from time to time it becomes necessary either to supplement them or to sacrifice medical services to fiscal realities. Ultimately, the level of resources the nation commits to health care may depend more on political than on economic or health considerations. Some national health insurance plans financed through payroll taxes may be subject to similar constraints.

National health service plans have no eligibility rules other than registration with a physician (for non-emergency treatment); generally, anyone can make use of all available medical services. The only limit on access is the capacity of the system. But because most providers of health care are directly or indirectly in the employ of the government, they have relatively little incentive to extend their working hours or to expand services to accommodate demand. The fee-for-service basis on which providers are paid under national health insurance plans does provide such an incentive and may be more effective in making the supply of medical services responsive to demand. National health service plans also tend to invite the use of subterfuge to obtain hospital beds and other services. At the same time, private practices may develop and grow outside the public system, reviving the inequalities of access to medical care that the public system was intended to eliminate. In Great Britain private practices have always existed alongside the health service plan and in recent years private health insurance enrollment has increased, although it is still relatively insignificant.[17]

It should not be assumed that these forms of national health insurance and national health service are the only alternatives to the methods presently used in the United States for financing medical care. National health care programs vary widely, including combinations of public and private, compulsory and voluntary systems. In West Germany, local, autonomous sick funds provide coverage essentially for physicians' services since most hospitals are publicly owned and operated. In the Netherlands, 20 percent of the population is enrolled in voluntary health insurance plans. Even in the Soviet Union some private practice is permitted.[18] The experiences of these countries suggest the complexity of the task of establishing a system of health care financing that can accommodate all segments of the population.

Scope of This Study

The pages that follow analyze the roles of the consumer (or the insured), the insurer, the provider, and prepayment plans in the present health care financing system of the United States. The separateness of the functions of consumer, insurer, and provider is at the root of the problem of utilization and resource allocation. When the consumer is in need of medical services, he is concerned only about the part of the cost that his health insurance will not cover, rather than about the cost of the insurance itself or the effect of his use of medical services on the cost of insurance. The insurer, in turn, is interested only in whether, in setting the premium rate, he correctly estimated the quantity and price of the medical services the insured would consume. He is not, as a rule, concerned with the cost or utilization of medical services. And, finally, the provider, in treating the insured, is not at all concerned about the effect of his treatment on the price of the insurance, which is the source of much of his income. None of these groups therefore constitutes an effective restraint on price increases or the utilization of services.

This analysis of the present system and the ways in which it serves or fails to serve the interests of consumers, insurance carriers, Blue plans, prepaid groups, government, physicians, and hospitals suggests some practical requirements for reform. The purpose of the analysis is to shed light on the current health insurance debate and the various proposals for reform. An examination of the American experience with health insurance is necessary to a full understanding of these proposals and to an assessment of their possible effectiveness.

2

Health Coverage and the Demand for Medical Services

Those even partly insured against medical costs tend to use medical services more than those not insured at all. Regardless of age, sex, family income, or place of residence, insured persons are more likely than the uninsured to undergo in-hospital surgical procedures. Hospital admission rates and average number of days per year spent in the hospital are also higher for insured than for uninsured persons. However, the uninsured have a longer average stay in the hospital than the insured, probably because the uninsured tend not to use hospital services except for very serious illnesses.[1]

That health insurance has a far greater effect on medical services than other forms of insurance have on the activities they cover can be attributed to the indefinite nature of many illnesses and the wide variety of medical services that can be applied in any case where doctor and patient consider treatment warranted. Under all other kinds of insurance, some specific, readily discernible event, which the insured individual is unlikely to initiate, must cause the loss for which insurance compensation is sought. Under term life insurance, for example, benefit payments are made only upon the death of the insured, a specific event that the insured does not normally hasten. Fire insurance benefits are paid only in the event of accidental fire. Even auto insurance, which, like health insurance, is characterized by a preponderance of small claims, requires that an automobile accident take place. Although insured individuals have been known to fake accidents, it is seldom in their interest, or worth the risk, to do so.

One might argue that an illness closely resembles an accident in that respect. But the situations in which an individual seeks medical care are not always clear-cut. How one defines "illness," how "ill" one must feel to seek medical help, and which treatment, if any, the physician administers or prescribes may depend on, among other things, whether and to what extent one is insured. Unlike smashed fenders and houses damaged by fire, the designation of one's condition as an "illness" is highly subjective and depends on such intangibles as one's degree of tolerance to discomfort, one's fears, or one's understanding of medicine. Under property or auto insurance, the insured can readily estimate what his potential loss may be. Under life insurance he can find some logical basis for determining the maximum coverage he may buy. But a person seeking to insure himself against the costs of medical services can never be secure in estimating his maximum potential loss because he does not know which of a vast range of illnesses may strike him or what kinds of services may be available to diagnose and treat them. It is as if auto insurance were to cover any repair or

15

adjustment desired by the insured or recommended by the mechanic because the automobile does not run smoothly or sound right. The "loss" against which health insurance protects thus differs from the concept used in normal insurance activities.

Cost-Sharing Mechanisms

Recognizing the potentially great demand for medical services health insurance can generate, health insurance programs in the United States, as well as in other countries, typically include disincentives to the utilization of medical services. The compulsory systems in Sweden and Belgium, for example, require the consumer to share the cost of medical services with the insurer. Sweden's system pays only 75 percent of the official fee schedule (which doctors usually exceed).[2]

Under the present voluntary system of the United States, the division of medical costs between insurer and insured is not standardized. Health insurance policies contain a wide variety of limitations, conditions, definitions, deductibles, exclusions and other restrictions that were intended mainly to limit the liability of the insurers and only incidentally to curtail utilization.

The insurer's principal concern is to limit his financial risk in a fairly new field, in which definitions are elusive and actuarial data imprecise, without endangering his competitive position vis-à-vis other carriers. Carriers have only recently acquired an adequate statistical basis for predictions of the incidence of illness; they still cannot accurately determine how many ailments remain untreated for financial reasons, and the potential utilization rate for medical services therefore remains unclear. Furthermore, even in the same locality, rates and fees for a given medical service vary greatly, depending on physicians' fee policies, the complications different cases may involve, and the accuracy of diagnosis. Under conventional health insurance plans (as opposed to prepaid group plans), the insurer has little control over the price the physician (or other provider) may charge. He therefore seeks to protect himself against these uncertainties by writing into the policies certain restrictions on coverage that will prevent anticipated claims from exceeding premium income.[3] The effectiveness of those restrictions in restraining the demand for medical services is not clear, in part because most consumers cannot understand—much less base their actions on—the terms of their policies.

Defining Medical Services
Covered by the Policy

One of the ways in which insurers limit their liability is by precisely defining the medical services that their policies will cover. The wide variety of definitions used for this purpose is often a source of confusion to the insured.

The 3 basic categories of health insurance are: (1) *hospital coverage*, which may include hospital room and board, certain specified ancillary expenses, and some services of hospital staff physicians;[4] (2) *hospital plus surgical* coverage, which may include in addition to hospital services, certain specified surgical services (usually only on an inpatient basis) and perhaps some inpatient nonsurgical treatments and some outpatient procedures; and (3) *major medical*, which may cover a great variety of medical services (depending on the price of the policy), including hospital and surgical costs not covered or covered on a limited basis in hospital and surgical policies, physicians' office and home visits, drugs, psychiatric care, even dental and optical care, although these are not common. Hospital-surgical coverage is frequently referred to as "basic coverage," and major medical is usually sold as a supplement to basic coverage. When hospital-surgical and major medical insurance are sold together, as they increasingly are, the coverage is called "comprehensive."

Within these categories, the specific procedures covered vary considerably. The ostensible purpose of defining a service specifically is to discourage fraudulent claims such as attempts to collect for a stay at a seaside resort by calling it a hospital. However, the definition may also permit the carrier to reject an otherwise valid claim on a technicality. The health insurance plan may cover care only in "approved" hospitals. Some Blue Cross plans, for example, cover only "participating" hospitals—those that have agreed to accept the Blue Cross fee schedules as payment in full. Other carriers may cover only hospitals with facilities for major surgery, or hospitals not used primarily for the treatment of alcoholism or drug addiction, regardless of what other facilities the hospital may have.

The ambiguity of the definition of "hospital" has been the subject of a number of court cases. In the case of *Aetna Life* v. *Adams et ux*, for example, a child suffering from dyslexia had been committed by his pediatrician to the Beaumont (Texas) Remedial Clinic for treatment. The carrier, Aetna Life, rejected the claim on the grounds that the Beaumont Clinic did not meet the definition of "hospital" set forth in the family's health insurance policy. The child's family sued, but the Appeals Court found in favor of Aetna.[5] The policy covered only hospitals engaged primarily in providing "diagnostic and therapeutic facilities for the surgical and medical diagnosis, treatment and care of injured and sick persons," including "twenty-four-hour-a-day nursing services by registered graduate nurses." The Beaumont Clinic had surgical facilities but did not normally treat patients requiring surgery. It did not provide round-the-clock nursing by registered nurses but claimed that registered nurses were on call.

The Court viewed as irrelevant the Clinic's membership in the American Hospital Association and Texas Hospital Association and the pediatrician's opinion that the Beaumont Clinic was appropriate to the patient's needs. Had the insured been treated in a less specialized hospital that met the requirements of the policy definition, Aetna would have had to cover the expenses, even though treatment might have been costlier and less efficient. The Court's decision, whatever its legal merits, concerned itself only with the definitional question and did not concern itself with whether the medical facility used was appropriate for the treatment. This implies no criticism of the Court itself; it demonstrates how definitions can be applied to deny claims even where the medical service appears to be proper.

Exclusions from Coverage

Another way in which carriers may limit their risk is by excluding illnesses that require expensive or long-term treatment. Psychiatric care, for example, is often excluded from coverage, or coverage may be accompanied by limitations that make it useful for the treatment of minor neuroses but not for more serious emotional problems. Renal dialysis is another common exclusion,[6] as are prosthetics and treatment for alcoholism and drug addiction (see Table 2-1). Many policies also exclude conditions covered by other insurance policies. For example, policies generally state that services covered by Workmen's Compensation laws are excluded from coverage. This exclusion is justifiable insofar as it serves to prevent overcompensation for medical services incurred through employment-related accidents or illnesses. However, when Workmen's Compensation provides only partial coverage of medical expenses, the insurer's payments do not necessarily result in overcompensation. Nonetheless, carriers have been upheld in the courts in their claims that they are relieved of liability if Workmen's Compensation covers any part of the expense.[7]

A policy need not specify that a service is excluded in order to exclude it. Carriers reserve the right to exclude from coverage any service not specifically listed as included on the grounds that the variety of medical treatments and the rate of introduction of new treatments makes it impossible to list all exclusions specifically, as shown in Table 2-1.

Limitations on Coverage

Policies may provide dollar maximums for daily hospital charges and surgery covered by the policy, and service maximums for procedures that are normally repeatable, such as psychiatric treatments (if psychiatric care is included in the policy as a covered expense).[8]

The maximum number of treatments, the maximum number of days of treatment and the maximum number of hospital days covered vary enormously from plan to plan, and the limitations may bear little relationship to medical requirements. These limitations (at the high end of the cost spectrum) are likely to work a greater hardship on the insured than do low-end limitations, and they probably have a less restraining effect on demand. For example, in cases of serious illness most employed individuals can afford to pay the cost of 2 or 3 days in the hospital, but the exclusion of the first 2 or 3 days of hospital costs from insurance coverage would discourage hospitalization for testing, observation, minor surgery, or the weekend convenience of the doctor. Limitations at the high end, on the other hand, are more likely to cut off coverage when the patient is seriously ill, is out of work and without income, and is really in need of hospitalization. And high-end limitations probably have very little effect on demand because few people are likely to stay in a hospital more than 60 to 90 days—common maximums for length of hospital stay—unless they have to.

Deductibles and Coinsurance Provisions

Most policies provide for coinsurance, usually on an 80-to-20 basis, which means that the insurer pays 80 percent of the cost of covered services, and the insured 20 percent. Many comprehensive plans—patterned after the Blue Cross-Blue Shield comprehensive plan consisting of basic plus supplementary or major medical coverage—cover 100 percent of expenses up to the maximum provided by the basic policy and 80 percent of covered expenses in excess of the basic coverage. For example, if the surgical schedule in the basic policy allows $150 for an appendectomy and the surgeon's fee is $350, the major medical portion of the plan may cover 80 percent of the $200 not covered by the basic plan. Unfortunately, coinsurance provisions, like maximums, often tend to shift to the consumer the responsibility at the high end of the cost spectrum where insurance is most needed. And they, too, limit the insurer's financial risk without really restraining demand.

Deductibles generally accompany coinsurance provisions; they range from $35 to $1,000 but most are $100 or less. In some comprehensive plans the insured pays the deductible on the first covered expenses incurred, in others on the first covered nonhospital expenses, and in still others on the first expenses incurred over and above basic (hospital-surgical) coverage. The amount is then called a "corridor deductible." Some policies feature an "integrated deductible," crediting benefits paid under the basic plan toward the deductible of the major medical supplement.[9] To add to the confusion, the deductible may be on a per-illness or a per-year basis, or the policy may require that the deductible amount of expenses be incurred within a certain time period—usually 90 or 120 days. The latter limitation, used to circumscribe the definition of an "illness," may deprive certain chronically ill individuals, whose recurrent medical expenses are not enough in any period of 90 or 120 days to exceed the deductible, of health insurance benefits.

Overall Maximum Dollar Limit

The overall maximum dollar limit may be the most important restriction on a policy. It may be on a per-illness, per-year, or per-lifetime basis or on a

Table 2-1
Exclusions and Limitations in National Postal Union Health Benefit Plan

General Exclusions

The following are not covered expenses and cannot be counted for any purpose under this Plan:

- Expenses incurred while not covered by this Plan

- Illness or injury for which any benefits are payable by employees' compensation or similar laws. (In case of illness or injury covered by employees' compensation, benefits are not payable under this Plan, and claim should be made to the proper compensation authorities)

- Routine physical examinations, routine eye examinations, eyeglasses, hearing aids and examinations for them, and immunizations

- Personal comfort services, such as telephone, radio, television, air conditioning, and beauty and barber services

- Injuries sustained while participating in a riot or committing a felony

- Speech therapy and visual training (orthoptics)

- Orthopedic shoes, arch supports, elastic stockings, corsets, and other similar attire or appliances

- Air purifiers, whirlpool bathing equipment, sun lamps, and heat lamps

- Any charge which is not reasonable and customary as defined on page 10

- Dental braces, and dental appliances except for replacement of natural teeth as specifically provided on page 9

- Blood or blood plasma which is donated or replaced

- Drugs and other devices prescribed for contraceptive purposes or for conditions of normal pregnancy

- Services of any practitioner not included in the definition of a doctor on page 10

- Diet supplements, vitamins, and drugs which can be obtained without a doctor's prescription

- Services rendered by a doctor, nurse, or physical therapist who is related to you or who lives in your household

- Hospital admissions primarily for physical therapy, rehabilitation, rest cure, or custodial care

- Charges by hospitals operated by State agencies, even if you are obligated to pay, unless admitted as the private patient of a doctor

- Services and supplies not certified by a doctor as being medically required, or for which you have no legal obligation to pay, or for which no charge would be made if the person had no health benefits coverage

- Services relating to circumcision of a member of a family during the first 90 days after his birth

- Diagnostic tests to determine the existence or nature of an allergy

- A service or supply not listed as covered.

Limitations

Maximum Benefit

There is a Maximum Benefit for you and each individual member of your family. This Maximum Benefit is $100,000 under the High Option, or $50,000 under the Low Option, for each person. Each person's Maximum Benefit is reduced by the amount of benefits that are paid by the Plan on his behalf.

Alcoholism or Drug Addiction

Benefits for treatment of alcoholism or drug addiction are limited to Supplemental Benefits as shown on page 9 and to persons enrolled in the High Option.

If Confined on Effective Date

A person confined in a hospital or other institution on the effective date of enrollment in this Plan will have his benefit for that confine-ment limited to $1,000 under the High Option, or to $500 under the Low Option. This limitation will be removed immediately upon discharge from the hospital.

Double Coverage

If you or any member of your family is eligible for benefits under Health Insurance for the Aged under Social Security ("Medicare") or any health benefits plan or insurance policy providing health benefits coverage (either in cash or in services or supplies) other than this Plan, the benefits under this Plan will be limited. In such a case, this Plan will pay benefits for covered expenses in accordance with its provisions up to an amount which, when added to the benefits available from Medicare or the other plan, will not exceed the total covered charges incurred. This provision applies whether or not claim is filed under Medicare or the other plan, and, if needed, authorization must be given this Plan to obtain information about entitlement or benefits available.

Coverage under any other plan which pays only for loss of time from work or for loss of income is not considered double coverage.

Source: *National Postal Union Health Benefit Plan* (Washington: Bureau of Retirement, Insurance, and Occupational Health, U.S. Civil Service Commission, January 1970), pp. 11-12.

combination of these, and it is the ultimate limit on the insurer's risk exposure. However broad a plan's coverage, the carrier can feel secure if its maximum limit is low enough. The dollar maximum may look very high by comparison with a family's normal medical expenses. It is difficult for a person whose use of medical services has been confined to an annual bout with the flu to imagine medical costs that would total as much as $10,000, for example, even in a lifetime. But just one serious illness requiring repeated hospitalization can easily exhaust a $10,000 maximum.

Even a $50,000 maximum may not save a family from financial disaster when a member contracts a serious illness such as cancer, serious cardiac disease, or some other ailment requiring expensive long-term treatment. Such cases are unusual; limits as high as $50,000 are rarely exceeded.[10] But for example, a thirty-seven-year-old woman in Washington, D.C., for the past 7 years has suffered from multiple sclerosis complicated by chronic leukemia. In this period, she has been hospitalized 25 times and has required special nursing care costing a minimum of $40.00 per week. She has spent $60 to $80 per month for medicines and $40 to $60 per month for physicians' services. Her husband, a government employee, is enrolled in one of the federal employee health plans with exceptional coverage and a lifetime maximum of $50,000 per person. Medical expenses such as those incurred by his wife can mount above $50,000 within a few years, but in these instances the high maximum can avert total bankruptcy.

Some policies feature "maximums within maximums," for example, a $20,000 lifetime maximum with a maximum of $10,000 per illness or per benefit year. But most maximums are stated on either a "per illness" or a "per year" basis. The relative merits of these restrictions depend on what kind of illness the insured may contract. The per-illness maximum will better serve the needs of a person who suffers a series of illnesses. The per-year maximum will better serve the needs of one who suffers a chronic ailment requiring long-term treatment. However, since most health insurance enrollees cannot anticipate their future medical needs, these distinctions have little meaning at the time the policy is purchased.

Effect on Demand for Medical Services

Research has turned up no conclusive evidence that copayment[11] provisions curtail utilization of medical services.[12] Blue Cross, which, philosophically, at least, eschews copayment has given considerable attention to this question. One recent study using 1967 Blue Cross data found that holders of service benefit policies providing for full hospital coverage had hospital admission rates 11.6 percent higher and, once admitted, hospital stays 10.8 percent longer than a contract group with a $25 daily maximum. However, the authors of the study, noting that the results could be attributed to many factors other than copayment, concluded that the effect of deductibles and coinsurance on utilization "still remains undecided."[13]

When the Blue Cross Association and the National Association of Blue Shield Plans asked all the Blue Cross and Blue Shield Plans to comment on the effectiveness of deductibles and copayment provisions, 13 plans agreed with the statement that deductibles curb utilization; 12 plans disagreed. However, of the 13 that agreed, 6 added that only large deductibles are effective. Two plans, reporting that the deductibles they employed did not significantly curb utilization, expressed the view that larger deductibles would be more effective.[14]

Experience under the present system thus suggests that a copayment requirement must be large if it is to affect the demand for medical services. But a large copayment requirement may result in underutilization or financial hardship, which insurance should avert. At present, most copayment requirements are too small to discourage unnecessary use of medical services, frequently too complicated for the average user to understand and respond to, or occasionally applicable only to major illnesses for which medical services are an absolute necessity.

Excluding certain services from coverage, on the other hand, may not reduce the demand for medical services but affects it in other ways if the exclusions are clearly stated. As one would expect, those services covered by insurance are more heavily utilized than those that are not. In addition, doctors can often make their treatment conform to the patient's insurance coverage. Exclusions thus encourage shifts in the utilization of certain kinds of services instead of restraining total demand. The exclusion of services from coverage may even have raised the total cost of medical services. Studies have shown, for example, that patients covered by surgical insurance have a higher rate of surgery than those without such coverage; and when more complete benefits are added to a hospital insurance contract, use of the added services increases. Holders of policies covering only inpatient services are more likely to be hospitalized for diagnostic tests that could be performed on an outpatient basis, even though inpatient services are more expensive.

Hospitalization appears to be one of the most discretionary of medical decisions and one very much influenced by the patient's insurance status. Sixty-two percent of the full-time, office-based physicians surveyed for this study, including 60 percent of surgeons, whose patients presumably require more urgent attention than the patients of primary physicians and of nonsurgical specialists, could recall deciding not to hospitalize a patient in part because of his or her lack of health insurance.[16]

Health Insurance in Practice

Differences in the coverage provided, for 1971, by a typical large group Blue plan and 2 major group plans—the Aetna Life and Casualty Company plan offered to federal employees, and Prudential's major medical plan for its full-time office employees—may illustrate the importance of internal restrictions and the difficulty of evaluating health insurance plans.

The Blue Cross-Blue Shield comprehensive plan has 2 components. The basic plan provides hospital-surgical coverage. A corridor deductible of $100 is applied toward expenses covered by the supplementary or major medical plan.

The Aetna plan covers about 20 percent of the employees and dependents included in the Federal Employees Health Benefits Program. The plan pays 80 percent of all eligible expenses, both inpatient and outpatient, over $50 per covered person per year, and pays in full for the first $1,000 of hospital expenses and all hospital expenses over $10,000. It has no internal maximums, no limits on hospital days, no surgical schedules, no restrictions on the number of psychiatric consultations. The lifetime maximum is $50,000, with an annual $2,000 restoration feature—that is, for each year the policy is in force after the lifetime maximum has been reached, $2,000 is restored to the maximum.

The Prudential Insurance Company's plan for its employees offers a relatively high lifetime maximum—$100,000 per person—and includes a variable corridor deductible. It follows the modified Blue plan format—that is, basic first-dollar hospital-surgical coverage and a comprehensive major medical supplement to which the deductible applies. The deductible, however, varies according to the insured's income. For those earning less than $4,000 per year the deductible is $50.00 per person per year; for those in the $12,000 to $15,000 bracket it is $100; for those earning over $40,000 it is $250. The Prudential plans's coverage is comprehensive, but not as broad as that of the Aetna plan for federal employees or the modified Blue plan. For example, it pays only up to 50 percent of the cost of psychiatric treatment or not more than $20 per visit. Although it has other internal limits, the most important are the relatively high deductible geared to income and the 90-day limit within which the deductible must be incurred.

Tables 2-2 through 2-6 show the compensation that these 3 policies would provide for a family of 4, with 1 employed member earning $20,000 per year and a number of medical expenses in a given year. Table 2-2 shows the family's covered expenses in a "healthy" year—probably typical of most families in most years. Only expenses covered by one or more of the 3 plans appear in the tables. Expenditures for eye examinations, eye glasses, dental work, nonprescription drugs, and other items not covered by any of the plans are not included. The family has no hospital, surgical, or other expenses that would be covered under the basic plan component of the policy. Family member A is assumed to be under treatment for an annoying, stubborn infection, difficult to diagnose.

The total of covered family expenses for the year is $384, an amount that should not be burdensome for a family with a $20,000 income even without insurance. The Prudential plan would not, in fact, pay any of these costs, because no individual family member incurred expenses exceeding the deducti-

Table 2-2

Assumed Annual Expenses for Covered Medical Services for a Model Family of in a "Healthy" Year

Month	Medical Service	All Family Members	Family Member A	Family Member B	Family Member C	Family Member D
Total expenditures during year		$384.00	$241.00	$14.00	$33.00	$96.00
January	Doctors' office visits		35.00			
	Laboratory tests		15.00			
	Drugs		8.00			
February	Doctors' office visits		25.00		15.00	
	Laboratory tests		15.00			
	Drugs		8.00		3.00	
March	Doctors' office visits		15.00			15.00
	Drugs		8.00			
April	Drugs		8.00			
May	Doctors' office visits		15.00	10.00		
	Drugs		8.00	4.00		
June	Drugs		8.00			
July	Drugs		8.00			
August	Doctors' office visits		15.00		15.00	10.00
	Laboratory tests		15.00			7.00
	Drugs		4.00			7.50
September	Drugs		4.00			7.50
October	Doctors' office visits					10.00
	Drugs		4.00			
	Laboratory tests					7.00
November	Doctors' office visits					25.00
	Drugs		4.00			7.00
December	Doctors' office visits		15.00			
	Drugs		4.00			

ble of $150 in any 90-day period. Aetna would pay 2 claims—80 percent of all expenses for member A over $50, and 80 percent of all expenses for member D over $50. The Blue plan, with a $100 deductible, would cover only one claim—that of member A.[17] Table 2-3 shows the compensation that each plan provides for the expenditures listed in Table 2-2.

The premium costs appear in the table even though the employer may pay all or part of them, because if he did not, presumably the family's income would be that much higher. For these expenses, as Table 2-3 indicates, the Aetna

Table 2-3

Comparison of Assumed Total Annual Expenses for Covered Medical Services for a Family of 4 Not Requiring Hospitalization or Surgery, under 3 Group Plans

Plan	Family Expenditures			Treatments Covered by Health Insurance Plan	
	Total (Col. 1 = Col. 2 + Col. 3)	Premium[a] (Col. 2)	Out-of-Pocket (Col. 3 = Col. 4 − Col. 5)	Total Cost (Col. 4)	Reimbursement by Plan (Col. 5)
Prudential	$909.12	$525.12	$384.00	$384.00	0.0
Aetna	825.12	630.72	194.40	384.00	$189.60
Blue	846.12	574.92	271.20	384.00	112.80

[a]1971.

Source: See text for description of policies.

Indemnity Plan would provide coverage at the lowest total price to the insured. The higher the proportion of outpatient treatments and the more even the distribution of treatments among family members, the greater are the advantages of the Aetna plan from a price standpoint.

Table 2-4 itemizes expenses totalling $4,480, incurred by family member B in connection with a back injury, in the same year and in addition to the expenses shown in Table 2-2. These expenses exceeded the deductible amount of $150 within the 90-day limit of the Prudential plan. Both the Prudential plan and the Blue plan would cover all hospital and surgical costs in this case; the Aetna plan would cover in full only the first $1,000 of hospital room and board. The Prudential plan would pay $4,220 in benefits, and the Blue plan would pay $4,260, but Aetna would pay only $3,744. Moreover, because family member B's expenses exceeded Prudential and Blue plan deductibles, his other medical costs would also be reimbursable. Table 2-5 shows the effect of family member B's expenses on total family expenditures. The Blue plan would be the least costly of the 3 plans in this situation, not only because it would provide the largest reimbursement for member B's medical expenses but also because its lower and less restrictive deductible would enable member A to be reimbursed for part of his expenses. If B were the only family member to incur covered medical expenses, the Prudential plan would be the least expensive, with a total family cost of $788.92; the Blue plan would have been next, at a total cost of $798.72.

Table 2-6 assumes that, instead of a back ailment, member B suffered a "nervous breakdown" and required weekly psychotherapy as well as some medication. All other family medical expenses remained the same. Fifty-two psychiatric consultations at $35 per session cost $1,820; medication, $75. The Prudential plan covers only up to 50 percent of the cost of psychotherapy and only for 50 sessions. The other 2 plans cover 80 percent above the deductible—

Table 2-4
Assumed Expenses of Model Family Member B for Treatment of a Back Injury[a]

Total	$4,480
First hospitalization—January	
7 days' room and board @ $80 per day	560
Miscellaneous hospital expenses	400
Surgeon's fee (myelogram)	100
Related visits to doctor's office before and after myelogram	175
Outpatient laboratory tests	50
Drugs	25
Second hospitalization—April	
14 days' room and board	1,120
Miscellaneous hospital expenses	900
Anesthetist	100
Surgeon's fee (spinal surgery)	600
Special nurses	200
Follow-up doctor care	
Office visits	175
Drugs	25
Back brace	50

[a]Incurred during same year as assumed expenses shown in Table 2-2.

$100 for the Blue plan and $50 for the Aetna plan. The Prudential plan would pay only $860 of family member B's psychiatric expenses plus medication, whereas the Blue plan would cover $1,436 and the Aetna plan $1,476.

In cases such as that of the woman with multiple sclerosis and leukemia described earlier, the Prudential plan, with its $100,000 lifetime maximum per person, would obviously be superior.

Thus the relative worth of different plans depends largely on the insured's medical needs which are unknown when the plan is selected. And even quite comprehensive plans, because of their internal limitations and maximums, may leave the insured with substantial out-of-pocket medical expenditures.

Emphasis on Low-Risk Coverage

The traditional purpose of insurance, other than health insurance, is to protect the insured individual against unforeseeable events that may cause damage too extensive for him or her to bear alone. Most health insurance plans, however, involve far less risk spreading, because they are frequently written to emphasize low risk coverage and because most of the insured incur small losses at a fairly

Table 2-5
Comparison of Assumed Total Annual Expenses for Covered Medical Services for a Family of 4, Requiring Hospitalization and Surgery, under 3 Group Plans

	Family Expenditures			Treatments Covered by Health Insurance Plan	
Plan	Total (Col. 1 = Col. 2 + Col. 3)	Premium[a] (Col. 2)	Out-of-Pocket (Col. 3 = Col. 4 − Col. 5)	Total Cost (Col. 4)	Reimbursement by Plan (Col. 5)
Prudential	$1,157.92	$525.12	$632.80	$4,864.00	$4,231.20
Aetna	1,561.12	630.72	930.40	4,864.00	3,933.60
Blue	1,054.92	574.92	480.00	4,864.00	4,384.00

[a]1971.
Source: See text for description of policies.

Table 2-6
Comparison of Assumed Total Annual Expenses for Covered Medical Services for a Family of 4, Not Requiring Hospitalization or Surgery but Requiring Psychiatric Care, under 3 Group Plans

	Family Expenditures			Treatments Covered by Health Insurance Plan	
Plan	Total (Col. 1)	Premium[a] (Col. 2)	Out-of-Pocket (Col. 3 = Col. 4 − Col. 5)	Total Cost (Col. 4)	Reimbursement by Plan (Col. 5)
Prudential	$1,932.32	$525.12	$1,407.20	$2,279.00	$ 871.80
Aetna	1,232.32	630.72	601.60	2,279.00	1,677.40
Blue	1,293.32	574.92	718.40	2,279.00	1,500.60

[a]1971.
Source: See text for description of policies.

constant rate.[18] The major private carriers polled for this study, reported that 40 to 60 percent of the claims they handled in 1969 represented amounts under $100. The nationwide survey conducted in 1970 by the Gallup Organization for this study (see Appendix C) found that only 38 percent of the respondents with health insurance had filed claims amounting to more than $500 in the 5 years from 1965 through 1969. (These figures suggest that slightly more than 7 percent of the insured public filed claims of this magnitude in any year. But as a result of inflation in medical costs and the expansion in coverage in recent years, more people may have filed claims for over $500 in 1969 than in 1965.)

The popularity of low-risk insurance coverage stems in part from the early days of Blue Cross-Blue Shield, which was intended to protect the providers (hospitals and doctors) of medical services from unpaid bills. The Blue plans therefore offered "first-dollar" coverage.[19] The policies of private carriers generally do not provide "first-dollar" coverage, but their deductibles are usually small and allow for the payment of many small claims.

Labor unions have generally favored policies providing broad coverage to meet the immediate needs of most of their members, rather than coverage for catastrophic and atypical medical expenses. Union efforts have helped to make low-risk coverage characteristic of employment-based group plans. The unions first showed marked interest in health insurance during World War II. At that time wage ceilings restricted wage increases, but fringe benefits were recognized as legitimate items for collective bargaining. It is natural, therefore, that unions considered health insurance primarily as an income supplement rather than as risk protection.

But under the present voluntary health insurance system of the United States, low-risk coverage is quite costly. The public's total expenditures for health care would probably be less if each person with an income paid for routine, relatively inexpensive medical services directly out of his own pocket.[20]

One major company estimates that the premium for a group plan with a $500 deductible would be 48 percent of the premium for the same plan with a $100 deductible. Thus, in 1971, a relatively comprehensive group policy with a $100-per-person, annual deductible cost about $600 annually per family in premiums. The same policy would cost $288 annually if the deductible were increased to $500 per person.[21] The lower deductible, for $312 per year, provides protection against possible medical expenses that most families with an income can bear themselves. Many may feel that the added coverage is worth $312. But the cost of administration and handling claims in the $100 to $500 range probably averages around 20 percent of the premium, an exorbitant rate at which to pay an intermediary for handling bills as predictable as many common household expenditures.

The public, nevertheless, demands low-risk coverage. Both the purchasers of group policies, which are usually employment-connected fringe benefits, and those who exercise their individual judgment in buying health insurance show a strong preference for low-risk protection. Companies queried for this study report that, in spite of their efforts to promote major medical policies not tied to low-risk basic plans but designed to stand alone and provide a wide range of protection above a high deductible, such plans have never been popular. This prejudice was, perhaps, best dramatized by the experience of the faculty of the University of Pennsylvania which, given the option of a major medical alone or a major medical plus basic coverage overwhelmingly chose the latter even though the $400 in first-dollar-coverage cost the insured $350 per annum.[22] The low-risk insurance system thus functions as a prepayment system. Most insured individuals apparently would rather make a predictable, fixed payment for routine and relatively small medical expenses than pay these expenses out-of-pocket as they occur. Yet a high deductible can be substantially more economical for all concerned. For example, in 1969, a family of 4 headed by a 40-year-old male could buy a major medical policy covering 80 percent of a wide range of medical expenses, with a $750 deductible and $15,000 maximum benefit per illness, at a premium cost of $380 per annum. Increasing the maximum to $25,000 per illness would raise the premium cost to $453 per annum—less than a 20 percent increase in premium for a 67 percent increase in maximum coverage. But a modest basic policy, supplementing the major medical by covering first-dollar hospital and surgical expenses (subject to limitations), would cost an additional $300.[23]

Carriers discount premiums disproportionately as deductibles rise, largely because of the high cost of handling claims relative to the value of claims at the lower end. In some individual policies a $50 deductible per illness for a family of four costs about $100 more per year than a $100 deductible. A $100 deductible eliminates all claims up to $100.01. If an insured family filed claims for expenses of 2 illnesses in one year and each illness cost $90, the insured with a $100 deductible plan would receive nothing. The insured with the $50 deductible would receive $40 per illness or a total of $80—$20 less than the $100 he paid in premiums for the lower deductible. And the cost to the carrier of processing these 2 small claims would probably consume most, if not all, of the $20. (See Chapter 3.)

However, the most serious drawback of low-risk insurance is not its effect on the insured's premiums or the insurer's profits, but rather its lack of constraint on the utilization of medical services and the prices charged by providers.

Cost Concern under Private Insurance

Until very recently health insurance underwriters in the private sector found it relatively simple to adjust to rising medical costs by raising premium rates. And because these rate increases met little significant resistance, insurers made little effort to control medical costs or to find more efficient ways of financing health care. (States that regulate Blue Cross-Blue Shield rates have tended to resist requests from the Blue plans for rate increases, but there is no evidence that these efforts have restrained either rising medical costs or rising health insurance premiums.)

How insurance is acquired and paid for can have only an indirect effect on the demand for the service the insurance covers, and this indirect effect is a function of the premium cost. If the premium rises inordinately fast the insured may find other ways to protect himself, possibly by buying less insurance and/or by modifying his use of the insured service. The rapid rise in automobile insurance premium rates, for example, was unquestionably a factor in bringing about requirements for more effective automobile bumpers.

If the insured reacted in this way to a rise in health insurance premiums he might, for example, develop an interest in large deductible, high-risk insurance and indicate a willingness to "self-insure" for the low risks, or show greater interest in prepaid group practice plans. Rising costs have not had this "indirect effect" on demand in health insurance to any significant degree because they are of limited concern to the insured. In fact, the insured have very little knowledge about the extent or cost of their health insurance coverage. Even people who are insured under individual policies and pay their own premiums often have an imperfect understanding of the real cost of their health insurance in terms of the coverage it provides. But it is under group plans, which account for two-thirds of the gross enrollments and over half of the benefit payments of public and private health insurance operations combined, that ignorance and indifference to the cost of health insurance is most widespread and significant.

Group Policies and Consumer Ignorance of Costs

Enrollment in a particular group plan is generally fortuitous, since most group health insurance is acquired as an employment fringe benefit. According to a recent Bureau of Labor Statistics study, 66 percent of urban factory workers and 53 percent of urban office workers in 1970 were enrolled in noncontributory hospitalization and surgical plans—that is, plans for which they paid no part of the premium. Noncontributory major medical plans covered 37 percent of urban factory workers and 45 percent of urban office workers. A recent article in the *Social Security Bulletin* estimates that employers pay at least 70 percent of the cost of health insurance premiums under employment-connected group programs.[24] If the employee contributes to the premium cost, his contribution is likely to take the form of a payroll deduction and to be listed on his pay voucher along with various other deductions such as taxes, retirement, and union dues.

In the Gallup survey conducted for this study each respondent was asked to choose from a list of 5 items—one of which was health insurance—the one that had increased the most in price from 1966 to 1971. Of those enrolled in group plans, 57 percent cited "food" and 27 percent "health insurance." Actually, food prices increased by 16 percent during this period, and medical costs increased by 29 percent.[25] There is no price index for health insurance, but, partly because of broadened coverage, the premiums of most group plans rose considerably more than medical costs. The respondents did show some awareness of the trend in health insurance costs relative to other costs; a large number of them replied correctly that the cost of health insurance premiums had risen more rapidly than the cost of rent, clothing, and automobiles. Only 22 percent of the women polled, as opposed to 31 percent of the men, believed that the cost of health insurance had increased more than the cost of other items. This difference has special significance for cost constraints on health insurance; women use medical services more frequently than men do and, in families with children, probably make most family decisions to seek medical care.[26]

The survey also indicated that few respondents knew the actual cost of their health insurance. Asked how much their own health insurance cost, 16 percent of married respondents with comprehensive coverage under group plans would not even hazard a guess. Of the remaining 84 percent, 45 percent estimated their premiums at less than $20 per month, 25 percent in the $21-30 range, 17 percent in the $31-40 range, 9 percent in the $41-50 range and the remainder (less than 5 percent) over $50 per month. No group plan found in the course of this study that could be considered "comprehensive" by any acceptable definition had a lower premium level than $20 per month—the most popular estimate in the poll. At the same time, only 17 percent of the respondents who attempted estimates put the premiums in the $30 to $40 range, the price range of most large group comprehensive plans. The low bias of these estimates suggests that most employees do not think of their health insurance premiums as foregone income or realize how much foregone take-home pay the premiums represent.

Trade Union Reactions to Rising Costs

Employee representatives who negotiate health insurance contracts with either employers or insurance carriers are, on the other hand, often quite knowledge-able as to cost and extent of coverage. Labor unions often hire consultants—many of whom are former officials of insurance companies—to assist them in buying health insurance.

But the union negotiator may not be able to use his knowledge to resist rising prices, because the membership he represents does not share his understanding of the issue. He cannot react to rising prices by, for example, choosing a plan with reduced coverage, because in the face of rising medical costs he is under considerable pressure to obtain still broader coverage. It is also difficult for employees to understand, for example, why an 8 percent wage increase may not be an 8 percent increase in take-home pay, because part of that 8 percent must pay the rising costs of a benefit won years ago.

The response of the unions to rising health costs has taken three forms, none of which involves resisting the rising price of health insurance. First, the unions have tried to negotiate larger collective bargaining packages to cover rising health insurance prices as well as to increase take-home pay and improve other fringe benefits. Second, in many cases they have attempted to broaden their health insurance coverage in order to justify the higher cost even though the additional coverage itself is not very costly. For example, the 1969 U.S. Steel contract increased the maximum number of days of hospital coverage for employees with

10 years or more service from 365 to 730. The unions have also obtained increases in maximum dollar limits and coverage of such illnesses as drug addiction and alcoholism. These are important but not costly changes that help explain rises in premium rates to the union membership.

Finally, unions have been in the forefront of efforts to transfer the responsibility for financing health insurance to the federal government. Both the AFL-CIO and the United Automobile Workers (UAW) support the Griffiths-Corman and the Kennedy bills which, by making health insurance a responsibility of the public sector, would eliminate it as a collective bargaining issue. These unions strongly oppose all bills which would leave health insurance in the private sector so that certain aspects of financing health insurance would remain issues for collective bargaining.

Reactions to Medicare Premiums

Employed people make the payments for Medicare Part A through payroll deductions in their working years. The only part of Medicare that enrollees pay for in their retirement years is the voluntary Part B plan that covers outpatient costs. But the payments of Part B subscribers are automatically deducted from their Social Security retirement checks by the U.S. Treasury Department. And many subscribers may have failed to notice changes in rates (all but one of those that have occurred to date have been increased) because they have frequently coincided with increases in retirement benefits. Few subscribers are likely to pay attention to small changes such as the recent ones from $5.00 to $5.60 per month and then from $5.60 to $5.80. Moreover, a fairly sizable number of Medicare enrollees may not be aware that they are enrolled in either Part A or Part B. (See Appendix C.) Still more may not know the amount of the premium payment. The response of the government—the insurance underwriter for Medicare—to rising costs is discussed in Chapter 5.

The High Cost of Individual Coverage

Many holders of individual policies are unaware of the rise in health insurance costs and do not exert even an indirect influence on health costs or utilization of medical services. Half of all individual policies (by premium value) sold in 1969 were noncancelable and guaranteed renewable.[27] The premiums on many such policies remain fixed or level until the insured reaches a certain age—usually 65—but the dollar maximums for each insured service are also fixed. Only a few years ago, for example, insurers were offering policies that provided a maximum of $8.00 per day for hospital room and board. By 1971, hospital room and board charges in most large cities were about ten times that amount. Yet, a healthy person might continue paying the monthly premiums on such a policy without realizing that it had become virtually worthless.

An individual purchasing a policy generally does not start with a fixed limit on the amount he wishes to spend, or have a well-defined view of the coverage he seeks. He starts, rather, with an undefined need (which, to be sure, he must tailor to suit his income), and he is apt to lack the technical knowledge on which to base his decision. To add to his difficulties, he must try to relate the price of the coverage to the coverage offered.

Most buyers of individual policies probably try to obtain the fullest coverage that they can afford for hospital room and board, surgical schedule, number of days of hospital care and overall dollar maximums. Health care is so expensive that no person of average income can contemplate meeting the financial costs of long-term serious illness out-of-pocket. But nongroup insurance coverage is also expensive. An individual who wants the kind of complete coverage offered by several group plans today may find that he can obtain it only by buying several different, although probably overlapping, individual policies. The premiums on these policies may prove more costly than the treatment of many major ailments.

Buyers of individual policies may obtain fairly broad coverage by combining basic and major medical insurance, but few comprehensive individual policies approach, in either completeness of coverage or dollar maximums, the coverage that some of the higher priced group plans now provide. The lowest-priced combination of basic and major medical coverage found in the course of this study cost a family of 4 (40-year-old husband and wife) $415 annually in 1970.[28] The major medical portion of this plan pays 75 percent of eligible costs not covered by the basic policy up to a per illness maximum of $10,000. The basic policy provides only $20 per day for hospital room and board (about one-third to one-fourth the prevailing rate in most cities in 1970) for 100 days, per illness, and a maximum benefit for surgery of $200—lower, at today's rates, than the fees for most surgical procedures. The deductible, which ranges from $500 to $1,000 must be incurred in 90 days and thus eliminates most physicians' visits from coverage. Clearly, this policy provides much narrower coverage than such lower-priced group plans as, for example, the low option Blue Cross-Blue Shield plan sold to employees of the federal government at a premium cost of about $300 per year. Individual coverage comparable to even medium-priced comprehensive group plans, costing around $420 per year, would have cost $900 to $1,000 per year in 1970 for the family of four used here as the model.

Summary

The health insurance system that has evolved in the United States essentially maintains intact the traditional relationship between the users of medical services and the providers. In other words, the patient is still free to choose his physician and to consume whatever quantity of medical services he and his physician decide upon, while the physician, for the most part, is free to charge for his services according to his own dictates (except for periodic price control situations). At the same time, the health insurance system makes available to most people a way to pay for some of the medical services they use at no direct cost to themselves. The variety and quantity of medical services being consumed through this system is growing rapidly and the insured individual's involvement in paying the cost of the insurance itself is diminishing apace as noncontributory plans grow more popular. The growth of insurance has, thus, greatly reduced and, in some cases, eliminated an element that in the pre-insurance era was critical to the rational functioning of the system: i.e., the market role of price in influencing the patient's determination of the quantity and variety of medical services he would use.

Since a number of national health insurance proposals would merely extend the present system by broadening coverage and expanding enrollment, it is worth noting what might be required to restore some measure of the consumer's traditional market role.

The essential elements of the consumer's incentive to perform his traditional market role—seeking the "best buy" among competing alternatives—are knowledge of price, participation in payment of the premium (so that the consumer can benefit financially from his choice), and knowledge of the coverage offered.

Knowledge of the price of insurance requires that cost-sharing and copayment requirements be standardized, for only standardization will permit the consumer to make valid comparisons of different plans. These requirements should also be large enough to affect the consumer's use of medical services.

The consumer should bear directly at least part of the cost of his health insurance premiums. Under the present system he bears these costs indirectly for the most part, through foregone income or through higher prices for medical services that an unforeseeable, uncovered illness may require him to pay out-of-pocket, but he generally has little knowledge about or interest in the actual premium.

If the consumer is to understand the coverage that is available to him, definitions of medical costs and medical services will also have to be standardized. This task would not be easy, for it can be argued with some justice that many services that do not involve traditional medical personnel (special doors for paraplegics, bathroom fixtures for paralytics) merit coverage, while many physicians' services such as cosmetic surgery do not.

It can be argued that the consumer should not be subject to the constraints of the market in seeking medical services in any case. But since no known system has succeeded so far in making unlimited medical care completely free to the consumer, some constraints are unavoidable, whether through some variation of the market mechanism, through arbitrary limits imposed by the state, through provider incentives, or through some other means. Other forms of restraining demand and allocating resources will be examined later. But if it is decided simply to extend the present system, the consumer's market role will have to be restored to a sufficient extent to make him respond to some degree to price, quantity and quality factors.

3

Health Insurance Bureaucracy: The Blue Plans and the Private Carriers

In June 1971, addressing a meeting of the Group Health Association of America, Senator Edward M. Kennedy referred to "those new monuments to inflation in health costs—the magnificent modern towers of insurance company office buildings dotting the sky lines."[1] At the same meeting, Leonard Woodcock, president of the United Automobile Workers, announced that private health insurance had failed Americans by not establishing effective cost and quality controls for medical care.

In fact, private insurers are not solely responsible for the inadequacies of our health insurance system, and their real failings are not an illustration of the evils of private enterprise for profit. As shown in Table 3-1, of the 12 largest private carriers (accounting for 38 percent of health insurance premiums in 1969), 5 are mutual companies that distribute "profits" only to policyholders, and 3 are nonprofit Blue Cross plans. The remaining 4 are profit-oriented stock companies, but such companies receive less than 35 percent of all private sector health insurance premiums. These percentages include income loss insurance, as do all data based on individual company statistics used elsewhere in this study. The published data on individual private carriers—Blue plans do not market income loss insurance—do not separate income loss premiums from conventional health insurance premiums. Separate figures for health and income loss insurance for the private carriers are available from a confidential trade association survey, but these data are published (by the Health Insurance Association of America and the U.S. Department of Health, Education, and Welfare) only on an aggregate basis for all carriers.

Insurers have only a limited opportunity to influence the price of medical care directly. Certainly they are not responsible for developing the medical techniques that account for perhaps a third of the increase in medical costs in the last 20 years. But insurers have made little effort to increase their influence on medical care costs and utilization. They have failed to provide complete, uniform, understandable health insurance coverage, and they have not done much to facilitate equitable distribution of medical services. But, given the nature and intensity of the competition that has historically characterized the health insurance business as well as the regulatory framework in which they have functioned, it is hardly plausible to expect that they would have played this role.

At the same time, reports to state insurance commissioners reveal that executive salaries of those engaged in conventional health insurance operations in the private sector are comparatively modest. The average salary—exclusive of

37

Table 3-1

Earned Health Premiums of the 12 Major Conventional Health Insurance Underwriters, 1969

Underwriter	Classification	Earned Health Premiums[a] (Millions)
Aetna	Life (stock)	$ 939.4
Travelers	Life (stock)	821.3
Metropolitan	Life (mutual)	739.2
Prudential	Life (mutual)	645.8
Equitable	Life (mutual)	465.6
Mutual of Omaha	Life (mutual)	428.4
Associated Hospital Service (N.Y.)	Blue Cross (nonprofit)	426.0
Connecticut General	Life (stock)	413.2
Continental Casualty	Casualty (stock)	375.5
Michigan Hospital Service	Blue Cross (nonprofit)	366.5
John Hancock	Life (mutual)	281.3
Massachusetts Blue Cross	Blue Cross (nonprofit)	236.3

[a]For private carriers figures include income loss insurance as well as health insurance.

Sources: *Argus Chart of Health Insurance 1970* (Cincinnati, National Underwriter Co., 1970); and *Blue Cross and Blue Shield Fact Book 1970* (Chicago: Blue Cross Association and National Association of Blue Shield Plans, 1970).

pensions, stock options and other fringe benefits, the value of which often equals or exceeds the salary—for the top 3 executives of the 6 largest private carriers selling health insurance, as listed in Table 3-1, was $107,000 in 1969, compared with an average of $202,000 for the 3 top executives of large corporations in other industries whose records were examined at random in company reports on file at the Securities and Exchange Commission.[2] The annual salary of Walter J. McNerney, president of the national Blue Cross Association, was $80,000 in the same year.

The private carriers as well as the Blue plans operate much as insurance enterprises have for generations. Fiscal conservatism and the pursuit of solvency are major concerns of both the nonprofit Blue plans and those private carriers that market private conventional health insurance (as opposed to prepaid group practice plans and similar health programs where the insurer and provider are part of the same organization). The pressures of competition and the direction of state regulations make it inevitable that the financial responsibilities of insurers are more important than their direct role in the health care system.

While both segments of the private sector have been forced by competition to a business behavior based largely on financial considerations, there are nonetheless important differences between the two systems. Of particular importance among these differences is the total concentration of Blue Cross-Blue Shield on the health care sector; their virtually complete reliance on health insurance for premium incomes and their unique relationship with health care providers. While the entry of the private carriers into the health insurance field has reduced the significance of these differences in present circumstances, they are nonetheless important in the health insurance reform context.

The Private Carriers

Health insurance is a new component of an old, well-established business. Only an estimated 5 percent of all those employed in insurance are engaged in the health insurance operations of these private carriers. Financially, too, the health insurance line is not yet of great importance to most private carriers, nor is it likely to become so in the next decade.

Both mutual and stock companies sell health insurance, generally, as a secondary line. Insurance carriers must register with the state as either life or casualty companies, and although both may sell health insurance, most that do so are registered as life companies. In addition, holding companies may control subsidiaries that sell life, casualty, and health insurance. Of the more than 1000 private carriers, only 40 specialize in selling accident and health policies, and of these only Mutual of Omaha ranks among the top 12 health insurance underwriters in premium volume (see Table 3-1). The large carriers dominate the health insurance field and control the major part of group business, even though many small companies manage to participate, mostly through sales of individual health policies and income loss insurance. The top 20 companies sell almost three-fourths of the private carrier premium volume, as shown in Table 3-2.

Table 3-2
Share of All Health Premiums Sold by Top 4, 8, and 20 Private Carriers, 1960 and 1969

Ranking of Carriers	Percent of Premium Volume	
	1960	1969
Top 4	31	29
Top 8	51	55
Top 20	65	73

Source: *Argus Chart of Health Insurance, 1970* (Cincinnati: National Underwriter Co., 1970.)

Some of these giants had annual health insurance sales of almost $1 billion in 1969, when the sales of most carriers were less than $1 million. But the private carriers have had a significant impact on health insurance. Prior to 1940, group health insurance, or "group hospitalization," was largely the domain of Blue Cross, which had twice as many hospitalization plan enrollments as the private carriers. But during World War II, wartime price stabilization regulations prohibited increases in money wages but permitted increases in fringe benefits, such as health insurance, that were thought to be less inflationary. At the same time, health insurance became a recognized demand in collective bargaining negotiations, and a new market of unknown proportions was opened up to the private carriers. By 1969 enrollment in group hospital coverage offered by private carriers exceeded Blue Cross group hospitalization enrollment by more than 25 percent.[3]

The private carriers achieved this dominant position in the group health insurance market through their ability to service nationwide groups and their willingness to set premiums on an "experience rating" basis—calculating financial risk on the basis of the age, sex composition, job hazards, and other characteristics of the particular group for which the policy is being prepared and adjusting premium levels accordingly. The tax exempt Blue plans used the system of "community rating," which takes into account the characteristics of all the citizens who might use the medical care of an area or region.[4] Under community rating, groups such as the elderly who were likely—statistically—to make extensive use of medical services paid the same premiums as groups such as single people and young persons whose utilization of medical service was likely to be low. Those with low claim levels subsidized those with high claim levels consistent with the true equity concept of insurance. Community rating made it possible for certain groups—the aged and those with chronic ailments—considered poor risks for health insurance to obtain insurance at a reasonable premium rate. Many Blue Cross-Blue Shield plans continued to determine premium rates on a community-wide basis for some years after the private carriers became significant competitors.

But employers and union groups, when offered the chance, found it advantageous to move away from the community rating system and profit from the lower premiums experience rating provided. If the Blue plans had refused to abandon community rating, they would have been left with a portfolio of adverse risks as their share of the health insurance business. The universal adoption of experience rating meant that certain groups could no longer obtain health insurance coverage at a reasonable cost. (Eventually the government took responsibility for providing coverage for these groups through the Medicare program and, to a lesser extent, the Medicaid program.)

The Blue Cross-Blue Shield Plans

From a program pioneered by a group of school teachers in Baylor, Texas, in 1929, the combined Blue Cross-Blue Shield organizations have grown to a point where, today, they employ 56,000 people, including those engaged in administration of the Medicare, Medicaid, and Champus programs under contracts with the federal government. (See Chapter 5.) Their close affiliation with the hospitals and medical societies, which dates back to their inception, has been a matter of some controversy over the years, with critics charging that the Blue plans are really instruments of the providers rather than the consumers.[5] The American Hospital Association (AHA) has, in fact, been an important element in the development of Blue Cross; far more important than the medical societies in the development of Blue Shield. In the early years, in fact, the guarantee given subscribers by participating hospitals that they would not look to them for payment (for the insured period) whether or not the Blue Cross Plan had the financial wherewithal to pay the bill was a critical factor in gaining public confidence and launching this fledgling organization on a successful growth path. Today, however, this guarantee is of little importance given the assets and volume of premium income Blue Cross plans have attained.

Another major change which has occurred in the *modus operandi* of the Blue plans and which has had an important effect on the evolution of health insurance in the United States concerns their method of establishing premium rates for group plans. The private carriers originally had an advantage over the Blue plans in competing for large groups, because they could use experience rating and did not have to go to the expense of dealing with the medical care providers. The Blue plans have competitive cost advantages of their own. Unlike the private carriers, the Blue plans are nonprofit and tax-exempt. Furthermore, the Blue plans operate on a "service benefits" basis, making payments directly to the hospitals and doctors on the basis of a negotiated cost figure, rather than reimbursing the insured as the private carriers normally do under "indemnity" plans. In most cases Blue Cross makes prior agreements with participating hospitals to pay actual costs that are generally somewhat less than the hospitals' usual schedule of charges, which include a share of the cost of welfare patient care, long-range building costs in some instances, research and other costs not directly related to treatment of paying patients, in addition to the actual per diem costs incurred by the individual patient. This discount, according to some private carriers, gives Blue Cross an advantage in setting premiums.[6]

Blue Shield, on the other hand, has failed to persuade participating physicians to accept its fee schedules as full payment except for some subscriber groups with very low incomes. In recent years, Blue Shield has begun reimbursing participating physicians on the basis of the fees that are "usual, customary and reasonable" (UCR) for the particular service in the area covered by the plan. Under this complex arrangement (discussed further in Chapter 7), Blue Shield expects participating physicians to accept payment at a given percentile of the UCR as payment in full, although physicians may of course charge less. While Blue Shield thus gains some control over physicians' fees, it probably does not derive a competitive advantage from selling service benefit insurance.

In addition to abandoning community rating in order to compete on a national basis, local plans were forced to yield some of their autonomy to their respective national organizations—the Blue Cross Association (BCA) and the National Association of Blue Shield Plans (NABSP). As the large trade unions, whose membership overlapped the jurisdictions of several local Blue plans, started negotiating uniform health benefits, the local plans involved had to form syndicates to offer uniform benefits and rates to all groups covered by a given union contract. For example, about 40 local Blue Cross plans, under the name of Blue Cross of Western Pennsylvania, acted together to draw up the Blue Cross-United States Steel-United Steel Workers policy. In some cases such syndicates were not feasible, and Blue Cross-Blue Shield local plans passed some of the negotiating function to the national organizations. Both the BCA and the NABSP have established separate nonprofit insurance companies for the purpose of underwriting and administering contracts or parts of contracts that local plans cannot handle.

The influence that Blue Cross and Blue Shield can exert on medical costs is limited (see Chapters 6 and 7) in part because most local plans enroll only a minority of the health insurance policyholders in the areas they serve. Blue Cross's share of total gross enrollments for hospital coverage dropped sharply after the private carriers entered the field, but it then leveled off and in recent years has begun a modest recovery (see Figure 1-1).

Even though the Blue plans have regained some ground in the enrollment race, wielding the kind of influence over providers the public sometimes expects requires more than simply gaining membership. In order to compete effectively with private carriers, the Blue plans have had to offer providers terms that are attractive enough to assure subscribers a choice of participating hospitals and physicians. Private carriers need make no demands on the providers such as the Blue plans are expected to do. Thus, many providers feel little incentive to respond to pressures from Blue Cross-Blue Shield since they can feel secure of an adequate clientele financed under private insurance plans. Furthermore, groups purchasing insurance cannot necessarily be induced to buy the kind of coverage that would produce the best utilization pattern for the entire community. Testifying before the Hart Subcommittee on Antitrust and Monopoly, in 1971, Blue Cross president Walter J. McNerney stated that Blue Cross-Blue Shield services 7 of the 10 largest industries in the United States, and that these plans emphasize inpatient hospital coverage, not at the instigation of the participating hospitals but because the labor unions specifically requested such coverage.[7]

Blue Cross and Blue Shield are not, as they have been called, merely collection agencies for the hospitals and medical societies that created them. They are, however, subject to many of the same pressures as their profitmaking competitors and must be just as responsive to operating cost considerations, which limits their ability to influence providers. The local Blue plan boards of directors can provide the services demanded by large groups only by remaining on good terms with hospitals and medical societies. At the same time they must maintain their staffs of trained and dedicated personnel. And they cannot, as their private carrier competitors can, pick up any slack through marketing other forms of insurance (although 2 plans—in Jacksonville, Florida, and in the state of South Carolina—have agency agreements to sell life insurance to group clients). They can accomplish these objectives only through continual growth—picking up their share, or more, of an expanding market, increasing subscription income, and protecting this growth with a reserve base to facilitate expansion into new programs. They must, in other words, compete with the private carriers on terms that, in many ways, are inconsistent with the community responsibilities they were created to meet. The policies and selling techniques of the Blue plans increasingly resemble those of the private carriers, although their organizations, their relations with medical care providers, and the treatment they receive from state regulatory agencies still differ widely.

State Regulation of Health Insurance

Insurance is the largest and most important interstate business activity still regulated almost entirely by the states, and the insurance companies have worked hard to keep the regulatory function at the state level. In 1944, the Supreme Court ruled that insurance companies were involved in interstate commerce and subject to federal regulation.[8] A year later, Congress passed the Insurance Regulation Act, which formally delegated regulative authority to the states by declaring "that the silence on the part of the Congress shall not be construed to impose any barrier to the regulation or taxation of such business by the several states." Although the 1944 ruling still stands, today the federal government controls insurance operations only in the traditional areas of securities regulation through the Securities and Exchange Commission, federal tax and antitrust laws, and advertising regulations of the Federal Trade Commission that apply mostly to mail-order business. Nonetheless, the Supreme Court's 1944 ruling makes it clear that the federal government can expand its regulation of the health insurance industry if it wishes.

The state insurance commissioners who are responsible for state regulation of insurance attempt to coordinate and standardize their activities through the National Association of Insurance Commissioners (NAIC). Reflecting the concerns and knowledge of the commissioners themselves, this organization is designed to deal with insurance problems—not health care. The principal aim of regulation of the private insurers is to keep them solvent. Some state commissioners—notably Pennsylvania state commissioner Denenberg—have tried to use their authority to influence health costs and medical services, but their terms of reference are too narrow to permit such efforts to have any real, lasting effect. Some insurance spokesmen recognize that health insurance differs from other forms of insurance and that its unique features require regulation at the federal level,[9] but the insurance companies' traditional fear of federal regulation inhibits them from putting forward proposals that might open this Pandora's box.

Private carriers are not subject to rate regulation. They have, in fact, only one general guideline—that is, to set premium rates high enough to meet the claims likely to arise under the coverage they have contracted to provide and to retain sufficient reserves to avert the danger of insolvency. State insurance regulations impose on the private carriers no incentive to analyze the costs of the medical services they cover or the effects of their coverage on the demand for those services, and no responsibility for questioning doctors' fees, hospital rates, hospital efficiency, duplication of services, or the necessity of certain medical treatments. Private carriers have been sharply criticized for failing to influence the cost and quality of medical care, but the regulations that guide their behavior have never required them to do so.

The relationship of Blue Cross and Blue Shield with the medical care providers does give them an opportunity and, as much of the public believes, a responsibility to influence costs. State insurance commissioners or rate-setting commissions in some states regulate the premium rate changes of the Blue plans, and in some states it has become politically popular to deny or delay requests for Blue Cross rate increases in order to pressure Blue Cross to resist rising hospital costs more vigorously. In Massachusetts, Michigan, New Jersey, New York, and Pennsylvania, where Blue Cross enrollment is concentrated and unionization is high, insurance commissioners have actively intervened in the rate-making process.

Some of the battles over rate increases have become quite acrimonious. In New York, for example, the city government tried through court action to force the state insurance department to bar Blue Cross-Blue Shield rate increases in the city. But ultimately, in most all cases, since the medical cost increases had already taken place, the rate adjustments had to be granted if the plans were to continue to service their subscribers. The publicity given these cases may have deterred the Blue plans from making additional requests for rate increases and helped, indirectly, to hold the costs of medical services down temporarily. In the meantime, the private carriers have been raising their rates without interference from state insurance commissioners or the publicity that accompanies such interference.

Competition and Operating Costs

With competition so keen, one would expect operating costs to be at a minimum. For group insurance, direct or "visible" operating costs—that is, those included in the premium costs—have been kept relatively low. Yet overall operating costs are enormous. Large numbers of individuals cannot obtain group coverage and are forced to seek coverage under individual policies with exorbitant operating costs. Moreover, even group policies carry a substantial "invisible" administrative cost, which does not appear in the premium calculations but which is a cost to society nonetheless.

Direct or visible operating costs in general cover the following functions:

Claims handling, which involves establishment and maintenance of enrollment records and eligibility dates, the processing and payment of claims amounts to as much as 4 percent of premiums and is the largest single item of administrative expense.

Statistical services, which provide actuarial data and analyses on such subjects as utilization of physicians' services and length of stay in hospitals.

Marketing, which includes some advertising and public relations as well as selling costs, including salesmen's commissions paid by the private carriers and salaries of Blue plan salesmen.

Collection, which essentially includes billing subscribers and policyholders. This cost is often included as part of selling costs.

Investment, which involves handling and investing the carrier's assets.

Taxes, licenses and fees, which, for the private carriers and a few Blue plans, amounts to 2.0 to 2.3 percent of premiums.[10]

Public relations, which is generally a minor item including such expenses as membership dues in insurance associations and the cost of collection and publication of data for public consumption.

Provider relations, which applies almost solely to the Blue plans and involves the cost of their dealings with local hospitals and medical societies about fees, hospital costs, regional planning, and other problems.

Since these functions overlap and definitions and accounting procedures differ from company to company, it is not possible to attribute precise costs to each function. Estimates of claims handling costs vary from company to company, for example, because some companies attribute activities that could legitimately be calculated as part of the claims handling cost to other functions.

The insurance business uses "operating expense ratio" (the ratio of operating costs to premium level) as an indication of efficiency. Despite variations in definition of functions and in accounting procedures, the operating expense ratio is a useful but imprecise measure that must be applied with great care. It is used, for example, to compare the performance of different companies selling the same type of insurance—that is, for similar age groups or for groups with the same mix of hospital and surgical coverage, and so forth—or to compare the performance of the industry as a whole—that is, only those companies selling the same type of insurance—in different years. Unfortunately, the operating expense ratio, as currently used by the industry, does not give a complete picture of the cost of health insurance to the consumer. The definition of operating costs does not include federal income taxes, net contribution to reserves or surplus, or any distribution of earnings to stockholders. Since the sum of these items is greater than the annual income from investments attributable to health insurance, which is excluded from the income side of the operating expense ratio, the ratio understates the cost of providing health insurance.

In 1969, the operating expense ratios for group plans of the 9 large private carriers studied range from 8.8 percent to 11.6 percent with the exception of Continental Casualty, which reported a ratio of 24.7 percent. (See Appendix Table D-1.) The ratio for individual or nongroup coverage is, of course, much higher. These figures have changed little in recent years, although in 1969, 5 of the 9 major carriers studied had operating expense ratios of less than 10 percent, while not more than 3 carriers achieved such low ratios in either of the previous 2 years.

Among the hundreds of small carriers, operating ratios for group plans vary widely—ranging from about 10 percent, like those of the large carriers, to as high as 50 percent. The higher figure in this range probably represents those small carriers which may, in any given year, have a preponderance of new groups in their portfolios, with the high operating costs involved in setting up records the first year. For large carriers handling many more groups, the high expenses of new groups are usually balanced by the lower expenses of the large number of old groups. These data do not necessarily mean, therefore, that the small groups are less efficient.

For all the Blue Cross-Blue Shield plans, the operating expense ratio for group as well as nongroup policies was lower than that of any of the major private carriers—7.3 percent in 1969—in part because the Blue plans are exempt from certain state premium taxes. But even with taxes added in, operating expenses of the Blue plans would probably still be slightly lower than those of the private carriers, in part because the average salary of Blue Cross and Blue Shield personnel is about 10 percent lower than that paid by most private carriers.

Cost and Function of Claims Handling

Claims handling is a complex process. Upon receipt of a claim, the insurance company must first establish that the claimant was a paid-up policyholder or dependent of a policyholder at the time of the illness. If so, the claim must be honored, although the policyholder may subsequently have dropped the policy or withdrawn from the group coverage.

Next, the company must determine what type of contract the insured holds. A claim handled by Blue Cross or Blue Shield, for example, may stem from one or more of the following types of coverage: Basic Blue Cross or Blue Shield, Supplementary Coverage to the Basic Coverage, Medicare Part A, Medicare Part B, CHAMPUS, Special Groups and National Accounts, and the Federal Employees Benefits Program. For most private carriers, especially those selling individual policies, the variety of contracts is even greater.

The next step is to verify coverage for the illness to which the claim applies. For example, the claim may be for a pre-existing condition not covered by the contract; the specified waiting period for the particular illnesses may not have been satisfied; the service may not have been provided in an insured location—that is, typically, in a hospital, rather than in a doctor's office.

The company must then make sure that payment has not already been made for the services the claim covers. Both patient and doctor may have submitted separate claims, either by mistake or in a deliberate attempt to defraud the company.

Next, the claims section must determine the amount of the coinsurance payment to be made by the insured and the difference between the charge for the service and the deductible. The bill for a physician's service may have to be checked against a fee schedule or the doctor's "fee profile." Finally, a check must be written to the claimant or provider, his account must be posted so that a record of the annual and/or lifetime maximum will be available for future reference, and his group account must be posted as a basis for future premium negotiations. A large company may process as many as 50,000 health insurance claims a day, using both computers and a considerable amount of manpower.

The company must also allocate staff for questions and complaints (many prompted by computer errors) from providers and patients; its legal department must handle complaints that cannot be settled by normal correspondence and procedures; and it must maintain a utilization review procedure to check against abuse.

The "visible" costs to the insurance company, and ultimately to the insured, of processing a claim average between $4.00 and $5.00 per claim, although they may range from $2.00 to $18.00.[11] These costs do not vary significantly with the amount of the claim and are therefore much higher percentagewise for small claims than for large ones. The cost of handling small claims represents approximately 80 to 90 percent of total claims handling costs. In 1970, claims under $100, according to a survey made by the staff of this study, constituted over half of all claims processed by the large carriers. The cost of handling these is considerably greater than the insurance risk cost of the typical policy and has a significant impact on premium rates.

In addition to these "visible" costs, incurred directly and reported by the insurer, the handling of claims involves certain "invisible" costs. These are the costs of paying for health care through the insurance mechanism which accrue to the doctor, the patient and, under some group policies, the employer. The example cited in Figure 3-1, which reflects the claims settlements process under indemnity type group plans, involves 6 separate transactions. While it is not possible to quantify these costs, they add substantially to the patients' real medical bill and may even detract from the quality of medical care as indicated in Chapter 7.

Sales Costs and Commissions

While total claims handling costs are generally underestimated, selling costs are probably exaggerated by critics of the health insurance system. The selling costs

48

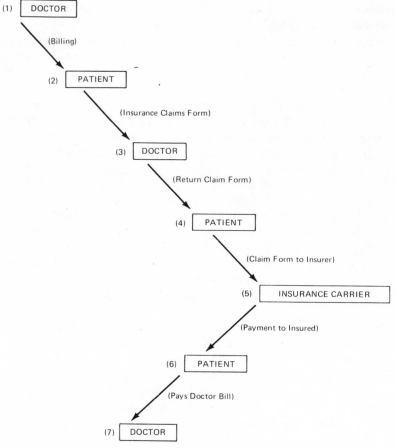

Figure 3-1. Transactions in Health Insurance (Indemnity) Claims Settlement

of group health insurance policies are not high. ("Selling cost" is sometimes used inaccurately as a synonym for "acquisition cost," which includes, in addition to selling cost, the initial cost of setting up records on a new insured.) The direct cost of selling group policies accounts for not more than 1 percent of the total premium value. Because group buyers are relatively sophisticated, advertising (a major selling cost in some industries) plays practically no role in the marketing of group policies. Selling costs consist of the salaries and commissions of those involved in marketing policies, plus the time of actuaries and others on the front office staff who design and determine the price of policies.

About 90 percent of the private carriers' health insurance plans are sold by agents who are paid on a commission basis. These agents are assisted by salaried "group representatives" or managers from the home office, who provide much of the technical expertise and who convey to the home office actuaries the type of policies desired by group buyers and how particular policies can be structured to fit group needs.

The buyers of group policies are generally well-informed, and the carriers strive to keep the cost of the premium as low as is consistent with group experience rating. Commission schedules, as a result, are low. Moreover the same amount of effort may be expended in selling a policy to a 100-member group as to a 2,000-member group, commission schedules decline rapidly as the premium level rises, as Table 3-3 illustrates. Commissions on group policies are usually paid on a level basis—that is, in equal annual payments for the first 10 or 20 years of a policy.

While the selling of group policies is thus a relatively efficient and economical operation, the marketing of individual policies is not. The operating expense ratios for individual policies run as high as 50 percent, as opposed to an average of 10 percent for group policies. Individual policies are sold on a person-to-person basis; the agent or broker deals directly, in most cases, with the buyer. The agent must explain the policy, which is always a complex document, to a buyer who is apt to be unsophisticated about health insurance coverage. The number of coverage combinations is infinite, and policy lapses are high. Commissions on individual policies therefore average 25 percent of the premium value.

Not all of the 25 percent is a true selling cost, however, since the agent may also assist the individual policyholder in claims processing or provide information and other services. But because the home office could probably perform these functions much less expensively, the agent's presence increases operating costs.

In addition to selling costs, the administrative expense of collecting premiums, the greater variety of coverage offered, the individual record-keeping involved, and the higher turnover rate also add to the premium costs of individual policies.

Table 3-3
Typical Commission Schedule (Level Basis) for Group Health Insurance Policies

	Commission Paid Per Year	
Premium Level	Amount	Percent
$ 10,000	$ 400	4.000
1,000,000	7,000	0.070
2,000,000	9,700	0.048
3,000,000	10,700	0.036

Source: Confidential field interviews conducted by staff of this study.

Summary

The conventional health insurance system thus emerges as an establishment that has been largely insensitive to the cost of medical care, utilization of services, and the use of resources by the health care sector. Regulation of health insurance—essentially the same as regulation of all insurance—has failed to recognize the great influence insurance has on the delivery of health care itself, and the insurers have therefore competed with each other in the financial arena to the neglect of the health care system.

In the administration of their financial responsibilities the conventional insurers have been relatively efficient. The question remains whether, in their pursuit of profits and growth, they have not in other ways added unnecessarily to the cost of health insurance, health care services, or both.

4 Profits, Reserves, and Motivations in Health Insurance

In a flier distributed in 1971, the AFL-CIO states that:

Private insurance is only interested in getting enough premium dollars to pay health care bills, overhead, commissions and advertising and still make a tidy profit. Last year, incidentally, out of $14 billion paid in as premiums, insurance companies pocketed more than $2 billion for profits, executive salaries, administrative costs and reserves.[1]

Some observers believe that the rise in the cost of health insurance and, indirectly, in the cost of health care has served mainly to expand profits in the health insurance industry. Others maintain that although health insurance is not profitable now, it may become so. As Harvard economist Rashi Fein puts it, "The reason industry wants in is to make money. They haven't been making money but they see a great potential."[2]

The ensuing analysis indicates that the present and potential profitability of the health insurance business is much more modest than these statements suggest. Nonetheless, though not likely to become a major source of profits to most private carriers in the next decade, health insurance premiums are growing rapidly, adding to the carriers' source of investment income. The rapid rise in medical costs has been a major cause of this growth, and it is an important factor when evaluating the role of the insurers in controlling medical costs since it makes inflation and the insurers natural allies whereas the welfare of the public might be better served if they were natural enemies.

Complicating the task of analyzing the effect of the pursuit of profits on health costs is a more fundamental disagreement among authorities on insurance finances about what constitutes "profit" in the insurance business as a whole. In fact, the insurance industry itself has under consideration a new accounting code for insurance that would center largely on profit measurement.[3] The Internal Revenue Code contains separate tax regulations for life insurance companies (Public Law 86-89, 86th Congress) in testimony of government recognition of the special nature of profit in insurance operations. These regulations have undergone many transformations. Prior to 1921 the government viewed insurance companies as ordinary corporations and taxed their dividends and increases in surplus. In 1921 a new law was passed taxing investment income as the "only true income of an insurance company." From 1921 to 1957 a number of definitions of "investment income" were used for tax purposes. Since 1957 a composite measure, described later in this chapter, has been in effect.[4]

51

The measurement of profits in health insurance presents some special problems in addition to those common to other lines of insurance. Over 40 percent of the premium income generated from conventional health insurance sales is attributable to the Blue Cross-Blue Shield plans. Although these organizations are nonprofit, they do accumulate surpluses to back up their operations. Mutual companies, which account for another 20 or 30 percent of the premium income, are also without a direct profit orientation; they distribute surpluses to policy holders as dividends, although such dividends are often programmed for promotional purposes.[5] Most of the private carriers that market health insurance also sell other forms of insurance, and the published data of both stock and mutual companies do not show what share of increases in surplus (in a sense a form of "retained earnings") is attributable to the health line. Insurance firms report income loss or disability insurance as health insurance, and it is not always possible to distinguish between the two.[6] Finally, underwriting gain—a popular indicator of the financial well-being of insurance operations—excludes certain income sources while reporting other sources on the basis of estimates that are subject to short-term manipulation.

The close integration of life and health insurance operations among the major stock companies means that traditional measures such as rates of return and price-earnings ratios cannot be used to determine health insurance profits. The carriers themselves consider that the profit on group policies should constitute 2 percent of operating costs or roughly 0.2 percent of premiums.[7] This amount does not seem excessive and in any case would not add appreciably to the cost of a group policy. The percentage of profit they anticipate on individual policies is undoubtedly higher.

The financial concepts used in the insurance business differ in several respects from those used in conventional business operations. The liabilities of the typical insurance company consist mostly of accounts payable called "reserves"—"incurred claims reserves," "unearned premium reserves," or "contingency reserves," according to the purpose for which they are intended—and "surplus," which is really an unassigned contingency reserve. The counterpart of the reserve accounts are the bonds, stocks, mortgages, and other investments held by the company that account for most of its assets. See, for example, Table 4-1, which is a balance sheet for Mutual of Omaha, the largest monoline health insurance company in the United States. The insurance company is basically a financial intermediary between the policyholders and the investors. Its principal activity is paperwork; traditional assets such as plant, equipment and inventory are thus not an important part of its asset holdings.

In examining the insurance business, figures on the amount of reserves and surplus that premiums generate and on underwriting gain or loss are frequently used as indicators of financial well-being. These indicators are applicable to both the private carriers and the nonprofit Blue plans.

Table 4-1

Mutual of Omaha Balance Sheet, December 31, 1970 (In Millions)

Assets	
Cash	$10.7
Investment in bonds	393.3
Investment in stocks	118.3
Other assets	46.3
Total	568.6
Liabilities	
Incurred claims reserve	210.4
Unearned premium reserve[a]	166.8
Reserve for taxes	7.4
Reserve for other liabilities	42.6
Total	427.3
Surplus Funds	
Contingency reserve	92.0
Unassigned surplus	49.3
Total liabilities and surplus funds	568.6

[a]Because of its heavy emphasis on individual and income loss policies, the unearned premium reserve for Mutual of Omaha accounts for a larger proportion of reserves than for other large sellers of health insurance.

Note: Figures shown are for Mutual of Omaha parent company only; assets of subsidiaries account for an additional $734 million.

Source: *Mutual of Omaha Annual Report: Financial Statement as of December 31, 1970* (Omaha: January 30, 1971).

Reserves and Profits

Although listed as liabilities, reserves are at the same time the major source of insurers' assets. In 1969, reserves constituted 84 percent of combined Blue Cross-Blue Shield assets and among the major private carriers, for all insurance lines combined, ranged from 66 percent of total assets for Mutual of Omaha to 83 percent for Travelers.[8]

The health insurance reserves of the 7 major life carriers increased 78 percent between 1965 and 1969. (See Appendix Table D-2.) Such reserve accumulations contribute to assets both directly and through their potential for investment income. For example, between 1966 and 1969, the investment income of the 7 major life carriers was nearly half the increment to reserves generated directly from premium income.

Reserve levels do not tell anything about profits per se or about rate of return on equity,[9] the usual economic measure of business profit. But when reserves grow year after year, the total assets of the insurance carrier are likely to grow as well. The upward trends in reserves and assets attributable to health insurance strongly suggest that the conventional carriers have not been losing money in recent years.

Underwriting Gains or Losses

A popular indicator of the financial outcome of an insurance carrier's operations in any given year is its reported underwriting gain or loss. This is the difference between earned insurance premiums or "subscription income" (the term used by the Blue plans) and the sum of benefit claims and operating expenses incurred in a given year. In any year in which a carrier's incurred claims—whether paid in that period or not—and operating expenses exceed earned premium income, the carrier is said to suffer an underwriting loss. From 1965 to 1969, the conventional insurance carriers (the Blue plans and private carriers) reported annual underwriting losses ranging from 0.7 to 6.7 percent of earned premiums, as shown in Table 4-2.

But underwriting gain or loss data should not be equated, as they often are, with "making" or "losing" money in the traditional business sense. Insurance companies rely heavily on estimated data in calculating underwriting results, and they exclude from the credit side of their calculations the income from both

Table 4-2
Underwriting Gains (or Losses), All Conventional Health Insurance Carriers, 1965-1969 (Millions)

Year	Earned Premiums	Claims Expense	Operating Expense	Underwriting Gain (or Loss) Total	As Percent of Earned Premiums
1965	$9,393.0	$8,177.9	$1,465.3[a]	−$250.2	−2.7
1966	9,922.8	8,560.4	1,548.0[a]	−185.6	−1.9
1967	10,413.3	8,919.8	1,566.3	−72.8	−0.7
1968	11,708.1[b]	10,631.6	1,863.8	−787.3	−6.7
1969	13,459.6[b]	12,209.1	2,067.2	−816.7	−6.1

[a]Estimated on basis of average operating expense ratio for other years.

[b]Figures shown here for 1968 and 1969 are lower than those shown in Mueller, op. cit. They reflect later data from the Health Insurance Association of America.

Sources: Majorie Smith Mueller, "Private Health Insurance in 1969: A Review," *Social Security Bulletin*, February 1971, Tables 13 and 17; Louis S. Reed, "Private Health Insurance, 1968: Enrollment, Coverage, and Financial Experience," *Social Security Bulletin*, December 1969; Louis S. Reed and Willine Carr, "Private Health Insurance in the United States, 1967," *Social Security Bulletin*, February 1969, Table 11; and Health Insurance Association of America, unpublished information.

unearned premiums and investments. Both "earned premiums" (the credit side) and "incurred losses" (the major part of the debit side) are, to some extent, fictitious.

Unearned premiums are premiums paid in advance, as opposed to premiums that have been earned up to the current date; for example, if a premium is paid on the first day of the month for the entire month, only one-thirtieth of that premium payment is "earned" on the first day and is included in calculations of underwriting gain or loss as of that day. The remaining twenty-nine thirtieths are "unearned" on the first day; they are held in reserve so that money will be available for refunds on policies that are terminated before the contract expires. Even though the carrier has collected these funds and is unlikely to have to refund all of them, they are not included in the calculation of underwriting gains. The growth of large group business in health insurance is reducing the importance of unearned premiums because more and more large group contracts are made essentially on a "cost-plus" basis—i.e., the buyer, for all practical purposes, guarantees to cover all claims plus the cost of handling. Individuals and small groups, as well as some large groups, still pay their premiums in advance.

In any case, the exclusion of unearned premiums in calculating underwriting gains of insurance operations is less significant than the exclusion of investment income, which has been a subject of debate among insurance experts for several years.[10]

Its importance is demonstrated by the experience of 8 life companies (all of the private carriers listed in Appendix Table D-1 except Continental Casualty) whose operations were examined for this analysis for the years 1965 through 1969. During this period, these companies reported underwriting losses in 26 of the 40 operating years covered (8 companies, 5 years each). In 17 of these 26 operating years, investment income exceeded underwriting losses.

Perhaps the most important shortcoming of underwriting gain or loss as a measure of profitability is that the exact amount of incurred claims can never be known. Claims are generally not filed until the insured has recovered from an illness or at least has received the bill for treatment. (The average lag between the treatment that generates a claim and payment of the claim is around three months.) The carrier's estimate of claims incurred but not paid is called the "incurred claims reserve" or the "incurred loss reserve." This estimated amount is added to claims that have been submitted and are being processed or have been paid to determine the "claims expense" for a given period—the debit side of the calculation of underwriting gain or loss.

Neither the insurance regulations nor the tax laws include formulas for estimating incurred claims, and there are no standards by which to judge the adequacy or inadequacy of the incurred claims reserves that the carriers report. The attribution of funds to the incurred claims account, rather than to surplus or some other reserve account is irrelevant to the real earning potential of the carrier, because the financial assets in these accounts are for all practical purposes interchangeable. The assets represented by reserves differ from surplus in only one way—they cannot be distributed to stockholders (or policyholders in the case of mutuals) until they are moved to a surplus account. But only those funds assigned to the incurred claims account are included in the underwriting gain computation; those in other reserve accounts and in surplus are not.

From 1962 to 1969, the 9 largest private health insurance carriers showed substantial increases in the ratio of incurred claims reserves to earned premiums in their annual reports to insurance commissioners. In the first 4 years of this period (1962-1965) the average annual ratio for these 9 companies combined was 25.7 percent; for the second 4-year period (1966-1969) it was 33.2 percent. If these carriers had applied the ratio for the first 4-year period in figuring the underwriting gain for the second 4-year period, many of them would have reported underwriting gains instead of underwriting losses.

An increase in incurred claims reserves would be called for when, for example, the carrier's records show an increase in the time lag between incurrence and payment of claims, since the incurred claims reserve should be sufficient to meet the lag in claims payment. An increase in the lag, in turn, may be caused by changes in the coverage provided by a large number of policies—from a per-illness deductible to an annual deductible, for example, or by expanded coverage of doctors' visits, for which the billing process may be slow and the cost to the patient not so large as to make it urgent for him to file an immediate claim. But between 1967 and 1970, the lag data of the major carriers changed very little.[11] For nearly all carriers examined, the lag between incurrence and payment of claims averaged approximately three months in the period 1967-1968, and increased by no more than a few days in 1969-1970. But incurred claims reserves, which represented from 3 to 5 months' claims for most carriers in 1967-1968, increased by the claims' equivalent of one half month or more in 1969-1970.

This apparent discrepancy may result from the growing popularity of group income loss insurance coverage, which requires greater reserves than health insurance coverage. From 1965 to 1969, the premium volume of group income loss coverage—sometimes referred to as disability insurance—increased slightly more than 70 percent,[12] while the conventional health insurance premiums volume of private carriers increased by less than 40 percent.

Another possible reason why incurred claims reserves are rising is that carriers with a large number of retrospective rating contracts may be shifting reserves to the incurred claims reserve account in order to avoid having to make the downward adjustments in premium rates that consistent underwriting gains under such contracts normally require.[13] Carriers may be able to use such tactics on small and medium-sized groups without experienced personnel who can properly analyze the reserve policies of their insurers, although probably not on most large group buyers of health insurance.

Federal income tax laws may also be responsible in part for the increases in incurred claims reserves. According to these laws, the taxable income of insurance companies consists of taxable investment income, 50 percent of the amount by which gains from operations (underwriting gains) exceed taxable investment income, and any amount substracted from the policyholder surplus account during the taxable year. If gains from operations are smaller than taxable investment income, then the former is excluded in calculating taxable income; if the carrier has sustained underwriting losses, the full amount of such losses is allowed as a credit against investment income.[14]

Incurred claims reserves are the primary expense allowable in calculating gains from operation for federal income tax purposes. The Internal Revenue Service requires carriers to justify changes in their incurred claims reserves-earned premium ratios on the basis of each company's own experience. Since this experience will inevitably change somewhat from year to year, the Internal Revenue Service cannot successfully challenge the accuracy of the carrier's computations until long after receiving its report. Moreover, it should be noted that although a carrier may have some flexibility in adjusting its incurred claims-earned premium ratio upwards in years when it would be advantageous to do so for tax purposes, this flexibility is limited.

Inflation and Reserve Growth

Carriers may also have increased their incurred claims reserves in response to continuing inflation, attempting both to anticipate increases in claims and to make up for the estimated underwriting losses of the previous years. In fact, the rapid inflation that accounted for one-half the increase in the cost of health care in the 1950s and 1960s has contributed directly to the growth of reserves, and has, therefore, benefitted the insurers. While the insurers cannot be rightly accused of deliberately fomenting medical cost inflation, the benefit they attain by its continuance must certainly be noted as a factor which diminishes any incentive they otherwise might have to sustain a vigorous fight against medical inflation.

Even in years when a carrier is experiencing real underwriting losses in its health insurance line, it may be increasing its reserves and, hence, its assets. This apparent paradox, which is of great importance to any consideration of the motives and interests of the insurers, occurs because of the lag between the time premiums are collected and claims are paid. Thus, in consecutive years, when premium volume is rising, expenses and claims actually paid may be less than premium income actually collected even though incurred claims plus expenses may exceed earned premiums and result in an underwriting loss. The insurance company's situation is something like that of a person earning $1,000 a month who, in a period of chronic inflation, incurs debts of $1,050, payable the following month. By the time the bills fall due, his income has been increased to

$1,100, so he can pay his bills and still have $50 in cash for other purposes. On an accrual basis this person is in deficit by $50; he has accrued more debts than income in this month. In cash terms, however, since the debt is not liquidated until a month after it is incurred, he has a $50 surplus. He can continue incurring liabilities greater than his income as long as he can be reasonably sure that his income will increase by as much as or more more than the deficit by the time the bills become due. Accrual accounting thus tends to obscure profits.

The carrier's situation is somewhat precarious, to be sure. The carrier cannot control the level of claims it may incur and, because of multi-year contracts and/or competitive pressures, cannot always increase its income from premiums sufficiently to meet rising claims costs, although as inflation in medical costs has accelerated, the tendency is more and more toward one-year contracts.

Moreover, the contingency that the premium volume of a particular carrier might decline and cause reserves to decline in a reverse process to the inflation illustration described above is cited as justification for maintaining a high incurred claims/reserve ratio. But premium income shows no likelihood of declining in the foreseeable future. The growth potential of health insurance, in terms of premium volume, is great, as shown in Figure 4-1. Conservative projections indicate that premium income from health insurance will surpass premium income from life insurance by 1978 and quite conceivably by 1976. If the share of national health expenditures paid by private health insurance continues to increase by about 4.2 percent per year, as it did in the 3 years prior to 1970, health insurance premiums will more than triple by 1980.

**Effect of Reserve-Premium Ratios
on Premium Rates**

A circumstance where reserve policy can add to the cost of health insurance is one where premium volume is rising and the carriers' competitive situation permits it to maintain reserves above the "self-generating" level. Most reserves are "self-generating"; unearned premiums accumulate as a natural consequence of the payment of premiums in advance, and incurred loss reserves accumulate as a natural consequence of the lag between incurrence and payment of claims. As long as reserves remain equal to unearned premiums and the actual lag in claims payments, the reserve level will not, in itself, affect premium rates.

If the carrier seeks to provide a contingency reserve or surplus, and therefore maintains reserves above the "self-generating" level when premium volume increases, it will have to make recurring increases in premium rates, (in addition to the increases required by growing claims) unless it can extend the lag between incurrence and payment of claims, and/or find ways to cut operating expenses. Table 4-3 presents a simplified model illustrating how this process might operate. Here, carrier #1 seeks to maintain a 50 percent reserve-premium ratio—well

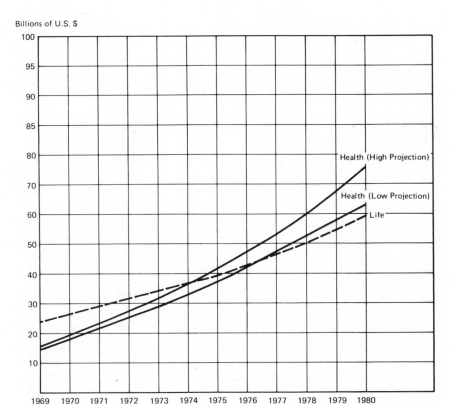

Figure 4-1. Projected Growth of Life and Health Premium Income, 1969-1980. Source and Explanatory Note: The projections are based on Dorothy P. Rice and Mary F. McGee, "Projections of National Health Expenditures, 1975 and 1980," *Research and Statistics Note*, No. 18 (Washington: U.S. Department of Health, Education, and Welfare, October 30, 1970). They assume that national health expenditures will increase from 6.6 percent of gross national product in 1968 to between 8 percent (low projection) and 9.8 percent (high projection) by 1980. Applying the growth rate in private health insurance coverage of recent years (increasing its share of civilian personal health care expenditures by approximately 1.5 percentage points annually) to the most conservative of these projections, health insurance premiums would exceed life insurance premiums, as estimated in *U.S. Industrial Outlook, 1971* (Washington: U.S. Department of Commerce) p. 433, by a minimum of $4 billion by the end of the 1970s. Should, on the other hand, the increase in national health expenditures come closer to the high projection, premium income from health insurance could exceed life insurance premium income by $17 billion—more than 25 percent—by 1980.

Table 4-3

Hypothetical Example of Effect on Premium Rates of Increases in Premium Volume at Different Reserve-Premium Ratios

	50% Reserve-Premium Ratio		30% Reserve-Premium Ratio	
	Year 1	Year 2	Year 1	Year 2
1. Premium	100.0	115.0	100.0	115.0
2. Total reserves	50.0	57.50	30.0	34.50
3. Required addition to reserves to maintain ratio		7.50		4.50
4. Self-generating reserves assuming 10% operating expense ratio				
a. Claims Incurred = 90% of premium	90.0	103.50	90.0	103.50
b. Claims Paid in Year 2:				
Year 1 claims paid in Year 2 (25%)		22.50		22.50
Year 2 claims paid in Year 2 (75%)		77.63		77.63
c. Total claims paid in Year 2 (b+c)		100.13		100.13
5. Financial claims on Premium Income (earned + unearned):				
a. Claims paid out (4c)		100.13		100.13
b. Desired reserve increases (2)		7.50		4.50
c. Operating Expenses (10% Premiums)		11.50		11.50
d. Total financial claims on Premium Income		119.13		116.13
6. Subsequent premium increase required to restore reserve-premium ratio		4.13		1.13

Note: To be more complete, the illustration should begin with a given increase in claims to which premium rates would respond. This response, plus new demand, would establish the basis for the new premium rate, against which the carrier would attempt to maintain his reserve/premium ratio.

Source: Authors' calculations.

above its self-generating level—while carrier #2 maintains a 30 percent reserve-premium ratio—approximately at the self-generating level. It is evident that carrier #1 cannot meet all of its claims and contribute enough to its reserve account to maintain the 50 percent ratio without increasing premium rates by approximately 4 percent in addition to the increase already in effect. Large group clients can usually avoid an accumulation of reserves above the self-generating level, except for contingency reserves agreed upon by both parties as a buffer against unexpected claims. But the carriers require larger contingency reserves for individual health policies, income loss coverage (included in the data), and smaller groups. These requirements are based to some extent, on fiscal prudence, but the forces of competition and consumer knowledge among individual and small groups are apparently insufficient to keep reserves at the level that such prudence alone would warrant.

Blue Plan Reserves as a Theoretical Reserve Ceiling

Competition with the nonprofit Blue plans and, to a lesser extent, with the mutual companies, may restrain the private carriers from acquiring and maintaining excessive reserves. Unlike the private carriers, which try to accumulate enough reserves and other assets to increase investment income and to permit some distribution of surplus to stockholders or to policyholders, the Blue plans do not distribute "surplus" (except in the form of lower subscription rates). The Blue plans, as nonprofit organizations, should strive to maximize enrollment and premium volume rather than reserves or assets. The fact that since 1950 the combined assets of all Blue Cross-Blue Shield plans have hovered around 50 percent of premium income and have consistently retreated from higher levels within a year or two while remaining in fairly constant ratio to reserves suggests that the Blue plans have, in fact, used any excess reserves largely to reduce premiums.[15]

The stock companies that compete with the nonprofit Blue plans and the mutuals that distribute surplus only to policyholders must either maintain greater efficiency of operations or offer product differentiation of some kind that will permit them to collect a higher premium for essentially the same risk in order to permit accumulation of enough surplus to enable some distribution to stockholders. There is no evidence that the stock companies as a group operate more efficiently than the mutuals and the Blue plans in the health field; the ratios of operating cost to premiums and of reserves to premiums of the 3 largest stock companies that account for about 40 percent of the premium volume sold by stock companies fall in the same range as those of the mutuals and are slightly higher than those of the Blue plans.[16] At the same time, group plans, especially large ones, afford only limited opportunities for product differentiation because groups generally predetermine either the coverage they want or the premium level they will pay. Better or faster service cannot easily be used to justify a higher premium rate, both because competitors can easily copy new techniques and because most insured groups are more interested in coverage and price than in services.

Unearned premium reserves are low or nonexistent in large group plans, and incurred claims reserves are also usually low relative to premiums because the insured and the insurer hold special reserves jointly to cover any underestimation in the premium level. Stock companies therefore have only a limited opportunity to accumulate excessive reserves in group competition.

Of course, the representatives of some groups are less expert than others in negotiating with carriers. Even under the Federal Employees Health Benefits Program, which is closely supervised by the U.S. Civil Service Commission and carries its own reserves, carriers can accumulate larger reserves than are apparently necessary. For example, from 1965 to 1969, Blue Cross-Blue Shield's incurred claims reserves averaged only 11 percent of premiums, while those of Mutual of Omaha, the underwriter for the American Foreign Service Protective Association, a much smaller group, averaged 66 percent. Although this large reserve is consistent with Mutual of Omaha's conservative overall reserve policy, it is not clear why a group protected by a back-up reserve held by the U.S. Treasury would be willing to pay for such a conservative reserve policy.

Many private carriers have found individual policies a better source of both reserves and underwriting gains than group policies. In fact in the years when carriers were generally reporting underwriting losses on overall operations, they were consistently reporting underwriting gains from the sales of individual health policies. But the individual health insurance market is dominated by small carriers rather than by the large stock companies. Individual policies comprise only about 12 percent of the enrollment of the Blue plans. The 3 large life stock companies—Aetna, Connecticut General and Travelers—derived only 5 percent of their total earned health premiums from individual health policies in 1969. On the other hand, the small mutual and stock companies and 1 large mutual—Mutual of Omaha—derive most of their income from such policies. In 1969 some 51 companies—38 stock companies and 13 mutuals—received a premium income of $10 million or more from sales of individual policies and accounted for over 70 percent of the individual health insurance business of the private carriers. Thirty-four small stock companies, several of which sell no group policies, dominate the field.

In general, only those private carriers whose portfolios are dominated by individual policies are likely to maintain reserves much in excess of those of the Blue plans. In 1969, when the reserves of the combined Blue plans were equal to only 5 months' claims, the 9 major private carriers maintained reserves equal to 6 months' claims or less, and 4 of these maintained reserves equal to 5 months' claims. Continental Casualty and Mutual of Omaha maintained reserves equal to

9 months' claims, but these carriers deal heavily in individual policies as well as income loss insurance.

One might expect that the Blue plans' nonprofit, community orientation should serve to restrain their reserve accumulation. But because each local plan is responsible for its own solvency, the composite reserve level of all the Blue plans is probably higher than it would be if, for example, the Blue Cross and Blue Shield national associations held part of the reserves of each plan, in the way central banks hold reserves for member banks. Nonetheless, the relation of reserve levels (5 to 6 months of estimated claims) to unearned premiums and the lag in settlement of claims (3 to 4 months) of the Blues and the large carriers suggests that their reserves exceed their needs only slightly.

Significance of Health Insurance
Reserves for Major Carriers

Except for the Blue plans, whose sole business is health insurance, and for Mutual of Omaha, health insurance is not of paramount importance to major insurance carriers and is not likely to become so even if health insurance premium volume should triple, a possibility that seems not unlikely, as can be seen in Figure 4-1.

For the 7 major life carriers combined, the rate of increase in health insurance reserves from 1965 to 1969 was 78 percent, more than four times the rate of increase in life insurance, which was 18 percent. But health reserves (and hence assets attributable to health insurance) are still insignificant in relation to total life reserves for these carriers, as shown in Figure 4-2; at the end of 1969, they accounted for only 2.5 percent of the total reserves of these companies. (See Appendix Table D-2.)

That the growing volume of health insurance premiums contributes so little to the total reserves of the major carriers is explained largely by the fact that a given increase in health insurance premiums generates a much smaller contribution to reserves than the same increase in life insurance premiums, or even property insurance premiums. As of 1969, among the 7 major carriers, the ratio of total accumulated life insurance reserves to annual life premiums—8.9:1.0— was much higher than the ratio of accumulated health insurance reserves to annual health premiums—0.42:1.0. (See Appendix Table D-3.) The reserve-premium ratio is high in life insurance because of the long-term, savings account nature of this kind of insurance; premiums are stretched over a long period representing the average time expected to elapse between initiation of the contract and payment of the claim. Reserve-premium ratio is low in health insurance because of the short-term, prepayment aspects of most health policies where most premiums are paid out in the same year in which they are collected.

Maintaining the reserve-premium ratio for life insurance, given an 8 percent

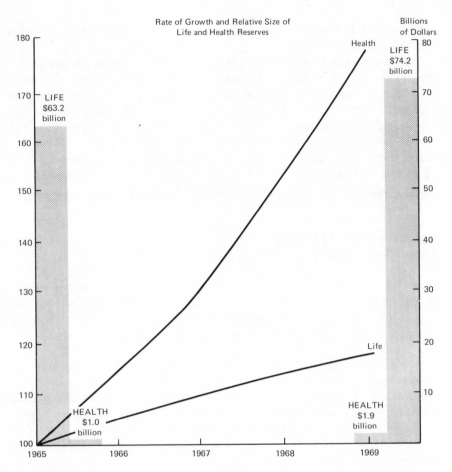

Figure 4-2. Health and Life Reserves of Major Life and Health Carriers, 1965-1969

increase in premiums in a year, would require adding about 60 percent of the year's premium income to reserves. Maintaining the ratio for health insurance, given the same increase in premiums, would require adding less than 3 percent of premium income to reserves. If the 7 major carriers maintain both their share of the life and health markets and their reserve-premium ratios through 1980, and if premium volume increases by 1980 according to the high projection shown in Figure 4-1, the accumulated reserves derived from health insurance could rise to more than five times those of 1969. But even this rapid rate of increase would bring health reserves to only 5.5 percent of the total reserves of these 7 life companies; life reserves would increase by about $108 billion, while health reserves would increase by only $9 billion. (See Appendix Table D-3.) The large private carriers already have such vast reserves that even the great increases expected in health insurance sales will not noticeably alter their investment capacity.

Motives of the Private Carriers

At a time when the Blue plans' adherence to community rating and local autonomy interfered with their ability to provide uniform coverage and service to groups whose membership extended over more than one region, the private carriers saw in health insurance an opportunity to capture the large low-risk group market on an experience-rated basis. But then Blue Cross and Blue Shield began to handle accounts on a uniform interplan basis and to use experience rating. These changes, together with their tax-free status and Blue Cross' special relationship with hospitals, made the Blue plans very strong competitors. Although in the 1950s they lost their dominant role to the private carriers, in the 1960s they stabilized and even improved their share of the health insurance market, as shown in Figure 1-1. In so doing, they reduced the profitability of health insurance for the private carriers.

And yet it costs the large carriers nothing to stay in the health insurance market, even if the expectation of future profits may not be what it was once thought to be. Group health insurance has become a virtually riskless enterprise. Most claims occurring in one quarter are paid from the premium income received in the same quarter or the next, and the insurer generally does not accept an obligation to reimburse the insured for claims incurred more than one year after termination of the contract. Even though some group contracts fix premium rates for more than one year, most provide for annual rate adjustments in response to adverse claims experience, generally using some kind of rating reserve mechanism to provide prospective or retrospective rate adjustments. Under retrospective rating agreements a special reserve is set up to cover claims in excess of estimates; any gains resulting from an overestimation of claims are either deposited in the special reserve to replace earlier drawings or used to reduce premiums. The insurers' gain and loss margins are thus limited. Under prospective rating agreements, each year's experience is the basis for adjustments in the next year's premiums if the insured continues to do business with the same carrier. A carrier can suffer from a bad initial year's experience, if the insured switches to another carrier, but his risk is limited to one year.

The role of insurance in general as a source of savings in the financial market is declining. Between 1946 and 1956, life insurance reserves constituted 16.5 percent of the financial assets acquired by households. Between 1957 and 1967 they constituted only 11.6 percent of the total financial assets acquired by households, and in the period 1966 to 1970 this figure dropped to just under 8 percent.[18] To reverse this trend and gain a more prominent position for insurance, not only as a supplier of investment funds but as an investor in its own right, has become a major goal for those in insurance circles who favor diversification and the formation of insurance-led conglomerates.[19] Health insurance can contribute little toward this objective during the 1970s, because it will have relatively little impact on total reserve growth, but its growth potential may influence plans for the more distant future. The major insurance carriers have been functioning for a long time, and the nature of their business compels them to plan well beyond the life spans of many of those who control their operations today.

The private carriers have two additional reasons for continuing to compete for health insurance premiums: first, selling health insurance enables carriers to maintain personal representatives in areas where the volume of business would otherwise not warrant them; second, under the "loss leader" principle, carriers are willing to sell health insurance at a loss in order to facilitate the sale of a more lucrative line such as life insurance. The assumption is that many buyers of group health insurance policies prefer to deal with one carrier for all group insurance. Nonetheless, the validity of the loss leader principle in this context is not clear. Seven of the 10 largest employee-employer plans buy health insurance from Blue Cross-Blue Shield, and other forms of insurance from other carriers, some of which also offer health insurance coverage. Many groups buy basic health insurance from Blue Cross-Blue Shield and major medical from a private carrier. Most of the groups examined in the course of this study used a diversity of insurers rather than package arrangements.

But perhaps the carriers' most important incentive to continue to sell health insurance is an interest in growth for growth's sake. Growth is a matter of interest to all insurance carriers, profit and nonprofit alike. For Blue Cross and Blue Shield, growth is the key to survival; only through maintaining or expanding their share of the market can Blue plans function as insurers and exert influence over the suppliers of medical services. The growth of health insurance operations is not essential to the survival of the major mutual and stock companies that sell health insurance (except for the monoline, Mutual of Omaha), but they are caught up in the mystique of growth that pervades all aspects of American life. Individual income, promotions and professional prestige hinge on organizational growth. And in their promotional material, organizations are more likely to cite their growth records than any other accomplishment. In their joint fact book for 1970, for example, Blue Cross and Blue Shield capsule their progress since 1948 by stating that they "have more people enrolled than ever before, have paid out more dollars in benefits to members than any other individual organization in the health insurance field." In its 1970 annual report, Mutual of Omaha boasts of being "the largest writer of individual and family health insurance in the world . . . First in new coverages ... First in benefits paid." Travelers, in its annual report for the same year points with pride to its "record earnings for the individual life, health, and annuity lines of insurance, a new high in investment income."[20] The concept of growth, of setting new records, of being "number one" is an aspect of the American spirit that transcends economic rationality.

5

The Public Sector and Health Insurance

Public agencies spend considerably more for the nation's personal health care than private insurers pay out in insurance benefits. (See Appendix Table B-1.) For example, in 1969, public expenditures for all types of health care and facilities totaled $23 billion, as shown in Table 5-1, which is nearly twice as much as paid out in benefits by private carriers. Thus, while the private sector insurers have borne much of the criticism for the deficiencies of the health care system and medical care inflation, the figures suggest that the public sector—whose role many would increase in seeking a better system—has had an even greater opportunity to exert an influence.

Between 1950 and 1969, federal, state and local governments' share of total national health expenditures increased from 26.4 to 36.1 percent, as shown in Table 5-2. In addition to direct expenditures the government contributes indirectly to the national health bill through income tax deductions for medical expenditures and tax exemptions granted to hospitals, Blue Cross-Blue Shield, and other nonprofit organizations in the health field (see Table 5-3). Moreover, during this period there was a striking movement toward concentration of public sector participation in the federal government whose share of public sector expenditures increased from 44 percent to 66 percent while the share paid by state and local government declined proportionately. In spite of the trend toward greater centralization of public sector health care expenditures in the federal government, public sector influence over the health care system is only slightly more perceptible than it was when a majority of public expenditures was scattered over the various states. Certainly government has not been any more successful than the private sector in restraining rising medical costs, controlling utilization of medical services, or achieving equitable distribution of available medical resources. In contrast to the private sector where rising medical costs are financially advantageous to the private insurers, normal budget restraints provide the federal government with incentives to keep costs down, at least in its own programs. But the government has had no overall policy on the financing or provision of health care. A recent study prepared by the U.S. Bureau of the Budget indicates that although the U.S. Department of Health, Education, and Welfare (HEW) accounts for 75 percent of federal health care expenditures, 24 other federal departments and agencies also engage in health-related activities, for which 7 of them spend over $100 million apiece annually.[1] These programs, created to meet the immediate needs of separate constituencies, have evolved in a haphazard and piecemeal fashion. Government efforts to restrain medical costs have consequently been uncoordinated and, usually, unsuccessful.

69

Table 5-1
Public Sector Expenditures for Health Care, by Type of Activity, 1969

Type of Activity	Amount (Millions)	Percentage Distribution
National health expenditures, total	$63,827	
Public sector expenditures, total	23,021	100.00
Insurance arrangements[a]	11,727	50.9
Medicare[b]	6,918	30.0
Medicaid[c]	4,597	20.0
Workmen's compensation (State agencies only)[d]	212	0.9
Other civilian medical services[e]	5,324	23.1
General hospital and medical care	3,071	13.3
Maternal and child health services	419	1.8
School health	247	1.1
Medical-vocational rehabilitation	138	0.6
OEO health and medical care	137	0.6
Other public health activities	1,312	5.7
Research and construction for civilian use	2,514	10.9
Research	1,647	7.2
Construction	867	3.8
Military and military related services	3,456	15.0
Department of Defense hospital and medical care for members of the armed services and their dependents	1,825	7.9
Veterans' Administration hospital and medical care	1,517	6.6
Military Construction	104	0.4

[a]With the exception of health care for members of the armed forces and their dependents, the role of the public sector as an employer is not accounted for in this table; for example, insurance benefits, workmen's compensation (medical benefits) and temporary disability (medical benefits) for federal and state employees and retirees are excluded because complete data are not available. These programs are substantial; federal government contribution toward employee-retiree health insurance (Federal Employees Health Benefits program) was $241 million in 1969 (and projected at $475 million for fiscal year 1972), while benefit payments to state government employees under temporary disability insurance (medical payments) were $55.3 million in the same year.

[b]Includes premium payments for supplementary medical insurance made by or on behalf of enrollees in the Medicare program.

[c]Includes, in addition to Medicaid, a small number of vendor medical payments administered under state public assistance programs.

[d]Excluded are the medical benefits under Workmen's Compensation which, although required by state law, are administered for private employers by private carriers.

[e]Includes three different types of government health care activities: transfer payments made to private sector providers, payments to autonomous public sector institutions such as municipal hospitals and completely public sector activities such as those conducted by the U.S. Public Health Service.

Table 5-1 (cont.)

Note: Discrepancies in addition are due to rounding.

Sources: Barbara S. Cooper and Mary F. McGee, "National Health Expenditures, Fiscal Years 1929-70 and Calendar Years 1929-69," *Research and Statistics Note*, No. 25–1970 (Washington: Social Security Administration, U.S. Department of Health, Education, and Welfare, December 14, 1970), Tables 1 and 8; and *Statistical Abstract of the United States, 1970* (Washington; U.S. Bureau of the Census, 1970), p. 62; and Alfred M. Skolnik and Daniel N. Price, "Another Look at Workmen's Compensation," *Social Security Bulletin*, October 1970, Tables 3 and 4.

Table 5-2
Public Sector Expenditures for Health Care, 1950-1969[a]

Year	Amount (Billions)	Total Percent of National Health Expenditures	Per Capita	Federal Expenditures as Percent of Total[b]
1950	$3.4	26.4[c]	$22.50	44.4
1960	6.3	23.3	34.93	45.6
1965	9.6	23.6	49.45	48.5
1969	23.0	36.1	113.57	66.5

[a]Definition of "public sector expenditure for health care" is that used in Table 5-1.

[b]Based on fiscal year data.

[c]Total public sector health expenditures as well as those of the Federal Government were increased above the historical trend somewhat in 1950 as a result of the Korean War.

Sources: Barbara S. Cooper and Mary F. McGee, "National Health Expenditures, Fiscal Years 1929-70 and Calendar Years 1929-69," *Research and Statistics Note*, No. 25–1970 (Washington: Social Security Administration, U.S. Department of Health, Education, and Welfare, December 14, 1970), Tables 1 and 8; *Statistical Abstract of the United States, 1970* (Washington: U.S. Bureau of the Census, 1970), p. 62; Alfred M. Skolnik and Daniel N. Price, "Another Look at Workmen's Compensation," *Social Security Bulletin*, October 1970, Tables 3 and 4.

Public sector health care activities fall into 5 categories: (1) provision of medical care to servicemen, indigents, mental and tubercular patients, and other special groups, either directly by government personnel in government facilities or by private sector providers financed by government; (2) underwriting of all or part of the medical expenses of enrollees in insurance programs such as Medicare or quasi-insurance programs such as Medicaid and CHAMPUS, where enrollees have substantial discretion in choosing their own physicians and hospitals in the private sector; (3) sponsorship of group health insurance programs (including income loss insurance) for public employees such as the Federal Employees Health Benefits Program and various state programs; (4) regulation of private sector health insurance programs under state Workmen's Compensation laws that require certain employers to purchase insurance to protect their employees

Table 5-3

The Federal Government's Indirect Contribution to the National Health Bill, Through Tax Deductions and Tax Exemptions[a]

Nontaxable Items	Estimated Federal Taxes Foregone
Total	$4.1 billion
Health insurance premiums paid by employers and health insurance claims paid	$1.5 billion
50 percent of health insurance premiums paid by individuals up to $150	$365 million
Unreimbursed medical expenses in excess of 3 percent of taxable income (including health insurance premiums paid by individuals not deducted under preceding item)	$1.6 billion
Charitable contributions to health organizations	$500 million
Income of nonprofit health care groups and organizations such as Blue Cross-Blue Shield, various prepaid practice plans, nonprofit hospitals	$255 million

Note: Because state tax laws vary, no effort was made to estimate the amount of similar indirect contributions to the medical care bill attributable to deductions for medical expenses under state and local tax codes and to the tax-exempt status given the nonprofit Blue plans, independent plans and hospitals under most state tax codes.

Source: Staff estimates.

against work-related injuries but involve little public sector expenditures; and (5) public sector medical research and construction and provision of funds for private sector research and construction.

Medicare and Medicaid account for about half of all public sector health care expenditures; the Defense Department and Veterans Administration health care programs account for about 15 percent, and research and hospital construction for about 10 percent. The remaining 25 percent is distributed among such public health activities as school health and immunization programs, rehabilitation services, welfare health programs and support of state and local hospitals, tuberculosis sanitariums and mental institutions. This public sector experience has been sufficiently long and varied to provide limited insights into how one might expect the public sector to behave with a larger role in financing health care costs.

73

Government as an Insurer: Medicare

The federal government became an underwriter of health insurance for the first time in 1965, when Congress passed an amendment to the Social Security Act establishing the Medicare program to finance health insurance for the aged. This measure represented the first real experiment with public sector health insurance in this country.

Medicare is divided into two parts: Part A, Hospital Insurance, covering care in hospitals and in extended care facilities and home health services; and Part B, Supplementary Medical Insurance, covering a wide variety of services provided by physicians and other medical personnel, both inside as well as outside the hospital.

Although virtually all persons, 65 years of age and over, are enrolled in Medicare, only those eligible for benefits under the Social Security and Railroad Retirement Acts, those who reached age 65 before 1968, and certain disabled individuals covered by the Social Security program are eligible for Medicare coverage.[2] Part A is automatically available upon registration for those eligible. Part B is a voluntary program open to anyone covered by Part A who is willing to pay one half of the Part B premium. (The other half is paid by the government.) In the fiscal year 1969-1970, roughly 95 percent of those enrolled in Part A were also enrolled in Part B. Table 5-4 summarizes enrollment, average

Table 5-4
Summary Data on Medicare Program, Fiscal Year, 1969-1970

	Part A, Hospital Insurance	Part B, Supplemental Medical Insurance	Total
Enrollment (millions)	20.3[a]	19.3[b]	20.3
Total benefit payments (millions)	$4,804	$1,979	$6,784
Administrative costs (millions)	$149	$217	$366
As percent of benefit payments	3.1	11.0	5.4
Average monthly premium	$20.33[c]	$8.00[d]	$28.33

[a]Estimated.

[b]Number of persons enrolled at the end of the year; gross enrollment for the year was 19.7 million.

[c]There is no premium as such for Part A; the premium was estimated by dividing benefit payments plus administrative costs by the estimated number of enrollments.

[d]The premium in 1969-70 was artificially low as the result of an administrative action; the average premium in the fiscal year 1970-71 was $10.30.

Sources: *Social Security Bulletin*, March 1971, Tables M-7 and M-8; "Medical Insurance Sample: January-June 1970," *Current Medicare Survey Report* (Washington: U.S. Department of Health, Education, and Welfare, July 1971), p. 8.

monthly premiums, total benefit payments and administrative costs as percent of benefit payments for both Parts A and B in that year.

Financing the Medicare Program

The financial structure of the Medicare program is patterned after that of the Social Security program (OASDI). It consists of two trust funds. The Hospital Insurance Trust Fund, for Part A, has been receiving about 85 percent of its income from an annual payroll tax—now 2.0 percent—which is part of the familiar "Social Security" tax deducted regularly from employees' pay checks and matched by employers and which is based on an individual's wage or salary—up to $10,800. Eleven percent has come from general revenue, and 4 percent from interest on investments and miscellaneous sources. These funds cover the benefits and administrative costs of those persons eligible for Medicare but not covered by Social Security or Railroad Retirements. The Supplementary Medical Insurance Trust Fund, for Part B, receives half its income from subscribers' premiums and half from general revenue of the federal government.

The premiums for Part A are based on 25-year actuarial projections of increases in unit medical costs, utilization rates and population trends measured against the growing taxable wage base and a series of assumed tax rates. As a long-term social insurance program, Part A was designed to show a surplus on both a cash and an accrual basis, and thus far it has done so, as shown in Table 5-5. But new projections, based on more rapid increases in medical costs than had been anticipated, indicate that in future years the program would be underfunded unless the payroll taxes that finance Part A are increased or benefits cut.[3]

Part B's financial structure is very much like the premium and reserve structure of the conventional carriers. During the first 5 years of the program, Part B did not compensate for the rapid increase in utilization rates, in physicians' fees, and related costs; as a result, the trust fund for Part B showed a growing underwriting deficit. The law requires that the premium rates for Part B be adjusted when necessary to show a surplus on an accrual basis. Part B premiums were accordingly raised in 1971 and again in 1972. But the trustees of the trust fund believe that the premium level cannot be raised indefinitely:

Enrollment is voluntary and government matching is legally limited. Due to the substantial variation in medical costs throughout the country, many enrollees receive only the actuarial value of their benefits—despite the government-matching contribution. The premium rate cannot be raised much above its actuarial value, since some of the lower cost enrollees would find it to their advantage to drop out, raising the average cost of the remainder, and thus the premium rate required.[4]

Table 5-5

Trust Fund Balance for Medicare Parts A and B, 1966-1970

(Dollar Amounts in Millions)

Net Surplus (or Deficit)

Calendar Year	Hospital Insurance (Part A)			Supplementary Medical Insurance (Part B)		
	Incurred Basis	Cash Balance[a]	Cash Balance as Percent of Premiums[a]	Incurred Basis	Cash Balance	Cash Balance as Percent of Premiums
1966	$888	$851	94.2	$45	$122	37.9
1967	1,325	1,343	44.1	−116	412	26.2
1968	2,072	1,431	37.2	−251	421	24.9
1969	2,413	2,017	38.4	−473	199	10.9
1970	2,522	2,667	48.9	−515	188[b]	8.6

[a]Cash balance and premiums (calculated as all income except interest on investment) for the Hospital Insurance Program are for fiscal years.

[b]On June 30, 1970, the cash balance in the Supplementary Medical Insurance Trust Fund was $57 million, only 8.2 percent of all outstanding obligations (incurred but unpaid). An unusual claims experience at that time would have forced the Fund to borrow from the Treasury to pay outstanding claims. On July 1, 1970, the premiums, and consequently the government contributions, were increased and the balance in the trust fund increased proportionately, as expected.

Sources: U.S., Congress, House, Committee on Ways and Means, *1971 Annual Report of the Board of Trustees of the Federal Supplementary Medical Insurance Trust Fund*, 92nd Cong., 1st sess., 1971, pp. 14-15; U.S., Congress, House Committee on Ways and Means, *1970 Annual Report of the Board of Trustees of the Federal Hospital Insurance Trust Fund*, 91st Cong., 2nd sess., 1970, pp. 12.

The insured's share, which was $3.00 per month in 1966, rose to $5.60 in 1971 and again to $5.80 in July 1972. This 87 percent increase—more than the price increase in doctor's services—has not been accompanied by a drop in enrollment even though enrollment is voluntary. Evidently the upper limit of Part B premiums has not been reached.

The low ratio of the Part B "cash balance" (analogous to the total reserves of the conventional carriers) to premiums, shown in Table 5-5, illustrates the problem of determining the appropriate reserve policy for a government-under-written insurance program. Because the government can temporarily "rescue" such a program through other treasury sources, unearned premium reserves, contingency reserves or surpluses seem unnecessary. But the ever-present political temptation to raise benefits while postponing increases in premiums justifies a legal requirement that the trust fund maintain an incurred claims reserve at least equal to the full amount of incurred but unpaid claims. Thus the reserve requirement in a government insurance operation such as Medicare Part B acts as a discipline by providing a ready measure of fiscal prudence and tends to avert such political experiences.

Since the government cannot usually raise premiums as readily as private insurers, it generally will feel compelled to restrain costs before seeking premium increases. The 1970 annual report of the Part B trust fund reports that the administrators of the Medicare program held benefit payments down in fiscal year 1969-1970 by imposing a stricter interpretation of the law on the Blue plans and private carriers who administer the program locally for the government. For example, the Social Security Administration distributed analyses of data on individual physicians with the highest amounts of reimbursement, issued stricter standards governing the use of physical therapy, increased their investigations of fraud allegations against the program, and began to submit apparently questionable practices to medical societies for review. Using these and other procedures, the Blue plans and private carriers, acting as administrator reduced or denied an estimated 40 percent of the bills submitted, with the result that total payments made to physicians were 10 percent less than total claims submitted.[5] As a result physicians' fees charged under Medicare increased by only 3 percent during the fiscal year 1969, compared with a national increase of between 6 and 7 percent.[6]

But lowering individual fees does not necessarily serve to lower total costs, because physicians can make up the difference by providing the patient with more services than might otherwise be offered or by billing separately for services normally included in a general fee.

And budgetary cutbacks may have other undesirable consequences for the insured. For example, Medicare Part A originally covered up to 100 days of "rehabilitation services" in extended care facilities (ECFs) such as nursing homes and convalescent hospitals. The purpose of this provision was to encourage convalescent patients to use these facilities rather than the more expensive hospitals. ECF coverage under Medicare was conditional on prior hospitalization of at least 3 days, a doctor's authorization, and admission to an ECF for other than "custodial services" within 14 days of hospital discharge. When Medicare costs began to increase much more rapidly than anticipated, the Social Security Administration issued directives that ECF claims were to be more carefully checked. As a result, the number of claims approved by the intermediaries for payment for care in ECFs declined by 12 percent in 1969 and by 38 percent in 1970. Many physicians alleged that cases rejected were similar to cases previously reimbursed, and that, for all practical purposes, the "more careful check" really amounted to an unannounced cutback in coverage. Moreover, prior to the enactment of H.R. 1 in 1972 claims were often rejected retroactively, causing economic hardship for the insured.[7] Many ECFs began turning away Medicare patients because retroactive denial often meant unpaid bills. By 1970, the American Nursing Home Association estimated that half of the nation's accredited nursing homes were cutting their participation in the Medicare program.[8]

It is hard to say how this unfortunate result might have been averted. On the one hand, failure on the part of the Social Security Administration to challenge rising costs in some manner might have actually encouraged abuses in the use of extended care facilities. On the other, raising premium rates to avoid cutting back services is not easily accomplished in the case of Medicare. The payroll tax is not paid by its current beneficiaries—but by employers and workers who might find it hard to relate a tax increase to their own future benefits from the program. They view the payroll tax as just another tax to be resisted, and government officials are always reluctant to propose tax increases. Often they find it easier to hold the line on costs, if necessary, by curtailing benefits.

Limitations and Loopholes in Medicare Coverage

Like that of private plans, Medicare coverage does not cover all medical expenses but is limited by deductibles and by provisions for coinsurance and maximums.[9]

Under Part A, hospital coverage is limited to 90 days per each illness and ECF coverage to 100 days per illness. The patient must pay the first $72 of hospital expenses and $18 for each day of hospitalization from the 61st to the 90th day. In addition, each person has a "lifetime reserve" of 60 hospital days, but in using this reserve, the patient must pay the first $36 of each day.

Under Part B, reimbursement is subject to a $60 deductible as well as a 20 percent coinsurance provision, and certain services such as psychiatric care are limited. As of 1969, Medicare was providing reimbursement for only 65 percent of the charges covered by the program—that is, charges for services listed as reimbursable under the plan.[10] The deductible accounted for 19 percent and the coinsurance provision for 16 percent of Part B charges. (Passage of H.R. 1, in October 1972, has eliminated the coinsurance provision for covered home health services.)

Part B does not cover such medical services as routine physicals, nonsurgical dental services, routine eye examinations, services performed by noncovered practitioners (such as chiropractors), private duty nursing, out patient prescription drugs, eyeglasses, hearing aids, and nursing home care.

(However, the 1972 amendments to the Medicare legislation did add the following to the list of covered services: services of a physical therapist in independent practice, outpatient speech pathology services, services of a licensed chiropractor, supplies related to colostomy care as prosthetic devices, and certain ECF services not explicitly covered previously.) Taking into account expenses not covered or only partially covered, the Social Security Administration estimates that, in 1969, Medicare patients were reimbursed for slightly more than half their total health care expenditures.[11] (By contrast, private insurers provided reimbursement for only 39 percent of total civilian personal health care expenditures in 1969, as shown in Appendix Table B-1.)

Forty-seven percent of Medicare enrollees also carry some kind of private health insurance, and another 15 percent are also covered by Medicaid. In fact, in 1969, 42 percent of all Medicaid expenditures—$1.8 million—went to pay for supplementary medical care for indigents enrolled in the Medicare program.[1] [2]

Administration of Medicare

About 50 private carriers and local Blue plans function as "fiscal intermediaries" for Medicare. They are responsible for determining the amount of the benefits to be paid (according to a formula supplied by HEW), making the payments, and auditing providers' records to assure that charges have been properly assessed. Blue Cross is the largest of the intermediaries.[1] [3] Blue Shield serves about 60 percent of the enrollees under Part B. In addition, 67 prepaid group practice plans provide medical services to Medicare enrollees.

The intermediaries, 21,000 of whose employees administer the Medicare program, are reimbursed, as the law requires, only for their costs. In addition, some 9,600 civil service employees supervise and service the program—1,000 in the central office in Washington and 8,600 in the Social Security Administration in Baltimore and in the field office. The field offices include 6 payment centers, 642 district offices, 118 branch offices and 3,600 regularly scheduled service locations. They provide information to local residents, channel inquiries, help with claims disputes, maintain records, conduct audits, and perform other functions necessary to this vast, nationwide health insurance operation.

The trust funds pay the salaries and related expenses of HEW employees involved in the administration of Medicare and the costs incurred by the fiscal intermediaries. But they do not pay all the expenses incurred by the government in connection with the administration of Medicare. The U.S. Treasury Department performs the functions of collection and investment—that is, the handling of the trust funds—for which its reimbursements probably cover only a portion of the real cost.[1] [4] Other expenses of Medicare administration not paid by the trust funds are the costs to the Office of Management and Budget for preparing and reviewing budgets; to congressional staffs for reviewing appropriations requests; and to the General Accounting Office—a part of the legislative branch—for auditing Medicare accounts. Medicare is a public function, and its records are kept in much more minute detail and published more frequently than records of private firms generally are. A powerful member of Congress interested in some special phase of the program can require HEW to maintain and furnish information that may be marginal to the operation of the program. Officials in policy-making roles must devote countless hours to essentially minor matters that might become issues in partisan politics. Adversaries and supporters, legislators and executives must keep abreast of details they could ignore if the program were not a government responsibility.

In recent years the reported operating expenses of the Medicare program (Parts A and B combined) have amounted to 5 to 6 percent of all benefits paid, a generally lower ratio of operating costs to benefits paid than those for the group health insurance plans of either the private carriers or the Blue plans. The operating cost data for Medicare and for the private plans are not entirely comparable, however, and do not permit valid comparisons of the relative efficiency of health insurance operations in the public and private sectors. Each entity sees its responsibilities differently and each is saddled with costs which the other need not face.

For its part, Medicare must meet heavier reporting requirements and must participate in supporting other government objectives such as Medicare's civil rights compliance program.

Moreover, the efficiency of the Medicare program in handling and paying claims depends on the ability of the private sector to carry out these functions. Approximately half of the total reported payments for administration from the trust fund accounts go to the financial intermediaries for processing and payment of Medicare claims. This use of the private sector as provided for in Medicare legislation is advantageous to Medicare because the average salaries of employees of the Blue plans and the private carriers that perform the inter-mediary tasks are about 20 percent lower than the average salaries of HEW employees, who would otherwise carry out these tasks. For instance, the average salary, including fringe benefits, of employees of the Social Security Adminis-tration, which performs many functions similar to insurance functions, in fiscal year 1970-1971 was over $11,000, according to the U.S. Bureau of the Budget. The estimated average salary of the employees of the Blue plans was less than $8,000 and of the employees of the major private carriers between $8,000 and $9,000. (See Chapter 3.) Government pay is higher in part because the federal government cannot take advantage of regional pay disparities as private busi-nesses can; government pay scales are uniform for all regions.

There are differences that affect operating costs of the two entities in several ways:

1. Medicare reports only those operating expenses paid out of the Part A and Part B trust funds, and excludes some expenses incurred by other government agencies.

2. The operations of the Department of Health, Education, and Welfare are not, as those of private health insurance underwriters are, subject to taxes nor to amortization of buildings and equipment, because amortization is not used in government accounting. (A portion of the amortization cost is, of course, included in the financial intermediaries' expenses in handling Medicare.)

3. Medicare's simple eligibility rules and uniform coverage make its claims handling and general administration far less complicated and costly than those of private carriers.

4. Finally, and perhaps most importantly, Medicare Part A claims are roughly twice as high on average as the claims for insured patients under 65 years of age, largely because the average hospital stay of those 65 and over is longer—15 days—than the national average of 8 days. Since it costs little or no more to process a large claim than a small one, Medicare Part A has a considerably lower ratio of operating costs to "premiums" paid than private hospital insurance plans. Part B's ratio of operating costs to premiums is 10 to 11 percent, roughly the same as that of the private carriers but slightly higher than that of Blue Shield, which, like Part B, does not cover hospital expenses. But these operating cost figures are also not very meaningful since the nonhospital coverage offered by the private sector varies so greatly that it is impossible to estimate average claim size from the data available in such a way that it would be comparable to the average claim size of Medicare, Part B.

The Blue Cross-Blue Shield plan offered under the Federal Employees Program is one large private sector plan that provides coverage more like the Medicare program than any other—that is, it includes comprehensive coverage, clear division between hospital and nonhospital coverage, and so forth. If the operating experience under this plan is adjusted to account for differences in average claims size, Blue Cross-Blue Shield comes out with a distinctly lower operating cost ratio for the years 1968, 1969, and 1970.[15] Nonetheless, even these calculations have to be taken with a grain of salt in light of the substantial differences which exist between the two approaches.

Government as a Quasi-Insurer: Medicaid

Unlike Medicare, Medicaid is not a true insurance program; it collects no premiums and holds no reserves. Medicaid is a grant-in-aid program under which federal and state (and sometimes local) governments share the cost of medical services for certain low-income groups. All of its funds come from general revenues.

In 1969, the Medicaid program, as shown in Table 5-6, financed medical care for an estimated 12.9 million enrollees—slightly less than a third of the nation's estimated 40 million "poor," who, according to the original intent of the Medicaid legislation, were to have been at least partially covered by the program.[16] Unlike Medicare, whose benefits are provided without regard to income level; Medicaid provides medical services only to those who continue to meet a certain income test. If their income status changes so that they no longer meet this test, they lose their coverage in much the same way that those insured under employee group plans lose their coverage when they become unemployed or change jobs.

Medicaid enrollees are made up of two groups: the "categorically needy" and

Table 5-6

Recipients of Medical Services and Expenditures under Medicaid, by Type of Recipient, 1969

Type of Recipient	Recipients	Expenditures
Total (millions)	12.9	$4,273
Percentage distribution, total	100.0	100.0
Children under 21	45.9	20.3
Persons 65 and over	22.5	42.2
Adults in AFDC families	17.3	8.8
Permanent and totally disabled	7.5	17.8
Other adults	6.2	10.1
Blind	0.6	0.8

Source: Dorothy B. West, assisted by Harold Coleman and Gloyd Robison, *Medicaid and Other Medical Care Financed from Public Assistance Funds: Selected Statistics, 1951-1969*, NCSS Report B-6 (Washington: National Center for Social Statistics, Social and Rehabilitation Service, U.S. Department of Health, Education, and Welfare).

the "medically needy." The former are those receiving cash assistance payments under four assistance programs: Old Age Assistance, Aid to the Blind, Aid to the Permanently and Totally Disabled and—most important numerically—Aid to Families with Dependent Children. Federal legislation requires states that establish Medicaid programs to provide certain minimum benefits to beneficiaries of these programs.

The "medically needy" are those whose incomes are inadequate to meet their current medical expenses but who are not eligible to receive assistance under any of the assistance programs. This category includes, for example, urban families of four whose total incomes are $90 a week or less. The law does not require states to provide benefits to this group, and in 1970 only 28 states had extended Medicaid coverage to the medically needy. Fewer than half the states that provide such coverage have established procedures under which medically needy individuals can apply for Medicaid coverage in advance of specific need for medical care. Without such procedures the state cannot make adequate budgetary estimates, give the patient financial security during a period of illness, or guarantee payment to the provider.

Medicaid paid $4.3 billion in benefits in 1969 (see Table 5-6). Of this amount, 42 percent went to pay for Part B Medicare premiums, copayments, deductibles and other expenses not covered by Medicare for persons aged 65 and over. (Federal law provides strong incentives for states to enroll Medicaid recipients 65 years of age and over in Medicare Part B.)

Although the federal government has established certain minimum standards for eligibility, services covered, and administrative procedures, Medicaid really consists of 48 separate state programs. (Arizona and Alaska have not established

Medicaid programs.) Not surprisingly, the state programs vary tremendously in coverage and quality. The amounts spent by the states on their programs illustrate these variations; 3 states—New York, California, and Massachusetts—account for half of all Medicaid expenditures.

The federal legislation that established Medicaid requires of each state "a satisfactory showing that it is making efforts in the direction of broadening the scope of the care and services made available under the plan and in the direction of liberalizing the eligibility requirements for medical assistance." But largely because of the steadily rising cost of Medicaid, most states have tightened eligibility requirements, reduced coverage, and failed to improve the quality of their programs. And Congress has repeatedly extended its deadlines for achieving comprehensive eligibility standards. In 1969, for example, Congress suspended for two years the operation of the provision quoted above, and changed the date by which the states were to have comprehensive eligibility standards from 1975 to 1977.

For the categorically needy, federal law requires the states to pay for: comprehensive medical services, including both inpatient and outpatient care in hospitals (except tuberculosis and mental hospitals); services of physicians, laboratories and X-ray units; and home health care, if the state program provides for the services of extended care facilities. The law gives the states some flexibility in establishing the financial criteria for eligibility and in determining the services it will provide for the medically needy.

Federal law does not place providers under any obligation to accept those eligible for Medicaid as patients, nor does it make any other provision regarding the actual availability of services for Medicaid recipients. As a consequence, many of both the categorically and the medically needy cannot gain access to medical services, even though Medicaid stands ready to pay the bill. Many of the poor live in areas where medical facilities are scarce, and those potential Medicaid patients who do have ready geographical access to services often find that physicians refuse to serve them. The reasons for this refusal are twofold:— (1) doctors have found that Medicaid not only has slow claims procedures but sometimes rejects claims and (2) some doctors believe that being known as "poverty doctors" or "Medicaid doctors" may drive away more affluent patients. In a few areas the Office of Economic Opportunity has established neighborhood health clinics to increase the access of Medicaid recipients to medical care, and Medicaid patients are eligible to receive treatment at existing HMOs.

In response to rising costs, state authorities have tried in various ways to limit both utilization and prices under the Medicaid program. For example, in December 1970, officials responsible for the Medicaid program in California ordered a 10 percent cut in fees for all Medicaid providers except hospitals, which, under federal law, must be paid on the basis of "reasonable cost" for services provided under the Mediplans. This reduction served mainly to make the providers of services even more reluctant to accept Medicaid patients. Some doctors, nursing homes, and pharmacists announced that they would no longer serve Medicaid patients if these and similar regulations were not rescinded.

The officials also announced that without prior authorization by a Medicaid consultant Medicaid would not pay for certain elective medical services, for more than 2 visits per month to a physician, more than 1 visit to a dentist within 6 months, nor all nonemergency hospital services. They instructed Medicaid consultants to authorize only those services that could not be postponed for 90 days or more.

They also revised the Medicaid drug formulary by establishing new wholesale price ceilings for many drugs and placing more than a thousand drugs on the list requiring prior authorization. And they tightened claims review procedures, limiting payments for services "only to those that are reasonable and necessary for adequate care of the patient."

The state of California maintained that these cost-cutting measures were necessary to cover a budget deficit of $140 million resulting from an unanticipated increase of 280,000 in the number of persons receiving medical services under the Medicaid program during the year. Ironically, in that year, the annual cost of services per recipient had decreased (largely as a result of previous administrative regulations) for the first time in the program's history. The net effect of the new regulations was to discourage eligibles from using and physicians from providing the services covered by Medicaid legislation.

Other states have handled the budgetary problems resulting from the rising costs of Medicaid by extending the time for payment of bills, by leaving bills unpaid altogether, by lowering the income threshold for eligibility of the medically needy, and by reducing covered services to this group.

Medicaid Operation and Administration

Medicaid's main function is the payment of claims, including Medicare copayment, deductibles, and Part B premiums, a function administered by the states in a bewildering variety of ways. Federal Medicaid legislation delegates to state agencies that administer the Medicaid program the job of selecting fiscal agents, who determine the amount to be paid on each claim, and in most cases also make the payment.

Twenty-two of the states use the state agencies themselves as fiscal agents; other states use private carriers and/or Blue plans for this purpose; still other states use both state agencies and the private health insurers. In 20 states the same private insurers serve as fiscal agents or intermediaries for both Medicare and Medicaid. The size of the workforce required to carry out this function has not been estimated.

The Medicaid program has established the country's commitment (as yet only partly realized) to provide medical services for those unable to pay for even minor treatment. It has also shown that the cost of such a program is much higher than anticipated and that its administrative structures are ineffective in controlling costs. Despite their efforts to reduce Medicaid fees and services, the states have failed to keep utilization within established budget limits, and as a result the state programs are in continual financial difficulty.

Like Medicare, the Medicaid program has filled an important need; it also dramatizes the problems of including those unable to pay either the cost of medical care or the insurance premium in a national health insurance plan while still maintaining cost and utilization control in an equitable fashion. Medicaid has also demonstrated that when the public sector finances medical care for the low-income population under a distinct and separate program, the providers of medical services may still discriminate against the program's "beneficiaries" and deny them equal access to medical facilities. It is this phenomenon that has led many proponents of national health insurance to insist that only through a monolithic, public sector program, which includes all segments of the population under the same financing system, can medical care be equitably provided to all.

Government as a Quasi-Insurer:
CHAMPUS

CHAMPUS (the Civilian Health and Medical Program for the Uniformed Services), sponsored by the Department of Defense, finances medical care for dependents of active duty military personnel, retired military personnel and their dependents, the dependents of deceased military personnel, and a small number of U.S. Public Health Service employees. In 1970, the program covered 6.1 million potential beneficiaries and paid claims totaling $276.1 million. CHAMPUS is intended to supplement the on-base health care programs of the various branches of the armed services by financing medical services that Defense Department medical facilities and personnel cannot provide. The Defense Department encourages those covered by the program to use on-base facilities when possible by keeping the fees charged by such facilities low compared with CHAMPUS coinsurance and deductibles. As a result, it is estimated that CHAMPUS finances only 43 percent of all inpatient care and 20 percent of all outpatient care of those eligible.[17]

CHAMPUS has uniform, nationwide coverage, which, although slightly more comprehensive, is similar to that provided by Medicare. The coinsurance and deductible provisions are also similar to Medicare's, and it covers a very comprehensive range of medical services prescribed by doctors, including routine physical examinations, obstetrics, and pediatrics, eye examinations, prosthetic devices, dental care, domiciliary or custodial care, and chiropractic services. Legislation has been introduced into Congress to extend the benefits and coverage still further.

The financial intermediaries or "contractors" who process claims operate in much the same way as intermediaries under the Mediplans. Blue Cross handles hospital claims in 33 states and Mutual of Omaha in 17 others. In most states the local Blue Shield plans handle the claims of doctors and other providers, but in some states local medical societies, private insurance companies, or some combination of these perform this function. CHAMPUS accounts for 2.6 percent of all Blue Cross-Blue Shield claims handled.

Like Medicaid, CHAMPUS is not a true insurance program. It does not collect premiums or maintain trust fund or reserve accounts. Like Medicaid enrollees, CHAMPUS enrollees must compete with others for providers' services in the private market, for the government makes no arrangements to assure availability of services. However, there is no evidence that CHAMPUS patients suffer from the discriminatory treatment that Medicaid patients often experience at the hands of providers, perhaps because CHAMPUS administrators have a more lenient attitude toward fees and a record of prompt claims settlement.

The CHAMPUS program is financed by the general revenues of the federal government through the budget of the Department of Defense. The government bases its annual appropriations on projections of the number of beneficiaries, utilization rates, and estimated costs in different areas of the country.

To avoid paying more than prevailing fees and reasonable charges for medical services to enrollees, CHAMPUS has adopted the Blue Shield system of fee profiles. But although cost overruns do occur and the annual budget is occasionally exceeded, these problems do not result in reductions of fee payments or coverage. Because of a lack of budgetary restrictions and a desire to secure local providers on the best available terms, charges and fees under CHAMPUS are not subject to the restrictions that the Social Security Administration and the state agencies have imposed on the Mediplans. The Department of Defense simply "borrows" the funds needed to make up CHAMPUS cost overruns from some other Defense Department program, includes the amount borrowed in the next year's appropriations, and repays it at that time. The characteristic that most clearly distinguishes CHAMPUS from the other public sector insurance or quasi-insurance programs is the absence of any practical budgetary constraint.

The direct cost to the Defense Department for administration of CHAMPUS is only 0.5 percent of claims, and the cost to the intermediaries for processing claims is roughly 3.2 percent. These costs, although not comparable with operating costs of private health insurers, indicate that CHAMPUS has the most straightforward payments procedures of all the government health programs and that its operation is relatively efficient.

Health Insurance for
Government Employees

The federal government and most state and local governments, like firms in private industry, offer group health insurance to their employees as a fringe benefit. A number of public employee health insurance programs are in operation. The largest and in many ways the most innovative is the Federal Employees Health Benefits Program (FEHBP).

The FEHBP, serving nearly 8 million federal employees and dependents, is the country's second largest health insurance program. (Medicare is the largest.) Incurred claims reported by the carriers under this program in 1969 amounted to $759.6 million—slightly less than 5 percent of the total claims under all health insurance policies for that year. The federal government does not underwrite the FEHBP and plays only a minor part in its administration. The government's main function in this program—other than sharing the cost of premiums—is to set standards and to enforce compliance with them among the insurers and the insured.

Private insurers and prepaid practice plans underwrite and administer the Federal Employees Health Benefits Program and negotiate with the U.S. Civil Service Commission regarding premiums and coverage. The Commission, which has primary administrative responsibility for the program, receives an amount totaling less than 0.2 percent of the program's annual premium volume for handling these annual negotiations, keeping statistical records, and monitoring the performance of the carriers. The government and the covered employees share the premium costs. The government's share, a flat amount equal to 40 percent of the average premium of the 6 top participating plans, is less than the average paid by private employers with similar health insurance plans. The employee's share is deducted from his salary. The U.S. Treasury Department disburses the premiums to the carrier and holds what is in effect an auxiliary contingency reserve. The law requires that this account be maintained but it adds unnecessarily to the cost of the program, since the carriers themselves hold similar reserves.

The FEHBP offers over 30 different health insurance plans to employees. (The health insurance program for employees of the state of California also offers a range of choices.) Not all these plans are available to all employees; many are local prepaid practice plans and others are available only to members of specific employee associations such as, for example, National Association of Letter Carriers and American Foreign Service Protective Association.

But the program offers each employee at least 4 plans to choose from and depending on location or membership in an employee organization as many as 8 or more, along with a further choice between high and low options—distinguished largely by level of maximum coverage—in most plans. Employees living in areas where prepaid plans are available can choose between them and conventional plans.

Nationally, the Government-wide Service Benefit Plan of Blue Cross-Blue Shield dominates the field, with almost 60 percent of total FEHBP enrollment. The Goverment-wide Indemnity Benefit Plan, administered by Aetna Life and Casualty Company on behalf of a consortium of private carriers, is second, with

20 percent of the total enrollment. A dozen or so different prepaid groups, about a half dozen individual practice plans, and 15 employee groups, mostly underwritten by private carriers (a few are self-insured) account for the rest of the enrollment.

The FEHBP offers coverage that is probably the most comprehensive of any program in the United States, if an employee wants to pay the additional cost. Employees have the opportunity to review and change plans once a year (formerly only every 3 years) during a 2-week period called "open season." While not openly presented as such, the right of the employee to change plans annually, for all practical purposes, means that the FEHBP has no upper limit. Thus, when an employee has reached the maximum-dollar limit under his present plan, he can start anew under another plan.

However, most employees are not likely to be able to evaluate the deductibles, copayment features, exclusions, and definitions of various plans comparatively beyond making such basic choices as that between conventional health insurance and a prepaid group. And in any case, the ultimate value of one plan compared with another depends on the kinds of illnesses insured family members may suffer.

Despite its size and the government's financial contribution to it, the FEHBP has been no more successful than private sector plans in controlling the costs of services to the insured, and it has not tried to bring about changes in the structure of the health care system. It has not experimented with ways of effecting a more efficient allocation of resources, such as encouraging the establishment of prepaid groups in areas where none exist or offering a high deductible plan as an option among the conventional plans. Nonetheless, with some important modifications, the FEHBP offers a significant model for a pluralistic national health insurance plan to be administered by the private sector but regulated by the public sector.

Government as a Regulator of Health Insurance: Workmen's Compensation

Workmen's Compensation programs are radically different from other government health insurance activities.[18] In most states such programs are not government-operated but required by state law, and regulated by state governments. In accordance with state-established standards, employers purchase insurance from private carriers or self-insure against work-related injuries suffered by their employees. The 18 states that have elected to underwrite and administer Workmen's Compensation themselves, either as a state monopoly or in competition with private carriers, account for 22 percent of premium volume.

In 1969, medical (including hospital) payments under Workmen's Compensation were estimated at over $800 million and represented roughly a third of all benefits paid under the program. Income loss payments made up the difference.

Few states require complete protection for employees with work-related injuries. In many states, employers are not required to provide coverage but those who fail to insure have no common law defense against employee suits. In other states, employers with fewer than a specified number of employees or with employees in certain types of employment, such as agriculture, domestic, work, and casual labor, are not required to provide coverage. The Social Security Administration estimates that, in 1968, only 84 percent of the employed labor force was covered by Workmen's Compensation. Workmen's Compensation pays less than half the cost of all work-related injuries in the United States. Since most private health insurance plans specifically exclude from coverage any medical expense falling under Workmen's Compensation laws—reimbursed or not—a job-related injury can be very costly to the worker.

The administrative cost of Workmen's Compensation insurance is high, especially for insurance sold to employers on a group basis. Its ratio of operating expenses to premiums is 31.4 percent, compared with an average ratio of about 10 percent for the large private carriers selling group health insurance. A major reason for this high administrative cost is the cost of settling Workmen's Compensation claims and disputes that arise from income loss settlements where disability must be established.

Workmen's Compensation provides close to 5 percent of all health insurance benefit payments and is thus an important source of medical care financing. It is, however, a very special kind of coverage and provides little experience of use in considering health insurance reform. This is a case where the public sector, as the regulator of this coverage, is more concerned with the liability of the employer than with the adequacy of the coverage.

Summary

The public sector's expenditures for personal health care are greater than those of the private sector, and unlike the private insurers who stand in the short run to benefit from rising medical costs, the public sector operates under budget constraints that serve as definite incentives to restrain costs. But government has been no more successful than the private insurers in checking inflation in medical costs, partially because the large public sector contribution to the total medical bill does not emanate from a single program but rather from several programs serving different groups. Moreover, the public sector, as an insurer or quasi-insurer, is in more or less the same situation as the private insurers. Although it can try to influence the prices of services as Blue Cross and Blue Shield do in the private sector, it cannot control the frequency with which patients will seek medical care or the quantity of medical service that physicians and hospitals will decide is appropriate. And since total cost is the product of price times quantity, the public sector can influence total cost no more than the private sector under the conventional system. The public sector has controlled, although with only moderate success, the costs of its own programs but, more often than not, in so doing is has arbitrarily curtailed coverage.

The operating costs of health insurance programs underwritten by the public sector are no lower, apparently, than those of the private insurers. To the extent that reasonably comparable data can be found, it appears, in fact, that the private sector has a slight edge.

Like Blue Cross and Blue Shield, the public sector can seek to control the providers by threatening them with denial of participation in its health care financing programs. This weapon could be more powerful than it now is if Medicare and Medicaid coordinated operations, for the two systems combined account for a fourth of expenses for hospital services and a sixth of expenses for physicians' services. Although the public sector does not, like the Blue plans, risk losing clients to the private carriers when it eliminates certain providers from the list of participants, it runs other risks. In denying participation to the one hospital in a community, for example, it effectively eliminates hospital coverage for the Medicare and Medicaid enrollees of that community.

The government as an insurer and quasi-insurer is also limited in its ability to experiment. It cannot use a high deductible to control costs and utilization, because many of the enrollees in public sector programs lack the means of paying even modest medical costs. It has, nonetheless, shown a greater willingness than the private sector to experiment with integrating insurer and providers in prepaid group practice plans to serve Medicare enrollees and has proposed a plan that might encourage more Medicare enrollees to subscribe to prepaid group plans.[19]

On the whole, however, the public sector has not used the influence its huge contribution to the total medical bill gives it to help reform the health care system or to help to control utilization and cost of medical services. It has been unable to bring its various health care and health care financing programs together under a common policy that would give recognition to the influence of financing on the quality and utilization of health care services.

6 Health Insurance and the Hospital

Payments to hospitals are the largest single item in the national health care bill. They represented over 40 percent of all personal health care expenditures in 1969, which was more than double the share spent for hospital services 40 years earlier. This increase reflects improvements in hospital services, an increase in the number of hospital beds, and, above all, rapidly rising per-unit hospital costs. Daily service charges in hospitals rose 127 percent in the 1960s—nearly three times the rate of increase in all medical care prices and more than five times the rate of increase in the overall cost of living.[1] By 1972, daily room charges in excess of $80 were common in hospitals in most large cities.

One explanation frequently offered for the dramatic increase in the cost of hospital services is the long overdue wage increases granted to hospital employees in recent years (see Tables 6-1 and 6-2). The inefficiencies in hospital operations, unnecessary duplication of costly services in hospitals in the same area, excessive expenditures for expansion and modernization, and the high cost of certain necessary services, such as those of pathologists, are other important factors that have been used to attempt to explain mounting hospital costs.

But although all of these aspects of hospital operations have contributed significantly to the rise in hospital costs, they are probably the results rather than the sources of the inflationary pressures; it is increased demand for hospital services rather than the hospitals themselves that has stimulated the price rise.

Through hospitalization insurance, 85 to 90 percent of the population has pooled a certain portion of its income and reserved it for expenditure on hospital services. The amount reserved in this way has increased year after year, generating an increase in demand that has enabled hospitals—most of which are nonprofit and, hence, under no pressure to distribute earnings—not only to accommodate the wage demands of employees but to expand, modernize, and introduce new equipment as well. The expenditures for expansion and modernization, in turn, represent the hospital's efforts to attract physicians with outstanding reputations and large clienteles and thereby to increase its share of the market.

Supporting the rising demand for hospital services is the fact that the need for hospital services is flexible. The decision to treat a given illness on an inpatient basis and the length of time the patient is kept in the hospital for treatment vary widely, depending on the doctor, the patient, and the method of payment available to the patient—that is, whether his bill will be paid by an insurance carrier, out of personal funds, or by a prepaid group practice plan.[2] Physicians

Table 6-1

Hospital Payrolls, as Percent of Hospital Costs, 1950-1969

Year	Percent
1950	56.7
1960	62.3
1965	61.7
1969	59.1

Source: *Hospitals, Guide Issue*, August 1, 1970, and various previous issues.

Table 6-2

Relative Importance of the Reasons for Increased Hospital Payroll Expense, 1960-1969

Reasons for Increased Payroll Expenses	1960-1965 (Percent)		1966-1969 (Percent)	
	Average Annual Increase	Share of Cost Increase	Average Annual Increase	Share of Cost Increase
Total increase in payrolls[a]	8.6	100	10.6	100
Higher earnings per employee[b]	3.3	40	3.3	32
Increased average daily census	3.3	40	3.7	36
Other reasons[c]	1.7	20	3.3	32

[a]Based on constant dollars.

[b]Based on average annual earnings per employee in constant dollars; hourly wage data for hospital workers for the years covered are not available.

[c]Includes changes in the quality of hospital service plus changes in productivity.

Source: *Hospitals, Guide Issue*, August 1, 1970, and various previous issues.

can directly influence the demand for all kinds of medical services including hospitals; hospitals can also stimulate demand for hospital services, although only indirectly, through improving or expanding facilities that are then readily consumed largely because insurance makes the demand for such services effective.

Whether hospital costs have risen because of forces, such as wage pressures, within the hospital that could not readily be resisted or because insurance has made it possible for the public to spend more money on hospital services is a distinction of great policy significance. If hospital inflation is mainly of the "demand-pull" variety—i.e., induced by more money in the hands of the public to spend on hospital services—then, efforts to restrain the price of hospital services through cost formulas, such as those employed by Blue Cross and the Mediplans, are not likely to be effective for any sustained period.[3]

Who Pays the Hospital?

The decline in patients' out-of-pocket expenditures for hospital care has been consistent and impressive. As shown in Table 6-3, these expenditures accounted for only 14 percent of the total operating revenue of hospitals of all kinds in 1969, compared with 21 percent in 1960 and 34 percent in 1950. The decline in patients' out-of-pocket expenditures at "community hospitals"—i.e., hospitals other than federal, psychiatric, and tuberculosis hospitals that receive 87 percent of their funding from public sources—has been even greater because of the greater share of income these hospitals receive from private insurance.

During the same period, the share of all hospital payments received from public grants and philanthropy also declined, while the share of all hospital care—community and other—paid for by public and private health insurance increased from 21 percent to 55 percent. Table 6-4 provides a breakdown by sources of community hospital operating income for 1969. The largest source, payments for Medicare enrollees, accounted for 23.3 percent of community hospital income; Blue Cross paid 22.2 percent of the bills, and the private carriers paid 20.1 percent. This growth of the insurers' role as a source of payments has vastly enhanced the financial well-being of hospitals.

In 1969, government programs (including Medicare) provided 40 percent of the operating income at community hospitals and almost half of the operating income at all hospitals (see Tables 6-3, 6-4, and 6-5), but by contrast, only about a fourth of total payments for the services of all other components of the medical care system. From 1950 to 1969, public sector payments to hospitals on a per patient basis (as opposed to cash grants) increased from 18 percent to

Table 6-3

Percentage Distribution of Sources of Financing for All Hospital Care, 1950-1969

Source	1950	1960	1965	1969
Total (billions)	$3.8	$9.0	$13.5	$23.9
Total, percent	100.0	100.0	100.0	100.0
Public grant programs and philanthropy	44.7	42.2	37.8	31.4
Health insurance (including Medicare and Workmen's Compensation)	21.0	37.8	44.4	54.8
Consumer out-of-pocket expenditures	34.2	21.1	18.5	13.8

Source: Barbara S. Cooper and Mary F. McGee, "National Health Expenditures, Fiscal Years 1929-70 and Calendar Years 1929-69," *Research and Statistics Note*, No. 25 (Washington: Social Security Administration, U.S. Department of Health, Education, and Welfare, December 14, 1970), Tables 8 and 9.

Table 6-4

Sources of Community Hospital Operating Income, 1969[a]

Sources	Amount (Billions)	Percent
Total	$18.9	100.0
Private insurance	8.4	44.4
Blue Cross-Blue Shield	4.2	22.2
Private carriers	3.8	20.1
Independent plans	0.4	2.1
Public programs	7.5	39.7
Medicare	4.3	22.8
Medicaid	1.7	9.0
Other	1.5	7.9
Consumer out-of-pocket expenditures	2.6	13.8
Philanthropy	0.4	2.1

[a]In so far as possible, data are for community hospitals only and therefore exclude expenditures in federal, psychiatric and tuberculosis hospitals because 87 percent of the funding for such hospitals comes from public sources and almost none from health insurance.

Sources: Barbara S. Cooper and Mary F. McGee, "National Health Expenditures, Fiscal Years 1929-70 and Calendar Years 1929-69," *Research and Statistics Note*, No. 25 (Washington: Social Security Administration, U.S. Department of Health, Education, and Welfare, December 14, 1970), Tables 7 and 8; and Marjorie Smith Mueller, "Private Health Insurance in 1969: A Review," *Social Security Bulletin*, February 1971, Table 15.

Table 6-5

Expenditures for Hospital Care from Public Programs, 1969

Program	Amount (Billions)	Percent
Total	$11.49	100.0
Health insurance for the aged (Medicare)	4.40	38.3
Public assistance (largely Medicaid vendor payments)	1.77	15.4
General and medical care	3.04	26.4
Defense Department and Veterans' Administration programs	2.12	18.5
Others[a]	0.16	1.4

[a]Includes Income Loss Insurance (medical benefits), Maternal and Child Health Services and Medical Vocational Rehabilitation. Figures are for current operating expenses only and exclude public funds spent for hospital construction and hospital-conducted research and for extensive public health programs administered outside of hospitals.

Source: Barbara S. Cooper and Mary F. McGee, "National Health Expenditures, Fiscal Years 1929-70, and Calendar Years 1929-69," *Research and Statistics Note*, No. 25–1970 (Washington: Social Security Administration, U.S. Department of Health, Education, and Welfare, December 14, 1970), Table 8.

roughly 60 percent.[4] Most of these payments come from Medicare, which has also greatly enhanced the financial security of the hospitals by reducing the risk that aged and poverty patients will not pay or will be covered only partially by public sector grants based on a lump-sum annual estimate.

These statistics do not mean that hospital costs are no longer a burden for patients or that hospitals have no trouble collecting bills. Hospital bills are still disastrous for patients with no hospitalization insurance or with limited coverage. Table 6-6 shows that only a small percentage of the population has no hospital insurance or institutional coverage, but much of the existing coverage is limited.

And although the ratio of consumer out-of-pocket expenses for hospital care to the total hospital care bill dropped sharply during the 1960s, the ratio of these out-of-pocket expenses to consumer disposable income dropped only 0.01 percent, from 0.53 percent in 1960 to 0.52 percent in 1969. In other words, the increase in hospital costs during the 1960s wiped out the consumer's gains from wider insurance coverage.

No exact figures are available on a nationwide basis, but estimates gathered in field interviews in the course of this study indicate that bad debts to hospitals average about 7 percent of gross revenues. Uncollected bills represent the costs of real services provided by the hospital, and the hospital must make up for them as best it can. The result is a vicious circle; bad debts increase as hospital charges are raised and charges are then raised still further to cover the

Table 6-6
Percent of Population with Insurance Coverage for Various Types of Hospital Services, 1969

Type of Service	Percent Covered
Basic hospital care	85.0-90.0
Related hospital services[a]	
X-ray and laboratory examinations	62.2
Private duty nursing	45.4
Nursing home care	14.0
Outpatient services provided by hospital	51.0
Doctor's in-hospital services[a]	
Surgical procedures	75.8
Hospital visits	66.6

[a]These estimates are made from consumer surveys of the U.S. Public Health Service and may underestimate the actual percent of the population covered by as much as 10 percent. (See Chapter 2 and Appendix C.)

Source: Marjorie Smith Mueller, "Private Health Insurance in 1969: A Review," *Social Security Bulletin*, February 1971, p. 3.

accumulation of bad debts. Those who are hospitalized and participate in insurance plans that pay hospital charges thus pay the price for what is, in reality, a community-wide welfare responsibility. How and to what extent uncollected bills may be included in reimbursement formulas are important issues between the hospitals and Blue Cross and the Mediplans.

How Hospitals Are Paid under
Insurance Arrangements

While Medicare, Blue Cross, and the private carriers share almost equally the major burden of financing hospital operations, none individually carries enough weight to control hospital costs.[5] Of these three components, in fact, only Blue Cross and Medicare make any direct effort to control hospital costs, but since each employs a different technique, their impact is less than it might be if their efforts were unified.

Although their techniques differ, both Blue Cross and the Mediplans[6] employ the principle of reimbursing hospitals only for the costs of the services actually performed for the patient rather than paying the price or "charge" on each service rendered for which hospitals usually assess patients. These charges, which are frequently unrelated to the actual cost to the hospital of the particular service, form the basis of payment for the self-insured and all those insured with private carriers.

The basic daily room charge and, to a lesser degree, the operating room charge are the hospital charges that are best known to the public and most affected by price competition. As a consequence, the daily room charge is customarily set at cost or slightly below, usually on a "follow-the-leader" basis for a group of community hospitals. (Nonetheless, demand for hospital services has been so strong that daily room charges have still increased more rapidly than other prices.)[7]

The hospitals make up their deficits on daily room charges by raising the charges well above costs for ancillary services, including those of hospital-based physicians—such as pathologists, radiologists, and other specialists whose incomes are paid out of hospital revenues—as well as for laboratory tests, X rays, and pharmaceuticals. The gradual adoption of modern cost accounting techniques by hospitals has narrowed but not eliminated differences between charges and actual costs of most services. To the extent that differences still exist, those who pay on the basis of charges are paying more for certain services than the cost of providing those services would seem to merit.

Most private carriers provide indemnity insurance—that is, the carrier's obligation is to the insured and not to the hospital, and the insured has no choice but to pay the hospital's charges. The private carrier, therefore, avoids involvement in the issue of whether hospital charges are just or unjust. But the failure of the private carriers to question the level or composition of charges makes it harder for Blue Cross and the Mediplans to influence the cost of hospital care through reimbursement on the basis of cost formulas.

Blue Cross—and for most purposes, Medicare—on the other hand, are associated with service benefit insurance, under which the provider—that is, the hospital—bills the insurer rather than the patient, and the insurer takes the responsibility for payment of all covered services. (Medicare and some Blue plans now have some deductibles related to hospital coverage.) Under service benefit insurance, as offered by Blue Cross, payment is always made directly to the provider, unless the provider is a nonparticipating hospital. This method thus assures payment to the provider rather than the beneficiary. The service benefit insurers, thus, can directly involve themselves in questioning hospital charges, and many of them have chosen to do so by arranging with hospitals to pay only the actual costs of services. Under cost reimbursement formulas, however, the insurers specify only what services and charges are reimbursable; they do not establish the maximum amounts they will reimburse for each service or charge, and they do not question the hospital's efficiency. For example, cost formulas do not state the number of nurses a hospital should have or what their wages should be, but only that "nurses' services" constitute a legitimate cost to be reimbursed in full, and the insurer agrees to reimburse at "reasonable" cost for covered services.

Some Problems of Cost Formulas

The components of cost formulas are a perennial subject of negotiation between the hospitals and the Blue plans and, in recent years, Medicare and Medicaid. For example, insurers paying claims according to cost formulas do not generally accept bad debts as a reimbursable expense. But the Medicare reimbursement formula accepts those bad debts arising from the deductible and coinsurance provisions of the Medicare program. Three other major controversial issues in the structure of the cost formulas are:

1. *Medical Research.* Most cost formulas reimburse costs related to hospital-based medical research programs only when they are incurred in conjunction with usual patient care and are not covered by separate funds for the research project. However, if the administrative overhead cost of a research project, which may run as high as 30 to 35 percent of direct research costs, exceeds the amount budgeted, these costs can usually be passed on to patients in the form of higher rates, with the result that they are reimbursed.

2. *Training and Education.* Most cost formulas reimburse the net costs of educational activities for nurses, medical students, and others, although these are largely community activities that may not benefit the patient. Incidentally, this source of income has made it easier for hospitals to grant large salary increases to

residents and interns in recent years. Training costs can amount to as much as 10 percent or more of the average daily hospital charge in non-teaching community hospitals. For university teaching hospitals, the cost is presumably more.[8]

3. *Depreciation and Charges for Growth.* Cost formulas usually accept depreciation charges as an expense for capital consumed during the year, or some equivalent cost-plus factor to cover such charges. But the accumulation of sufficient capital for growth is a chronic problem for hospitals, and the real issue in negotiating cost formulas is not whether a depreciation allowance based on historical cost should be reimbursable but whether it should include a "growth charge."

Blue Cross usually permits the direct inclusion of a growth charge, which may amount to from 1 to 5 percent of the patient's bill, with the provision, in some localities, that the accumulated capital be spent in accordance with the decisions of local planning boards. The Medicare formula originally included a 2 percent cost-plus factor, largely to generate capital for expansion, but the Social Security Administration dropped this factor when increasing hospital costs made it necessary to economize on Medicare benefit payments.

Underlying these issues are broad questions involving the community interest. Hospitals will have expenses whether or not cost formulas reimburse them. The community as a whole benefits from hospital research and training, but the costs of these activities are only tangentially related to an individual hospital's services and should not necessarily be charged by hospitals to their patients. Under the present system, not only do different hospitals spend different amounts on research and training, but because different insurers have different cost formulas and some patients' bills are not calculated on the basis of cost formulas, the costs are also unevenly divided among patients of the same hospital. More important, hospitals do not coordinate their research and training activities or provide any opportunity for the community to approve or disapprove them.

Depreciation costs provide money for expanding services and also affect the community, as well as the individual hospital, which has a responsibility for replacement and modernization of its equipment. Hospitals may reasonably be required to fund depreciation charges fully, but pooling such funds on a regional or community basis might facilitate planning and prevent costly duplication of facilities. Depreciation charges are often used to cover current operating deficits, a practice that imposes an unfair burden on patients. Often the hospitals inflate depreciation allowances to permit the inclusion of what are in fact growth charges; for example, they may adopt an accelerated depreciation formula or use the current cost of replacement rather than the historical cost. A strong case can be made for placing some limits on capital expansion by eliminating from the reimbursement formulas all growth charges above a fair depreciation allowance, however labeled. Hospitals could still, as they do today, add to their capital facilities from internally generated net income, depreciation, outside borrowing, and grants.

But depreciation charges also raise the much broader question of how large and how elaborate a community's hospitals should be. Presently the community as a whole has little voice in such decisions. The participation of insurers in cost formula negotiations, which focus on research, training, depreciation, and other items of community interest, is no substitute for this community voice, because the insurer's major concern is to limit its risk, and it cannot adequately represent the community's interest in determining the form and extent of hospital expansion.

Blue Cross Efforts to Control
Hospital Costs

Blue Cross has attempted, from time to time, to limit its costs for reimbursable services and to obtain a voice in budgeting, hospital wage policy, or capital expenditure planning, but few hospitals would sign participating contracts with Blue Cross that would permit that degree of intervention.[9] Given the competition from private carriers, Blue Cross cannot insist on its standards. The hospitals have other alternatives; Blue Cross does not. If the hospitals refused to participate, Blue Cross would be left with nonparticipating hospitals and, for all practical purposes, would be forced to abandon its service benefit insurance and, functioning as an indemnity insurer, would find it even harder to influence costs.

In Massachusetts, New York, New Jersey, and Pennsylvania, insurance commissioners have tried to force Blue Cross to take a harder line with hospitals by refusing to approve Blue Cross requests for rate increases to keep pace with rising hospital costs. These efforts, often aired in politically charged public hearings, have served mainly to delay subscription rate increases and force Blue Cross to pay claims from accumulated reserves and surpluses and thus reduce reserve levels that in some cases had been unnecessarily high but in others were forced too low and had to be reestablished later through larger rate increases. In any event, there is little evidence that these tactics have had any significant effect on hospital costs, although the publicity may have prompted hospital administrators to strive for greater efficiencies in the short run.

Blue Cross plans do, however, have a strong incentive to be persistent in negotiations with participating hospitals, because the more successful Blue Cross is in limiting the number and scope of items, such as bad debts, growth charges, and training, included in the negotiated cost formulas, the greater the spread between Blue Cross rates and the rates applied to patients with indemnity insurance. Since Blue Cross does not distribute profits, it is in a position to pass on this discount, net of the cost of negotiation and auditing, to subscribers in the form of lower premiums. Along with tax-free status, this discount is the major competitive advantage Blue Cross has vis-à-vis the private carriers.[10]

Experimenting with Cost Formulas

A 1967 amendment to the Medicare legislation has encouraged the Department of Health, Education, and Welfare to promote experimental agreements between hospitals and insurers from which would evolve a formula that, in addition to specifying reimbursable items, would restrain costs and support high quality hospital services. Local Blue Cross plans also experiment with payment systems; for example, in some areas, they offer a choice of cost formulas to participating hospitals. Several experiments now under way include payment to hospitals on a capitation basis, "prospective" reimbursements for particular services and various "average cost" formulas basing reimbursement on the average cost increase for hospitals in a particular area. The prospective reimbursement approach, strongly supported in certain quarters,[11] would require the insurers and hospitals to negotiate fixed rates for specified services in advance, on the basis of prior agreement as to the hospital's budget or of projections of historical costs. The purpose of this method is to induce hospitals to plan costs more precisely in relation to projected income, and it might indeed force the hospitals to plan better, particularly if all insurers coordinated their negotiations. But it probably would not in itself, be effective in curtailing rising hospitals costs—especially if, as postulated in this analysis, cost pressures are mainly demand induced. Enforcement would also be a problem. As long as hospital administrators are independent of insurers but under pressure from hospital boards and the medical societies, they will tend to incur expenditures according to these pressures. Even if hospital expenditures exceeded the income provided by the negotiated rates, hospitals would probably not be forced to close their doors for lack of funds. Either the insurers or the community would have to come to the rescue. And it would be difficult to fix the blame for the gap between expenditures and income, since the prospective rates would have been based on estimates.

Hospital Performance and
Third-Party Payments

Health insurance as presently structured has contributed to rising hospital costs by simultaneously increasing demand and diminishing traditional checks on costs, such as consumer resistance to price and the influence of philanthropists, without providing a satisfactory substitute.

During the 1960s, hospitals were able to vastly improve their financial status as hospital insurance coverage expanded. Third-party payments increased the demand for and utilization of hospital services, which in turn provided funds to expand the size of the basic hospital plants, so that the hospitals could meet and possibly stimulate demand further; to improve the quality of hospital services by modernizing facilities and equipment and expanding the work force associated with new technology; and to raise the wage rates of the basic hospital work force.

The per capita use of inpatient hospital services increased 32 percent between 1950 and 1969—from 0.9 days per person per year to 1.2 days per person per year. The "average daily census" of hospitals—that is, the average number of patients in hospitals each day, increased 75 percent from 1950 t0 1969 and 36 percent from 1960 to 1969, as shown in Table 6-7. Nonetheless, hospital capacity is believed to be more than adequate in most areas.[12]

During the 1960s, the number of hospital admissions increased from 129 to 142 per thousand, while the average length of hospital stay increased from 7 1/3 days to 8 days. Although exact data are not available, the use of hospital outpatient services has grown even more rapidly, particularly in recent years, with the trend toward greater use of hospital emergency rooms.[13]

The most obvious benefit for hospitals from the changes in the payments mechanisms has been growth in revenues, net income, and plant assets. The data on community hospitals shown in Table 6-8 indicate a satisfactory financial position during the first half of the 1960s and a noticeable improvement since 1965, when the legislation establishing Medicare and Medicaid was passed. The ordinary business experiencing cost increases of this magnitude would not expect, at the same time, to improve its net income position. But despite the steady rise in expenses, hospitals have been able to pass cost increases on to patients during this period of insurance growth and have increased their net income, which they have then applied toward improving the quality of services and enhancing their position vis-à-vis other hospitals.

The ability of hospitals to improve their internally generated cash flow (net

Table 6-7
Utilization of Nonfederal, Short-Term Hospitals, 1950-1969

Measures of Utilization	1950	1960	1969	Percentage Change 1950-1969	Percentage Change 1960-1969
Admissions					
Total (millions)	16.7	23.0	28.3	69.6	23.0
Per 1,000 population	110.5	128.9	141.5	28.1	9.8
Average length of stay					
(days)	8.1	7.6	8.3	2.5	9.2
Patient days					
Total (millions)	136	174	237	74.3	36.2
Per 1,000 population	900	977	1,188	32.0	21.6
Average daily census					
(thousands)	372	477	651	75.0	36.4

Source: *Hospitals, Guide Issue*, August 1, 1970, and various previous issues.

Table 6-8
Changes in Financial Position of Community Hospitals, 1960-1969

	1960-1964	1965-1969
Annual percentage change		
Total revenue	10.0	14.9
Total assets	7.6	8.6
Net income as percent of −		
Total revenue	.020	.036
Plant assets	.015	.033

Source: *Hospitals, Guide Issue*, August 1, 1970, and various previous issues.

income plus depreciation) has in turn improved their ability to borrow outside funds for capital expansion. Citing the greater stability of operating income under the Mediplans, improved hospital administration, and new freedom from charitable contributions, one investment analyst has stated that, "While there are problem investments in hospitals, there is generally a high degree of credit worthiness in loans to this group of borrowers."[14] This new financial independence has led the government to replace federal grants, under the Hill-Burton Act, which initially provided federal matching grants for hospital construction, with federal loan guarantees and, in 1973, to propose elimination of this type of support entirely. Figure 6-1 shows the extent to which this improved financial picture has permitted hospitals to expand and improve their medical services.

Most of the equipment and techniques that have been introduced since 1960 are not labor-saving or cost-saving and do not substitute for existing hospital functions; rather, they add directly not only to capital costs but to manpower costs as well, since they usually involve more highly skilled and better paid technicians than do basic hospital services. Table 6-9 provides a rough measure of the cost per patient for the additional services showing the number of employees and the plant assets per patient. Moreover, the number of new services offered increases with hospital size, and hospitals have grown dramatically since 1950.

A much smaller share of the increase in the incomes of profit-making than of nonprofit hospitals has been committed to expansion of facilities. For equivalent size hospitals, the ratio of plant assets per bed (one measure of the number of specialized facilities) is twice as high for nonprofit as for profit-making hospitals. Each of the specialized facilities listed in Figure 6-1 is found in roughly 50 percent more of the nonprofit than of the for-profit hospitals. Profit-making hospitals are, predictably, more concerned with financial result, and their occupancy rates and rates of increase in patients served are generally higher (when corrected for differences in hospital size) than are those of nonprofit hospitals. Not surprisingly, the ratios of net income to total revenue and to plant assets are for profit-making hospitals also considerably higher.[15]

Nonprofit hospitals claim that these statistics do not reflect better management, on the part of the profit-making hospitals, so much as patient selection—fewer long-term and terminal cases, tighter scheduling of short-term patients admitted on a nonemergency basis, and fewer patients requiring expensive night care services. Since short-term patients usually make more intensive use of hospital facilities, the for-profit hospitals benefit by directing their services toward this group, leaving the nonprofit hospitals with patients who will bring in lower reimbursements per patient-day.[16]

The inducements that prompt hospitals to add new services include the availability of financing, a need to improve the quality of care and a desire to attract the best physicians to the hospital staffs. According to one hospital administrator who is also a past president of the American Hospital Association:

One of the goals of our hospital is the attraction and retention of the best possible medical staff available. Naturally, a physician's view of a hospital is affected by the kinds and quality of its service facilities.[17]

In other words, given the strong demand created by health insurance, hospitals are able to compete with one another and to attract high quality medical staff by providing the latest, best, and usually most expensive, equipment, rather than through the pursuit of efficiency and lowered costs. The unfortunate result is duplication, and often subsequent underutilization, of expensive capital equipment that must eventually be paid for by higher per-diem costs, even though the new equipment may actually adversely affect the quality of care in hospitals that have infrequent occasion to use it and do not have adequately trained staffs to handle it.

Hospital Labor Costs

One of the reasons why wage increases of the hospital labor force are often cited as an explanation for rising hospital costs is that the rate of increase in wages of hospital workers has indeed been higher than that for other workers. Between 1960 and 1969, the earnings of hospital workers increased by 66 percent, while the earnings of workers in manufacturing industries increased by 43 percent, and those of workers in retail trade increased 36 percent.[18] This rapid increase, which has brought hospital wages closer to the level prevailing in other industries, is the result of productivity gains in hospital work, the application of minimum wage legislation to hospital workers, and the growth of unionism in the hospitals. Wages in hospitals are still relatively low, however. The average for all full-time workers—supervisory and nonsupervisory—was $5,380 in 1969.

Hospitals are labor intensive; payrolls account for roughly 60 percent of their total costs. Wage increases therefore have a substantial impact on hospital costs. But the impact of increases in wages paid to hospital workers on rising hospital

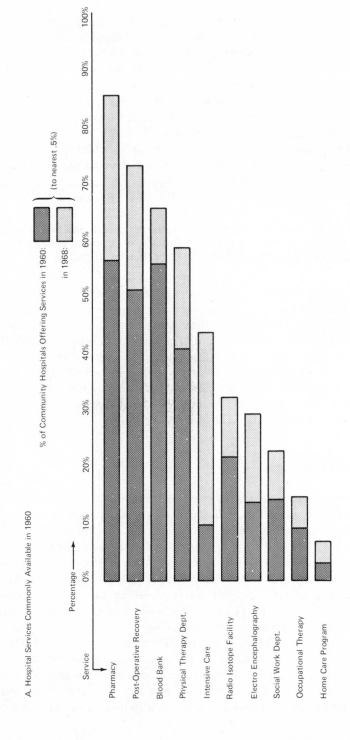

Figure 6-1. Percent of Community Hospitals Offering Specific Services, 1960-1969. Source: Services for which no American Hospital Association data before 1960 are available. *Hospitals, Guide Issue,* August 1, 1970, and various previous issues.

B. Additional Services Available in Community Hospitals by 1969

% Offering Service ⟶

Service

0% 10% 20% 30% 40% 50% 60% 70% 80% 90% 100%

Inhalation Therapy
Histopathology Lab
Intensive Cardiac Care
Organized Out-Patient Dept.
Radium Therapy
Psychiatric Dept.
Renal Dialysis
Cobalt Therapy
Rehabilitation (In-Patient)
Extended Care Unit
Open Heart Surgery
Family Planning
Self-Care Unit
Organ Bank

Table 6-9

Growth of Community Hospital Facilities and Services, 1950-1969

Facilities and Services	1950	1960	1965	1969	Percentage Change 1950- 1969	Percentage Change 1960- 1969
Number of hospitals	5,031	5,407	5,736	5,853	16.3	8.2
Beds per hospital	100	118	129	141	41.0	19.5
Beds per 1,000 population	3.35	3.59	3.86	4.14	23.6	15.3
Employees per patient[a]	1.78	2.26	2.24	2.80	57.3	23.9
Plant assets per patient[b]	$747	$1,738	$2,187	$2,537	239.6	46.0

[a]Employees divided by the average daily census.
[b]Plant assets divided by the average daily census.
Source: *Hospitals, Guide Issue*, August 1, 1970, and previous years.

costs has been overstated. Nonlabor costs in hospitals have been growing even faster than labor costs; labor's share of total costs, which increased substantially from 1950 to 1960, actually declined between 1960 and 1969, as was shown in Table 6-1.

The increase in total payroll itself results not only from higher wage rates but also from the increased manpower requirements generated by increases in hospital utilization (shown in Table 6-7). Improvements in the quality of hospital care have also necessitated increases in both the number of employees per patient and the number of higher paid workers. Many of the new services listed in Figure 6-1, although more capital intensive than the traditional hospital services, require skilled and highly paid technicians. Intensive care units, for example, employ several skilled nurses per bed, around the clock. Physical therapists are college trained. Renal dialysis requires a large, skilled staff.

The relative contribution of increased wage rates, greater utilization of hospitals and other factors (primarily improved services) to higher hospital payrolls during the 1960s was estimated in Table 6-2. Between 1960 and 1965 higher wage rates accounted for 40 percent of the real increase in hospital payrolls, but during the second half of the 1960s the share of the increase caused by higher wage rates dropped to less than one third; greater utilization and improvements in the quality of service (plus small increases in productivity) accounted for over two thirds. The increasing importance of "other factors" for increases in payrolls reflects the additional services hospitals have begun to provide as the proportion of hospital income from third-party payments has increased.

Productivity

Productivity gains in hospitals, although difficult to measure, are generally believed to have lagged noticeably behind those in other industries, despite the increasing use of mechanical equipment in certain diagnostic and treatment procedures. The day-to-day care of patients is still a labor-intensive activity. If hospital productivity continues to lag (as seems likely), and if the demand for inpatient service permits hospital wage rates to rise to the level of those activities competing for the same labor supply, hospital costs will continue to increase faster than other costs. Future changes in medical technology are likely to accentuate this trend, increasing the need for incentives to improve hospital productivity and to rationalize capital expenditures.

Summary

Utilization of hospital care has grown rapidly, partly because many doctors find it a convenient way to treat patients, particularly if insurance will cover the bills, and partly because many health insurance policies favor medical care administered on an inpatient basis. The basic distortions that have taken place in hospital utilization and, concomitantly, in hospital costs, can be at least partially corrected by placing all types of care—non-hospital as well as hospital—on an equal insurance footing, and by providing doctors and patients with appropriate incentives to use outpatient facilities when feasible. Obvious substitutes for inpatient hospital care are available: for long-term patients, home care or nursing-home facilities; for diagnostic testing, outpatient services at a hospital or clinic; for minor surgery, outpatient facilities; and for consultative work, closer working relationships between doctors.

Minimizing hospital cost inflation, in the final anslysis, will depend on the demand for and utilization of hospital services, and further experimentation with cost formulas is not likely to contribute much toward achievement of that objective. Effective control of hospital utilization will require building into the system some way of inducing physicians and patients to take into account the costs and benefits of hospital treatment in relation to substitute forms of medical treatment.

7

Health Insurance and the Doctor

Once a patient has initiated the demand for medical care and decided that he wants to continue treatment for an illness, he is largely dependent on the decision of his doctor as to the kind and quantity of medical services he will consume. The patient can buy certain drugs only if prescribed by a doctor; except in emergencies, he can be admitted to a hospital only on the orders of a doctor; he undergoes laboratory tests under doctor's orders, and the results of these tests are generally reported to the doctor; and he cannot collect on his health insurance until a doctor has certified the nature of the illness and the kind of treatment administered.

The analysis in this chapter is limited to physicians in private, office-based practice, almost all of whom are paid on a fee-for-service basis. Excluded are the growing number of doctors employed by prepaid group practices or public institutions, attached full-time to hospital staffs, or not practicing but involved in research, administration, or teaching. In 1969, 84 percent of all licensed physicians were practicing medicine and 57 percent were in office-based private practice.[1]

These doctors perform three general functions that affect the costs of providing health care: (1) they provide medical services themselves and charge fees for them; (2) they determine what other medical services may be required; and (3) they devote a surprising amount of time to supporting patients' insurance claims by certifying that treatment has taken place. Directly or indirectly, this cost also has to be paid by patients.

But while the doctors' influence extends over all aspects of the health care delivery system, it is his role in determining the disposition of his services and the exceptional income he has attained in the process that has commanded the greatest attention. Figure 7-1 shows a comparison of the net median incomes, before taxes, of physicians in the United States with the median incomes of other high-paid professionals—including chief accountants, attorneys, chemists and engineers—which reveals that during the 1960s doctors' incomes increased faster than the incomes of the other professionals. Because physicians' incomes are high and have increased rapidly, many have concluded that one way to attack medical cost inflation is to control doctors' incomes. These efforts have, for the most part, taken the form of controls on the level of fees they may charge. As in the case of the hospitals, such efforts at dealing with unit costs have had only limited success because they ignore the demand-pull nature of medical cost inflation and the fact that physicians can minimize the effect of fee

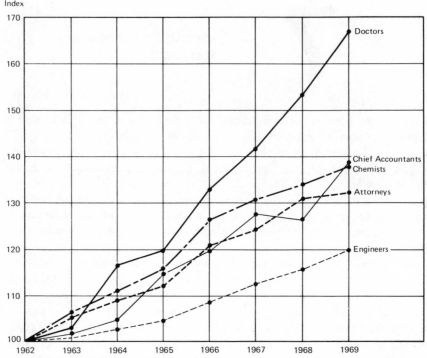

Figure 7-1. Indexes of Median Annual Incomes of Doctors and of High-Paid Chief Accountants, Attorneys, Chemists, and Engineers, 1962-1969. Source: "Continuing Survey of Full-Time Practicing Physicians Under Age 65," *Medical Economics* (various issues, 1962-1970); also *National Survey of Professional, Administrative, Technical and Clerical Pay*, 1962-1970, Bureau of Labor Statistics, Department of Labor (Washington: Government Printing Office, 1962-1970).

controls on their income by varying the nature and quantity of services they provide or prescribe.

Comparisons of the ratios of doctors' incomes to incomes of other high-paid professionals in several countries, shown in Table 7-1 indicate that doctors in these countries earn more than other professionals no matter what payment method is used or how doctors' fees are regulated. The figures suggest that in these countries a higher value is placed on the services of doctors than on the services of other professionals and that doctors elsewhere also possess substantial economic power just as they do in the United States.

Between 1950 and 1969, the estimated net median income (before taxes) of full-time physicians in private practice in the United States more than quadrupled, rising from $8,744 to $40,550.[2]

Table 7-1

Ratios of Doctors' Incomes to Incomes of Other Professionals, Selected Countries and Years[a]

Country	Year	Type of Medical Practice	Ratio of Doctors' Incomes to Incomes of:		
			Engineers	Attorneys	Other Professionals
France	1963	All types	1.94:1	2.29:1 1.72:1	1.71:1 University professors
Sweden	1959	All types			2.76:1 Professionals
Netherlands	1966	Specialist	.875:1	2.08:1	1.67:1 Accountants
		General	.619:1	1.47:1	1.19:1 Accountants
West Germany	1963	All types	3.51:1		1.45:1 Top civil servants
Great Britain	1955-1956	Specialist	2.59:1	1.93:1	2.00:1 University graduates in industry
		General	1.79:1	1.30:1	1.38:1
United States	1963	All types	2.39:1	1.91:1	1.06:1 Highest level attorney

[a]Latest year for which data are available in each country shown.

Sources: William A. Glaser, *Paying the Doctor: Systems of Remuneration and Their Effects* (Baltimore: Johns Hopkins Press, 1970), pp. 174, 175, 198, 199, 237, 279 copyright © 1970, The Johns Hopkins University Press; and "Continuing Survey of Full-Time Practicing Physicians Under Age 65," *Medical Economics*, 1964.

The most significant factor contributing to this rapid increase apparently has been the growth of health insurance coverage of physicians' services. In 1950, approximately 36 percent of the resident population had some coverage of surgical expenses but comprehensive coverage, which includes outpatient physician services, was virtually unknown.[3] In 1955, 3.1 percent of the total population was protected by comprehensive health insurance; by 1960, 17.3 percent had such coverage. By 1965, more than one third of the population was enrolled in comprehensive plans and by 1969, about 60 percent, if those under 65 who are eligible for Medicaid are considered to have such coverage. Moreover, by 1969, the portion of the population with insurance covering at least surgical expenses had increased to approximately 80 percent. Today both doctors and patients know that for most Americans a third party will pay part—often a major part—of the cost of many physicians' services.

From 1950 to 1969, the share of doctors' income paid by health insurance, including Medicare Part B and Workmen's Compensation, increased from 15.5 percent to nearly 50 percent, as shown in Figure 7-2. Predictably, as health insurance coverage has increased, the gap has widened between the fee actually

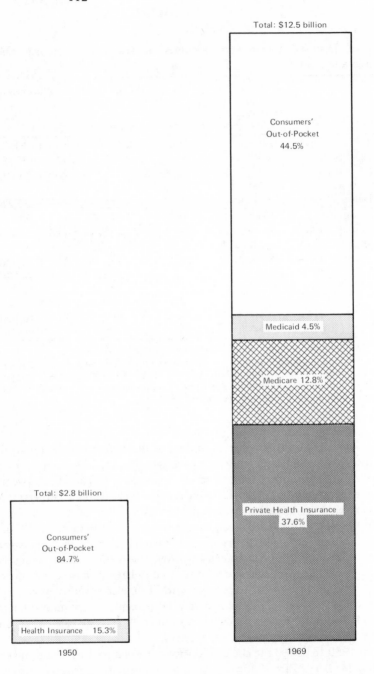

Figure 7-2. Share of All Payments for Physicians, Services, Paid by Health Insurance and Directly by Consumers, 1950 and 1969

charged by the doctor and the amount paid out of pocket by the patient. The ratio of actual fees charged to fees charged net of insurance rose from 106 in 1958 to 149 in 1966. But although the proportion of the population with insurance, as well as the level of coverage, increased substantially, the overall increase in doctors' fees was so great that "the average price net of insurance (paid by the insured) not only did not fall but actually increased by 2.1 percent per year."[4]

The growth of comprehensive insurance coverage has not only added to the share of doctors' fees paid by third parties, but more important, encouraged patients to seek treatment or diagnosis for discomforts or symptoms they might otherwise leave untreated. The rise in doctors' incomes as a result of this growth in health insurance appears to fit the classical pattern of the effects on prices of a rapidly rising effective demand juxtaposed with a much slower increase in supply.

Doctors' Responses to Rising Demand

To some extent, the response to rising demand has been an increase in the supply of physicians and physician services. From 1962 to 1969, the number of practicing physicians *per capita* increased roughly 10 percent. The median work week of physicians in private practice, however, stayed roughly the same, changing only from an average of 60.5 hours between 1962 and 1965, to an average of 61 hours between 1966 and 1969.[5] At the same time, doctors have assumed somewhat higher patient loads. Between 1962 and 1969, the median weekly patient load for full-time practicing physicians of all specialties rose by about 11 percent, from 120 to 133; by 1970, it had risen to 137 visits per week. Office visits accounted for most of the increase while the number of house calls, which are very time-consuming, decreased virtually to a statistical minimum.[6]

The 11 percent increase in patient load obviously does not account for the 66.9 percent increase in median income of doctors in this period. It is evident, therefore, that the response of physicians to rising demand has, in the main, taken the form of higher fees.

According to the Consumer Price Index of the Bureau of Labor Statistics, doctors' fees increased by 38.9 percent during the period 1962-1969. But this measure must be analyzed with some care. It is based on the "usual, customary and reasonable" fees for 7 medical procedures, weighted by estimated frequency of use. (Usual, customary and reasonable fees represent fees most commonly charged for a particular service.)

"Visits to the family doctor" account for about half of the total weight. The weighting system was not changed from 1962 to 1969 and therefore does not reflect the changes in average doctors' fees that have resulted from the increased use of specialists in recent years.[7] The use of usual, customary and reasonable fees, rather than the average of actual fees charged, also distorts the financial picture.

The price of doctors' services may have risen even more than the prices of other services under similar supply-demand conditions, because prior to the spread of health insurance, doctors' average fees were artificially low; moral considerations and community pressure caused doctors to reduce their fees for patients to whom the usual fees represented a financial hardship. Due to the vast increase in the number of patients who have comprehensive health insurance since the 1960s, doctors have apparently felt less pressure to lower their fees to meet patients' needs. Sixty-two percent of the doctors responding to the Twentieth Century Fund Survey of Practicing Physicians expressed the view that when ability to pay is a consideration in assessing fees, it is fair to take into account the patient's health insurance coverage.

Thus, the advent of comprehensive insurance has enabled doctors to charge a larger portion of their patients on the basis of regular fee schedules. As a consequence, average fees in the early 1960s were lower than the index would suggest, and a comparison of 1962 figures with 1969 figures understates the real rise in physicians' fees. Between 1949 and 1966, the official index of physicians' fees used in the Consumer Price Index increased at an average annual rate of 3.2 percent, but according to Martin Feldstein, the actual annual rate of increase in physicians' average charges was 4.1 percent.[8]

As Martin Feldstein has shown, these increases in doctors' fees have been closely related to wider insurance coverage. Feldstein's multiple regression model indicates that between 1949 and 1966 a 1 percent increase in insurance coverage was accompanied by a .36 percent increase in the average fee level. In summarizing the results of his study, Feldstein states:

From 1948 to 1966, average fees rose 71 percent more than the CPI. . . . [The model] indicates that 31 percent of this increase (a price rise of 22 percent) can be attributed to the increased level of insurance protection during this period. Society is thus indirectly forced by the market to pay physicians a high price for the risk-pooling advantages of health insurance.[9]

The correlation between the growth of doctors' incomes and the growth of comprehensive health insurance is particularly striking in the period since the Medicare and Medicaid programs were established. Thus, the ratios of doctors' incomes to the incomes of the other professionals in the United States increased by a greater amount from 1966 to 1969 than from 1962 to 1965 (see Figure 7-1). But it was not Medicare and Medicaid alone that added to the demand for physicians' services. During the same period the private health insurance system brought comprehensive coverage to an additional 26 million persons, adding to the demand for physicians' services among the non-aged as well.

However, in a survey of insured adults conducted by the Gallup organization for this study (see Appendix C), 73 percent of the respondents indicated that, if they knew that their physicians were padding fees for services covered by insurance, they would object. Unfortunately, few patients know enough about fees to recognize overcharges (unless they were markedly high). Regulations established by the Cost of Living Council in 1971 require that physicians make available upon request a schedule of principal fees, a practice that many doctors followed before it was officially required. But it is doubtful that many patients ask to see the fee schedules. In any case, fee schedules usually represent maximum fees, and doctors have a great deal of leeway in adjusting fees up to the maximum.

Attempts to Limit Doctors' Fees

The effect of expanded health insurance coverage in increasing doctors' fees has generated considerable interest regarding Blue Shield's and the Mediplans' fee controls. Although no comprehensive attempts to control doctors' fees or incomes have been made in the United States (other than a rather loose arrangement under the Cost of Living Council mentioned above), Blue Shield in the private sector and the Medicaid and Medicare programs in the public sector have experimented with fee controls. (The maximum reimbursement schedules for specific procedures, which are found in many insurance policies, are intended to limit the insurer's liability rather than the amount that the doctor receives, but sometimes patients interpret the fee listed as the "going rate," and refuse to pay more.)

The community independent practice plans, such as Group Health Insurance, Inc., (GHI) of New York City, control fees by contracting with participating doctors to accept the stated fee as "payment in full," much as Blue Cross does with hospitals. Although Blue Shield has also employed fee schedules, its participating doctors have never accepted the listed fees as "payment in full," except for low-income Blue Shield patients. Patients above a stated income level are held responsible for payment of any charges over the listed fees, just as they are responsible for any charges over the dollar maximums in indemnity health insurance policies.

Since 1968, Blue Shield plans have been gradually abandoning fee schedules in favor of reimbursing doctors on the basis of "usual, customary and reasonable" charges (UCR). For Blue Shield this change represents a realistic compromise between what patients would like and what doctors are willing to accept. But it also represents an effort on Blue Shield's part to influence fees as well as to meet the competition of private carriers who often offer plans covering full charges, subject to coinsurance and deductibles.

According to Blue Shield's current practice, participating physicians are allowed to charge Blue Shield patients the same fees that they charge to other patients (subject to coinsurance provisions of patients' major medical policies, if applicable), provided that: (1) charges fall below a designated maximum percentile of the fees charged for similar procedures by the participating physicians in the region (generally between the 85th and the 92nd percentile); and (2) the physician agrees to accept the reimbursement as "payment in full." If a Blue Shield plan reimburses at the 85th percentile, and the fee of a participating doctor is higher than the fees of 85 percent of his colleagues for the same procedure, he must agree to accept as payment in full the fee charged by the physicians at the 85th percentile. As other physicians change their schedules, the prevailing charge at the 85th percentile also changes. Blue Shield determines the UCR fees by compiling "fee profiles" on each participating physician. These profiles and the reimbursable UCR fee levels are kept secret by Blue Shield on the theory that published schedules would invite those charging less than the designated percentile to raise their fees. Thus, a physician becomes aware of the reimbursable fee levels only if he raises his own fees above the 85th percentile.

The UCR fee system has been in effect for too short a time in most areas to permit an evaluation of its effectiveness. Michigan Blue Shield, which has been applying UCR since 1969, ran into financial difficulties very early. It overcame them partly through freezing UCR fee levels on some procedures and rolling back others. A number of participating doctors have complained about the new fee system, but few of them have actually withdrawn from participation in Michigan Blue Shield.[10]

Whether the initial financial problems of Michigan Blue Shield were due to excessive fee increases by Michigan physicians in response to the UCR system, to subscription rates that may have been too low, or to an underestimation by Blue Shield of the difference between the previous fee schedules and UCR cannot be determined until more data are available. Michigan Blue Shield alleges that Michigan doctors raised their fees 27.2 percent between June 1967 and June 1970, while the national average increase was 21.8 percent. It is not clear what Michigan Blue Shield's calculation is based on, or whether the Blue Shield doctors in Michigan started with a lower base.[11]

Blue Shield has encountered a similar problem in its participation in the Federal Employees Health Benefits Program. For this program it also uses the UCR system rather than fee schedules. In 1971, claims exceeded expectations, as they had in Michigan after fee schedules were abandoned; and in 1972 Blue Cross-Blue Shield had to increase the premiums for its Government-wide Service Benefit Plan by more than 22 percent, which was later reduced when it was discovered that the level of claims had been over-estimated.

The task of maintaining and adjusting individual fee profiles for participating doctors also raises the administrative costs of the UCR system. It is too early to tell whether the system will reduce the rate of increase in fees and if so, whether the reduction will be enough to compensate for the higher administrative cost.

The federal government has used a system similar to Blue Shield's UCR system in reimbursing physicians under Medicare Supplementary Medical Insurance (Part B). Medicare reimburses doctors who agree to accept Medicare assignments for charges up to the 75th percentile of physicians' charges in the region. These doctors are paid directly by the fiscal intermediaries and are assured of payment. Other doctors may bill Medicare patients for whatever amount they may feel is warranted, and take their chances on collecting the entire amount charged from patients who are reimbursed directly (up to the UCR level) by the fiscal intermediaries. Officials of the U.S. Department of Health, Education, and Welfare have stated informally that there is no evidence that the average charges of doctors who have agreed to accept Medicare assignments are higher than the average charges to Medicare patients of those who have not. (No formal study has been made on a per-procedure or per-service basis.)

As might be expected, doctors generally are opposed to any form of fee control. In the survey of full-time practicing physicians conducted by the staff of this study, 78.3 percent of the respondents indicated their opposition to fee control by any organization, government or private. Many of the doctors criticized Blue Shield, Medicare and the fee schedules of private plans as unnecessarily restrictive. (See Appendix A.) Some expressed the opinion that, for practical purposes, "fee controls are already here."

Although the efforts of Medicare and Blue Shield have probably had some restraining effect on fees for services covered by these insurance programs, they do not appear to have had much effect on doctors' fees in general. In fact, the rate of increase in doctors' fees as measured by the BLS rose from an average of approximately 4.8 percent annually from 1962 to 1969 to 7.5 percent in 1970 and 7.9 percent in the first 10 months of 1971. (On the other hand, fees increased only 3.1 percent in 1972, the first full year of controls under the Cost of Living Council.)

In any event, the effect of fee controls on doctors' incomes can be circumvented in a number of ways that do not add greatly to the patient's financial burden or specifically violate laws or government regulations. For example, if the physician believes the full charge for a consultation will not be reimbursed, he may itemize various minor procedures for which he would ordinarily not submit a bill or even add a few procedures that are harmless to the patient but of questionable therapeutic or diagnostic value. In an article entitled "Look What Medicare's Doing to Medical Ethics," Dr. William A. Nolen examines with amazing frankness the various ways Medicare controls are circumvented. He claims that doctors find these subterfuges distasteful, "But that's what we'll continue doing until the Government realizes we're the only ones who can do what needs to be done for the patients' health, and until it stops shoving rules, regulations, and schedules down our throats."[1][2]

Although fee controls may restrain increases in fees for specific medical procedures, they do not necessarily restrain total costs and utilization of doctors' services. Doctors can manipulate the description of a given procedure to justify a higher fee. The vast number of procedures, their interrelationship and the legitimate variations in treatment, depending on the complications and seriousness of illness, add to the difficulties of policing fees.[13]

When doctors find fee schedules unacceptably low—as in the Medicare program—evidence suggests that they try to compensate by prescribing additional treatment. A California pathologist reports:

... I'm constantly seeing what seem to be cases of more diagnostic and therapeutic procedures on Medicare patients than would be done on private patients. ... It's obviously a matter of what ... is necessary in order to get a day's pay for a day's work—scheduling more procedures than you might if you were getting an adequate unit cost for each procedure.[14]

European experiences described by William A. Glaser suggest some of the problems that can result from attempts to control fees. Germany has had chronic problems of overutilization of doctors' services, because fees are held below levels acceptable to doctors. Doctors' salaries are paid out of "sick funds" (health insurance funds) and are prorated among participating doctors on the basis of services rendered. Each doctor tries to increase his share by increasing the number of services he performs, but as they increase the quantity of services, the amount paid physicians per service declines, and doctors must perform still more services in order to keep their incomes from falling. There is, thus, a tendency to have patients return for more follow-up consultations than doctors might otherwise deem necessary.

The government of the Netherlands has sought to prevent such overutilization by providing lower fees for follow-up visits than for the initial visit for each illness, and by permitting the full fee to be charged only for the major service rendered a patient, if more than one service is performed in one visit. But doctors can circumvent these safeguards by having the patient return for additional services at later dates, a practice that is risky for patients who may urgently need the delayed services. As Glaser remarks, overutilization is not a problem "when fees are high and all doctors are busy." He cites the example of Sweden, with its high doctor-population ratio and its generously financed, government-subsidized insurance fund that pays high fees. The average annual rate of patient visits to doctors is less than 3 per year, compared with an average of slightly more than 4 per year in the United States and an average of more than 5 per year in most European countries.[15]

These experiences suggest that fee controls, even if universally applied, may lead to overutilization and may cause the quality of care to deteriorate by giving doctors an incentive to perform unnecessary services, carry heavy patient loads, and reduce the time they spend with each patient.

Doctors and Demand Creation

Their spectacular income level notwithstanding, doctors contribute to rising medical costs less through increases in their own fees than through their decisions as to patients' needs for additional treatment such as surgery, laboratory tests, prescription medicines, and hospitalization. Doctors create demand for both their own services and those of other providers. The prevalence of health insurance facilitates this kind of demand creation, and fee controls do nothing to discourage it. In fact, fee controls may even encourage the use of other facilities if doing so permits a doctor to see more patients or charge for additional procedures, such as interpreting a laboratory result.

In no other economic activity does a key supplier have so much power to dictate the kind and amount of his services and of related services the consumer will consume. Since the patient can rarely determine the seriousness of his condition, whether or not an ailment is self-limiting or progressive, or what treatments are required, he must rely almost completely on the judgment of the doctor. The doctor can urge frequent follow-up visits, prolong postnatal care, or even recommend surgery, and few patients will seriously question his advice. Hence the comment of one doctor, in a letter accompanying his response to the questionnaire of practicing physicians conducted by the staff of this study: "As you know, it is not difficult to sell a patient on the need for surgery (even unnecessary surgery) if that person has faith in you."

A patient's financial means—whether he is poor or rich, insured or uninsured—influence the doctor's choice of treatment for him. Dr. Martin S. Gumpert, in his book on doctor-patient relationships, discusses this point:

There can be no doubt that a doctor who remains blind to the financial implications of his patient's sickness cannot be a good doctor. . . . I prefer to admit frankly that a doctor cannot often work for nothing and that, before the treatment starts, a fee should be agreed on which takes into consideration the prospective length and kind of treatment and the economic situation of the patient. Otherwise, I am quite disturbed by the gleam in the patient's eyes while he discusses his troubles, a gleam which indicates that he is wondering nervously: What will this cost me? The patient's worries are often fully justified, because there are many ailments easier to bear than a financial setback, and in the end the financial blow will also aggravate the physical ailment. Often there exists also a queer inclination to prefer money to health and to subordinate physical well-being to economic well-being. Some people obviously prefer death to financial loss.[16]

According to the results of the survey of practicing physicians undertaken by the staff of this study, approximately 65 percent of the responding physicians try to determine, during the initial examination, what kind of health insurance coverage the patient has. Only 27 percent of the doctors responding maintained that doctors are "never influenced" by insurance coverage in deciding what type of treatment to provide or to recommend. More than 60 percent could recall deciding whether or not to hospitalize patients on the basis of their insurance coverage.

The initiative in choosing expensive treatment does not come exclusively from patients. Only 20 percent of the respondents to the survey questionnaire reported that insured patients "frequently" ask doctors to perform expensive treatments (that are covered by their insurance); 76 percent said that their insured patients either "never" or "infrequently" make such requests.

Data on prepaid groups, whose staff doctors usually receive bonuses for achieving economies in utilization, indicate that their patients spend roughly half as many days in the hospital per 1000 members as patients of doctors in private practice, who have no incentive to keep costs down for patients with insurance coverage. (See Chapter 8.)

The doctor's power to influence the level of demand for medical services is further demonstrated by a comparison of U.S. and British experiences. Surgeons in the United States perform routine operations at two to three times the rate of British surgeons. This fact, coupled with the fact that there are twice as many surgeons in the United States in relation to population as there are in Great Britain,[17] suggests either that British surgeons are overworked and must devote their time to the most urgent cases, or that American doctors are less busy and tend to intensify treatment—partly to augment their incomes or to pursue their professional interest in better treatment of illness.

None of the foregoing should be construed to mean that the additional treatment prescribed by doctors is not justifiable, medically speaking. A doctor's decision to hospitalize a patient, for example, can have any one or more than one of a number of motivations. A very busy doctor may find it convenient to hospitalize a patient for observation, especially if the patient's ailment cannot be readily diagnosed in the brief time the doctor has to examine him, and the symptoms indicate that the illness might be serious. Doctors in individual practices, who cannot consult with colleagues as readily as those in group practices, are particularly likely to hospitalize patients for observation and tests if serious illnesses are suspected. Such use of hospital services are all the more "justifiable" if the patient is insured, and the doctor knows he is not causing his patient financial hardship.

In the same way, doctors may sometimes consider it necessary to run diagnostic tests or prescribe medicine for patients who continue to complain of ailments, even though the doctors may be convinced that the additional tests or medication will contribute nothing more than psychological support for the patients. If the doctors do nothing, they may lose such chronically ailing patients to other doctors.

If diagnosis and treatment are complicated, doctors usually prefer to have patients in the hospital where professional personnel can have complete control over the patients and where the patients can be observed by trained observers twenty-four hours a day.

The use of other medical services to supplement a doctor's own treatment usually contributes more to total medical costs than do the doctor's own services. In 1971, room and board and ancillary charges for a day in the hospital cost $130 to $140, which was perhaps ten times the cost of a visit to the doctor. It is, thus, more the doctor's creation of demand for these other services which generates important additional medical costs under the present system and far less his power to raise fees.

Handling Insurance Claims—The Hidden Cost to the Patient

Finally, doctors contribute to the cost—direct and indirect—of providing medical services through an unwanted requirement that they participate in the handling of insurance claims of their patients. A recent *Medical Economics* survey indicates that the average full-time private practitioner spends almost 5 percent of his office time each week working on insurance forms. He also spends time on other health insurance activities such as answering patients' questions, instructing staff, and communicating by telephone and correspondence with insurance companies.[18] The Twentieth Century Fund Survey of 1510 Physicians in Private Practice, conducted by the staff of this study, raised this question:

According to a *Medical Economics* survey, a prominent patient complaint is that doctors' bills are often not itemized, causing either delay or loss of insurance coverage. Do you find that the need to meet insurance requirements in billing significantly detracts from time you could spend with patients?

Of those responding to the questionnaire, 44 percent answered "yes." Of the primary physicians (general practitioners, pediatricians, internists—those whom the patient generally contacts initially when symptoms appear) responding, 50 percent answered "yes." Many who answered explained that the reason why dealing with insurance claims did not decrease the time they spent with patients was that they had delegated this task to someone on the staff. Some doctors, most of them in partnership or group practice, reported the addition of a staff position devoted entirely to this function. But whether handled by the doctor or by his staff, paperwork adds to administrative costs.

According to *Medical Economics*, some doctors charge a fee, ranging from $0.50 to $5.00, for filling out insurance forms.[19] In any case, the doctor passes this cost on to the patient in the form of either the shorter consultation or higher fees. Moreover, for professionals, valued as highly as doctors are, to spend so much time on essentially clerical tasks is costly to the community as a whole.

Much of the reason why filling out health insurance forms is so time-consuming is that the forms and the information required vary for each plan. Some of the information requested is irrelevant to the claim and some is not likely to be known by the doctor (for example, "Does the patient have other health insurance?"). If the forms are not filled out satisfactorily the insurer may reject the claim; the doctor may therefore feel obliged to give his personal attention to these tasks, even though he has formally assigned them to someone on his staff. The doctor frequently finds himself in the midst of continuing paperwork as the patient pursues his claim and the insurer requests additional information and justification. Moreover, it is not unusual for a patient to delay payment of the doctor's fee pending settlement of a disputed claim, or to refuse to pay the fee if the claim is rejected.

Patients often do not know which procedures their insurance will cover, and equally often they misinterpret schedules of maximum benefits for medical and surgical procedures. For example, if an insurance policy provides for payment of a maximum of $100 for an appendectomy, the insured is apt to assume that $100 is the "going rate" for this procedure and that any charge above that is excessive. The medical profession regards the publication of fees as tantamount to advertising and hence "unethical"; few patients therefore know the going rates for most medical procedures, and many assume that the maximum benefits listed in their health insurance policies reflect the carriers' knowledge of average prevailing fees.

In short, claims handling is a nuisance for doctors, and it often provokes resentment. The remarks of one general practitioner are fairly representative of the attitudes expressed by a number of doctors surveyed for this study:

I may be somewhat paranoid but I feel that both the patient and the insurance company are causing me problems I should not have. Because of this I do what's best for me in each case and if it costs the insurance company or the patient either one that's just tough luck.

Summary

It is as legitimate to try to regulate physicians' incomes as it is to try to regulate the incomes of other economic entities that have monopoly power. The medical profession is already so attractive to young people that nearly 3 out of 5 qualified applicants can find no space in medical schools.[20] The exceptional income levels to which physicians have climbed, therefore, have not evoked the usual economic response of an increase in the supply of doctors.

But it is difficult to find an effective way to control physicians' incomes. The usefulness of fee controls for this purpose is, at best, unclear. The experience under Medicare indicates that doctors can circumvent limitations on specific

123

fees, and such controls may even have adverse effects that would more than offset their benefits. For example, doctors might try to make up for losses that result from fee controls by stimulating demand for unnecessary services. And by setting cheaper rates for certain services, fee controls could also increase the demand for doctors' services on the part of roughly one half of the population not covered by comprehensive insurance and thus add pressure to a supply already under strain. Policing controls also involve administrative costs (which can be substantial) as well as the cost (which cannot be measured) of antagonizing the medical profession.

The spread of insurance and the ability of doctors to generate additional demands indicate that there will be a continuing rise in the demand for doctors' services and that the upward pressure on doctors' fees relative to other prices is also likely to continue. The supply of doctors seems unlikely to expand sufficiently to serve as a restraint on fees in view of the prospect of growing demand and the obstacles to increasing the supply of doctors.

The problem of controlling doctors' incomes without radically changing the system or making doctors unwilling participants in the system, is one that other countries have tried to solve in various ways, with spotty results.

It may well be impossible to devise a suitable formula for controlling doctors' incomes within the fee-for-service system. The issue then to be faced is whether that system should be changed. A decision to change the system should not be made merely in order to control doctors' incomes. The cost of doctors' incomes to the public is small compared to the additional costs that could be incurred because doctors can direct the use of other medical services when they are relatively unconcerned about the financial burden on their patients. Reform of the means of paying doctors, therefore, should be designed not only to control their incomes but to deal with their influence in the utilization of other and more expensive medical services.

8 Cost Savings under Nonconventional Health Insurance Plans

A small but significant number of Americans—about 5 percent of the population in 1971—participate in health care financing systems other than the conventional system of the Blue Plans and the private insurance carriers (see Table 8-1).

Among such systems, community prepaid group practice and individual practice plans are of particular importance because evidence indicates that they have delivered quality health care at a lower cost than the conventional system. They have therefore, with some modifications, been prominently considered as models for health insurance reform.

Prepaid Group Practice Plans

Prepaid group practice plans have been in operation in the United States since the 1930s. The largest of the groups—the Kaiser-Permanente Medical Care Program—was started in 1938 by Henry J. Kaiser, who established the first of the Kaiser centers for his own employees. In 1971, prepaid group plans enrolled less than 3 percent of all insured persons. Enrollment in these plans still has grown more slowly in the past 2 decades than that in either the Blue plans or the health insurance programs of the private carriers (see Figure 1-1). The experience of the prepaid groups is thus too limited to permit us to predict with any assurance that the efficiencies that such systems have realized in the past could also be realized by a system with a vastly increased enrollment.

Prepaid group plans differ from conventional health insurance in a number of ways, but the basic difference is that the prepaid group plan or association is both the insurer and the provider, either supplying the services covered under the plan directly through its own personnel and facilities or arranging for the use of local medical facilities on a contractual basis. Except for certain exceptional, specified circumstances, members of prepaid group plans can obtain insured medical care only from those providers under contract to the plan. In contrast, patients under conventional systems can seek services from any eligible provider who meets the definition of "provider" under the insurance contract.

Prepaid group plans achieve some savings through centralized administration and support functions, through elimination of such insurance operations as claims handling, and in some plans, through the integration of the medical staffs and facilities—that is, medical centers or clinics with hospitals. But the most important way in which prepaid groups economize is probably by offering

Table 8-1

Enrollment in Independent Health Insurance Plans and in Dental Insurance Plans, 1971

Type of Plan	Total Enrollment[a] (Thousands)
Total independent health insurance plans	11,100
Group practice plans	5,450
Community	3,450
Employer-employee or union	2,050
Individual practice plans	5,650
Community	1,650
Employer-employee or union	4,000
Private group medical clinic	130
Private dental clinics and dental service corporations[b]	3,500

[a]Enrollment figures are for those enrolled in plans offering some of the following outpatient services: X-rays, laboratory tests, medical treatment in office, clinic or health center.

[b]Private dental clinics and dental service corporations, while offering "prepaid group medical care," are shown here separately because of the distinct character of their operation. Dental service corporations are individual practice plans sponsored by local dental societies.

Source: Marjorie Smith Mueller and Jeffrey Furnish, "Independent Health Insurance Plans in 1971," *Research & Statistics Note*, No. 6 (Washington: Social Security Administration, U.S. Department of Health, Education, and Welfare, May 2, 1973).

financial incentives to staff doctors to find the most economical ways, consistent with accepted medical standards, to treat ailments. Recognizing the influence of doctors in determining the kind and quality of treatment a patient receives for a given illness, the prepaid group plans usually provide bonuses for the staff doctors if they achieve certain economies in the operation of the plans. Quality care and efficiency are encouraged because the knowledge that the performance of any member of the medical staff can affect the income and reputation of the other members strengthens the peer review that arises naturally out of the close professional relations characteristic of group practices.

Dr. Ernest W. Saward, formerly Medical Director of the Permanente Clinic in Portland, Oregon, has described a "genetic code" of prepaid group practice, which, he states, cannot be violated "without the result being either a still-born plan or a plan that will be defective in its growth and maturity," as follows:

It is fundamental that the program be nonprofit and that it be self-sustaining without philanthropy or tax support, although the poor and the elderly need tax support to participate in the system. The program must be conducted in the paramount interest of the membership. The principal characteristic of the program is the assumption of the responsibility, by the providers of medical services, for the organization and delivery of such services on a prepaid basis. It is not an insurance program that trades dollars of premiums for benefits. Dollars are only available for use as services.

The Kaiser-Permanente Medical Care Program, according to Dr. Saward, illustrates the application of these principles:

Prepayment. Medical care is paid for in advance, usually by monthly dues, paid by the subscriber or on his behalf, "to mutualize the cost of medical care for the population covered." The program is community-rated, which means that "subscribers pay equal rates for equal benefits."

Group practice. The medical group (i.e., the doctors and, possibly, auxilliary medical personnel hired to provide medical services to subscribers) is an autonomous, self-governing unit under contract to the prepayment organization. Virtually all members of the group work full time for the prepaid group plan.

Medical center. A central medical center with integrated facilities, including a hospital, maintains inpatient and outpatient records of all members. Satellite clinics serve neighborhoods in the area. Centralized laboratory services, accounting, and administration contribute to economy of operation.

Volunteer enrollment. All members join voluntarily. This means that employers, unions, or other groups must give participants in the groups a dual choice—between the prepaid group plan or a conventional plan such as is offered by Blue Cross-Blue Shield or by private carriers.

Capitation payment. Both the doctors and the hospital "are paid by capitation for the services they contract to render [i.e., the group collects so much per member per year regardless of how many covered services each member may require]. This creates a predictable, budgetary operation in which the only unknown is the size of the membership. From past experience this, too, is relatively predictable." This system of payment of the providers is the reverse of the fee-for-service system, under which the providers "are paid only for illness, and usually the more illness, the greater the payment."

Comprehensive coverage. This includes outpatient care, inpatient care, extended care, home health services, drug coverage, and mental health services.

Comprehensiveness directs an appropriate use of the budgeted dollars. The least expensive, effective modality will be the one used. Prevention, health education and early disease detection are obviously good for the population covered but can also be a cost saving to the providers. The medical group is motivated to use appropriate ancillary personnel. Budgetary systems without fee-for-service assure that if a particular type of work doesn't have to be done by a physician, someone more appropriate, such as his nurse, health aide, or other personnel will be substituted for the expensive physician.[1]

While no plans as yet strictly obey all principles of the "genetic code," the Kaiser plans and the Group Health Cooperative of Puget Sound, in Seattle, follow them to a greater extent than most prepaid group practice plans. For example, the Health Insurance Plan of Greater New York (HIP) contracts with 30 medical groups to provide comprehensive medical service on a capitation basis. But HIP does not insist on dual choice for members who join under sponsorship of an employer, a union, or other group. And HIP doctors are not required to devote full time to HIP members. They may accept private patients on a fee-for-service basis (though HIP is considering a change, requiring that all HIP doctors work exclusively for HIP).[2] The Group Health Association (GHA) of Washington, D.C., has a full-time staff of doctors organized into a full-service integrated clinic but still relies on outside community hospital facilities, as do the prepaid group practice plans in Boston, Denver, New Haven, and Columbia (Maryland). Moreover, coverage is not completely comprehensive in any plan and use of nonphysician personnel is not extensive.

Sources of Savings in Prepaid Group Plans

The best-known characteristic of prepaid group plans is probably the integrated medical center with its staff of doctors with various specialties, its laboratories, and other facilities, its complete medical records of all members, and its supporting staff to facilitate efficient use of doctors' time. But this feature is less important as a source of cost savings than generally thought. The favorable comparisons with the conventional system related to this feature stem largely from the unwillingness of physicians in the conventional sector to take advantage of similar integrated facilities available to them.

In the first place, evidence provides no clear indication that a doctor in a large group or clinic practice sees more patients either in office or hospital visits than a doctor in a small group or solo practice. The common belief that large group practices are inherently more efficient than small group or solo practices stems from the large number of doctor and nondoctor functions that are combined and carried out within the office, as well as the high gross income and staff-physician ratios of large group practices. But these figures are not what they seem. They do not reflect the assignment to staff members of nondoctor functions performed in conventional practices by physicians. In fact, in conventional small medical practices such nondoctor functions as X rays and laboratory tests are performed elsewhere (by commercial laboratories, for example), in roughly the same proportion to doctor functions as in large group practices.[3]

Some economies of scale do, of course, result from the integration of doctor and nondoctor services. But most of these economies are available to all doctors in urban areas. Those in solo practices can purchase specialized services, including such administrative services as bookkeeping, from outside concerns, while those in large group practice can integrate these services into their overall operations. The newly developed electronic multiphasic testing clinic is an example of a facility with evident economies of scale that is available to doctors in both group and solo practices at virtually the same cost per patient.

The availability of these economies to doctors not in prepaid group practices does not mean that all doctors in conventional practices take advantage of them. Many doctors in solo and small group practices operate with expensive, underutilized, and unnecessary capital equipment and refuse to delegate many normal nondoctor tasks to their staffs. This kind of inefficiency increases the costs of conventional practices relative to prepaid group practices. In other words, solo and small group practices in urban areas can achieve many economics of scale if they take advantage of various services available to them.

The integration of staff and facilities also offers opportunities for paramedical personnel to perform certain medical functions normally performed by doctors, as opposed to nondoctors' functions, discussed above. For example, midwives could handle routine deliveries, as they do in many countries, and clinical specialists could handle the routine work of prenatal care, freeing gynecologists for work in more demanding cases. Well-baby care could be delegated to specially trained pediatric nurses. The time of the orthopedist could be used much more efficiently when a trained orthopedic technician is assigned to work with him. Optometristics can be used for routine eye examinations, freeing ophthalmologists to concentrate their attention on eye diseases that require their special skills.

But much to the disappointment of proponents of prepaid group practice, the available evidence indicates that the prepaid group plans do not make significantly greater use of paramedics than conventional practices to perform traditional doctor tasks. In 1967, the National Advisory Commission on Health Manpower reported that the Kaiser plans, although innovative in many ways, did not differ essentially from conventional practices in the use of paramedics. Their report stated, "Kaiser physicians use standard medical practices and procedures during their contacts with patients, and there does not appear to be unusual substitution of auxiliary personnel for physicians."[4]

One of the reasons why paramedical personnel are not more widely used in prepaid group practices is that in some localities laws and administrative rulings governing medical practice require a doctor's presence for many routine procedures.

Moreover, as Richard M. Bailey points out:

Group as well as nongroup physicians receive the same type of training in medical school and in postgraduate internships and residencies, in which the concept of following accepted patterns of health care are instilled into them. Indeed, various surveys of physician work habits have demonstrated that physicians in a given specialty allocate a remarkably similar amount of time to each kind of patient visit.[5]

Prepaid groups are sensitive to charges that they achieve their economies by lowering the quality of the care that they provide. In principle, appropriate use of paramedics should improve the overall quality of medical care by allowing doctors to devote their attention to those medical procedures that demand their special skills. But the prepaid groups seem to fear that the public might interpret extensive use of paramedics as lowering the quality of medical care in order to save money.

In fact, the integrated aspect of prepaid groups results in efficiencies that are mainly qualitative and not readily translatable into cost savings. Peer review, which is relatively rare in conventional practice—at least among solo practitioners—is built into group practice, as each doctor's work is subject automatically to the scrutiny of his colleagues. Where referrals are called for, prepaid group practice plans create efficiency by saving the patient's time—an item that does not appear in the medical cost statistics. Patients benefit from the convenience of a one-stop medical facility for the family. In multispecialty groups, primary physicians can refer patients to specialists when necessary without excessive delays and without fear of thereby losing patients. And the medical records and histories of all members are centrally located and readily available to all doctors associated with the group.

*Integration of Insurer and
Provider Functions*

Integration of the staff and facilities of prepaid groups is less important as a source of savings than integration of the functions of insurer and medical provider. For example, in 1969, the cost of all nonmedical functions of the Kaiser-Permanente plan was 3.2 percent of total costs; among the major health insurance carriers administrative costs of group policies amount to roughly 10 percent of written premiums. (See Chapter 3 and Appendix D.) Prepayment eliminates much of the cost of handling claims, which is usually the largest item of administrative expense for conventional group health policies. In prepaid groups, subscribers submit claims only for emergency treatment received outside the areas of their group plans. Doctors in prepaid groups have fewer insurance forms to process and hence more time to practice medicine. Prepayment also spares patients a good deal of paperwork—filling out insurance forms, calculating the copayment and deductible, and paying several doctor bills.

Selling and enrollment costs are somewhat lower for prepaid group plans than for conventional group policies, principally because groups sell only a limited number of standard plans to both group and individual subscribers.

Prepaid group plans are not required to pay state insurance premium taxes or federal income taxes and thus enjoy, along with most Blue Cross-Blue Shield plans, a competitive advantage vis-à-vis the private carriers. In some states, prepaid groups are totally exempt from insurance commission regulation and thus are not subject to the reserve requirements imposed on conventional insurance carriers. Even in those states where prepaid groups are considered to be health insurance organizations and, hence, must operate under insurance laws, the reserve requirements are lower for prepaid groups than for conventional insurers.

The savings accruing to prepaid groups because of the virtual elimination of claims handling are inherent in the concept of prepayment; the conventional sector cannot duplicate them without radically changing the system of remunerating providers or by introducing major deductible policies under which the insured would pay most small claims. (See Chapter 10.) The savings made possible by exemption from the reserve requirement, on the other hand, are primarily due to present government policy regarding the insurance obligations of prepaid groups, which is subject to change.

The exemption of prepaid groups from reserve requirements and general insurance regulation is consistent with their position that they are not health insurance organizations but are medical care providers. Prepaid group plans budget fixed amounts, each year, to be paid in the form of salaries to doctors and other staff members for services performed in the clinic or in the hospital if the prepaid group has its own hospital. When the demand for services exceeds expectations, additional staff must be hired or the staff will be required to work overtime, and the staff salary budget will have to be enlarged to meet this cost.

Perhaps prepaid groups should be required to hold some unearned premium and incurred claims reserves, or assets in some form, to assure that they can carry out the insurance function inherent in prepayment. When an insurance carrier ceases operations, another carrier usually picks up the risk on a comparable basis; if a prepaid group plan were to cease operations, the subscriber would have to switch to less comprehensive coverage under a conventional plan. Subscribers to prepaid plans may thus be more in need of unearned premium reserves than conventional health insurance policyholders are.

Savings Attributable to Integrated
Hospital-Clinic Facilities

Hospital-clinic integration is another factor that has permitted prepaid groups to achieve economies, although, to some extent, at the expense of the rest of the community.

Officials of the Group Health Association of America and of various prepaid groups maintain that much of the impressive economic performance of the Kaiser-Permanente health plan is due to the integration of the plan's hospitals and clinics.[6] Estimates of the savings in the per-diem hospital rates attributable directly to integration of prepaid group hospitals and clinics range from 16 to 30 percent.[7]

During the 1960s the Kaiser health plans were able to maintain the ratio of hospital expense to total plan revenues at a constant level, while for Group Health Association in Washington, D.C., which does not have a hospital, the ratio of hospital expense to total revenues doubled.[8]

One way in which the integrated hospital-clinic achieves these savings is through avoidance of duplication of testing when hospitalization is necessary. Hospitals customarily subject patients to various tests, often duplicating tests performed prior to admission, in order to avoid the risk of inappropriate treatment and to protect themselves from malpractice suits. The extra cost of this duplication is borne by the patient (or his insurance carrier). When clinic and hospital comprise an integrated unit, staffed by the same doctors and technicians who are all subject to the same discipline, with centralized medical records of all members readily available, the hospital has no need to repeat the preadmission testing. Assuming, for example, an average of 0.24 hospital admissions per family enrolled in group prepaid practices (see Table 8-2) and an average preadmission testing cost of $57.50 per admission,[9] the average saving per family of avoiding duplicate tests after hospital admission is $13.80 per year. This saving is not enormous, but it helps prepaid groups to compete with conventional health insurance on premium costs.

The integration of the clinic and the hospital also saves the time of the doctors in travel from office to hospital and allows hospital duties to be delegated to the medical staff of the prepaid group plan, rather than to a separate hospital staff with its own priorities, responsibilities, and allegiances.

Prepaid group plan hospitals may also have lower costs as a result of better management and economies in purchasing supplies, if several hospitals are operated by the same group, as in the Kaiser-Permanente health care program.

In addition, prepaid group plan hospitals have achieved higher occupancy rates than conventional hospitals, thereby lowering the average per-diem cost per patient. The National Advisory Commission on Health Manpower reported in 1967 that Kaiser Foundation Hospitals in California required 40 percent fewer beds than conventional hospitals in the state. Of this difference, one fourth can be explained by higher average occupancy rates, while three fourths can be explained by lower utilization rates, which are discussed below.[10] Because of their better defined patient group, prepaid group plans can schedule hospital admissions so that they have fewer empty beds and require less space than hospitals operated for the community at large. This efficiency results in cost savings and permits more effective use of staff.

In part, the savings that prepaid group plans achieve through clinic-hospital integration are at the expense of the conventional medical service community. The difference in relative efficiency of the two sectors therefore seems greater than it is. Prepaid group hospitals can function more economically than conventional hospitals, in part because they are rarely teaching institutions and are not obliged to take patients who cannot pay their hospital bills. Both these functions are performed in the community interest by voluntary and training hospitals, which must pass part of the costs on to patients in the form of higher charges, if charity or government grants do not pay them. These costs are substantial.

Lower Utilization Rates: The
Main Source of Savings

The most important source of savings for prepaid plans is the relatively low rate of utilization of hospital services. The prepaid group plans emphasize outpatient care and the medical staffs are conservative in their attitudes toward surgery. Since the cost of one day's stay in the hospital is equal to the cost of 8 to 10 visits to the medical center, the savings achieved are substantial.

Under the Federal Employees Health Benefits Program (FEHBP) in 1968, the number of days of hospitalization of nonmaternity patients per 1,000 prepaid group members was about half the number per 1000 Blue Cross subscribers, as shown in Table 8-3. The average length of stay for prepaid group members admitted to hospitals is virtually the same as for those covered by Blue Cross, but prepaid group practice plan members have lower hospital admissions rates (see Table 8-2) and lower rates of surgery than Blue Shield subscribers, as shown in Table 8-4.

One reason for the lower utilization rates of prepaid groups is that many conventional health insurance policies provide more complete coverage of

Table 8-2
Comparison of Nonmaternity Hospital Admission Rates for Surgical and Non-surgical Procedures of Subscribers to Blue Cross and Prepaid Group Practice Plans, under the Federal Employees Health Benefits Program, 1968

| | Nonmaternity Hospital Admissions per 1,000 Subscribers | | | |
Type of Plan	Total	For Surgical Procedures	For NonSurgical Procedures	For Surgical Procedures as Percent of Total Admissions
Blue Cross	117	75	42	64
Prepaid group practice	58	34	24	59

Source: *The Federal Employees Health Benefits Program: Enrollment and Utilization of Health Services, 1961-1968* (Washington: Public Health Service, U.S. Department of Health, Education, and Welfare, June 1970).

Table 8-3

Nonmaternity Hospitalization Utilization Rates for Subscribers to Blue Cross and Prepaid Group Practice Plans, Under the Federal Employees Health Benefits Program, 1968[a]

Employment Status of Patient	Blue Cross	Days of Hospitalization of Nonmaternity Patients per 1,000 Subscribers[a]	
		Prepaid Group Practice Plans[b]	Prepaid Group Practice Plans as Percent of Blue Cross
Active employee	1,085	560	52
Dependent of subscriber	715	305	43
Annuitant	3,180	1,530	48

[a]Figures are for nonmaternity inhospital services for subscribers covered under the high option plans of the FEHBP.

[b]Figures are drawn from a sample including over 85 percent of prepaid group practice enrollees.

Source: *The Federal Employees Health Benefits Program: Enrollment and Utilization of Health Services, 1961-1968* (Washington: Public Health Service, U.S. Department of Health, Education, and Welfare, June 1970), Fig. 5.

Table 8-4

Nonmaternity Inpatient Surgical Procedure Rates for Subscribers to Blue Shield and Prepaid Group Practice Plans, under the Federal Employees Health Benefits Program, 1968

Type of Procedure	Blue Shield[a]	Surgical Procedures per 1,000 Subscribers	
		Prepaid Group Practice Plans	Prepaid Group Practice Plans as Percent of Blue Shield
All procedures	75.0	34.0	45
Tonsillectomy and/or adenoidectomy	6.9	2.4	35
Female surgery[b]	9.2	4.8	52
Appendectomy	2.1	1.1	52
Cholecystectomy[c]	2.1	1.5	71

[a]Among health insurance subscribers under the FEHBP, Blue Shield subscribers have the highest rate of surgical procedures.

[b]Includes mastectomy, dilation and curettage (nonmaternity), and hysterectomy.

[c]Removal of the gall bladder.

Source: *The Federal Employees Health Benefits Program: Enrollment and Utilization of Health Services, 1961-1968* (Washington: Public Health Service, U.S. Department of Health, Education, and Welfare, June 1970), Fig. 6.

hospital costs than of nonhospital costs and thus tend to encourage hospitalization. Prepaid group plan doctors do not have to hospitalize a patient solely to assure insurance coverage, as doctors in conventional practice sometimes do. Likewise, solo practitioners who do not have facilities for extensive testing often hospitalize patients suffering from ailments not easily diagnosed, in order to have tests performed and to obtain the opinions of specialists. Doctors in group practices—prepaid or conventional—that have integrated medical staffs and facilities may resort to hospitalization less frequently for these purposes. The utilization and hospital admission review procedures built into prepaid group practice, fortified by the pecuniary incentives to doctors, discourage unnecessary hospitalization in a way that conventional practice—as it now operates—cannot duplicate.

Roughly two-fifths of the lower rate of hospital admissions for prepaid group practice plan members results from a lower rate of inpatient surgery (see Table 8-4). The differences in hospital admissions for "elective surgery"—procedures that involve organs that are not vital to normal body functioning and can be removed with little risk—are especially striking. Conventional insurance provides fairly complete coverage for such elective procedures as tonsillectomies and adenoidectomies, female surgery, appendectomies, and cholecystectomies. A fee-for-service doctor may justify such surgery, if symptoms vaguely indicate that one of these organs is the source of the ailment, on the grounds that even if postoperative analysis proves the surgery unnecessary, the patient will have lost nothing except time and money. And if the patient is insured, he will not even have lost money directly. The incomes of fee-for-service doctors rise as the number of surgical procedures increase, whereas the incomes of doctors in prepaid groups, who receive bonuses for achieving cost savings, rise when surgical procedure rates are kept low.

The lower hospital utilization rates achieved by prepaid group plans apply to all age groups, including Medicare patients and annuitants covered under the FEHBP (see Table 8-3). At the Permanente Clinic in Portland, Oregon, Dr. Ernest W. Saward reports a rate of 1700 hospital days per 1000 members of the clinic who are participants in Medicare; the national coverage is 2700 days of hospitalization per 1000 Medicare participants.[11]

Hospital utilization rates for prepaid group practice plans have been decreasing for more than a decade reflecting a steady decline in the rate of admissions. At the Group Health Cooperative of Puget Sound, in Seattle, for example, days of hospitalization per 1000 members declined from 569 in 1961 to 483 in 1969, or 15 percent in 8 years. Under the Federal Employees Health Benefits Program, hospital utilization decreased generally between 1962 and 1968 for the prepaid individual and group practice plans, but increased for the Blue Cross-Blue Shield and indemnity plans.[12]

However, in utilization of outpatient services, prepaid group practice plans and conventional practice apparently differ relatively little. Unfortunately, differences in presentation of statistics do not permit precise comparisons. The data on prepaid groups define "doctors' visits" as direct doctor-patient contacts, whereas the data for the population as a whole use the term to refer to any services provided by doctors' offices. But to the extent that comparisons can be made the statistics suggest that prepaid group members use total outpatient services, including direct and indirect doctors' services, at a somewhat higher rate than the population as a whole.[13]

This difference in utilization reflects the major difference in approach between the two types of practice. In conventional practice, patients may hesitate to make the initial visit to the doctor, because their insurance either does not cover outpatient services at all or is limited by deductibles and coinsurance provisions. When the patient does see his doctor, his insurance encourages hospitalization for services that could be performed on an outpatient basis. In prepaid group practice, the initial visit is free of extra charges, or subject to only a nominal extra charge in a few cases, and the doctor has financial incentives to perform services on an outpatient basis. And since hospital services are so much more costly than outpatient services, it is here that the major savings accruing to prepaid groups are achieved.

Comparing Costs to Subscribers:
Prepaid Groups and Conventional Plans

The results of numerous studies indicate that the costs of medical care are lower for subscribers in prepaid group practice plans than for enrollees in conventional health insurance plans and hence, that the cost savings of prepaid groups are passed on to consumers.[14] Studies comparing the Kaiser-Permanente Medical Care Program with conventional health insurance plans have consistently shown that the cost of medical care for Kaiser-Permanente members is lower.[15]

But in most of these studies, the conventional and prepaid groups are not strictly comparable in terms of age distribution, occupation, sex, inclination to use medical services, geographical location, and regional standards for prices of services; nor has any definitive study determined the extent to which subscribers of prepaid group practice plans use services outside the plan at their own expense, although there is evidence that they do so.[16]

In 1964, the state of California conducted a study of the medical insurance program for state employees.[17] The individuals whose medical expenditures were studied represent a more homogeneous group than most of those reported on in other studies. Of course, those individuals who choose to participate in prepaid group plans may have a different orientation toward medical care than other insured employees, and it is known that they occasionally resort to nonplan services, paying for them out of their own pockets. It is speculated, in

137

fact, that the use of outside services by plan members may be substantial, although the exact frequency has yet to be determined.[18] But the difference between the medical expenditures of prepaid plan (Kaiser and Ross-loos) members and those insured under a private indemnity plan or Blue Cross-Blue Shield was enough to outweigh even liberal allowances for these factors. The total medical care expenditures—insurance plus out-of-pocket—for Kaiser-Permanente members were 77 percent of those of Blue Cross-Blue Shield subscribers and 95 percent as much as the private carriers' subscribers, as shown in Table 8-5.

Although prepaid group practice plans provide medical services at a lower cost to their subscribers as a whole, an individual may find a prepaid group more costly than conventional health insurance. Because of the lack of uniformity in coverage and definitions of the various health insurance plans, the least expensive plan for any individual depends on the illnesses that he and members of his family will contract. No plans—conventional or prepaid—cover all treatments of all illnesses fully, and a particular individual may find any relatively comprehensive plan perfectly suitable or substantially unsuitable to his eventual needs.

Table 8-6 summarizes the results of applying to 2 large prepaid group practice plans—the Kaiser plan for federal employees in Southern California and the Group Health Association (Washington, D.C.) plan—the same hypothetical family medical experience presented in Chapter 2 (see Tables 2-3, 2-5 and 2-6). Both prepaid plans offer more comprehensive coverage than any of the conventional plans described in Chapter 2.

Table 8-5

Comparison of Total Family Medical Costs to Subscribers, under Various Health Insurance Plans

Plan	Annual Premium or Subscription Payment	Average Additional Out-of-Pocket Expenditures for Medical Services of Members or Subscribers	Total Average Cost to Members or Subscribers
Kaiser-Permanente	$284	$89	$373
Ross-Loos	271	125	396
Private carrier	227	189	416
Blue Cross-Blue Shield	285	200	485

Source: *Final Report on the Survey of Consumer Experience Under the State of California Employees' Hospital and Medical Care Act* (Sacramento: Board of Administration, Public Employees' Retirement System, October 1964).

Table 8-6

Variations in Assumed Annual Expenses for Covered Medical Services for a Family of 4, According to Type of Illness and Medical Services Required, under 3 Conventional Group Plans and 2 Prepaid Group Plans[a]

Medical Services Required	Conventional Plans			Prepaid Plans	
	Prudential	Aetna	Blue Plan	Group Health Association, Washington, D.C.	Kaiser-Permanente
1. Minor illnesses not requiring hospitalization or surgery	$909.12	$825.12	$846.12	$829.92	$635.49
2. Minor illnesses and back injury requiring hospitalization and surgery	1,157.92	1,561.12	1,054.92	929.92	735.49
3. Minor illnesses not requiring hospitalization or surgery and illness requiring psychiatric care	1,932.32	1,232.32	1,293.32	2,465.72	815.49

[a]Assumed expenses are based on premiums in 1971.

Source: See Tables 2-3, 2-5 and 2-6 and text of Chapter 2 for description of conventional plans and types of assumed illnesses. See text of Chapter 8 for description of prepaid plans.

The prepaid groups cover all visits, including routine physicals. But they do have certain restrictions. For example, for psychiatric services Kaiser requires the subscriber to pay $5 per visit beyond the first 20 visits in a year; GHA covers only the first $15.00 of charges per visit for only the first 16 psychiatric visits in a year. Neither plan covers the cost of blood or corrective appliances. Kaiser charges 50 percent of the wholesale book price of prescription drugs; GHA covers 80 percent of annual prescription charges over a $50 deductible for each family member. Kaiser limits coverage for renal dialysis and organ transplants to $10,000. GHA has no such restriction. Kaiser provides full coverage for the first 150 days of hospitalization and covers 50 percent of the charge for the next 215 days (using charges applied by non-Kaiser hospitals to calculate the 50 percent charges to patients). GHA has no limit on hospital coverage. The total annual premium as of 1971, for the GHA plan (family membership) was $745.92; for Kaiser, it was $609.24. (Regional price differences may account for some of the difference in premiums, particularly for the higher GHA rates, since medical costs in Washington, D.C., are relatively high.)

The first hypothetical case presented in Chapter 2 was that of a family of four that experienced only minor illnesses throughout the year. One member of the family accounted for $241.00 of a total of $384.00 of the family's medical expenditures for the year. The Kaiser plan, costing a total of $635.49 for the premium plus the family's out-of-pocket expenditure for drugs, would be the least expensive of the 5 plans used as examples in Table 8-6. The family's expenses under the Group Health plan would total $829.92, approximately the same as 2 of the conventional plans. The reason for the wide discrepancy in cost between the two prepaid plans is that Group Health's premium rate is higher and it has a large deductible for drug costs. If the hypothetical family's expenditures included eyeglass fittings and routine physicals—both of which are covered by both GHA and Kaiser but not by the conventional health plans—the cost under GHA would have been less than under the conventional plans but not less than under the Kaiser plan.

In the second hypothetical case presented in Chapter 2, one member of the family suffered a back injury necessitating 2 hospitalizations, surgery, and a back brace, all in the same year. Neither of the 2 prepaid plans would cover the cost of the brace, but either of them would be less costly in this case—$929.92 under the GHA plan and $735.49 under the Kaiser plan—than the conventional plans, each of which would involve over $1,000 of expenses to the family.

In the third hypothetical case described in Chapter 2, one member of the family required psychiatric treatment. Although both of the prepaid group practice plans limit coverage for psychiatric care, the Kaiser plan would result in total costs of $815.49 for the year and would thus be the least costly of the 5 plans. The GHA plan, on the other hand, would cost the family $2,465.72, over $500 more than the Prudential plan, the most expensive of the conventional plans in this case.

Because of the kinds of illnesses presented in each of these 3 hypothetical cases, the Kaiser plan would cost the family the least, in each case. The GHA plan would be less costly than all 3 conventional plans only in the second case, requiring surgery and hospital care. On the other hand, the GHA plan is also more economical than the Kaiser plan for cases involving prolonged hospital treatment (beyond the 150 days covered in full by the Kaiser plan). In these "catastrophic" cases, the Kaiser plan is likely to be the most expensive and the GHA plan the most economical, followed closely by the Blue Cross-Blue Shield plan. Where more intensive psychiatric care is needed, the Blue plans would be clearly superior. Other hypotheses would yield still other results.

Individual Practice Plans

Prepaid individual practice plans have received less attention than prepaid group practice plans in discussions of health insurance reform. Evidence that the individual practice plans also can provide health care at lower cost than the conventional system is rudimentary and results from rather special circumstances, but the plans merit attention because they demonstrate that effective peer review is possible even if doctors are more loosely affiliated than in the clinic-based prepaid group practice plans.

The 18 individual practice plans listed by the Social Security Administration in 1970[19] have some of the characteristics of both prepaid group practice plans and conventional health insurance. They resemble prepaid group practice plans in that subscribers pay a fixed monthly or annual fee in advance, in return for which they are entitled to receive unlimited amounts of the covered services, generally without payment of further fees, provided they are treated by any of the doctors who are participating members of the plan. Individual practice plans may also cover treatment by nonparticipating doctors, although only up to the amount of the fee schedule, which is generally somewhat below the "usual, customary and reasonable" rate.

A more basic difference between group practice plans and individual practice plans is that the latter own no facilities and do not hire any medical personnel. The participating doctors and other providers operate independently and may serve nonsubscribers as well as subscribers to the plan. The integration of insurer and provider is therefore not complete, as it is in the group practice plans. Moreover, physicians do not generally participate in bonus plans or other financial inducements for achieving savings as they customarily do in prepaid group practice plans.

In individual practice plans such as Group Health Insurance, Inc., of New York City and the Foundation for Medical Care of San Joaquin County, in California, participating doctors are largely solo, fee-for-service practitioners who maintain the traditional doctor-patient relationships. But these doctors agree to accept the lower than average fees set by the plans as payment in full, sacrificing the hope for higher fees for assurance of payment and established clientele. Hospital coverage is usually provided for subscribers to the plans by Blue Cross. In spite of lower fixed fees, there is some indication that the individual practice plans have been able to hold utilization, particularly of hospital services, to a lower rate than Blue Cross-Blue Shield, as shown in Table 8-7. The explanation appears to lie in the strong management of the plans and their effective "peer review," under which unnecessary or excessive treatment is closely questioned. It is also significant that individual practice plans are found in neighboring areas to prepaid groups. This proximity suggests that the threat of competition from prepaid group practice plans may have induced doctors in these areas to form these individual practice plans and to cooperate in making peer review an effective cost-saving tool.

The experience of the individual practice plans thus suggests that prepaid group practice plans have an effect on costs beyond the confines of their own operations by forcing other providers to organize and compete. More important, the lower utilization rate of medical services under both individual and prepaid group practice plans provides additional evidence that medical treatment is often

Table 8-7

Nonmaternity Hospitalization Utilization Rates of Blue Cross, Individual Practice Plan, and Group Practice Plan Subscribers, under the Federal Employees Health Benefits Program, 1968

Area	Days of Hospitalization per 1,000 Subscribers			
	Blue Cross	Individual Practice Plans	Prepaid Group Practice Plans	Prepaid Group Practice Plans as Percent of Blue Cross
California	825	440	422	51
Washington, D.C., Maryland, Virginia	838	a	379	45
Hawaii	1,364	436	404	30
New York	725	661	468	65
Oregon	879	490	272	31
Washington	791	427	341	43

aNot available.

Source: *The Federal Employees Health Benefits Program: Enrollment and Utilization of Health Services, 1961-1968* (Washington: Public Health Service, U.S. Department of Health, Education, and Welfare, June 1970), Fig. 4.

elective and that doctors can influence costs through their decisions about the treatments they will prescribe. The integration of insurer and provider that characterizes prepaid group practice provides perhaps the most effective way yet discovered to induce doctors to use their influence in the interests of economy. Despite certain drawbacks to the universal application of this system, the experience of prepaid groups should be useful to those concerned with health insurance reform.

9

Prepaid Group Practice—A Basis for a National System?

The two most prominent national health insurance bills introduced in the 92nd Congress, one proposed by the Nixon Administration[1] and the other sponsored by the committee for National Health Insurance,[2] included provisions designed to foster the growth of prepaid group practice plans or health care organizations with the basic attributes of prepaid groups, and to expand the total share of health care provided by such plans.

These provisions represent a response to the cost savings the prepaid groups have been able to achieve. It is natural that the search for a better system has focused on cost. But the future growth of prepaid group practice plans and their chances of becoming the dominant health care financing system in the United States will depend not only on cost but also on certain important nonfinancial considerations: wider acceptance of the prepaid group concept by consumers, the willingness of doctors to participate in prepaid group plans, the availability of financing and of managerial personnel, and the adaptability of the system to different population densities.

Consumer Acceptance of Prepaid Group Plans

During the 1960s, enrollment in prepaid group plans roughly doubled, increasing from 1.5 million to just over 3.0 million, while enrollment in conventional comprehensive plans in the private sector tripled, increasing from 30 million to more than 90 million (see Table 1-3). However, unlike conventional insurance coverage, prepaid group plan participation is available only in certain geographical areas, and in many of these areas, prepaid group practice plans have significantly increased their share of the health insurance market in recent years.

Among the various Kaiser-Permanente groups participating in the Federal Employees Health Benefits Program, for example, enrollment rose during the 1960s not only in absolute terms but also in relation to the number of federal employees located in the metropolitan areas where Kaiser plans are in operation. The proportion of federal employees in these areas who subscribe to Kaiser plans increased from 34.4 percent to 41.5 percent. In other areas, enrollment in prepaid group plans also increased, from 4.6 percent of eligible federal employees to 7.3 percent, as shown in Figure 9-1. These increases are small, but they show that in areas where prepaid group plans are in operation they have been

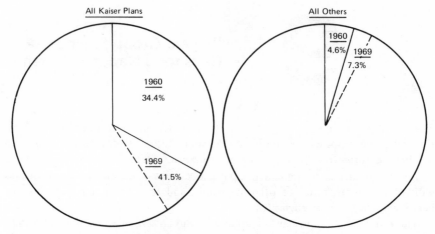

All Kaiser Plans

All Others

1960
34.4%

1969
41.5%

1960
4.6%

1969
7.3%

Figure 9-1. Federal Employees Health Benefits Program Enrollment in Group Practice Plans, as Percent of Federal Employees in Areas Where Plans are in Operation. Source: *Federal Employees Enrollment in Group Practice Plans, by Metropolitan Area* (Washington: U.S. Civil Service Commission, 1969).

able to overcome some of the general resistance of subscribers to switching from a plan they are already enrolled in to another plan.[3] Since most of the population is already enrolled in conventional health insurance plans, future growth of the prepaid groups will depend not only on the establishment of new groups in areas where they are not now available but also on their success in overcoming this resistance. The factors that seem most likely to determine consumer acceptance of prepaid group plans are subscription or premium rates (in relation to benefits), impressions of the quality of care provided by prepaid groups, and accessibility of prepaid group facilities.

Subscription Rates and Consumer Acceptance

Most health insurance enrollees belong to employment-related group plans the premiums for which are paid in large part or in full by the employer. (See Chapter 2.) Hence, the employee himself is not greatly concerned (and probably not well informed) about premium or subscription rates. However, premium costs, especially for noncontributory plans—that is, plans for which employers pay total premiums—are important to employers. If employers are to give their employees a choice between a prepaid plan and one or more conventional plans, the prepaid group subscription rate must be roughly equivalent to the premium rates of the conventional plans. Since prepaid plans are generally more comprehensive and cover a larger number of routine procedures such as annual physicals, well-baby care, eye examinations, they frequently make certain supplementary charges (e.g., $1.00 or $2.00 for an office visit, and/or $5.00 for a house call, and so forth) or exclude from coverage such seemingly trivial items as the cost of blood for transfusions in order to keep their subscription rates low enough to compete with those of conventional plans.[4]

These supplementary charges and exclusions, however, are evidently not looked upon as seriously diminishing the extent of coverage prepaid groups offer. In fact, a number of studies have shown that the principal attraction of prepaid groups to new subscribers has been their broad, comprehensive coverage, and the impression that prepaid groups offer a smaller risk of heavy, out-of-pocket costs than most conventional plans.[5]

The figures in Table 8-5, comparing out-of-pocket plus premium costs under certain prepaid groups plans with certain conventional plans suggest that consumers do benefit from the efficiencies achieved by prepaid group practice plans, although to what extent is not entirely clear.

However, experience under the Federal Employees Health Benefits Program, with numerous plans competing for subscribers, provides data that permit some comparisons of conventional and prepaid group systems over time. The premiums for both the conventional and prepaid group plans have increased, but those for conventional plans have increased more than those for the prepaid groups. From the inception of the program in 1960 to 1971, the Aetna plan increased its total premium 201 percent and Blue Cross 147 percent. Of the 10 prepaid group plans, 3 increased their premium rates by a higher percentage than Blue Cross-Blue Shield, 6 by a lower percentage, and 1 by approximately the same percentage. During this period, the share of prepaid plan income derived from supplemental charges, representing out-of-pocket expenses for consumers, declined. Between 1960 and 1968, the share of Kaiser's total income derived from supplementary charges declined from 19.9 percent to 8.1 percent, and that of the Group Health Association declined from 16.5 percent to 7.7 percent.[6]

Part of the reason why the conventional plans had such large premium increases is that they expanded their coverage considerably more than the prepaid group plans during the 1960s. But the coverage offered by the prepaid group plans was from the beginning more comprehensive and devoid of overall dollar maximums, so that the increase in the premium rates in prepaid group plans was largely a function of inflation, whereas that in conventional plans, was largely due to increased coverage. Whether prepaid groups continue to pass on their savings to consumers will depend on the relative strength of such competing demands on prepaid group surplus as capital requirements and the income demands of physicians, and whether prepaid groups will have to use improved benefits or lower subscription rates in order to attract new members. In part, the outcome will depend upon trends in conventional health insurance. Today only a minority of the conventional plans offer coverage approximating the comprehensiveness of prepaid groups, but the trend is toward expanded coverage. As the conventional plans broaden their coverage to include many of the popular services now offered by prepaid groups, whatever additional services prepaid group plans offer will seem marginal to many subscribers and potential subscribers.

Quality of Service and
Potential Acceptance

In years past, organized medicine's opposition to prepaid groups was strong enough to persuade many states to prohibit their activities and to leave a residue of public skepticism about them even after organized medicine had changed its position.

Whether the prepaid group system sacrifices quality to achieve cost efficiencies is, in fact, still an unanswered question. Prepayment may give a physician financial incentives to postpone treatment in precisely the same way that the fee-for-service system gives him financial incentives to perform excessive or premature treatment. After all, keeping treatment to a minimum reduces costs and, in many group practice plans, reduced costs mean higher incomes for the physicians. The advocates of prepaid groups maintain that the best way to reduce costs is to keep the patient well, and that the prepaid group system encourages the doctor to practice preventive medicine. The term "Health Maintenance Organization (HMO)," popularized by the health care proposals of the Nixon administration, emphasizes the preventive medicine aspect of the prepaid group concept.

The quality of medical care is difficult to measure. The available statistical evidence does not suggest that the care provided by prepaid groups is not as good as that provided on a fee-for-service basis. Indeed, though mortality and morbidity data for prepaid group subscribers do not differ greatly from those for comparable age groups enrolled in conventional plans, the findings of some studies based on these data indicate that the record of the prepaid groups is better.[7] But the patient's impression of the quality of the care he receives is more important to the future of prepayment systems than are morbidity and mortality data.

The patient's definition of high quality medical care may be very different from the doctor's. Doctors are likely to judge quality by the professional expertise—the prompt and perceptive diagnosis or surgical skill—their colleagues display in handling difficult problems. The patient, on the other hand, is only moderately aware of differences in professional skills. His judgment of quality is based on the accessibility of the physician, the physician's attitude—whether friendly, firm, confident—and whether he appears willing to continue searching for the right solution to what the patient perceives as a difficult problem.

Morbidity and mortality data reveal only the final result of medical care and tell little about the patient's comfort or discomfort, his concerns and fears. If the patient is not acutely ill, many physicians do find his vague symptoms somewhat boring, and the patient, sensing his doctor's impatience, anxiously wonders whether he is receiving the medical attention that he regards as his right.

By the physician's standards, prepaid groups apparently provide quality medical care. In 1970, of 1000 full-time hospital staff members, faculty members, house officers, and senior medical students surveyed by the magazine *Hospital Physician*, more than half gave the opinion that prepaid groups are superior to any other form of practice.[8] In 1967, the National Advisory Commission on Health Manpower reported that the quality of medical care provided by the Kaiser plan was "equivalent, if not superior, to that available in most communities."[9]

Subscribers to prepaid plans do not always concur with these professional judgments. Some complain that prepaid group doctors are interested in them only if they are seriously ill, that waiting times are too long, and that because their "personal" physicians are often not available, they have to discuss intimate medical problems with different doctors on each visit. The prepaid groups' quest for efficiency has resulted in some sacrifice of quality by these standards. Group Health Association of America (GHAA) considers the "impersonal" nature of prepaid group service one of the major problems the system has yet to solve.[10] But many patients do not consider a close, personal patient-physician relationship essential to quality service. Some may also feel that the convenience of the one-stop service compensates for the impersonality characteristic of prepaid group plans.

The question of whether prepaid groups practice preventive medicine and whether by doing so they raise the quality of their medical care and at the same time lower costs is also difficult to answer. The term preventive medicine usually refers to such activities as conducting periodic examinations to facilitate detection of disease, immunization, dietary instructions, and public education programs regarding, for example, the use of seat belts. But though it is no doubt beneficial to the patient, there is no hard evidence that "preventive medicine" in its broadest sense reduces medical costs. Obviously, if medical treatment could prevent serious illness, overall medical costs would be reduced. The most effective preventive medicine in this sense is immunology, and prepaid groups that cover the costs of injections may encourage immunizations more than conventional systems do. But prepaid group plans do little more to inculcate in their membership such good health habits as improving their diets, giving up smoking, and using seat belts when driving than exhorting members to develop better habits. There is nothing in the make-up of prepaid groups that gives them any more success in these areas than any number of public service agencies engaged in public health education.

Prepaid groups very likely do contribute to early detection of diseases by offering their members an annual physical examination and encouraging periodic chest X rays and such tests as glaucoma tests, "Pap" smears, glucose tests. But although these measures facilitate early detection and thus improve the quality of medical care, they do not necessarily reduce total medical costs. Indeed, the result may be the opposite. Failure to detect some ailments early can result in the patient's early demise and eliminate the cost of his care (notwithstanding the unhappy result for the patient). Early detection, on the other hand, may save the life of a patient but then require years of expensive treatment.

It is not clear, in any case, that an annual physical examination contributes much to lowering costs or to preventing disease. Many officials of prepaid groups look upon the annual physical examination provision as an unnecessary burden. Officials of Group Health Association (GHA), in Washington, D.C., interviewed in the course of this study, indicated that annual physicals are continued as a covered service only because the members of this cooperative plan refuse to give it up, in spite of the heavy cost it entails and even though GHA doctors question its value. After conducting a series of interviews with Permanente Medical Group physicians, medical writer Greer Williams concluded that:

Permanente physicians tend to be less enthusiastic about promotional emphasis on preventive medical services—"keeping people well"—than do Kaiser health plan representatives. Except for those doctors involved in the automated multiphasic screening program or other aspects of preventive medicine, the typical medical attitude toward disease prevention is one of skepticism with the obvious exception of immunizations. The doctors not only say healthy patients "clog the system"—this could be a misperception of the primary care program— but they question the general effectiveness of annual health examinations in reducing morbidity, mortality, and disability. They also point out that the uncovering of many abnormalities that may not progress to clinical disease requires follow-up observations and further stresses the demand-supply balance.[11]

To summarize the quality issue, then, from a professional standpoint, few have disputed the high standards of medical care and the impressive medical results prepaid groups have achieved. From the patient's point of view, symptoms of illness cause anxiety, and the most important objective of a visit to the doctor is to attain freedom from this anxiety. When the patient's symptoms do not point to any treatable illness, he gains nothing by prolonging treatment, and it behooves the physician in prepaid groups to discourage further visits. Under conventional plans providing comprehensive coverage, the patient may pursue his case by consulting many physicians and trying as many treatments as may be available, and receive reimbursement for these services, subject to the maximums, deductibles, and copayment features in his policy. Such patient persistence ultimately increases the overall costs of medical care. If, on the other hand, the patient belongs to a prepaid group plan, he may appeal to other doctors on its staff, but once the group has decided that it will provide no further treatment, the patient who wishes to pursue his case further must do so at his own expense.

Many patients are reluctant to accept the finality of a chronic physical impairment, no matter how slight, and they may resent an abrupt cutoff of consultations by prepaid group doctors. Large numbers of the population will probably be hesitant to join prepaid groups if other forms of comprehensive coverage are available. In particular, those individuals with family doctors who are accessible and whom they consider effective are likely to subscribe to prepaid group plans only if their family doctors precede them into group prepayment plans or if no other option is available.

Accessibility: An Obstacle to Prepaid Group Growth

The goal of geographical accessibility for prepaid group facilities conflicts with the principle that a prepaid group must be clinic-based—i.e., housing all medical services and facilities under one roof—in order to maximize economies. Clinic-based facilities must serve a large number of subscribers if they are to be economically sound, and many people, especially the increasing numbers living outside metropolitan areas, may find the locations of the clinics inconvenient.

From 1950 to 1969, the number of residents of "standard metropolitan statistical areas"—that is, counties or groups of counties with at least one central city of 50,000 or more—living outside central cities increased from 42 percent to 55 percent of the population.[12]

In response to this continuing movement of population toward the suburbs, many groups have established satellite clinics with small staffs to help make medical services more accessible. The Kaiser-Permanente group in California has established a number of satellite facilities, and Group Health Association, in the District of Columbia, has added two suburban satellite clinics, but they are located within easy driving distance of only a small part of the vast suburban population. Problems of access may be much of the reason why only 7.3 percent of federal employees in the Washington metropolitan area are enrolled in GHA.[13]

In any event, the satellite solution is feasible only for groups with memberships large enough to bear the additional cost. And not even the largest groups can afford to maintain enough satellite clinics to compete with the accessibility of solo physicians or two- or three-physician partnerships.

Access to medical services involves more than access to primary physicians, of course. Although independent general practitioners, internists, and pediatricians may be more conveniently located for many people than prepaid group clinics, specialists, and medical laboratories may be less so, and the patients who use them are more likely to be acutely ill and to find travel burdensome.

150

But most patients consider accessibility only in terms of the location of the primary physician. Geography therefore, is likely to remain an important obstacle to public acceptance of prepaid groups that adhere to the principle of clinic-based service.

Physicians' Willingness to Participate in Prepaid Groups

In the final analysis, the growth prospects of prepaid groups will probably depend more on the willingness of doctors to work in a prepaid group practice than on public acceptance of this system of providing medical care.

Many doctors are vehemently opposed to the prepayment system, and a number, apparently, regard group practice unfavorably, whether it is prepaid or fee-for-service. The findings of a survey conducted by the magazine *Medical Economics*, in 1971 indicate the strength of this opposition. Full-time practicing physicians not already in group practices were asked if they would join a group, "if required to qualify for reimbursement under national health insurance." Less than half (42 percent) answered "yes"; 36 percent said that they would refuse to join groups even with this strong inducement; and 22 percent were undecided.[14] Presumably, without the incentive of qualifying for health insurance reimbursement, an even greater number would have answered negatively.

However, fewer young doctors than old doctors responding to the *Medical Economics* survey were opposed to joining prepaid groups. If young doctors are generally more favorably disposed toward prepaid groups, a steadily increasing supply of doctors may be available for prepaid group employment in future years. The evidence of such an attitudinal shift is inconclusive, however, and in the short run, a rapid expansion of prepaid group practices seems likely to encounter recruitment bottlenecks. Doctors doubtless cherish the operating independence that the unstructured fee-for-service system offers. Prepaid, clinic-based groups will have difficulty in attracting doctors who consider the freedom to choose the location of their practices, to set their own hours, and generally to be their own bosses more important than regular hours, established pension plans, and opportunities for consultation.

While "independence" may be a more important consideration for many, the incomes doctors can expect to earn in prepaid groups will also influence the willingness of many doctors to become part of group plans. Many doctors assume that the fee-for-service system offers opportunities for greater income. Prepaid plans do not provide data on the salaries of the physicians they employ, but it is alleged that their policy is to provide compensation at levels comparable to what the physicians could earn in private practice.[15] According to Dr. Earnest Saward, formerly Medical Director of the Permanente Clinic in Portland, Oregon, the starting salary for physicians is competitive with the incomes of doctors in the community, and the physicians are expected to reach peak income in 10 years after joining the clinic.[16]

The prepaid group practice plans keep each other informed of their salary scales. Some groups use a point system, which includes, among other things, the number of years the physician has spent in residence, experience after formal training, and number of years in the group. The Puget Sound group grants annual salary increases during the first 10 years of membership, with cost-of-living adjustments thereafter and an additional increase after 15 years.[17] This pattern of increases (similar to that of most prepaid groups) concentrates income gains in the early years of practice, and keeps physicians' incomes relatively stable and prevents them from receiving a disproportionate share of the prepaid group practice plans' revenues.

Fringe benefits constitute an important part of the income of prepaid group plan physicians. The annual value of fringe benefits to physicians in one prepaid group plan was estimated at $4,000; the package included life insurance, a pension, full medical insurance coverage, malpractice insurance, sick leave for 90 days and disability income insurance thereafter, one month's paid vacation, and one week for postgraduate training.[18] Other groups provide even more.

Available data indicate that incomes, including the value of fringe benefits, of physicians in prepaid groups are about the same as *average* earnings of physicians in full-time private practice. Full partners in Kaiser-Permanente groups in 1969 averaged $35,198 to $44,780, plus benefits valued at $4,000 to $10,000, depending on region and specialty. For physicians at the Community Health Association in Detroit the average salary, exclusive of fringe benefits, was $35,000 in 1970, about the same as for physicians at the Group Health Association in Washington, D.C. The national median income before taxes of doctors in 1969 was $40,550, and the arithmetic average was probably about 10 percent more.[19] (See Chapter 7.)

However, the range of earnings is somewhat narrower in the prepaid plans than in conventional practice, so that the incomes of a few fee-for-service doctors may be a great deal more than the highest salary offered by a prepaid group. For example, in 1969, 17 percent of full-time physicians in private practice earned $60,000 or more (net before taxes), which was apparently above the top pay offered by any prepaid group.[20] This higher earning potential—even though only a small percentage of fee-for-service doctors achieve it—probably contributes to the attraction of fee-for-service practice.

Capital and Management Requirements
of Prepaid Group Practice

A third consideration that will affect the growth prospects of prepaid group practice plans is the availability of capital and of managerial talent. Figures supplied in 1969 by the Kaiser Foundation Medical Care Program indicate that hospital and clinic facilities and equipment require a capital expenditure of roughly $83,000 per thousand members.[21] Of course, a prepaid group plan that can use existing hospital facilities will avoid this expense and cut its capital needs by considerably more than half.

Not all existing plans are growth oriented, despite the thesis that prepaid plans must constantly bring in new, young members in order to avoid a steadily rising median age and the higher medical risks associated with advancing age. It is more likely that plans grow or seek to grow for the same reasons conventional health insurers seek growth.[22] (See Chapter 4.)

Of all the prepaid group plans, Kaiser-Permanente has been the most growth oriented, having established centers in 6 new areas since 1950 and increased the number of facilities in its original areas of operation. Kaiser-Permanente's capital for new facilities comes largely from internally generated earnings—net income from operations and depreciation—and the proceeds from long-term borrowing. In 1969, Kaiser-Permanente's internally generated contribution to capital development was 7.2 percent of total gross revenues and 16 percent of hospital revenues. This internally generated cash flow was supplemented by the net proceeds from long-term borrowing, which accounted for an additional 4.6 percent of gross revenues. The total capital resources acquired by the Kaiser-Permanente plan in 1969 were equal to 11.8 percent of total revenues; the annual average in the preceding 7 years was over 15 percent. The internally generated capital of 7.2 percent in 1969 was also less than the 7-year annual average of 8.9 percent.[23] This decline may be transitory, or it may result from the effects of the rising costs of providing medical care on the ability of the Kaiser plan to generate capital. On the other hand, having expanded so rapidly in recent years, the plan may now be deliberately slowing its capital formation.

The problem faced by Group Health Association of Washington, D.C., is a good example of how capital needs threaten to offset economies of operation. Although it already has a high subscription rate—its high option is the most expensive of all the plans under the Federal Employees Health Benefits Program—GHA may have to increase its premiums further or curtail benefits if it is to generate internally even part of the capital needed for the hospital it wants to build. Hospital ownership will ultimately result in cost savings for GHA, but they will be consumed for a time by debt payments, and will not benefit present subscribers for many years.

Since the capital required by prepaid groups is substantial, particularly if they plan to build integrated hospital-clinics, and since capital for hospital construction has traditionally been difficult to obtain, newly formed prepaid group practice plans in Boston, Denver (a Kaiser-Permanente group), New Haven, and Columbia, Maryland, are beginning their operations with only a clinic and making use of existing hospital facilities. The clinics themselves are costly. The Community Health Center for the New Haven prepaid group plan is to cost $1.7

million for construction alone, while GHA in Washington, D.C., recently completed purchase of its clinic for $3.34 million.

In financing capital facilities, prepaid group plans have made use of several different sources of funds: savings generated from current operations; long-term borrowing from traditional capital sources, including private insurance companies; direct participation of local Blue Cross-Blue Shield plans; and grants or loans from philanthropic foundations and the federal government. The new prepaid group practice plan in Columbia, Maryland, for example, is sponsored and financed by a private insurance company, Connecticut General, which has an overall investment in Columbia itself as a planned community. Connecticut General is investing $3.75 million in mortgage money, plus $500,000 to cover the costs of starting the plan. The company will also market policies for the prepaid group plan and underwrite all losses for the first 5 years. Boston's Harvard-based prepaid group plan received $1.5 million in grants and short-term loans from major foundations during its first year of operation. The Blue plans, in particular, are showing a great interest in investing in prepaid group plans and have recently purchased the Community Health Association in Detroit.

Outside capital is important if the prepaid group system is to expand rapidly and make its benefits available to a large number of consumers in the early years of its existence. The use of outside capital sources, whether private or public, enables the prepaid group plan to expand its operations considerably faster than it could from the use of internally generated funds alone. In this regard, a prepaid group plan is no different from most conventional business operations. If they borrow the outside capital, the prepaid plan will have to budget to make loan repayments from operating revenues and spread the cost of capital facilities over a number of years. If they cannot borrow but must rely on current operating revenues, they will have to increase premiums so much that current subscribers would not benefit from the potential cost savings. For this reason, plans relying exclusively on internally generated funds should not be expected to grow rapidly.

To keep the lack of capital from inhibiting the growth of prepaid groups or similarly oriented plans, a number of bills in the Congress authorize federal funding for investment and initial costs. The proposed Health Maintenance Assistance Act (H.R. 5615 and S. 1182, 92nd Congress), for example, would authorize the use of public funds as seed capital to foster the growth of "Health Maintenance Organizations" that would embody many prepaid group concepts.

The Department of Health, Education, and Welfare, in conjunction with other financing agencies, is already providing a limited amount of financial assistance to help establish prepaid groups.[24] This kind of assistance provides the resources to help recruit the necessary personnel, but it does not develop the managerial talent that is essential to a properly functioning prepaid group practice plan.

Managing the prepaid groups involves bridging the sizable communication gap

154

between the medical profession and the laymen who make up the membership. A unique aspect of the prepaid group system is the expectation on the part of its membership (or subscribers) that the medical partnership will practice the kind of medicine the membership desires. In the conventional system, patients can simply change doctors if they are dissatisfied. But when subscribers to prepaid group plans are not satisfied, they complain to the plan management, who must then translate the complaints into action. This change in doctor-patient relationships requires some shift in the thinking and attitudes of the participating physicians. Managers who can understand both the physicians' and the memberships' viewpoint and reconcile them so that the organization will function smoothly are rare. Managers of prepaid groups are expected not only to exercise organizational control over members of a profession that prizes its independence, takes glory in its professional separateness and generally disdains nonprofessional interference, but to oversee other personnel functions and to display considerable expertise in financing and capital budgeting.

Adaptability of Prepaid Groups to
Diverse Population Densities

Prepaid group practice plans in their present form can be effective in urban areas only if the main medical centers and the satellite clinics are within ready commuting distance of the subscribers. And to achieve the efficiencies that have made this form of medical care attractive, group practice plans must have a fairly substantial membership. To function efficiently without a hospital, GHAA estimates that membership must be at least 20,000 though Kaiser-Permanente considers a membership of 50,000 to be the minimum without an integrated hospital and 75,000 with an integrated hospital.[25]

Prepaid group practices can increase their savings if the hospital and clinic are integrated, but according to the Kaiser-Permanente estimate a plan-owned hospital is not feasible unless the plan has a membership of at least 75,000. Even with a membership of 75,000, only a small hospital—perhaps in the neighborhood of 100 beds—could be justified, but a hospital of this size cannot operate at maximum efficiency.[26] For group plans without an integrated hospital the degree of efficiency is also reduced, as membership falls below a certain point. For example, a plan with 20,000 members probably supports no more than 20 full-time physicians; as a result some specialties are not covered and patients who need them must use outside specialists, who are costlier and more difficult to control.

But on a voluntary basis, relatively few metropolitan areas could provide the minimum membership necessary to support a prepaid group practice plan. Assuming (somewhat optimistically) that a prepaid group plan could initially enroll 10 percent of the population of a metropolitan area, that population would have to number at least 200,000 to achieve the minimum membership. In the United States in 1970 approximately 40 percent of the total population resided in metropolitan areas with populations of less than 200,000.

The prepaid group concept may have to be adapted if those in less populated areas are to have access to it. The principle of clinic-based practice will probably have to be sacrificed or modified. The "Health Maintenance Assistance Act" now pending in Congress would permit doctors hired by the plan or "Health Maintenance Organization" to work in small satellite clinics or in their traditional office-based facilities at various locations. The HMO would retain most of the other desirable features of prepaid group plans, particularly the integration of the functions of insurer and provider. Doctors could be paid by capitation, salary or fee-for-service, but would receive monetary incentives to seek the most economical ways of treating patients. The system would retain incentives for consultation and peer review, because all members of the physician partnership would stand to gain by high standards, just as they do in the clinic-based group plans. The physician partnership and hospital could still be integrated, as they are in the prepaid groups, even if they were not housed in the same building. The HMO's would retain the savings due to elimination of the insurance function. And modern communications devices such as closed circuit TV and computerized records retrievable by telephone could compensate for the loss of such benefits of clinic-based practice as quick referrals and readily available medical records and laboratory facilities.

In rejecting the principle of clinic-based practice, the HMO would lose economies of scale and the convenience of "one-stop" service. But it would gain the kind of accessibility that is most important to the public. Prepaid group practice is one way of providing medical services at lower cost than the conventional system. Whether prepaid practice is a better way to provide medical care or not is another matter. Cost is not the only criterion and one cannot ignore either the preconceptions of the public or the prejudices of doctors in judging the quality of this system. Yet there is much to be learned from the limited prepaid group experience to date and, with some modifications, it could provide a desirable option for those who are attracted to lower cost and may prefer a more integrated system.

10 The Requirements of Health Insurance Reform: A Summary

The most frequently mentioned objectives of health insurance reform—though not necessarily all common to all of the current proposals—are: (1) enrollment should be universal but not necessarily compulsory; (2) coverage should be "comprehensive" (though definitions vary); (3) everyone should have equal access to medical services, to the extent possible and to an extent consistent with other objectives; (4) medical cost inflation should be held to a minimum; and (5) the cost of administering the health insurance system should be held to a minimum.

Congress is now reviewing several proposed approaches to reform of the health insurance system. None of these achieve all 5 objectives; in fact, they confirm the difficulty of achieving all 5 objectives simultaneously. Indeed, striving even for limited objectives seems to create additional problems in delivering and paying for medical services.

Proposals for a National Health Insurance Plan

For the purposes of analysis, the health care financing proposals put forward either in bills introduced in the First Session of the 92nd Congress or in leading publications can be regarded as falling into 6 categories, although the classification of a given proposal may be somewhat arbitrary. To simplify the task of classification, it is necessary to ignore some of the very features that the proponents of a given approach consider most important. For example, the extent of coverage of a proposal is considered important in classifying plans only when coverage is an important component of the proposed plan's attack on medical sector inflation. Beyond that, the specific benefits of one plan can easily be adapted to any other plan. Similarly, techniques to foster the growth of HMOs are easily adapted to any plan and are generally included in all proposals. This analysis excludes a number of proposals for partial coverage, such as catastrophic health insurance and expansion of Medicaid and Medicare, and concentrates on universal, comprehensive plans. The first 3 categories are largely adaptations of existing systems; the last 3 contain many innovations.[1]

1. *Extended Present System—Proposals to Broaden Both Coverage and Enrollment:* Fulton-Broyhill bill, H.R. 4960,[2] supported by the American Medical Association; and Burleson bill, H.R. 4349, sponsored by the Health Insurance Association of America.

Proposals in this category would employ a voluntary approach to achieve universal coverage by extension of the present mixed system. The public sector would encourage broad enrollment, mainly by providing income tax credits to purchasers—employers or employees or both—of private health insurance and issuing vouchers for the purchase of health insurance to those whose incomes are too low to pay income tax. The law would establish a minimum level of coverage that health insurance enrollees would have to purchase in order to qualify for tax credits. The Medicare and Medicaid programs would be continued. Individual policies providing at least the minimum coverage would be available, but they would still be expensive relative to group policies, as they are now.

2. *Extended Medicare—Proposals to Achieve Universal Coverage Through Government Underwritten Plans Employing Insurance Principles:* Javits bill, S. 836; Dingell bill, H.R. 48; and Scott-Percy bill, S. 1598.

Essentially, these proposals would extend Medicare to the entire population. The federal government would take over the health insurance underwriting function but leave the provider and insurance administration functions to the private sector, subject to the kinds of controls and requirements now applied to Medicare. (See Chapter 5.) The system would be financed mainly though payroll taxes (unlike Medicare Part B).

All residents would be covered on the same basis, and coverage would be uniform. Deductibles and coinsurance provisions would be modest.

The proposals in this category would expand the present public sector health insurance system in the same way that proposals in the first category—*Extended Present System*—would expand the existing private sector system, except that these proposals call for compulsory enrollment.

3. *Regulated Private Sector:* Byrnes bill, H.R. 7741; and Bennett bill, S. 1623, supported by the Nixon administration in the 91st Congress but dropped in the 93rd Congress.[3]

These proposals would rely primarily on the private sector for administration of the insurance and claims handling functions, but unlike plans in the first category, they would require employers to offer a uniform standard health insurance plan or, as an alternative option, an HMO plan for all employees working a minimum number of hours per week. Additional benefits could be negotiated. Stricter regulation of insurers is contemplated. To control cost and utilization, deductibles and copayment would be fairly high ($100 per person annually for physicians' expenses, the first 2 days' hospital per-diem charges, plus 25 percent of per-diem charges thereafter, with a $50,000 lifetime maximum per person). Similar group policies would be offered to the self-employed, those employed by small employers or in casual trades.

These proposals would establish a dual health care financing system—one for families of employed persons—the vast majority—and another "Family Health Insurance Plan" for low-income families. Medicare would continue in operation for the aged; Medicaid would be limited to the aged indigent, the blind, and the disabled.

4. *Quasi National Health Service:* Griffiths-Corman bill, H.R. 22; and the identical Kennedy bill, S. 3, sponsored by the Committee for National Health Insurance and supported by the United Automobile Workers of America and the AFL-CIO.

This proposal promises to provide, eventually, almost all medical services, to the extent available, to all residents with virtually no maximums, no direct charges, and no deductibles or copayment provisions. The federal government would underwrite and administer the program and finance it through payroll taxes matched by general revenues.

The health care system would be restructured, in an effort to keep the total cost within the projected revenues. The cost control mechanism would entail budgeting of revenues and expenditures by functional category—that is, hospitals, physicians, and other health care providers—and, subsequently, by region. These budget ceilings could be altered only if receipts or expenditures proved to differ significantly from original estimates or if an epidemic or other catastrophes required higher expenditures. Each hospital and nursing home would be subject to specific budget ceilings. Physicians and dentists in each region would be subject to a budget ceiling. They could choose to be remunerated by fee-for-service, capitation, or salary, but payments to those choosing fee-for-service would be limited to the residual in the doctors' and dentists' budget after all physicians and dentists on salary and capitation had been paid. The administrative system would establish 100 local health service areas and 10 regional offices, headed by a 5-man Health Security Board, supported by a National Advisory Council, serving under the Secretary of Health, Education, and Welfare.

The sponsors of this proposal claim they would increase the quantity of medical services while holding increases in the health insurance budget at a constant ratio to the national wage bill. The implication is that the incomes of providers would increase less rapidly than average national incomes.

5. *Major Deductible or Major Copayment:* No legislation in this category has been introduced, but the major deductible concept is proposed by Martin S. Feldstein.[4]

The underlying concept of this proposed approach to national health insurance is that the main benefit of health insurance is the provision of high-risk protection and that low-risk coverage encourages abusive use of medical services and high administrative costs. To discourage overutilization but provide high-risk protection, the insured would be required to share the expense of medical services either by a deductible that would be related to the size of family income up to a certain level or by a smaller deductible (perhaps 5 percent of income) combined with a 50 percent copayment requirement up to an additional 10 percent of income. (In 1971, Feldstein suggested 10 percent up to $8,000 annual income, with a minimum of $500 per family. Naturally, the minimum would have to be adjusted periodically to account for inflation.) The second of these alternatives would make the consumer and provider cost-conscious in regard to a broad range of medical services without increasing the insurer's maximum risk.

This proposal would permit postpayment of the major deductible so that the insured would be able to finance his share of the insured medical expenses and need not refrain from seeking treatment for lack of funds. (Some way would have to be found to keep the availability of credit from undercutting the purpose of the large deductible—perhaps by making repayment subject to terms and interest charges, as in installment buying.)

Feldstein's article does not deal with such details as the extent and definition of coverage, the source of financing, the kind of regulation required, its relation, if any, to other health care proposals, whether the program should be compulsory or voluntary, public or private. Nor does it suggest ways to cope with the tendency of employee groups to negotiate coverage below the anticipated deductible level, a practice which, if permitted, would obviously render the major deductible proposal useless.

6. *"Free Choice" or FEHBP Model:* No concrete legislative proposal has been made in this category, but it embodies the suggestions of Anne R. Somers and of Odin W. Anderson and J. Joel May of the Center for Health Administration Studies of the University of Chicago.[5]

The suggestion that the Federal Employees Health Benefits Program (FEHBP) be used as a model for a national health insurance system does not necessarily mean that the system (described briefly in Chapter 5) should be applied on a universal basis, but is based on three important characteristics that set FEHBP apart from other plans: (1) "controlled competition" between carriers, with a government agency approving each carrier's plan and setting reserve and other financial requirements; (2) free choice of an approved plan by the employee, and the right to change plans at specified times despite any preexisting conditions; (3) sharing of premium payments by employer and employee, which allows insurers to compete in terms of price as well as quality of administrative services.

This approach would give the population at large a choice of various plans offered by the private sector and would subject the plans to close government scrutiny and regulation. The proposal is similar to proposals in the third category, "Regulated Private Sector," except that it could automatically offer several alternative types of insurance, including group prepaid plans and plans providing for major deductibles, as options to the consumer. The proponents of this approach have not spelled out ways to achieve universal enrollment or to make the program available to those who would require some kind of subsidy.

Regulating Demand and Costs under Universal and Comprehensive Plans

One important test of the efficacy of any of the proposals described above is whether they provide an effective means of regulating the health care sector's claim on total resources. The popular slogan, "medical care is a right, not a privilege," suggests that under the right system everyone could use medical services in any quantity at any time. But in a world of limited resources, it can, at best, mean only that "some minimum amount of medical care is everyone's right." Regardless of the system used to pay for medical services, unrestricted access to every form of medical care is simply not feasible.

An effective system of health care financing must not only limit demand and restrain inflation but also give clear signals when there is a genuine public desire (as opposed to a public desire for more "free" care) to shift resources into or out of the health sector. It must also efficiently allocate resources within the medical sector. Probably no system that provides even moderately comprehensive coverage can accomplish all of this in a wholly satisfactory way.

The proposals outlined above employ—in various combinations—the following 4 basic ways of restraining demand, controlling costs and allocating resources:

1. *Requiring that the consumer bear some direct responsibility for the cost of his medical care.* This requirement encourages both providers and consumers to weigh the costs of optional medical services against the desire for other goods and services. The traditional fee-for-service method of compensating physicians theoretically causes doctor and patient to weigh the cost of each service and to determine jointly the most efficient way of meeting the patient's medical requirements. The theory works somewhat imperfectly in practice, and it loses all validity if insurance covers much of the cost of medical services, particularly of low-cost services.

The *Major Deductible or Major Copayment* concept, which offers protection against major medical costs, comes the closest of all the proposals to applying price principles to restrain demand, but under the present health insurance system the effectiveness of this concept has not been adequately tested in practice.

Under a major deductible plan, the signal to move additional resources into or out of the health sector would take the form of upward or downward pressure on prices. Inevitably, some medical cost inflation would have to be tolerated from time to time. Also government intervention would probably be required to stimulate an increase in the supply of some medical services—particularly the services of physicians—in the event of training bottlenecks and other such problems.

2. *Using provider incentives addressed to the physician's major role in determining the patient's need for medical services.* This method is used by prepaid group practices and presumably would be used by HMOs. All proposals, to the extent they support HMOs, reflect recognition of the value of this method of utilization control.

Provider incentives do not curtail the initial demand for medical services, although follow-up treatment is generally under virtually total physician control as is the type of treatment. Dr. Sidney Garfield, formerly of the Kaiser-Permanente group, has, however, put forward a proposal—the "Garfield Plan"—

that would also restrain initial demand by giving all patients computerized, multiphasic tests when they initially seek help, in order to screen out the "worried well" before they see the doctor.[6]

The provider incentives in prepaid group practice plans consist of the provision of services on a fixed cost basis and the integration of the functions of provider and insurer which gives providers a direct interest in controlling the cost of providing service. As a means of signaling public desire for more or less health care resources, provider incentive plans would probably be effective only if they operated in competition with each other. Under monopoly conditions, consumer dissatisfaction with the quantity or quality of services would be difficult to discern. Competition among plans, on the other hand, forces each plan not only to consider ways of economizing on treatment but also ways of satisfying consumer desires for expanded service.

3. *Imposing an arbitrary, budget-determined ceiling on the total cost of services.* Proposals that call for public sector financing—that is, those under *Extended Medicare* and *Quasi National Health Service* categories—would attempt to limit the funds available for medical services each year to revenues derived from payroll taxes matched by general revenues.

Under the *Extended Medicare* proposals, if utilization of services covered by the plan exceeded expectations, the authorities would have to decide whether to increase the payroll tax and matching revenues; to try to cut the price of services, through such measures as fee controls, closer scrutiny of hospital costs; or to adopt stricter interpretations of "covered services" that would in effect reduce coverage. (Medicare, and Medicaid programs have applied all 3 methods with mixed results.)

The *Quasi National Health Service* proposals call for detailed budgeting of expenditures, as explained earlier, and presumably would require providers to absorb the cost of utilization in excess of amounts budgeted. The proposals assume that the total cost can be held firm, even if the number of doctors and other providers is increased. Given the projected increase in the number of doctors,[7] this approach might well cause the average income of physicians actually to decrease. In the absence of experience with a plan of this type in the United States, or with any exactly comparable plans in other countries, one can only speculate as to how effective this approach would be in achieving the objectives of cost restraint and resource allocation.

The arbitrary ceiling on health care expenditures would probably make it difficult to determine the degree of public desire to increase or decrease the share of total resources allocated to the health care sector. Since medical services would be "free" to the user, each person would expect to receive the maximum amount of service he felt he "needed," but he would not have a clear sense of what other things he would have to give up to acquire this service. Unfulfilled demand would no doubt be substantial but hard to interpret. Such indicators as increases in the use of services outside the system or long waiting lists for elective surgery and other elective treatments, as have occurred in England.[8] would not necessarily mean that the public was willing to move resources from one sector to another. Only through the political process could the public express its dissatisfaction with the quality, quantity, and distribution of services under this system. But protests expressed in the political arena become intermingled with other protests and often do not clearly reflect public priorities. The response to changing public attitudes is likely to be slow and somewhat arbitrary. The British Minister of Health, speaking before the House of Commons on October 27, 1960, gave his seasoned judgment on this issue in defending the British National Health Service:

Policies which are formed centrally and executed administratively are bound to be slower to change and less adaptable to alterations of circumstances and demand, than if responsibility were diffused and decisions were independent. The great machine is bound to have a one track mind, to be cumbrous and unresponsive, to abhor variations, to be insensitive to the world around it.[9]

4. *Controlling the costs of the health care system through resistance to the cost of insurance.* Today officials in the public sector and employers and unions in the private sector are under pressure from those covered to extend coverage and thus facilitate greater utilization of medical services. At the same time those who are insured are seeking coverage that involves less and less of their own participation in the payment of premiums.[10] When the insured individual participates in the payment of premiums, he acquires a direct, financial interest in the cost of the insurance covering medical services, if not the cost of the services themselves. If all those insured had a choice of plans and a financial reason to choose one plan over another, as well as a standard for evaluating different plans, insurers might become more involved with the cost and quality of the services of the providers in order to meet competition. Maximizing this indirect influence on the cost of medical services, however, would require elimination of noncontributory group health insurance plans—a step which would pose serious political problems. Noncontributory plans, which cover the majority of persons under group plans,[11] are the hard fought gains of labor unions, which would not readily give them up even to encourage insurers to take an interest in the cost and quality of the services of the providers.

Achieving Optimum Rational Resource Allocation—Monolithic Versus Pluralistic Systems

The demand control technique one ultimately favors will depend on which of the health insurance reform objectives one feels is most important and which of the techniques one feels has the most chance of success in the real world. Each of the proposals for a national health insurance plan described above has features that seem superior to others in their likely effectiveness for controlling costs, achieving a rational allocation of resources within the health care sector, and determining the health sector's claim on total resources. For these purposes a pluralistic system, consisting of various insurers and various plans incorporating the best features of all the proposals would be superior to a monolithic national health care financing system.

The main objective of the model pluralistic system described below is to achieve optimum cost control and efficiency of resource allocation while offering comprehensive coverage for everyone. The model—which is illustrative and not a detailed suggestion for a new health insurance plan—assumes that the national health plan would include a standard definition of medical cost coverage at 2 levels: minimum and optimum (definition of "medical costs" is discussed later in the chapter), so that the insured would have a meaningful basis for choice among the plans offered. It also assumes that the employer's contribution would be made in such a way that, by choosing a less expensive plan, the insured would gain money income. (How this feature might be made politically acceptable is discussed later in this chapter.) On this basis, 6 plans—2 main categories of plans, each with 3 subcategories—might be offered:

1. *Comprehensive HMO-type plan:* (a) offering optimum coverage according to the standard definition, with no deductibles, no copayment, no maximum limits; (b) offering the same optimum coverage, subject to a deductible or copayment, with no maximum limits; (c) offering minimum coverage under the standard definition, with no maximum limits.

2. *Major deductible conventional plan:* (a) offering optimum coverage under the standard definition, with no maximum; (b) offering the same optimum coverage, subject to an additional deductible or copayment, with no maximum; (c) offering minimum coverage under the standard definition, with no maximum.

All insurance carriers would have an opportunity to offer any or all of the 6 alternative plans, which would be the only ones acceptable under the national health insurance system. It would probably not be administratively feasible for most employers to deal with more than one carrier for each plan, but most employers would be able, and should be required to offer at least 2 plans supplied by each of 2 insurers.

However, with competition strengthened by giving each insured person, rather than the group representative, a wider choice and a financial stake in making a choice, it is conceivable that the insurers might be encouraged to seek ways of combining small groups so as to reduce costs.[12]

This range of choices, combined with a modification of noncontributory plans giving the employee the benefit of savings, would put into operation 3 of the 4 basic demand-restraining methods. Fully comprehensive plans offering low-risk (first-dollar) as well as high-risk coverage would be available only in

HMO-type plans that give the physician an incentive to provide medical services efficiently. The only conventional plans available would be those with provision for major deductibles, which theoretically, at least, would bring traditional consumer (and physician) responses to price into play. Most families do not need full coverage of low-cost medical services, but those who wanted it as a convenience would be able to obtain it in HMO-type plans in which the provider could regulate utilization. Of course, many people still prefer coverage in the "first-dollar" or low-deductible range and are not yet prepared to accept HMOs as the only source of coverage in this range. The addition of 2 additional plans (i.e., optimum and minimum-no maximum plans under standard definitions) with low deductible coverage would weaken demand restraint somewhat, but if employees realized the premium savings when opting for a lower-price plan, the indirect effect would still apply. Moreover, since HMOs should be able to provide the standard coverage at lower price than conventional plans offering the same coverage, one might expect that those with a preference for complete coverage would tend to gravitate toward HMOs once they realized that the premium savings accrued to them.

Monolithic public sector systems, such as *Extended Medicare* and *Quasi National Health Service*, could also limit total expenditures either, at worst, by rationing services on a "first-come, first-serve" basis, or, at best, through HMO-type physician incentives. But they would be less efficient than a pluralistic system in implementing the public's desire to move resources from some other sector into health care.

Equal Access to Medical Services and
Optimum Resource Allocation

Although the optimum system in terms of efficient use of resources would seem to be a pluralistic system (or a major deductible plan alone) for the employed or otherwise financially self-sufficient and a separate system for those considered medically indigent, such a dual system would probably perpetuate many of the present inequalities in medical care. Those who place great emphasis on the need for equality argue that separate treatment inevitably leads to inequality in medical care, as it does in education.

It is, unfortunately, difficult to devise a pluralistic system that can provide medical services of uniform quality for those financially able to contribute on the same basis. If they were not required to contribute, medically indigent families would, quite properly, choose the most complete coverage offered. If they had to do otherwise, the community would still have to pay for any uncovered medical services they might need. In any pluralistic system offering the insured a meaningful choice, those in need of public support would find themselves receiving separate and in many respects probably inferior treatment. The Medicaid experience is an example of this process. (See Chapter 5.)

A monolithic system supported by payroll taxes or general revenue, on the other hand, would not create distinctions between those able and unable to pay, because everyone would be eligible on exactly the same basis. Collection of premiums and payment of providers also on the same basis would eliminate all financial reasons for discrimination. It is largely due to these considerations that monolithic, public sector plans find support.

Enrollment under Monolithic
and Pluralistic Systems

Monolithic, public sector plans also have a greater potential than pluralistic approaches for achieving universal enrollment.

Universal enrollment is not as easy to achieve as it may seem, even under a compulsory system. Few countries have achieved 100 percent enrollment in national health insurance or health service plans, because, virtually every system, no matter how free or open, imposes some eligibility requirements on those who wish to use it. They must pay part of the premiums directly or through payroll taxes; be employed, if employers pay the premiums; take some action to qualify for welfare support; or, if capitation systems are used for paying physicians, register with a physician. The unemployed, the self-employed, itinerant workers, employees of small organizations, domestics, and rural workers sometimes fail to participate in such systems because of ignorance, carelessness, fear that they will in the end have to pay for the service, or desire to avoid contact with officialdom.

In Great Britain, for example, everyone is eligible to participate in the National Health Service, irrespective of his contribution to the insurance fund. But because all treatment—except for emergencies—must be initiated at the general practitioner level, and because general practitioners are paid on a capitation basis, each person participating in the British program must register with a physician.[13] Even a monolithic system, therefore, would require some kind of registration mechanism for participants but would present fewer obstacles to enrollment than a pluralistic system.

Even though monolithic systems may have some advantage in this regard, a pluralistic system could incorporate measures to encourage more and better medical care for the poor and medically indigent than have been tried heretofore. For example, fee controls, which are of doubtful usefulness in controlling costs and of negative value in restraining demand (see Chapter 7), could be used to favor services to the medically indigent. Many physicians prefer not to treat Medicaid or Medicare patients because reimbursement for services to these patients is generally too little and too late. The regulations fixing fees for subsidized groups should not, as they now do, require physicians to reduce their fees to the 75th percentile of "usual, customary and reasonable" charges, while

Blue Shield is reimbursing charges between the 85th and 90th percentile. Instead, they should provide for rates above those reimbursed by Blue Shield and other carriers. In other words, the system should reward providers who serve the poor and medically indigent. Since providers tend to induce greater utilization of medical services to compensate for "losses" of income caused by fee controls, a higher fee level is not likely to increase total expenditures by any significant amount.

Other measures might also be considered toward the same objective. Computers, for example, could be used to standardize identification and means of payment, even though the coverage and source of payment would remain differentiated. Each citizen could be provided with a health care charge card that would specify, in the computer code, his coverage and carrier. Centralized agencies could be established as clearing houses for medical bills and insurance payments, paying providers what they may correctly charge and billing insurance carriers and patients as appropriate. The insurance carriers themselves could underwrite this billing procedure and guarantee one another against any loss due to unpaid bills, and include the cost in premiums as a legitimate operating expense. Moreover, this billing cost would not be an additional cost to the community but very likely a net saving, particularly because it would relieve high paid physicians of a burdensome and costly chore.

And standardization would make the billing procedure easier and cheaper than it now is. By this mechanism physicians would have no disincentive to treat a patient simply because of his source of financing.

Equality of access can be provided for in those areas where medical services are critical, but need not be provided for in the much larger area where medical care is sought for personal satisfaction or comfort and does not involve debilitation or threat to life. What this means is that initial access has to be assured for everyone and that treatment in life or death cases or where lack of treatment may result in permanent handicap has to be assured on the same basis for all participants. But, it is as impractical to say that every individual has a right to any kind of medical care in any quantity as to say that every individual has the right to unlimited quantities of any other consumer goods or services.

Probably no system can provide complete equality of medical care. Patients differ in their understanding of symptoms and of the kinds of treatment available. Doctors differ in their professional competence; some hospitals are better than others; and few patients know the difference or are able to choose the best. Location will always affect the quality of medical services available; rural areas and small towns, obviously, cannot support the extensive facilities available in large urban areas. Finally, human nature cannot be readily controlled. A doctor with strong prejudices against an individual or a group can simply not be forced to provide the same quality of treatment to the objects of his prejudice that he would give to others.

Voluntary Versus Compulsory Systems

The concept of equality in the context of a national health insurance system often applies not only to treatment but also to payment. Equality of payment can be interpreted to mean charging participants either the same premium without regard to preexisting serious ailments, or a rate based on the individual's ability to pay. In either case, a compulsory system is more likely than a voluntary system to conform to the principle of equality. A system intended to include both high and low risks on a community rating basis, would not serve its purpose, if the wealthy, or those who consider themselves favorable risks, were free to choose not to participate or to seek more favorable, experience-rated premiums. (See Chapter 3.) The objective of cost-sharing according to ability to pay thus implies a compulsory, single plan system, financed through payroll taxes or general revenues.

But concern for equality of payment is not the only argument for a compulsory system. A compulsory system offers greater assurance that providers will be paid for their services. Unpaid bills account for about 7 percent of hospitals' gross revenues (see Chapter 6), and probably about 5 percent of physicians' bills go unpaid.[14] The unpaid bills of physicians may be partly absorbed by the physicians themselves, but unpaid hospital bills are generally passed on and distributed among hospital users. This cost is, in turn, reflected in health insurance premiums, so that the insured and the uninsured who are hospitalized and pay their own bills share the cost of the medically indigent. Compulsory participation in the system would assure a wider, more equitable distribution of medical costs.

Compulsory participation in a system offering standard protection would also facilitate job mobility by removing differences in the degree of medical cost protection that exist from one place of employment to another. Although differences in premiums are often slight under the present system, differences in coverage may be crucial for an employee who requires a certain kind of medical treatment.

Another argument for compulsory participation is that the consumer has to be protected "for his own good"; that people who have not experienced serious illness cannot appreciate the huge costs that medical care can entail and, left to their own devices, might not acquire the protection they need.

The choice between compulsory and voluntary participation would not affect the efficiency of resource allocation as would the choice between monolithic and pluralistic systems. Both types of system could be either compulsory or voluntary, but compulsory participation would further the objective of maximum equality of access.

Defining "Medical Costs"

Any system aimed at achieving the substantive objectives of health insurance reform will require more precise definitions of the "medical costs" or "medical services" covered than health insurance plans now provide. Under a pluralistic system, the several plans available need not offer the same coverage, but they should be required to use a standard meaning for all terms such as "hospital," "laboratory tests," "prosthetics and appliances," and should standardize the combinations of coverage they offer, which would reduce the variety of health insurance plans to a number that would make meaningful choice possible (as suggested in the model presented earlier in the chapter) and lower costs by simplifying claims handling.

Standardizing the definition of "medical costs" could also promote public health policies. As an extreme example, health insurance could support a public policy of population control (if one were adopted) by including birth control devices, abortions, and family-planning counseling in the standard definition while limiting coverage of maternity costs.

The standardizing of definitions and of combinations of coverage under a national health insurance plan should be the responsibility of the federal government. A concomitant responsibility should be effective monitoring of health status and program experience. For this purpose the government might appoint a committee consisting of representatives of the medical profession, hospital administrators, certain research foundations, labor unions, industry, the insurers, and the public-at-large, represented by two or three noted citizens of different disciplines. This committee would meet annually to review the existing standards in light of technological developments, possible abuses in interpretation of the standards that might make clarification necessary, distortions in utilization, and general national health policy. It would report its findings and recommendations to the Secretary of the Department of Health, Education, and Welfare, who would resolve disputes that could not be reconciled in committee.

The task of determining the standard definitions would undoubtedly be difficult. The definitions should be based on medical considerations and the potential financial hardships that medical care can entail—not the "popularity" of certain illnesses, which is the principal concern of buyers of most group health insurance under the present system. (As a result, the system serves more to supplement income than to protect against the cost of serious medical risks.) Nor should the standard definitions be considered rationing devices, as they frequently are today by some sellers of insurance. The main methods of restraining demand would be those outlined earlier in this chapter.

If a national health insurance plan is to provide genuine protection against high-risk illnesses, it should have no maximum limitations, in keeping with the objective of comprehensive coverage. This goal leads to complications in defining covered medical costs, however, particularly for such needs as psychiatric care. Psychiatric patients often need long-term treatment, but unlimited coverage of such treatment is easily abused. On the other hand, limiting psychiatric care to 20 visits per year, as in some proposals or in some present plans, is of benefit only to those with minor neuroses. It leaves those with serious emotional problems the choice of absorbing the enormous cost of psychiatric treatment or resorting to state mental institutions.

Coverage of prosthetics and devices such as special bathroom fixtures presents similar problems. The prosthetics field is growing and has recently seen the rapid development of electronically operated artificial limbs and supportive devices of great utility and high cost.[15]

Perhaps insurance should be designed to cover, in general, all medical services that contribute to the diagnosis, cure or relief of an ailment that is sufficiently unpredictable that one could not reasonably be expected to anticipate it and be financially prepared for it, or the treatment of which could entail costs greater than the person of average income could be expected to handle alone. Such services as normal dental care, which is required in fairly even amounts and is fairly predictable, would probably be excluded from standard coverage under this guideline.

No criteria for definitions of coverage can be absolutely objective and workable; all would involve some arbitrary distinctions. But standard definitions and definite rules regarding combinations of coverage (applicable under a pluralistic system) would at least give providers, insurers, and consumers a clear understanding of the medical costs against which coverage was being provided, and enable consumers to treat deductibles and copayment features as demand restraints.

Insurance or Health Care—State or Federal Regulation?

Mention of the usefulness of a government authority to determine standard definitions of medical costs leads inevitably to the sticky question of regulation.

Insurance carriers have strongly resisted federal regulation of insurance, including regulation of health insurance. But health insurance is different from other forms of insurance. Because the financing mechanism influences the delivery of health care so profoundly, because the "loss concept" in health insurance differs so much from that in other forms of insurance, and because health care in the private sector is financed in so many different ways—through private insurance carriers, Blue plans, prepaid groups, individual practice plans—the financing of health care should be considered and regulated more as a health care function than as an insurance function.

The solvency of carriers, which is the principal concern of insurance commissioners, may be one of the least important elements of health insurance regulation, given the trend toward group plans that are essentially riskless, cost-plus operations. The problems of defining medical costs, of hospital planning and coordination, of peer review among physicians, of fee schedules, of the use of paramedical personnel, and of regulating prepaid groups or HMOs are, on the other hand, of great importance. The state agencies that deal with these problems seldom if ever coordinate their efforts with those of the state insurance commissioners, who regulate the financial aspects of health insurance. This separation of responsibilities is inefficient, since all of the problems mentioned above are in some way responsive to the financing mechanism.

Under a national health plan the guidelines for this integrated regulation would have to be determined at the federal level, and the federal government would have to retain authority to alter the guidelines in response to changing conditions. Administration of the regulations might be delegated to the states, though this decision would require careful consideration of the advantages of uniformity and the problems of decentralization.

Private or Public Sector Program?

Regulation would, of course, take on a different form under a public sector program. A monolithic system designed to provide equal access to medical services would have to be largely a public sector operation. It would have to have at least as much public sector involvement as the *Extended Medicare* proposal, although, as under Medicare, the administration of the program could remain largely in the hands of the private sector.

The basic arguments for and against increased public sector control of the economy are well known and are, in any event, beyond the scope of this study. As to specific arguments, it should be noted that federal assumption of responsibility for the financing of personal health care services would mean a large increase in taxes and in public sector employment. Total federal, state, and local taxes in 1969 were 28.5 percent of the gross national product; if all health care costs had been financed through the public sector in that year, the tax burden would have increased to about 33 percent of GNP, or by about 16 percent. The increase in federal employment would depend on the extent of public sector involvement in financing medical services. At the extreme, the government could take over the entire health care system, which employs some 4 million people, and thereby more than double federal employment.[16] Less extreme and more plausible would be for the public sector to follow the example of Great Britain and West Germany and take over the hospitals, which in 1969 had approximately 1.9 million full-time employees, about one third of whom were on state and federal payrolls.[17] Under the Griffiths-Corman and Kennedy bills (described above in the *Quasi National Health Service* category) all hospitals would come under federal budgetary control, but they would apparently retain their present juridical status, with administrators responsible to the hospital boards and other hospital employees responsible to the administrator. (The ability of the government to exercise budgetary control in the absence of an employer-employee relationship with the administrators seems less certain than in an arrangement under which the government assumed direct control of hospitals.)

It is often argued that health costs are incurred in any event and that channeling them through the federal budget system does not increase them or substantially alter the way total resources are allocated. The counterargument is that public sector expenditures affect the economy in a different way from private sector expenditures and that high taxes, in particular, distort work incentives and lead to a generally inefficient use of resources.[18]

A more narrow issue is the relative efficiency of the 2 systems. The experience to date of the public sector in financing health care does not show clearly that either sector is superior to the other in efficiency of administration or in adopting policies in response to public need. Some evidence suggests that in comparable situations the private sector can handle claims under group policies at lower cost than the public sector, but the evidence is not conclusive. Greater uniformity of coverage and standardization of definitions—which the public sector programs already enjoy—should further reduce private sector claims handling costs. (But to lower its total administrative costs, the private sector would have to provide some way of "grouping" those now insured under individual plans, without bunching adverse risks in a single group with rates far higher than the community average.)

Although it might be less effective in control of expenditures, a uniform public sector system financed by payroll taxes or from general revenues or both would undoubtedly be administratively simpler than a pluralistic system. The accountability of the government for funds entrusted to it is far greater than that imposed on the private sector, although the direction of public sector expenditure is susceptible to much more political interference than private sector operations. From the standpoint of financing, however, a public sector program would have a clear administrative advantage. The public sector can assess a payroll or other tax to meet all financing requirements of a public sector health insurance program, but a private sector program would require the establishment of income-level criteria for those individuals whose insurance is paid for in full or in part by public funds. The Byrnes-Bennett bill, earlier supported by the Nixon administration, proposed a system of graduated premiums, with premiums diminishing as incomes decline and with no premium payments for those below a certain income level. Administration of such a system would be awkward for a number of reasons, but particularly because people move in and out of income ranges as employment situations change or work weeks increase or decrease. The establishment of an arbitrary income ceiling, below which no one would be required to contribute, would penalize those whose incomes exceed the ceiling by less than the amount of the insurance premium, although any program not requiring contributions from those below a certain income level would present this problem.

Consolidation of Health Insurance

Whether monolithic or pluralistic, voluntary or compulsory, public or private, a universal health insurance system should bring about some consolidation of the

myriad programs now in existence and a consequent lowering of total administrative costs. Such programs as automobile, school bus, and summer camp
accident coverage, many of which pay benefits to claimants regardless of other
insurance payments, would be totally inconsistent with a national health
insurance system.

Policy decisions will be required on certain other programs such as the
medical portion of Workmen's Compensation, disability income insurance, and
the special program financed by the Veterans Administration. Some argue that
medical coverage under Workmen's Compensation should be retained and
excluded from national health insurance coverage as an inducement to employers to maintain safe working conditions. But the disability and income loss
portions would remain in effect in any case, and they would seem to be
adequate inducements for the maintenance of safety standards.

Income loss or disability insurance sold privately presents a somewhat
different problem. Many of these plans pay flat amounts, such as $40 per day of
established illness, regardless of other insurance coverage. Several plans cover the
patient only for the number of days he is hospitalized, and thus encourages him
to seek hospital treatment—the most expensive form of medical treatment now
available. Since it pays benefits regardless of other insurance coverage, income
loss insurance would continue to be attractive to many people even if a universal
health plan were adopted. This inducement to overutilization and distortion in
the use of health care resources should be eliminated, and the sale of this kind of
insurance should be limited to coverage of the actual income loss due to injury
or illness.

Today, 75 percent of Veterans Administration hospital treatment involves
illnesses or injuries that are not service-connected. In these circumstances, it
would be hard to justify continuation of a separate medical program for veterans
if a universal health plan were adopted. The Veterans Administration employs
extensive facilities, physicians and other health care personnel to service a
narrow sector of the total population. These resources could probably be
utilized more efficiently if they were integrated under a national plan.

The Vanishing "Crisis"

Even without a universal health insurance program, the trend toward broader
coverage is likely to continue. More and more group programs are offering
coverage maximums of as much as $250,000, and even these maximums are
likely to be raised. Comprehensive coverage including more outpatient treatment
is also on the increase. Procedures falling under the "preventive care" heading—
pap smears, glaucoma tests, immunizations, proctoscopies, and so forth—that
were once covered mainly in prepaid group plans, are now covered more and
more by conventional plans as well. And in the public sector, Medicare has been
expanded to cover the disabled, to defray most of the expenses of renal dialysis,
and to make access to extended care facilities easier. Congress will probably pass

more and more bills providing at least partial protection for various treatments whose costs might otherwise bankrupt the patient. Moreover, as HMOs spread and the self-employed and small employers find ways to group, fewer people are likely to have to rely solely on costly individual coverage.

If the trend toward broader coverage continues, while an estimated 95 percent of the population has some protection against the cost of medical care, it will be hard to justify using the term "crisis" in referring to the financial side of the health care delivery system. Of course, 5 percent of the population still has no coverage, and, given the experience elsewhere in the world, it is hard to see how this component can be reduced much more under the present voluntary system. But as coverage of the other 95 percent broadens and improves, medical care for the 5 percent without protection will be less of a burden on providers and should, therefore, be more readily available. This situation would not be ideal, but it would certainly be far from critical.

Although the thought that medical care will cause less personal financial hardship in the future is heartening, the prospect of broader coverage will still pose the problems of medical cost inflation, of distortions in the use and distribution of medical services, and, above all, of resource allocation both within the medical sector and between the medical sector and all other sectors. Broader coverage, combined with another trend mentioned elsewhere—the steady increase in noncontributory or "employer-pay-all" group plans—will tend to make consumers less concerned about these problems and, hence, less interested in reform. Pressure for reform will, thus, be left to such groups as the labor unions, who would prefer to remove health insurance from wage negotiations; employers, who would like some help in defraying health insurance costs; providers, who want to minimize interference in their activities; and insurance carriers, who want to avoid any regulations more stringent than now apply. With public interest diminished, the interested parties remaining are likely to work toward stalemate or a somewhat collusive form of mutual accommodation.

On the other hand, a sweeping, comprehensive revamping of the health care system, centered around a monolithic financing mechanism, seems premature at this time. Many of the changes proposed to establish such a system are distrusted by large numbers of consumers and providers. With so much opposition, attempts to introduce a new system would certainly lead to serious confrontations and, perhaps, to deterioration in the quality of health services. Broadened coverage, diminished pressure from the general public, and the crowded Congressional calendar, which seems certain to put off serious consideration of health insurance reform until at least 1975, may permit a period of experimentation with various approaches to health insurance reform. In this period the various participants in the system would have an opportunity to become more acquainted with the larger issues of universal health insurance coverage and their ramifications. Reform at this stage should therefore permit as much experimentation as possible while still achieving the maximum feasible universality in a context where consumers and providers have some way of understanding and expressing their preferences. In other words, what is called for in the immediate future is a pluralistic system that assures the consumer and provider of a certain number of distinct options, leaving the way open for further changes as the participants develop and refine their attitudes through experience with these options.

Private Sector—The Right of First Refusal

The private sector would, of course, play a major role in a reformed pluralistic system. The public sector could also participate, although its role should be minimal. The threat of a public sector takeover should give private carriers a strong incentive to accept needed changes in the rules under which they operate. They are aware that, unlike doctors, they can be replaced by the public sector as the underwriter. But the vast assets they control and the extensive experience they have acquired in the health field should not be lightly cast aside. They can spare the community much of the great burden of mobilizing resources for expansion and experimentation if in doing so they can also serve their own interests. And the two interests need not be incompatible; private carriers and Blue Plans, for example, are already showing a willingness to underwrite some of the initial costs of establishing HMOs. By encouraging the private carriers to expand their activities in this field, the federal government could avoid using its own revenues—as it now plans to do—for HMO start-up costs.

A centralized, monolithic health care financing system dominated by the public sector would not lend itself to experimentation and evolution. Government operations are difficult to change, especially if the change requires legislative action. Bureaucracies functioning without the clear guidelines of cost and profit tend to resist innovation and to become preoccupied by self-perpetuation. Moreover, taking over the health care financing system would burden the federal government with another heavy operating responsibility that would vastly increase the number of policy decisions forced upon the limited number of officials responsible to the electorate. Even now, for example, Congress finds it difficult to complete action on something as basic as appropriation bills in many cases until the fiscal year is well under way. This delay attests to the heavy workload of the legislative branch, which therefore seems unlikely to deal effectively with the additional problems of a vast and complicated health care financing system. Given, in addition, the difficulties of the public sector in perceiving and responding to the public's desires to shift resources into or out of the medical sector, placing the health care financing system entirely in the public sector should be a last resort measure, an approach to be tried only when all else has failed.

Private Sector Requirements in
a Pluralistic System

In the meantime, a reformed pluralistic system with enough leeway to permit experimentation and evolution, should certainly not follow the lines of such proposals as AMA's Medicredit and the proposals of the Health Insurance Association of America, which would in effect merely extend the present system by broadening coverage, and change little else.

The system that is needed would permit evolutionary development toward better quality health care, in quantities suited to popular tastes, and consistent with an appropriate division of resources between the medical sector and all other sectors according to people's desires. Such a system cannot be based on the meaningless meanderings of an unstructured, imperfect market where choices of coverage are infinite and little understood. An effective system must generate vigorous competition based on price and quality, as perceived by the consumer. It should be based on a number of changes in existing rules and adoption of new rules:

1. Participation must be compulsory, financed through such means as payroll deductions for all employed, check-offs for pensioners, surcharges on tuition payments for students, and so forth. Enrollment could be enforced, among other ways, through the Internal Revenue Service, which could assess a tax penalty against those who failed to participate, rather than offer a deduction from taxable income for participation as is now the case. Some form of Medicaid would continue for the unemployed.
2. Some degree of standardization is a *sine qua non*; definitions should be standardized, only a limited number of standard coverage combinations should be offered, and these should be comprehensive with no upward limit.
3. Each individual should have a choice of at least 2 coverage combinations and at least 2 carriers, to foster active competition.
4. Laws that prohibit grouping for insurance purposes should be amended so that employees of several small firms can obtain the benefits enjoyed by larger groups. Although standardization would substantially diminish the operating cost advantages that group policies now have over individual policies, group arrangements would still offer the advantages of easier premium collection and a broader choice of plans.
5. The so-called adverse risk selections should be distributed among the insurance carriers. If Medicare and Medicaid remain in operation—and there is no reason why they should not—the private sector would have only a small number of adverse risks to absorb and could probably accommodate them through regional pooling arrangements.
6. The consumer must have a financial stake in his choice of plans. Noncontributory plans now constitute over half the group arrangements, and while

labor unions and other employee groups are unlikely to give up a valuable and hard-won fringe benefit, perhaps this benefit could take the form of a nontaxable "health insurance voucher" that could be used to pay the employee's health insurance premium and would provide a refund if he chose a less costly plan or require him to pay the difference if he chose one more costly.

7. Regulation of the health care financing mechanism should be in the hands of a body with broader responsibilities and greater involvement in the health care delivery system than state insurance commissioners.

8. Community costs—such as those for training physicians and nurses, research, technological experiments, major construction and expansion of hospitals, and such welfare care as would remain—should be separated from general hospital and clinic costs and financed independently. The carriers themselves may eventually pick up some of these costs, if competitive pressures move the system toward a network of health care corporations or other institutional arrangements whereby the carriers find it more efficient actually to take over control or ownership of facilities. Initially, however, such costs can best be financed through tax on health insurance premiums or subscription rates, including the premiums or subscription rates of nonprofit organizations. An earmarked tax of this sort would help keep the health care sector intact and avoid the temptation to trade these vital activities off against activities outside the health care sector. A tax on health insurance payments would also keep the public aware of the total health care bill.

9. The system should support peer review and community planning by refusing to reimburse, within the compulsory health program, any entity not participating in these arrangements.

10. A system of payment through the use of coded credit cards and centralized collection agencies (as described earlier in this chapter) should be introduced to facilitate payment and obscure differences in the source of financial support as a way of minimizing discrimination.

These arrangements should stimulate lively competition among either a limited number of carriers or a larger number of carriers working in consortium alongside such community-oriented organizations as prepaid health group cooperatives. The system would provide consumers as well as providers with clear-cut choices. These circumstances would encourage the carriers to become more innovative in trying to cut the cost of services and in providing services that the public wants. The carriers would be free to experiment with methods of paying physicians, so that the system itself could determine the relative merits of capitation and fee-for-service payment.

On an experimental basis, the carriers might make contractual arrangements with groups of physicians that would give them financial incentives, like those provided by prepaid group practice plans, to seek the most economical ways of treating patients. Blue Shield, for example, already has arrangements with participating physicians and, with some modifications in its *modus operandi*, could offer its participating physicians bonuses as prepaid groups now do. Such an approach would not encourage physicians to economize on the services they themselves (the HMO case) provide, but it would encourage prudence in admitting patients for hospital care and in limiting the length of hospital stay. And since hospital costs are the heaviest of health care costs, the potential savings from such an arrangement could be substantial.

No health care financing system will be "perfect," and this system would be no exception. But it would at least permit close to universal coverage without the disadvantages of a monolithic system, leaving a residual small enough for providers to accommodate without great difficulty. It would give its participants the financial freedom to seek medical care initially and protect them from being bankrupted by the prolonged or expensive treatment that life-threatening or debilitating illness might require. Standardization would reduce operating costs as well as eliminating differences in health insurance coverage as a bottleneck to job mobility. The system would permit the consumer to express his preferences, including his preference for more or fewer medical services out of the total resources available.

The basic premise of this approach is that the greatest satisfaction for the greatest number can be achieved by providing the widest possible freedom of choice to consumers as well as providers, consistent with the objective of universal and adequate coverage and maximum efficiency. No doubt some patients would receive less care than others. But inequality is not unique to medical care; it also characterizes activities of equal or greater importance, and it is found in all societies to a greater or lesser extent. In general, medical care is not a necessity of life in the sense that food is a necessity of life. Some illnesses, or course, are fatal or may leave permanent injury if not treated, but they are relatively rare. Most of us would live reasonably long and pleasant lives with a fraction of the medical care we now receive. We seek it, however, as we seek other comforts and to rid ourselves of fears and doubts. The real justification for universal health insurance is not that medical services are so expensive but rather that illness is, to most of us, mysterious and unpredictable and that science has provided an effective but expensive array of treatments and diagnostic procedures of which we do not want to be deprived on the random chance that they will one day be required. We, as a community, have the right, if we so choose, to commit increasing amounts of our total resources to improving the quality of our lives through more and better health care. But to make a valid choice, we must know how much this activity is costing us, so that we may all judge whether it is worth the price of other goods and services foregone.

Appendixes

Appendix A: The Twentieth Century Fund Survey of 1,510 Physicians in Private Practice

Age:

    Under 35 _____

    Over 35 _____

Location of Practice:

    Rural _____

    Urban _____

    Suburban _____

Specialty _____

1. Are you generally familiar with the health coverage provided by the most prevalent group plans in your area of practice, (i.e., Blue Cross-Blue Shield, Employer-Union Plans, etc.)?

    Yes _____

    No _____

    Not aware of any group plans in your location _____

2. Do you make a special effort to keep abreast of changes in the most prevalent forms of health insurance coverage in your location?

    Yes _____

    No _____

    Not aware of any group plans in your location _____

3. As part of your initial work-up of a patient, do you attempt to find out what type of health insurance coverage your patient has (e.g., Major Medical, Medicare, Plan B, etc.)?

    Yes _____

    No _____

4. Do you find that few, about half, or most patients have a very specific understanding of their insurance coverage?

    Few _____

    About half _____

    Most _____

5. Do you think a doctor's decision as to the kind of treatment to provide a patient may be influenced by the type of insurance coverage the patient may have?

    A. Minor Illnesses: B. Major Illnesses:

        Rarely _____   Rarely _____

Frequently   _____   Frequently   _____
Never   _____   Never   _____

6. Can you recall cases in your own practice where the fact that the patient did *not* have insurance coverage was a factor (among others, of course) in deciding *not* to hospitalize a patient?

Yes   _____
No   _____

7. How often do patients request you to perform more expensive procedures or prescribe more varieties or more expensive types of drugs on the argument that "insurance will cover it"?

Frequently   _____
Infrequently   _____
Never   _____

8. How often do patients ask you to try to "stretch" the definition of services performed to assure eligibility for insurance coverage?

Frequently   _____
Infrequently   _____
Never   _____

9. According to a *Medical Economics* survey, a prominent patient complaint is that doctors' bills are often not itemized, causing either delay or loss of insurance coverage. Do you find that the need to meet insurance requirements in billing significantly detracts from time you could spend with patients?

Yes   _____
No   _____

10. Do you find that insured patients are more cooperative and generally easier to treat than noninsured patients with comparable ailments, or do you think there is no difference?

More cooperative   _____
Less cooperative   _____
No difference   _____

11. Do you find that insured patients generally show less concern about fees than uninsured patients, or do you find no consistent pattern one way or another?

Less concern   _____
More concern   _____
No difference   _____

12. Does the fact that an increasing part of medical costs is now paid by "third parties" (i.e., private insurance, Medicare, etc.) make it easier or more difficult for you to adjust your fees to keep up with rising costs, or doesn't it matter?

Easier   _____

More difficult   _____

No effect   _____

13. Which do you find most "difficult" to deal with in terms of simplicity of claims, information required, prompt payment of claims, etc.? (Please rank "most difficult" No. 1, etc.)

Blue plans   _____   Workmen's Compensation _____

Pvt. carriers   _____   Medicaid   _____

Medicare   _____

14. Is it your impression that few, many, or most doctors still take into account the patient's "ability to pay" in charging fees?

Few   _____

Many   _____

Most   _____

15. For those doctors who take into account the patient's "ability to pay" in setting fees, do you think it appropriate to consider the patient's insured status in determining his economic potential?

Yes   _____

No   _____

16. Do you find "Relative Value Scales" helpful in setting fees, or are they of little use?

Helpful   _____

Not very useful   _____

17. Do you think some form of fee fixing—not necessarily by government agencies (perhaps Blue Shield)—would be preferable to the present system, where the decision falls entirely on your shoulders?

Yes   _____

No   _____

Additional Comments. If you wish to add any comments regarding health insurance, private plans, Blue Cross-Blue Shield, Medicare, Workmen's Compensation, how any of these plans affect you or the practice of medicine or health care in general—anything you wish to add—please feel free to write such comment in long hand, pencil, or in any form, on the back of this page.

Appendix B: National Health Expenditures

The most widely accepted measure of the total cost of health care is "National Health Expenditures," as used by the Social Security Administration.[1] It consists of 2 broad categories of expenditures: health-related "Research and Construction" and "Health Services and Supplies." It measures total current expenditures (public and private) for medical care plus research and construction, and does not represent the contribution, or "value added," of the health sector to the gross national product, which is smaller by the amount of goods and services the health sector purchases from other sectors of the economy. However, given the labor-intensive nature of health care, the difference between total health expenditures and value added is much less than for most other sectors of the economy.

"National Health Expenditures" includes depreciation, or the cost of capital equipment used up by the health care sector during the year, as well as the value of any new construction. Therefore "National Health Expenditures" is not an appropriate figure to use to determine the completeness of health insurance coverage, since insurance would not be expected to cover depreciation charges and the cost of new construction.

A narrower concept of the cost of health care is "Personal Health Care Expenditures," which excludes expenditures for research and construction, the costs of prepayment and administration (that is, the cost of handling insurance), expenditures for certain public health activities and the expenditures for certain activities of private voluntary agencies. In this study the health care expenditures of interest are the civilian population expenditures that could conceivably be covered by health insurance (public and private) if coverage were complete. The expenditure figure for 1969 cited in Chapter 1 is therefore "*Civilian* personal Health Care Expenditures" ($53.5 million), which is "Personal Health Care Expenditures" minus personal health care expenditures of the Department of Defense. Another measure used by the Social Security Administration is "Consumer Expenditures for Personal Health Care," which is those personal health care expenditures solely attributable to the private sector, except private philanthropy. It excludes programs such as Medicare and Medicaid which are administered by the private sector but for which the financing is channeled through the public sector.

The relationship between these various measures of health care expenditures is shown in Appendix Table B-1.

Appendix Table B-2, showing the source of funds of National Health Expenditures, further clarifies the composition of the category of expenditures, "Health Services and Supplies." Particularly important because of their expanding role are public expenditures, which include all government health programs

Table B-1
National Health Expenditures, by Type of Expenditure, 1969

Type of Expenditure	Amount (Billions)
Total	63.8
Research and construction	4.9
Health Services and supplies	58.9
Expenses of prepayment	1.9
Government public health activities	1.3
Expenditures of private voluntary agencies	0.4
Personal health care expenditures	55.3
Department of Defense expenditures	1.8
Civilian personal health care expenditures	53.5
Civilian health care expenditures, public sector	17.0[a]
Private philanthropy	0.8
Consumer expenditures for personal health care	35.6
Health insurance benefits	14.0[a]
Direct payments	21.6

[a]Medical benefits under Workmen's Compensation are excluded from public sector expenditures and included with health insurance benefits under consumer expenditures for personal health care.

Note: Discrepancies in addition are due to rounding.

Source: Barbara S. Cooper and Mary McGee, "National Health Expenditures, Fiscal Years 1929-70 and Calendar Years 1929-69," *Research and Statistics Note*, No. 25–1970 (Washington: Social Security Administration, U.S. Department of Health, Education, and Welfare, December 14, 1970), Tables 1, 4, 8, 9.

such as Medicare, Medicaid, temporary disability insurance and Department of Defense and Veteran's Administrations expenditures, among others.

Table B-2

National Health Expenditures, by Purpose of Expenditure and Source of Funds, 1969

| | (Billions) | | |
| | | Source of Funds | |
Type of Expenditure	Total	Private	Public[a]
Total	$63.8	$40.0	$23.8
Research and medical facilities construction	4.9	2.3	2.6
Research	1.8	0.2	1.6
Construction	3.1	2.1	1.0
Health services and supplies	58.9	37.8	21.2
Hospital care	23.9	12.1	11.8
Physicians' services	12.5	9.5	3.0
Dentists' services	4.0	3.8	0.2
Other professional services	1.4	1.2	0.2
Drug and drug sundries	6.6	6.2	0.4
Eyeglasses and appliances	1.7	1.7	–
Nursing-home care	2.6	0.9	1.7
Expenses for insurance administration	1.9	1.6	0.3
Government public health activities	1.3	–	1.3
Other health activities	2.9	0.8	2.1

[a]In accordance with Social Security Administration procedure, medical benefits under Workmen's Compensation programs are treated in this table as public sector expenditures; in Table B-1 they are included with health insurance benefits under consumer expenditures for personal health care, since they are administered for private employers by private carriers.

Source: Barbara S. Cooper and Mary McGee, "National Health Expenditures, Fiscal Years 1929-70 and Calendar Years 1929-69," *Research and Statistics Note*, No. 25–1970 (Washington: Social Security Administration, U.S. Department of Health, Education, and Welfare, December 14, 1970), Table 6.

Appendix C: Various Methods of Estimating Net Enrollment in Hospital Insurance Plans

Statistics of enrollment in health insurance plans vary greatly, depending on source and concept.

One widely quoted survey is that conducted annually by the Health Insurance Association of America (HIAA). This survey covers member insurance companies of the HIAA plus some nonmembers—about 80 percent of all health insurance carriers. To data collected in this survey must be added enrollment in the various Blue Cross-Blue Shield Plans and in independent health care plans to arrive at total private sector enrollment.

The HIAA attempts to correct for duplication figures collected from private carriers. The HIAA can obtain with some (but not absolute) accuracy, the total gross number of persons insured by the health insurance carriers. An individual carrier cannot, of course, know how many of those insured by it are insured under more than one plan or more than one policy. Experts in the field of health statistics have therefore questioned whether the HIAA correction for duplication is adequate.[1]

That duplication of coverage occurs with some frequency is unquestioned. Some people wish to supplement insurance provided as a "fringe benefit" by their employers or to supplement Medicare or other coverage. More commonly, two or more members of the family may be provided health insurance by their respective employers under plans that automatically cover all dependents.

The HIAA estimated that 203.6 million gross enrollments in 1969 in the private sector under plans providing at least hospital coverage[2] actually represented only 175 million people of all ages. The 10 million Medicare enrollees who had no supplemental private insurance represented a net addition to the total insured.

Estimates of private hospital insurance coverage resulting from sample surveys of households rather than of the insurance companies have consistently resulted in net enrollment estimates significantly lower than those of the HIAA. U.S. Department of Health, Education, and Welfare (HEW) estimates are based on household surveys conducted by the U.S. Public Health Service in 1963, 1967, and 1968 and on Social Security Administration projections for 1969 that used the 1968 survey results as a base. The Health Information Foundation conducted a similar survey in 1963. The results of these surveys compared with those of the HIAA in the same years are shown in Appendix Table C-1. In November 1970 Gallup International of Princeton, New Jersey, conducted a sample survey of individuals specifically for this study and, again, the results indicated a lower percentage of the population with hospital insurance coverage than did the HIAA's 1969 survey. (The questionnaire and survey sample for the Gallup survey are shown at the end of this appendix.)

190

Table C-1
Estimates Resulting from Various Surveys of Net Enrollment in Public and Private Health Insurance Plans that Include Hospital Coverage, Selected Years

Source of Estimate and Year	Resident Civilian Population (Millions)	Total		Estimated Net Enrollees Private Plans (Millions)		Medicare (Millions)
		Millions[a]	Percent of Resident Civilian Population	Total	Under Age 65	
1963 Health Insurance Foundation						
HEW		126.1	67.0	126.1		
HIAA		144.6	76.8	144.6		
1967	195.7					
HEW		156.9	78.8	146.1	137.6	19.4
HIAA		173.2	86.9	162.9	153.8	
1968						
HEW		162.4	80.7	152.1	142.8	19.8
HIAA		179.1	89.0	169.5	159.3	
1969	199.7					
HEW		167.3	82.3	157.3	147.4	20.0
HIAA		184.4	90.7	175.2	164.4	
1970	202.0					
Gallup		157.6[b]	78.0[b]	b	b	b

[a]The Health Insurance Association of America (HIAA) and Health, Education, and Welfare (HEW) surveys cover insurance in private plans only. Total net coverage for the years 1967, 1968 and 1969 resulting from HEW and HIAA surveys has been estimated by adding estimated net enrollees in private plans under age 65 to Medicare enrollees for those years.

[b]Survey included Medicare enrollees.

Sources: Louis S. Reed and Willine Carr, "Private Health Insurance in the United States," *Social Security Bulletin*, January 1969; *Source Book of Health Insurance Data* (New York: Health Insurance Institute, 1970), p. 17; Marjorie Smith Mueller, "Private Health Insurance in 1969: A Review," *Social Security Bulletin*, February 1971, Tables 6 and 8, p. 9; Medicare—*Health Insurance Statistics*, HI-11, HI-17 and HI-24 (Washington: Social Security Administration, U.S. Department of Health, Education, and Welfare, January 31, 1969; April 15, 1970; February 19, 1971).

That there is wide agreement that the HIAA estimates are too high does not necessarily mean that the lower estimates are more accurate. The real net enrollment in hospital insurance plans is likely to be somewhere between Gallup's low estimate of 78 percent (1970) and HIAA's high estimate of 91 percent (1969), shown in Appendix Table C-1. (For purposes of this study, it has been assumed that total net enrollment in hospital insurance plans—private plans plus Medicare—is between 85 and 90 percent of the total population.) Insurance carriers cannot know the exact magnitude of duplication because there is no central registry of enrollment information. It is to be expected that a survey of carriers would result in some overestimation.

It is less obvious why numerous sample surveys of the public would result in underestimation. An important factor in underestimation seems to be that a not insignificant number of people with health insurance coverage are unaware that they are insured. In the Gallup survey those conceding that they were unsure whether or not they were covered by health insurance constituted only 2 percent of the population.[3] However, there is evidence that among the respondents indicating they were not covered by health insurance some actually were covered. For example, in attempting to find out whether the respondent was aware that his coverage was "group," "individual" or "government" (essentially Medicare and Medicaid) only 7 percent of those who claimed to be insured indicated "government," whereas HEW statistics indicate that approximately 26 million persons are covered by Medicare and Medicaid which represents 16.5 percent of the total number estimated to be insured as a result of the Gallup survey. Even by distributing those indicating coverage under more than one health insurance plan, and by allowing for the maximum sampling error, the result would be about 10 percent less than the known number eligible for Medicare benefits.[4] If this 10 percent apparent underestimation also holds true in the non-Medicare-Medicaid category—and there is no definitive way of proving or disproving such an assumption—then the correct total net enrollment level could be as high as the HIAA estimate.

How can it be that such a large number of Americans seem to be unaware that they are insured? And of what significance is it? The phenomenon seems to be more than a statistical discrepancy. Encountered in the course of this study, for example, were participants in the Federal Employees Health Benefit Program who were not certain whether or not they were insured, though health insurance is not automatically provided but requires some employee actions to enroll—that is, indication of a choice of one of the several plans, signing of a payroll deduction form. One can expect that in areas where workers are employed on a less permanent or on a seasonal basis—construction workers, for example—or where health insurance is automatically provided and employers pay the entire premium (noncontributory group plans), employees may not absorb all of the indoctrination data usually passed out by unions and employers and may not discover that health insurance is one of their fringe benefits until they acquire medical bills.

The "ignorance factor" is most likely a function of the way health insurance premiums are paid. About three fourths of the people insured outside of the Medicare system obtain their coverage through group arrangements and premiums are either paid entirely by the employer or are at least shared, and may be automatically deducted from wages. In either case, the employee does not participate directly in the payment of premiums and, hence, is less likely to be aware of the composition of his fringe benefits.

National Survey on Medical Insurance

The overall objective of the study conducted for The Twentieth Century Fund by Gallup International, was to measure current public knowledge of and attitudes toward medical insurance.

A total of 1668 interviews with civilian adults were conducted in late November, 1970. The following questions were asked:

1. Do you now have Blue Cross-Blue Shield or some form of insurance that covers medical costs, other than disability income or Workman's Compensation?
2. Is your insurance "group" insurance—that is, insurance with your place of employment—or is it your own individual policy with payments made to an agent—or is it government insurance, such as Medicare?
3. Looking at your own medical insurance coverage, does it cover in-hospital costs?
4. Looking at your own medical insurance coverage, does it cover surgical costs?
5. Looking at your own medical insurance coverage, does it cover most visits to the doctor?
6. Just your best guess, how much do you—or you and your employer together—pay in premiums for your medical insurance per month?
7. Almost every family has at one time or another filed an insurance claim for medical costs. What is the highest amount of medical expenses you have had in any one year since 1965 that you asked the insurance company (or your health plan) to pay?
8. Did you find that your insurance covered more, less, or about what you expected?
9. Do you think it is justifiable for a doctor to exaggerate the description of his treatment on insurance forms to make sure the patient gets paid by the insurance company?
10. Suppose you discovered that your doctor increased or "padded" his fees because he knew his fees were covered by your medical insurance. Would you, yourself, raise an objection to this practice, or not?

11. Here is a list of items that have gone up in price in the last 5 years. From what you have heard or read, which of these do you think has had the highest rate of increase in price over the last five years—food, rent, medical insurance, clothing or cars?

The national adult civilian population, 21 years of age and older, excluding the institutional population, was estimates as of September, 1970, at 119,600,000.

Composition of the Sample
(Gallup Survey)

	Number of Interviews
National	1,668
Men	815
Women	853
Total insured	1,324
Total uninsured	323
Total group	980
Total nongroup	252
Male insured	648
Male uninsured	159
Female insured	676
Female uninsured	164
Male—group	490
Male—nongroup	117
Female—group	490
Female—nongroup	135
Total—hospital coverage only	36
Total—hospital and surgical	691
Total—comprehensive	519
Male—hospital coverage only	17
Male—hospital and surgical	313
Male—comprehensive	293
Female—hospital coverage only	19
Female—hospital and surgical	378
Female—comprehensive	226

Appendix D: Health Insurance Carrier Financial Data

Table D-1

Ratios of Operating Expenses to Written Premiums for Group Policies. 9 Largest Private Carriers and Combined Blue Plans,[a] 1967-1969

Carrier	1967	1968	1969
Aetna	10.1	10.0	9.7
Connecticut General	11.0	11.3	11.6
John Hancock	11.7	11.2	10.6
Continental Casualty	25.0	24.0	24.7
Equitable Life Assurance	10.4	10.3	10.6
Metropolitan	7.8	8.4	9.0
Mutual of Omaha	8.4	9.0	8.8
Prudential	11.0	10.6	9.6
Travelers	9.0	8.6	8.8
Blue Cross			
Blue Shield	6.8	7.2	7.4

[a]Covers all policies for Blue plans, which do not keep financial records on a group, nongroup basis.

Sources: *Argus Chart of Health Insurance, 1970* (Cincinnati: The National Underwriter Co., 1970); and *Blue Cross and Blue Shield Fact Book, 1970* (Chicago: Blue Cross Association and National Blue Shield Plans, 1970).

Table D-2

Comparison of Life and Health Insurance Reserve Growth, 7 Major Life Carriers, 1965-1969[a]

	Health Reserves		Life Reserves		Life and Health Reserves Combined	Health Reserves as Percent of Life and Health Reserves
Year	Amount (Millions)	Index (1965=100)	Amount (Millions)	Index (1965=100)		
1965	$1,048.0	100.0	$63,178.0	100.0	$64,226.0	1.6
1966	1,199.8	114.5	65,984.3	104.6	67,184.1	1.8
1967	1,374.0	131.1	69,081.3	109.5	70,455.3	2.0
1968	1,618.2	154.4	71,690.8	113.7	73,309.0	2.2
1969	1,867.9	178.2	74,186.9	117.6	76,054.7	2.5

[a]Carriers include Aetna, Connecticut General, Equitable Life Assurance, John Hancock, Prudential, Travelers and Metropolitan.

Source: *Argus Chart of Health Insurance* (Cincinnati: The National Underwriter Co., 1963-1970); "Health Insurance Statistical Review," *The Spectator*, various years; unpublished annual insurance reports to the Washington, D.C., Commissioner for Insurance.

Table D-3

Calculation of Projected Growth in Life and Health Insurance Reserves, 7 Major Life Carriers, 1980[a]

Line No.	Steps in Projecting Reserves, 1980		Amounts in Billions
	Life		
1.	Life premiums, all carriers, 1969		$24.3
2.	Life premiums, 7 carriers, 1969		8.3
3.	Life premiums, 7 carriers as percent of all carriers (Line 2 ÷ Line 1)	34.3	
4.	Life reserves, 7 carriers, 1969		74.2
5.	Ratio of life reserves to premiums, 7 carriers, 1969 (Line 4:Line 2)	8.9:1.0	
6.	Projected life premiums, all carriers, 1980		59.7
7.	Projected life reserves, 7 carriers, 1980 (Line 6 × Line 3 × 8.9 [Line 5])		182.2
	Health		
8.	Health premiums (including income loss[a]), all carriers, 1969		17.3
9.	Health premiums, 7 carriers, 1969		4.4
10.	Health premiums, 7 carriers, as percent of all carriers (Line 9 ÷ Line 8)	25.4	
11.	Health reserves, 7 carriers, 1969		1.9
12.	Ratio of health reserve to premiums, 7 carriers, 1969 (Line 11:Line 9)	0.42:1.0	
13.	Projected health premiums (including income loss[a]), all carriers, 1980		100.0
14.	Projected health reserves, 7 carriers, 1980 (Line 13 × Line 10 × 0.42 [Line 12])		10.7
	Life and Health Combined		
15.	Total life and health reserves, 7 carriers, 1980 (Line 7 + Line 14)		192.9
16.	Health reserves as percent of total life and health reserves, 7 carriers, 1980 (Line 14 ÷ 15)	5.5	

[a]Carriers include Aetna, Connecticut General, Equitable Life Assurance, John Hancock, Prudential, Travelers and Metropolitan.

Source: Unpublished annual insurance reports to the Washington, D.C., Commissioner for Insurance.

Appendix E: Aggregate National Health Expenditures, by Type of Expenditure, Selected Calendar Years, 1929-72

198

Table E-1

Aggregate National Health Expenditures, by Type of Expenditure, Selected Calendar Years, 1929-72

(In Millions) Type of Expenditure	1929	1935	1940	1950	1955
Total	$3,649	$2,936	$3,987	$12,662	$17,745
Health Services and supplies	3,436	2,875	3,868	11,702	16,884
Hospital care	663	763	1,011	3,851	5,900
Physicians' services	1,004	773	973	2,747	3,689
Dentists' services	482	302	419	961	1,508
Other professional services	252	153	174	396	562
Drugs and drug sundries[a]	606	475	637	1,726	2,384
Eyeglasses and appliances	133	133	189	491	604
Nursing-home care	–	–	33	187	312
Expenses for prepayment and administration	110	95	167	316	624
Government public health activities	96	117	153	361	377
Other health services	91	64	112	666	924
Research and medical facilities construction	213	61	119	960	861
Research[a]	–	–	3	117	210
Construction	213	61	116	843	651

[a]Research expenditures of drug companies included in expenditures for drugs and drug sundries and excluded from research expenditures.

Source: *Research and Statistics Note*, DHEW Pub. No. (SSA) 74-11701, Note No. 3–1974 (Washington: U.S. Department of Health, Education, and Welfare, February 6, 1974).

1960	1965	1966	1967	1968	1969	1970	1971	1972
$26,895	$40,468	$44,974	$50,696	$56,588	$64,139	$71,619	$79,658	$89,516
25,185	37,087	41,440	46,987	52,533	59,348	66,405	73,864	83,173
9,092	13,605	15,583	18,145	20,926	24,089	27,528	30,850	34,215
5,684	8,745	9,156	10,287	11,099	12,654	14,294	15,822	17,325
1,977	2,808	2,964	3,360	3,623	4,047	4,419	4,860	5,200
862	1,038	1,123	1,158	1,271	1,313	1,466	1,557	1,615
3,657	4,850	5,309	5,652	6,165	6,812	7,405	7,800	8,475
776	1,230	1,413	1,609	1,731	1,765	1,865	1,984	2,065
526	1,328	1,526	1,858	2,280	2,650	3,070	3,355	3,610
861	1,293	1,681	1,877	2,007	2,109	2,098	2,647	3,680
414	698	885	942	1,098	1,316	1,568	1,986	2,542
1,336	1,492	1,800	2,099	2,333	2,593	2,691	3,003	4,426
1,710	3,381	3,534	3,709	4,055	4,791	5,214	5,794	6,343
662	1,469	1,574	1,703	1,795	1,818	1,848	1,949	2,163
1,048	1,912	1,960	2,006	2,260	2,973	3,366	3,845	4,180

Notes

Notes

Chapter 1
Why Health Insurance Reform

1. For instance, The Capper Bill, 1933, was introduced by Senator Arthur Capper of Kansas; the so-called "National Health Bill of 1939," introduced by Senator Robert Wagner of New York; the two Wagner-Murray-Dingell bills of 1943 and 1945; and several bills similar to the Wagner-Murray-Dingell Bill that were introduced during the Truman administration from 1945 to 1950.

2. James G. Burrow, *AMA: The Voice of Medicine* (Baltimore: Johns Hopkins Press, 1963).

3. See, for example, the following articles from *The Washington Post*: Eve Edstrom, "Meany Strongly Endorses National Health Insurance," September 25, 1970; Stuart Auerbach, "HEW Doctor Praises Proposal for U.S. Health Insurance Plan," September 17, 1970; and "Major Health Reforms Backed in Business Polls," June 8, 1971.

4. Anne R. Somers, *Health Care in Transition: Directions for the Future* (Chicago: Hospital Research and Educational Trust, 1971), p. 128.

5. Consumer Price Index of the Bureau of Labor Statistics. *Statistical Abstract of the United States 1970*, 91st ed. (Washington, D.C., 1970) Tables 79 and 523.

6. *Statistical Abstract of the United States, 1971* (Washington: Bureau of the Census, U.S. Department of Commerce, 1971), pp. 62 and 339.

7. The 1971 Argus Chart of Health Insurance (Cincinnati: The National Underwriter Company, 1971).

8. "Health Insurance Plans other than Blue Cross-Blue Shield or Insurance Companies," U.S. Department of Health, Education, and Welfare, Office of Research and Statistics, Research Reports # 35, 1970 Survey (Washington, 1971), p. 11.

9. Ibid.

10. Ibid.

11. *Research and Statistics Note* # 25, December 14, 1970, U.S. Department of Health, Education, and Welfare, Social Security Administration, Office of Research and Statistics.

12. "Main Features of Selected National Health Care Systems," Note No. 9 (U.S. Department of Health, Education, and Welfare, Office of Research and Statistics, May 18, 1973).

13. Estimates of net enrollment in health insurance plans vary widely. The Health Insurance Association of America (HIAA), on the basis of surveys of insurance companies, estimated enrollment at 184 million for 1969. The U.S. Department of Health, Education, and Welfare (HEW) gave an estimate of 167

million for the same year, based on projections of earlier U.S. Public Health Service surveys of households. The Gallup survey conducted for this study indicated that the HIAA estimates may be more accurate than those of the HEW. (See Appendix C for further discussion of these estimates and for a description of the Gallup Poll.)

14. *Health Resources Statistics*, Public Health Service Publication No. 1509, 1970 ed. (Washington: Public Health Service, U.S. Department of Health, Education, and Welfare, February 1971). Excluded from the HEW health manpower statistics are persons engaged in health insurance operations; the manufacture, sale and distribution of pharmaceuticals and medical equipment; and health-related activities such as construction of hospitals and other medical facilities.

15. Payments to hospitals and doctors accounted for 57 percent (37.5 percent to hospitals and 19.5 percent to doctors) of all health care expenditures in 1969 but 94 percent (55 percent to hospitals and 39 percent to doctors) of all health insurance benefit payments including those paid under the Medicare program. (See Marjorie Smith Mueller, "Private Health Insurance in 1969: A review," *Social Security Bulletin*, February 1971; and Barbara S. Cooper and Mary F. McGee, "National Health Expenditures, Fiscal Years 1929-70 and Calendar Years 1929-69," *Research and Statistics* note (Washington, Social Security Administration, HEW, December 14, 1970.)

16. William A. Glaser, *Paying the Doctor: Systems of Remuneration and their Effects* (Baltimore: Johns Hopkins Press, 1970), pp. 15, 16.

17. Joseph Simanis, "Health Insurance in West Germany and Great Britain," *Social Security Bulletin*, October 1970, pp. 39ff.

18. Glaser, *Paying the Doctor*, pp. 14, 15 and 226.

Chapter 2
Health Insurance Coverage and the
Demand for Medical Services

1. See various studies conducted during the 1960s such as Ronald Andersen and Odin W. Anderson, *A Decade of Health Services* (Chicago: University of Chicago Press, 1967), Chapter 2.

2. William A. Glaser, *Paying the Doctor: Systems of Remuneration and Their Effects* (Baltimore: Johns Hopkins Press, 1970), p. 195.

3. A premium rate adequate to pay claims is important to the insured as well as the insurer for "there is nothing more useless than a bankrupt insurance company." See Duncan M. MacIntyre, *Voluntary Health Insurance and Rate Making* (Ithaca: Cornell University Press, 1962) p. 26.

4. Very few policies today provide hospital coverage alone; only 7 or 8 percent of health insurance enrollees have such limited coverage.

5. 447 S.W. 2nd 453, Court of Civil Appeals, October 16, 1969. A rehearing was denied on November 6, 1969.

6. With the passage of HR 1 in October 1973 (92nd Congress, 2nd Session), renal dialysis is now extended to most people—over or under 65—through Medicare. See Chapter 5.

7. *Phillips v. Prudential Insurance Co.*, Alabama Supreme Court, 1 Div., 564 (April 2, 1970); appeal from Mobile Circuit Court, Affirmed, 8 CCH Life Cases (2d) 930. The insured received $2,400 for medical, surgical, and hospital benefits under the Alabama Workmen's Compensation laws, but the court ruled that Prudential was not obliged to pay any part of an additional out-of-pocket expense of $2,244.

8. The dollar maximums applied to a surgical procedure do not necessarily conform to the fee schedule of the surgeon performing the service, but many insured individuals assume that the amounts shown in their insurance schedule represent a "fair" rate. Patient-doctor relationships sometimes become strained over such misinterpretations. (See Chapter 7.)

9. Marjorie Smith Mueller, *The Benefit Structure of Private Health Insurance, 1968* (Washington: Social Security Administration, U.S. Department of Health, Education, and Welfare, 1969), p. 69.

10. Medical inflation is, however, making $50,000 claims more common. William E. Ryan, Senior Vice President of the National Association of Blue Shield Plans, has noted that in recent years the Blue Cross-Blue Shield Government-wide Service Benefit Plan has made benefit payments in excess of $50,000 to more than one thousand subscribers. (*The Blue Shield*, December 1971, p. 1.) Mr. Ryan referred to this fact in explaining the 1972 Blue Cross-Blue Shield rate increase under the federal employee program.

11. As used in this study, the term *copayment* refers to all mechanisms that require the insured to share in the costs of covered services (fixed maximums on dollar amounts and on specific services, deductibles and coinsurance provisions). The term is sometimes used more specifically to refer to a flat fee the insured is required to pay per day or per treatment.

12. Charles P. Hall, "Deductibles In Health Insurance: An Evaluation," *Journal of Risk and Insurance*, June 1966, p. 262.

13. Charles T. Heaney and Donald C. Riedel, "From Indemnity to Full Coverage: Changes in Hospital Utilization," *Blue Cross Reports*, Research Series 5 (Chicago: Blue Cross Association, October 1970), p. 11.

14. "Survey on Deductibles, Coinsurance, and Copayments," internal circular letter of the Blue Cross Association (Chicago: September 28, 1971).

15. In addition to Andersen and Anderson, op. cit., see for example, Burton A. Wersbrod and R.J. Fresler, "Hospitalization Insurance and Utilization," *American Economic Review*, March 1961.

16. See Appendix A for questionnaire used in the survey.

17. The number of claims—that is, pieces of paper submitted to the carrier for

processing—may be far more than 2 or 3. The administrative cost of handling a claim ranges from $2 to $5. An insured can submit each bill separately once his deductible amount has been reached; thus, in the Aetna case, the reimburseable claims of the 2 family members whose expenses reached the deductible level could have been submitted in as many as 21 segments. (See Chapter 3.)

18. Andersen and Anderson, op. cit., p. 57, estimate that approximately two thirds of all families spent less than $600 annually for medical care in 1963.

19. "First-dollar" coverage requires the insurer to pay for all covered expenses up to an agreed ceiling; the insured does not have to pay a deductible in order to qualify for benefits.

20. Of course, under a compulsory, universal system, those financially unable to pay for medical care would require total coverage including low-risk coverage in order to have equitable, nondiscriminatory access to medical services. Some believe that if the system is to provide such coverage for the medically indigent, it must provide low-risk coverage for all insured. The implications of low-risk coverage under such a system are discussed in the concluding chapter.

21. These figures are based on a confidential survey of major insurance carriers undertaken for this study. The actual premium would, of course, be affected by the maximum limits, exclusions, copayments and other provisions.

22. Robert Eilers and Sue S. Meyerman, *NHI Conference Proceedings Sponsored by the Leonard Davis Institute for Health Economics* (Philadelphia: Richard D. Irwin, Inc.) July 1971. This point is also made in "Major Medical Is Also Important to Your Client," *The Health Insurance Underwriter*, January 1971.

23. *Timesaver*, 1970, pp. 123-24.

24. See Lester Petermann, "Fringe Benefits for Urban Workers," *Monthly Labor Review*, November 1971, p. 43; and Walter W. Kolodrubetz, "Trends in Employees' Benefit Plans in the Sixties," *Social Security Bulletin*, April 1971.

25. Consumer Price Index of the Bureau of Labor Statistics, *Statistical Abstracts 1970*, Tables 79 and 523.

26. Andersen and Anderson, op. cit., Table 34.

27. *Argus Chart of Health Insurance, 1970* (Cincinatti: National Underwriter Co., 1970), p. 112.

28. *Timesaver*, 1970, p. 259; and field interviews conducted in connection with this study.

Chapter 3
The Health Insurance Bureaucracy:
The Blue Plans and the Private Carriers

1. *Best's Review*, July 1971, p. 5.
2. The corporations examined include a business machine corporation, a

banking establishment with international affiliation, 2 utility companies, a nationwide retail chain establishment, a tire and rubber manufacturer, and an automobile manufacturer.

3. Marjorie Smith Mueller, "Private Health Insurance in 1969: A Review," *Social Security Bulletin*, February 1971.

4. Rate-making in health insurance is a complex and detailed subject beyond the scope of this book. For an excellent discussion of health insurance rate making in theory and practice among both the Blues and the Private carriers, see Duncan M. MacIntyre, *Voluntary Health Insurance and Rate Making* (Ithaca, N.Y.: Cornell University Press, 1962). This section draws heavily on MacIntyre's work.

5. According to the *Blue Cross and Blue Shield Fact Book of 1972* (Chicago: Blue Cross Association and National Association of Blue Shield Plans, 1970), p. 2, 48 percent of Blue Cross Plan board members represent the general public, 38 percent have hospital affiliation, and 14 percent are identified with the medical profession. The composition of the boards has thus changed substantially since 1959 when only 32 percent of all Blue Cross board members represented the general public, 51 percent were hospital affiliated, and 17 percent represented the medical profession.

6. See, for example, letter from the Travelers Insurance Co. to Senator Philip A. Hart, *High Cost of Hospitalization, Part II: Hearings on S. Res. 334*, January 26-28, 1971, p. 261. Recently the Travelers Insurance Company of Pittsburgh filed an antitrust suit against the local Blue Cross plan, alleging that the plan was engaging "in unreasonable restraint of competition and monopolistic practices in the business of providing hospitalization coverage" by reimbursing hospitals on the basis of a negotiated cost formula. In this case, in which the court denied Traveler's claim, Blue Cross indicated that the reimbursement discount averaged 4.4 percent and that hospital expenses not covered by Blue Cross under the agreement were made up from other sources. See *Travelers Insurance Corporation v. Blue Cross of Western Pennsylvania*, District Court for the Western District of Pennsylvania, January 6, 1972.

7. *High Cost of Hospitalization Part II: Hearings on S. Res. 334*, January 28, 1971, p. 220.

8. *U.S. v. South-Eastern Underwriters Assn.*, 322 U.S. 533 (1944).

9. See, for example, a statement by E. Paul Barnhart, a consulting actuary, in *The National Underwriter*, March 13, 1971, p. 1, criticizing the federal government for having failed to provide, among other things, "better community and regional planning for utilization of health care resources; more effective development of cost and utilization control techniques . . . Instead, government has concentrated its attention primarily on benefits . . ."

10. *1969 Loss and Expense Ratios, Insurance Expense Exhibits* (Albany: New York State Insurance Department, December 31, 1969) Table 7, p. 54. "Taxes and fees" include premium taxes, payroll taxes, licensing fees, expenses

of Insurance Department examinations and related expenses. Excludes federal income taxes, which are not considered part of operating expenses under National Association of Insurance Commissioners accounting rules. For the stock and mutual companies who pay them, federal income taxes in recent years have ranged from 0.5 to 1.5 percent of premiums annually.

11. All cost figures quoted are net of federal income tax. The cost of handling an individual claim is extremely difficult to determine because it requires calculating, for example, what proportions of overhead (building costs and salaries of top management) and of the expenses of the complaints, legal, and customer services departments support the claims paying function. Moreover, some companies consider each individual bill related to an illness as one claim, whereas others consider one illness, regardless of how many individual bills it generates, as one claim.

Chapter 4
Profits, Reserves, and Motivations
in Health Insurance

1. *Q & A on Health Security* (Washington: American Federation of Labor and Congress of Industrial Organizations, 1971) p. 5.

2. "Kennedy Says Nixon Plan Falls Short on Health Care," *The Washington Post*, February 23, 1971.

3. "Interview with Lorne R. Worthington," *The Spectator*, November 1970, p. 13; and "Regulators Again Eye Need for Guidelines on Adjusted Earnings," *National Underwriter*, January 23, 1971.

4. The 1957 composite measure is described in "Parts 10I and 10E Study Notes, the United States Federal Income Tax As It Applies to Life Insurance Companies" (Chicago: Society of Actuaries, February 1971), p. 16. It would distract from this study to examine in detail the reasons for the differences between calculation of insurance profits and of profits of banks and other businesses to which the general internal revenue code provisions apply. Those who wish to pursue the subject will find an excellent discussion of it in *Measurement of Profitability and Treatment of Investment Income in Property and Liability Insurance* (Milwaukee: National Association of Insurance Commissioners, June 1970).

5. It is widely believed that many mutual companies keep their premium rates high enough to generate policyholder dividends. Mutual companies receive a minor tax benefit from distributing dividends to policyholders. Under the Life Insurance Tax Code, mutual carriers may deduct up to $250,000 of dividends to policyholders in determining "gains from operations." Health insurance policyholders' dividends of mutual companies generally amount to 3 or 4 percent of earned premiums.

6. For the private carriers as a whole, income loss premiums were $2.9 billion in 1969, and health insurance premiums were $7.3 billion. Data based on annual industry-wide surveys published by the U.S. Department of Health, Education, and Welfare in various publications and by the Health Insurance Institute (New York) in its annual *Source Book of Health Insurance Data* show health insurance and income loss data separately on an aggregate basis but not for individual firms.

7. Field survey of major carriers conducted by the staff of this study.

8. Reports to state insurance commissioners and *Argus Chart of Health Insurance, 1970* (Cincinnati: National Underwriter Co., 1970). A breakdown of assets by insurance line is not required in the annual report to state insurance commissioners and is consequently unavailable for analysis.

9. The problem of calculating rate of return in insurance operations is discussed in *Measurement of Profitability and Treatment of Investment Income in Property and Liability Insurance* (Milwaukee: National Association of Insurance Commissioners, June 1970).

10. See, for example, *Measurement of Profitability and Treatment of Investment Income in Property and Liability Insurance*, pp. 758-83. The Blue plans, in their joint annual *Blue Cross and Blue Shield Fact Book* (Chicago: Blue Cross Association and National Association of Blue Shield Plans), present the operating results of the Blue plans in terms of "net income," which includes investment income among income sources.

11. Data regarding previous years' claims paid—the basis of the lag calculation—were reported differently in annual reports to insurance commissioners prior to 1967 than since that time. Comparisons for years prior to 1967 were, therefore, not possible.

12. *Source Book of Health Insurance Data* (New York: Health Insurance Institute, 1970), p. 40.

13. Ibid., pp. 4-22.

14. Parts 10I and 10E Study Notes, Society of Actuaries.

15. *Blue Cross and Blue Shield Fact Book, 1970*. For example, the combined Blue Cross-Blue Shield reserves of all kinds—unpaid claims and unearned subscription income as well as other reserves listed in the annual *Blue Cross and Blue Shield Fact Book*—remained at about 85 percent of assets for most years during the 1960s.

16. *Argus Chart of Health Insurance, 1970*. Operating cost data are available for group plans only. They do not include stockholders' or policyholders' dividends.

17. *Argus Chart of Health Insurance, 1970*; estimate for the Blue plans provided by Blue Cross Association, Chicago.

18. James A. Genry and Charles M. Linke, "The Life Insurance Company—Mutual Fund Combination Movement: An Overview," *Best's Review*, July 1970, p. 12. The reserves of life companies are considered assets of the public

("households") in the national account maintained by the U.S. Department of Commerce, because such reserves are held largely as backing for life insurance policies, which are eventually repayable to the public.

19. See, for example, Chandler Currier Jordan, *Insurance Holding Companies and Other Fiscal Fauna* (a monograph published by the *Insurance Advocate*, New York: 1968).

20. *Blue Cross and Blue Shield Fact Book, 1970; Mutual of Omaha Annual Report: Financial Statement as of December 31, 1970* (Omaha: January 1971); and *Travelers 1970 Annual Report* (Hartford: February 1971).

Chapter 5
The Public Sector and Health Insurance

1. U.S., Congress, Senate, Committee on Government Operations, Subcommittee on Executive Reorgnization and Government Research, *Health Activities*: Federal Expenditures and Public Purpose, 91st Cong., 2nd sess., 1970, Table 2, p. 11.

2. This is a simplified summary of the eligibility requirements under Medicare Part A. For a detailed description of the requirements see U.S., Congress, House, Committee on Ways and Means, *1970 Annual Report of the Board of Trustees of the Federal Hospital Insurance Trust Fund*, 91st Cong., 2nd sess., 1970, p. 31.

In 1972, with the passage of H.R. 1, the Medicare legislation was amended to make eligible for both Parts A and B those persons or families qualifying for income payments related to disability under the Social Security program as well as (on a more limited basis) those who require hemodialysis or renal transplantation for chronic renal disease. The new legislation also permits persons reaching age 65 who were previously ineligible for hospital insurance (Part A) to enroll on a voluntary basis, although such persons are required to also enroll for Part B and to pay the full cost of the Part A premium of $33 a month. As a result of this later change, everyone 65 or over with access to funds—either their own or institutional—can now qualify for Medicare benefits. In addition, those covered by Part B are now given the option of having their covered health care provided through "a Health Maintenance Organization," which is essentially a loosely organized prepaid group practice system. (See Chapters 8 and 9.)

3. "Material Related to H.R. 1," Senate Finance Committee, 92nd Congress, 1st sess., July 16, 1971, p. 12.

4. U.S., Congress, House, Committee on Ways and Means, *1971 Annual Report of the Board of Trustees of the Federal Supplementary Medical Insurance Trust Fund*, 92nd Cong., 1st sess., 1971, pp. 1-2.

5. Barbara S. Cooper and Mary F. McGee, "National Health Expenditures,

Fiscal Year 1929-70 and Calendar Years 1929-69," *Research and Statistics Note*, No. 25 (Washington: Social Security Administration, U.S. Department of Health, Education, and Welfare, December 14, 1970).

6. U.S., Congress, House, Committee on Ways and Means, *1970 Annual Report of the Board of Trustees of the Federal Supplementary Medical Insurance Trust Fund*, 91st Cong., 2nd sess., 1970, p. 11.

7. Under H.R. 1, beneficiaries will be "held harmless" in situations such as those in which claims are disallowed but the beneficiary is without fault. In such cases, liability will be shifted to Medicare or to the provider where it is found that he has acted without due care. The new legislation permits exceptions to the regulation that a patient's transfer to an ECF take place within 14 days of his discharge from a hospital, for patients whose condition would not permit provision of the skilled services of the ECF within 14 days or where ECFs are not available.

8. Ralph M. Thurlow, "Medicare Is Double-Crossing Our M.E.C.F. Patients," *Medical Economics*, October 26, 1970, pp. 19-39.

9. The 1972 amendments to the Medicare legislation (H.R. 1) introduce several additional cost control techniques, including the establishment of Professional Standards Review Organizations consisting of a substantial number of practicing physicians in a local area (usually 300 or more) to assure that the institutional care covered by Medicare is medically necessary and "provided in accordance with professional standards"; the limitation of payment under federal programs (including Medicare) of capital expenditures for plant and equipment (including depreciation, interest and return on equity) that are determined to be inconsistent with State or local health facility plans; the requirement that each institutional provider of services have a written plan reflecting an operating budget and a capital expense budget; the experimentation with various methods of making payment to providers on a prospective basis and with methods of payment designed to increase efficiency and economy in the provision of services; the establishment of new regulations covering fee increases of physicians and other health providers. This brief summary obviously cannot do justice to the potential importance and far reaching consequences of some of these cost control techniques. The interested reader is referred to the legislation.

10. See Gretchen Y. Wolfe, "Medical Insurance Sample—January-December 1969," *Current Medicare Survey Report* (Washington: U.S. Department of Health, Education, and Welfare, July 12, 1971), p. 7.

11. Wolfe, "Medical Insurance Sample," p. 7. Of those enrolled in Part B, in 1969, only 49 percent had covered medical expenses greater than the deductible (and hence received any reimbursements from the supplemental insurance); 30 percent used covered services but did not meet the deductible, and 21 percent did not use the covered services.

12. Ibid.

13. Louis S. Reed, assisted by Maureen Dwyer, *Private Health Insurance*

Organizations as Intermediaries or Fiscal Agents Under Government Health Programs, Staff Paper No. 7 (Washington: Social Security Administration, U.S. Department of Health, Education, and Welfare, January 1971).

14. In fiscal year 1969-70, according to information received from the Office of Management and Budget, the Treasury Department was reimbursed $6.2 million out of the Hospital Insurance Trust Fund and $26,000 out of the Supplementary Medical Insurance Trust Fund for these functions—less than 0.1 percent of all Medicare income.

15. "Health Insurance: Can the Government Do It Cheaper?" John Krizay, *Best's Review*, January 1973, p. 14.

16. *Recommendations of the Task Force on Medicaid and Related Programs* (Washington: Office of the Secretary, U.S. Department of Health, Education, and Welfare, June 1970), p. 3.

17. *Fourteenth Annual Report, Civilian Health and Medical Program of the Uniformed Services of the United States, Canada, Mexico and Puerto Rico*, calendar year 1970, prepared by the staff, Office for the Civilian Health and Medical Program of the Uniformed Services.

18. Data in this section are from: Alfred M. Skolnik and Daniel N. Price, "Another Look at Workmen's Compensation," *Social Security Bulletin*, October 1970, pp. 3-25; and *Insurance Arrangements Under Workmen's Compensation*, Bulletin No. 317 (Washington: Wage and Labor Standards Administration, U.S. Department of Labor, 1969).

19. A provision of H.R. 1 would permit prepaid groups to apply the difference between their actual cost of care and 95 percent of the cost of care under conventional health care systems toward increasing Medicare benefits beyond those prescribed by law.

Chapter 6
Health Insurance and the Hospital

1. *Social Security Bulletin*, March 1971.

2. See Ronald Andersen and Odin W. Anderson, *A Decade of Health Services* (Chicago: University of Chicago Press, 1967), Chapter 2; and discussion and studies cited in Chapters 7 and 8 of this book.

3. Corroborative evidence of this point of view is presented by Dr. Martin S. Feldstein in "Hospital Cost Inflation: A Study of Nonprofit Price Dynamics," *American Economic Review*, December 1971, p. 853.

4. Barbara S. Cooper and Mary F. McGee, "National Health Expenditures, Fiscal Years 1929-70, Calendar Years 1929-69," *Research and Statistics Note*, No. 25 (Washington: Social Security Administration, U.S. Department of Health, Education, and Welfare, December 14, 1970), Tables 8 and 9.

5. See Herman Somers and Anne R. Somers, *Medicare and the Hospitals:*

Issues and Prospects (Washington: The Brookings Institution, September 1967); *Reimbursement Incentives for Hospitals and Medical Care, Objectives and Alternatives* (Washington: Social Security Administration, U.S. Department of Health, Education, and Welfare, 1968); and *Principles of Payment for Hospital Care* (Chicago: American Hospital Association, 1962).

6. About two-thirds of the Blue Cross plans reimburse hospitals on the basis of cost formulas agreed to in negotiations with the hospitals. State Medicaid plans are required to use Medicare cost formulas.

7. *Statistical Abstract of the United States 1970* 91st ed. (Washington, D.C., 1970) Tables 79 and 523.

8. U.S., Congress, Senate, Committee on the Judiciary, *High Cost of Hospitalization, Part I: Hearings on S. Res. 334*, 91st Cong., 1st sess., February, April, and May 1970, pp. 93, 94.

9. The effort of Blue Cross to place a ceiling on reimbursement costs of all Washington, D.C. area hospitals illustrates the limitations on Blue Cross's ability to influence hospital costs. The formula the local Blue Cross attempted to apply would have limited reimbursable costs to the average increase in costs of all the hospitals in the area. The hospitals refused to participate on this basis and Blue Cross had to abandon its effort. (Interview with Blue Cross officials, Washington, D.C.)

10. See Chapter 3. One of the private carriers took Blue Cross to court to challenge its legal right to negotiate a discounted rate with the community hospitals, on the ground that it gives Blue Cross an unfair competitive advantage and is discriminatory against patients with indemnity insurance. (*Travelers Insurance Corporation v. Blue Cross of Western Pennsylvania*, District Court for the Western District of Pennsylvania, January 6, 1972.) The Court, however, found for Blue Cross, upholding its special relationship with hospitals.

11. See, for example, testimony of John F. O'Leary of the Massachusetts Rate Setting Commission, U.S., Congress, Senate, Committee on the Judiciary, *High Cost of Hospitalization, Part II: Hearings on S. Res. 334*, 91st Cong., 2nd sess., January 26-28, 1971, pp. 125ff.

12. Although the average bed occupancy rate in community hospitals has now grown to 78 percent (from 74 percent in 1950), there is a growing belief that the usual benchmark of 80 percent for hospital occupancy is unrealistically low, especially in large hospitals. Many hospitals now operate efficiently with occupancy rates of 90 percent or more. See Herman M. Somers and Anne R. Somers, *Medicare and the Hospitals: Issues and Prospects* (Washington: The Brookings Institution, 1967), pp. 57-59.

13. *Hospitals, Guide Issue*, August 1, 1970, and various previous issues.

14. James A. Tate, "Hospital Investments—Policy and Experience," *Best's Review*, January 1971, p. 25.

15. For more detail, see Karen Davis, "Economic Theories of Behavior in Nonprofit, Private Hospitals," *Economic and Business Bulletin*, Winter 1972, pp. 1-13.

16. For a discussion of profit versus nonprofit hospitals, see *High Cost of Hospitalization, Part I: Hearings on S. Res. 334.*

17. George E. Cartwill, "Increased Productivity and Better Utilization," Report of the National Conference on Medical Costs (Washington: U.S. Department of Health, Education, and Welfare, June 27-28, 1967), p. 140.

18. These figures are not strictly comparable, because average annual earnings in hospitals—the only data available—are compared with weekly earnings in the retail and manufacturing sectors. In addition, the average annual wage figures available for hospital workers include supervisory as well as nonsupervisory personnel, whereas the figures for the other industries include nonsupervisory workers only. *Employment and Earnings* (Washington: Bureau of Labor Statistics, U.S. Department of Labor).

Chapter 7
Health Insurance and the Doctor

1. See *Health Manpower and Health Facilities, 1970* (Washington: Public Health Service, U.S. Department of Health, Education, and Welfare, 1971), Table 82, p. 134.

2. These estimates are based on the "Continuing Survey," *Medical Economics.* Median income is usually about 10 percent less than the arithmetic average, which reflects (as the median does not) the exceptionally high earnings of a few physicians. See Louis S. Reed, *Studies of the Incomes of Physicians and Dentists* (Washington: Social Security Administration, U.S. Department of Health, Education, and Welfare, December 1968).

3. Marjorie Smith Mueller, "Private Health Insurance in 1969: A Review," *Social Security Bulletin*, February 1971.

4. Mart S. Feldstein, "The Rising Price of Physicians' Services," *Review of Economics and Statistics*, May 1970, pp. 123, 124.

5. "Continuing Survey," *Medical Economics.*

6. Ibid.

7. Fewer doctors have been entering the generally lower paid categories of general practitioner and pediatrician, and more are choosing the higher paid specialties. See Ann R. Somers, *Health Care in Transition: Directions for the Future* (Chicago: Hospital Research and Educational Trust, 1971), pp. 6-7; and *Health Resources Statistics*, Public Health Service Publication No. 1509, 1968 and 1970 eds. (Washington: Public Health Service, U.S. Department of Health, Education, and Welfare, December 1968, February 1971), Chapter 18. If this trend continues the amounts spent on doctors' services can also be expected to continue to increase.

8. Feldstein, op. cit., pp. 121-33. Also see Ann A. Scitovsky, "Changes in the Cost of Treatment of Selected Illnesses, 1951-67," *American Economic Review*, December 1967.

9. Feldstein, op. cit., p. 129.

10. About 69 percent of Michigan's doctors participate fully in Blue Shield; others participate on a case-by-case basis, accepting, for some specific cases, the Blue Shield payment as payment in full. Ninety-two percent of Michigan Blue Shield payments were on a paid-in-full basis in December 1971, according to officials of Michigan Blue Shield interviewed by the staff of this study.

11. Jay W. Grossett, "Is Blue Shield Still 'The Doctors' Plan'?" *Medical Economics*, February 15, 1971, pp. 35ff.

12. *Medical Economics*, February 15, 1971, pp. 93-97. Copyright © 1971 by Medical Economics Company, Oradell, N.J. 07649. Reprinted by permission.

13. For example, the German *Gebührenordnung für Ärzte* (Fee Schedule for Doctors) lists over a thousand procedures, fills nearly a hundred pages, and requires constant updating as new procedures are introduced and old ones modified. The Dutch fee schedule is even longer. See William A. Glaser, *Paying the Doctor: Systems of Remuneration and Their Effects* (Baltimore: Johns Hopkins Press, 1970), pp. 27-32. In the U.S., the California Relative Value Studies lists 113 double-columned pages of procedures. See "California Relative Value Studies, 1969," Fifth Edition (San Francisco: California Medical Association, 1970).

14. Nolen, op. cit., p. 95. Copyright © 1971 by Medical Economics Company, Oradell, N.J. 97649. Reprinted by permission.

15. Glaser, op. cit., pp. 152-53.

16. Martin S. Gumpert, *You and Your Doctor* (New York: Bobbs-Merrill, 1952), p. 46.

17. *Medical World News*, June 11, 1971.

18. "Time Well Spent: The Norms Will Help," *Medical Economics*, December 6, 1971, pp. 79-87.

19. "Professional Briefs," *Medical Economics*, October 28, 1968, pp. 35-36.

20. According to the Association of American Medical Colleges, 43.1 percent of medical school applicants were accepted for the 1969-70 term; down from an acceptance rate of 60.4 percent in 1961-62. The Association estimates that 75 percent of the applicants were qualified by grades and test scores. (Lawrence K. Altman, "Medical School Applications Up Despite Lag in Funds and Space," *New York Times*, February 21, 1971, p. 1).

Chapter 8
Cost Savings under Nonconventional
Health Insurance Plans

1. Ernest W. Saward, "The Relevance of Prepaid Group Practice to the Effective Delivery of Health Services," paper delivered at the 18th Annual Group Health Institute, Ontario, Canada, June 18, 1969 (reprint; Washington: Public Health Service, U.S. Department of Health, Education, and Welfare, 1969), pp. 8-12.

2. Group Health Association of America field interview.

3. Richard M. Bailey, "Economies of Scale in Medical Practice," in *Empirical Studies in Health Economics*, ed. Herbert E. Klarman (Baltimore: Johns Hopkins Press, 1970), pp. 255-73.

4. "Kaiser Foundation Medical Care Program," *Report of the National Advisory Commission on Health Manpower* (Washington: U.S. Government Printing Office, November 1967), Vol. II, p. 207.

5. Bailey, op. cit., p. 269.

6. Interviews with officials of GHAA and of Group Health Association, of Washington, D.C., by the staff of this study.

7. "Kaiser Foundation Medical Care Program," *Report of the National Advisory Commission on Health Manpower*, Vol. II, Table 1, p. 209; and field interviews conducted by the staff of this study.

8. Annual reports, Kaiser-Permanente Medical Care Program (Oakland, California) and Group Health Association (Washington, D.C.).

9. Estimated by the staff of this study for the year 1971.

10. "Kaiser Foundation Medical Care Program," *Report of the National Advisory Commission on Health Manpower,* Vol. II, p. 211.

11. Op. cit., p. 14; see also George S. Perrott, "Federal Employees Health Benefits Program, Utilization of Hospital Services," *American Journal of Public Health*, January 1966, pp. 57-64.

12. Ray Bloomberg, "Group Health Cooperative of Puget Sound: How Seattle Plan Works, How Doctors Are Paid," *Modern Hospital*, May 1969; and George S. Perrott and Jean C. Chase, "The Federal Employees Health Benefits Program, Sixth Term Coverage and Utilization," *Group Health and Welfare News, Special Supplement*, October 1968, pp. i-viii.

13. See Greer Williams, "Kaiser—What Is It, How Does It Work, Why Does It Work," *Modern Hospital*, February 1971, p. 82; Jocelyn Chamberlain, "Selected Data on Group Practice Prepayment Plan Services," *Group Health and Welfare News, Special Supplement*, June 1967; Ronald Andersen and Odin W. Anderson, *A Decade of Health Services* (Chicago: University of Chicago Press, 1967), pp. 28-31; and *Volume of Physician Visits—United States, July 1966-June 1967,* Series 10, Number 49 (Washington: Public Health Service, U.S. Department of Health, Education, and Welfare, November 1968).

14. See Avedis Donabedian, "An Evaluation of Prepaid Group Practice," *Inquiry*, August 1969, for a comprehensive review of the available comparative cost studies of prepaid group plans.

15. *Final Report of the Survey of Consumer Experience Under the State of California Employees' Hospital and Medical Care Act* (Sacramento: Board of Administration, Public Employees' Retirement System, October 1964); and *The Federal Employees Health Benefits Program: Enrollment and Utilization of Health Services, 1961-1968* (Washington: Public Health Service, U.S. Department of Health, Education, and Welfare, June 1970), Fig. 4.

16. Donabedian, op. cit. In 1971, the U.S. Department of Health, Education, and Welfare embarked on such a study, analyzing the behavior of federal employees enrolled in the Group Health Association (Washington, D.C.) plan under the Federal Employees Health Benefits Program.

17. *Final Report of the Survey of Consumer Experience Under the State of California Employees' Hospital and Medical Care Act.*

18. Donabedian, op. cit.

19. Louis S. Reed, assisted by Maureen Dwyer, *Directory of Health Insurance Plans Other than Blue Cross or Blue Shield Plans Or Insurance Companies* (Washington: Social Security Administration, U.S. Department of Health, Education, and Welfare, March 1970).

Chapter 9
Prepaid Group Practice—A Basis
for a National System?

1. The "National Health Insurance Partnership Act," S. 1623, introduced by Senator Wallace F. Bennett, and H.R. 7741, by Representative John W. Byrnes.

2. The "Health Security Act," H.R. 22, introduced by Representatives Martha W. Griffiths and James C. Corman, and S. 3 introduced by Senator Edward M. Kennedy.

3. Studies indicate, for example, that when participants in an existing group health insurance plan are offered a choice between remaining in a conventional plan or changing to a prepaid group, most of them choose to continue with the existing plan. But if the members of a new group are offered a choice between a conventional and a prepaid plan, about half of them choose the prepaid plan. See Avedis Donabedian, *A Review of Some Experiences With Prepaid Group Practice*, Bureau of Public Health Economics Research Series No. 12 (Ann Arbor: School of Public Health, The University of Michigan, 1965), p. 4.

4. In 1968, the share of the Kaiser plans' total income derived from supplementary charges was 8.1 percent; for Group Health Association, of Washington, D.C., the share was 7.7 percent. See Annual Reports, Kaiser-Permanente, Oakland, California, and Group Health Association, Washington, D.C.

5. See, for example, B. Wolfman, "Medical Expenses and Choice of Plan: A Case Study," *Monthly Labor Review*, November 1961; and C.A. Metzner and R.L. Bashshur, "Factors Associated with Choice of Health Care Plans," *Journal of Health and Social Behavior*, December 1967. Whether the coverage offered by prepaid groups results in lower out-of-pocket costs, depends, of course, on the illnesses afflicting those covered. See Chapters 2 and 8.

6. Annual Reports, Kaiser-Permanente and Group Health Association.

7. See Avedis Donabedian, "An Evaluation of Prepaid Group Practice," *Inquiry*, September 1969, pp. 3-27, for a summary of various studies.

8. "Professional Briefs," *Medical Economics*, September 14, 1970, p. 41.

9. "The Kaiser Foundation Medical Care Program," *Report of the National Advisory Commission on Health Manpower* (Washington: U.S. Government Printing Office, November 1967), Vol. II, p. 206.

10. Field interview, GHAA, Washington, D.C., June 1971.

11. Greer Williams, "Kaiser—What Is It, How Does It Work, Why Does It Work," *Modern Hospital*, February 1971, p. 89.

12. "Population of the United States by Metropolitan-Nonmetropolitan Residence: 1969 and 1970," Current Population Reports, Series P-20, Number 197 (Washington: Bureau of the Census, U.S. Department of Commerce, March 6, 1970), Table A, p. 1.

13. "Financial and Statistical Data, Fiscal Year 1970," mimeo. (Washington: Bureau of Retirement, Insurance, and Occupational Health, U.S. Civil Service Commission, 1971).

14. "America's Doctors Write Their Prescription for National Health Insurance," *Medical Economics*, August 30, 1971.

15. Ray Bloomberg, "Group Health Cooperative of Puget Sound: How Seattle Plan Works, How Doctors Are Paid," *Modern Hospital*, May 1969, p. 4.

16. *Proceedings; Part I, 17th Annual Group Health Institute, Seattle, June 12-14, 1967; Part II, Group Health Association of America, Luncheon and Annual Joint Session, GHAA and Medical Care Section, American Public Health Association, Miami Beach, October 25, 1967* (Washington: Group Health Association of America), p. 92.

17. Ibid. The Puget Sound salary schedule is designed to provide for a 75 percent increase in the base salary during the first 5 years.

18. Answer to confidential questionnaire.

19. "Professional Briefs," *Medical Economics*, September 14, 1970, p. 41; Williams, op. cit.; and surveys of the major plans by the staff of this study.

20. "1969 Continuing Survey," *Medical Economics*, December 21, 1970, p. 64.

21. *Kaiser Foundation Medical Care Program, 1969* (Oakland: 1970).

22. However, there is some fear that if prepaid groups are induced or required to pass on part of their savings to Medicare eligibles in the form of greater benefits, they will attract such large numbers of the aged population as to distort the age composition of the group. Under H.R. 1, passed in October 1972, prepaid groups may offer such inducements to Medicare eligibles, but the reimbursement formula provides less reimbursement for prepaid groups than the average amount paid to providers in the fee-for-service system. No data are yet available to indicate whether Medicare enrollment in prepaid groups has increased as a result of H.R. 1.

23. Ibid.

24. For example, in June 1971, HEW made a grant of $500,000 to help establish a pilot project prepaid plan in Rochester, N.Y. The plan will be

operated by Blue Cross-Blue Shield. The purpose of the project is to prove that a plan serving a membership of 20,000 to 50,000 can be established and made economically viable in 12 to 18 months. See *Group Health and Welfare News*, July 1971.

25. Field interviews by members of the staff of this study with GHAA officials.

26. Assuming hospitalization of 422 days per 1000 subscribers per year (the average under the Federal Employees Health Benefits Program), prepaid plans with 75,000 members would hospitalize approximately 87 patients per day. At 87 percent occupancy, a 100-bed hospital would exceed the average of community hospitals. (See Chapter 6.)

Chapter 10
The Requirements of Health Insurance
Reform: A Summary

1. See U.S., Congress, House, Committee on Ways and Means, *Analysis of Health Insurance Proposals Introduced in the 92nd Congress*, 92nd Cong., 1st sess., August 1971 (prepared by the U.S. Department of Health, Education, and Welfare for the Committee on Ways and Means) for a complete description of major proposals.

2. Senate and House numbers are those assigned in the 92nd Congress.

3. Another bill that falls in this category is the Pell-Mondale bill (S. 703), which would require employers to pay 100 percent of the premium. A unique feature of this bill is its provision for the establishment of public-supported "Health Care Corporations" in areas where the Secretary of Health, Education, and Welfare determines they are needed. Their role would be extensive, including the training and education of health care personnel as well as the provision of health care services.

4. Martin S. Feldstein, "A New Approach to National Health Insurance," *The Public Interest*, Spring 1971, p. 93.

5. Anne R. Somers, *Health Care in Transition: Directions for the Future* (Chicago: Hospital Research and Educational Trust, 1971), p. 135; and Odin W. Anderson and J. Joel May, "The Federal Employees Health Benefits Program, 1961-1968; A Model for National Health Insurance?" *Health Administration Perspectives*, A 9 (Chicago: University of Chicago Press, 1971).

6. Sidney R. Garfield, "The Delivery of Medical Care," *Scientific American*, April 1970, pp. 15-33.

7. Somers, op. cit; and Anderson and May, op. cit.

8. Joseph Simanis, "Health Insurance in West Germany and Great Britain," *Social Security Bulletin*, October 1970.

9. John and Sylvia Jewkes, *The Genesis of the British National Health Service* (Oxford: Basil, Blackwell and Malt, 1961), p. 30.

10. Mike Causey, "Firms Paying Full Health Plan Costs," in "The Federal Diary," *Washington Post*, November 18, 1971.

11. Lester L. Petermann, "Fringe Benefits of Urban Workers," *Monthly Labor Review*, November 1971.

12. The National Association of Blue Shield Plans has recommended an amendment to the National Health Insurance Partnership Act (the Byrnes-Bennett bill, H.R. 7741 and S. 1623) that provides for combining small employee groups, self-employed individuals, and other individuals in one group with a single rate structure. See *The Blue Shield*, April 1972, p. 4.

13. The Griffiths-Corman and Kennedy bills would eliminate this requirement by making registration with a primary physician voluntary and permitting anyone who does not wish to register with one physician a free choice of physicians. But without some method of policing this free choice, those registered with a physician might resort to services of other physicians, and physicians paid on a capitation basis would be reimbursed for services performed by others.

14. "Continuing Survey of Full-Time Practicing Physicians Under Age 65," *Medical Economics* (various issues, 1962-1970).

15. See "Making the Impossible Possible," *Medical World News*, March 10, 1972, pp. 47 ff, for a description of some of the amazing new developments in the field of prosthetics and rehabilitative medicine.

16. Total civilian federal employment was approximately 2.9 million in 1970. Of these, 193,000 were employed in civilian hospitals and other health care functions, and another 9,600 in health insurance functions in support of Medicare. (See Chapter 5.) In addition, state and local governments employed 10.1 million persons, including 1 million in hospitals and other health care functions. See *Statistical Abstract of the United States, 1971* (Washington: Bureau of the Census, U.S. Department of Commerce), Table 639.

17. Estimated on the basis of *Health Resources Statistics* (Washington: National Center for Health Statistics, U.S. Department of Health, Education, and Welfare, 1970), Tables 7, 10, 11, and 177.

18. This argument is advanced, for example, by Feldstein, op. cit.

Appendix B
National Health Expenditures

1. See Barbara S. Cooper and Mary McGee, "National Health Expenditures, Fiscal Years 1929-70 and Calendar Years 1929-69," *Research and Statistics Note*, No. 25–1970 (Washington: Social Security Administration, U.S. Department of Health, Education, and Welfare, December 14, 1970).

Appendix C
Various Methods of Estimating Net Enrollment
in Hospital Insurance Plans

1. Louis S. Reed and Willine Carr, "Private Health Insurance in the United States," *Social Security Bulletin*, January 1969; Marjorie Smith Mueller, "Private Health Insurance in 1969: A Review," *Social Security Bulletin*, February 1971.

2. More people have health insurance covering hospital expenses than any other kind, even though only a very small percentage have hospital insurance alone. Most plans are combined with surgical coverage and, increasingly, with major medical. Few, if any, people carry coverage only against nonhospital medical costs; therefore, enrollment for hospital coverage is the measure used in estimating the maximum number of people with some kind of health insurance coverage.

3. Given the margin of error, the range of "don't knows" could be from 0 to 4 percent.

4. It is estimated both by the HIAA and by the HEW that approximately half of the Medicare category (about 10 million) also are insured under private insurance plans. Counting the Medicare duplication, gross enrollments probably exceed net enrollments by as much as 30 to 40 million. Thus, the duplication in the Medicare category is about one-fourth to one-third of the total duplication in all health insurance. Adding one-third of those answering "more than one" in the Gallup survey, or 2.67 percent to the total responding they were covered under "government" (7 percent) plus an additional 2 percent calculated to be the possible sampling error at the upper end, would yield a maximum of 11.67 percent of all insured, or 18.4 million in the "government" category.

Index

Accessibility, of medical services, 149-150, 165-166
Accounting, accrual, 58
Adenoidectomies, 134, 135
Admission rates, hospital, 132t
Aetna Life and Casualty Company, 62, 86
  v. Adams et ux, 17
  annual coverage of, 28t
  earned health premiums of, 38t
  family medical costs under, 138t
  financial data on, 195t
  group plan of, 24
  indemnity plan of, 23, 26
  maximum coverage of, 25
  supplementary charges of, 145
AFDC families, 81t
AFL-CIO, 2, 33, 51, 159
Aid to the Blind, 81
Aid to Families with Dependent Children, 81
Aid to the Permanently and Totally Disabled, 81
Alcoholism, 18
AMA. See American Medical Association
American Bar Association, 2
American Foreign Service Protective Association, 62, 86
American Hospital Association (AHA), 41
American Medical Association, 2, 157
American Nursing Home Association, 76
Anderson, Odin W., 160
Annual physicals, 145
Appendectomy, 134, 135
Appliances, 169
Associated Hospital Service, 38
Attitudes, toward medical insurance, 51, 192
Automobile insurance, 30

Back injuries, 27t
Bailey, Richard M., 129
Belgium, compulsory systems in, 16
Benefit payments, 15
Bennett bill, 158
Blood bank, 104f
BLS. See Bureau of Labor Statistics
Blue Cross, 5, 6, 10t, 13
  competitive advantages of, 99
  copayment, 22
  and hospital costs, 99
  hospitalization utilization rates under, 141t
  and participating hospitals, 17. See also Blue plans
Blue Cross Association (BCA), 38, 42
Blue Cross-Blue Shield, 39, 137
  comprehensive plan of, 24
  family costs of, 137t
  for federal employees, 34
  government-wide Service Benefit Plan of, 86

history of, 28, 40-43
incurred claims reserves of, 62
premium income of, 52
Blue Cross of Western Pennsylvania, 42
Blue Cross-United States Steel-United Steel Workers, 42
Blue plans, 38
  annual coverage of, 28t
  family medical costs under, 138t, 139
  group, 23
  maximum coverage of, 25
  operating expense ratio for, 46
  relations with hospitals, 42
  reserves of, 61-63
  state regulation of, 30
  tax exempt, 40. See also Blue Cross; Blue Shield
Blue Shield, 5, 6, 10t, 13
  fee controls of, 115
Boston, prepaid group practice plans in, 152, 153
British National Health Service, 163, 166
Budget ceiling, 159
Bureau of the Budget, 69
Bureau of Labor Statistics, 31, 113, 117
Burleson bill, 157
Byrnes-Bennett bill, 172
Byrnes bill, 158

California, Medicaid program in, 82-83
Capitation, 127, 159
Carriers, private, 62
  solvency of, 170
Center for Health Administration Studies, of Univ. of Chicago, 160
CHAMPUS (Civilian Health and Medical Program for the Uniformed Services), 7, 41, 46, 71, 84
  operation of, 85

Chest x rays, 148
Child health services, 70
Children, on Medicaid, 81t
Chiropractic services, 84
Cholecystectomy, 134, 135
Civil Service Commission, U.S., 62, 86
Claims handling, 45, 48, 121-122
  cost of, 46-47
  function of, 46-47
Clinics, electronic multiphasic testing, 129
  satellite, 149
Cobalt therapy, 105f
Coinsurance provisions, 19
Collection, 45
Collective bargaining, 32, 40. See also Unions
Columbia, Maryland, prepaid group practice plans in, 152, 153
Commissioners, state insurance, 37, 44
Commissions, 47-49
  on group policies, 49

223

About the Authors

John Krizay is Director of the Office of Monetary Affairs, U.S. Department of State. He received the A.B. in foreign affairs and economics from George Washington University and the M.A. in economics from Yale University. His interest in the economy of medicine and health insurance is recent, dating from his return to the United States in 1966 after ten years of service in the American embassies of Germany, Brazil, and the Republic of Zaire (formerly known as the Belgian Congo). In 1970, the Twentieth Century Fund commissioned Mr. Krizay to head a project to do an objective study of the present system of third party financing medical costs in the United States, emphasizing the implications for health insurance reform.

Andrew Wilson is a labor economist; he received the Ph.D. from Claremont College in 1966. His fields of interest are welfare economics and the application of economic tools to further social justice. He has been employed with the Agency for International Development both in Bolivia and in Washington, D.C.